CLASSIC ESSAYS IN ENGLISH

Classic ESSAYS in English

Second Edition

Edited by
JOSEPHINE MILES
University of California, Berkeley

Little, Brown and Company
Boston *Toronto*

LIBRARY OF CONGRESS CATALOG CARD NO. 65-16298

Third Printing

Published simultaneously in Canada
by Little, Brown & Company (Canada) Limited
PRINTED IN THE UNITED STATES OF AMERICA

Foreword

If you have ever tried to work out an idea that seemed to you worth while, you realize the pleasure of seeing it take shape. This is the pleasure of the essayist – first the tentative thought, then the steps of development through positive and negative evidence, finally the restatement and clarification of the thought in its developed form.

You may ask, how generally true is your idea? What connections and associations does it have? Who cares about it? How may it grow, take on breadth and depth, lead others to think about ideas like it? What is your feeling toward it, your manner in writing of it?

You may ask, what are the main concerns of your ideas? They may be what you like to do – "Fishing is pleasanter than hunting," or "It's a good plan to read the end of a book first." Or they may be concerns about people, with puzzling complexities of character, with a question such as "Why do I like the people I like?" or "What is the difference between an acquaintance and a friend?" Or they may be about concepts of groups and organizations – "Why do people enjoy excluding others?" "How does a church differ from a religion?" "How important are settings in theatrical productions?" "What are the consequences of one vote in an election?"

If you think as you read these suggestions that no one of them is an idea that would ever cross your mind, then ask yourself what you think about instead, when you are philosophizing on matters larger than one person or one event, when you are thinking, that is, about matters that may be at least proposed to be generally true.

Some concerns for such matters keep recurring through the centuries. Others change from era to era, as events and situations change. In this book are gathered a number of essays that have come up for discussion over and over during the past four centuries.

An essay tries to develop an idea. The concept of trying, of tentative effort, is in the term *essay* itself—*essaier* in French is *to attempt.* So it differs from a formal report or a technical work of any kind which supplies evidence as complete and thorough as possible. The evidence offered by the essay is usually just that available to the author at the moment of writing. He searches his mind, maybe asks his friends what they think, but does not necessarily do further research. Much of the finest prose-writing of our day we would not call essay-writing because it is too technical, too loaded with materials which are themselves as interesting as the argument. An essayist's main interest is his idea, his argument; he is more interested in developing an attitude, a clarification of a thought, than in adding to knowledge.

Why does he usually write in prose rather than in verse? Because, as the word *pro*-se suggests, it *pro*gresses, it carries his idea straight *for*ward, while *verse,* related to *versus,* turns back upon itself, stops at the end of one line and re*verses* its position to the beginning of the next line, using all sorts of repetitions in sound, such as rhythm and rhyme, to create a stronger sense of pattern than the development of an idea may require. A clear idea, in other words, might find a close repetitive emphasis on sound qualities distracting; it would call for emphasis less on syllables, more on words, phrases, and clauses, and thus establish a larger rhythm of repetition, in the straightforward motion of prose. A closely repetitive sound-pattern in prose may cause it to be called "poetic," while, on the other hand, verse, if it stresses sound as little as possible, especially in places that emphasize the argument, comes close to being justly called verse-essay: some of Pope's writing, for example, or of Wallace Stevens' in our own day. The essay is written by those most interested in the general and thoughtful powers of language.

What form do these powers usually take in prose? What shape does the artist in prose give to language by his selection and arrangement of it? The principles of arrangement are similar from art to art. Repetitions in balance, in contrast, in culmination, in analyzed portions of repeated wholes, serve to give first emphasis and then connection to the selected materials, which in prose are the words, phrases, clauses, sentences, paragraphs.

So as we look for the shaping of an idea in an essay, we may look first for its most basic unit—the sentence that states its idea. Then we may look to see how this sentence is repeated, or analyzed, or varied, in each larger paragraph unit. Then finally we may look for supporting patterns: the main ways in which phrases and clauses are combined into sentences, the main ways in which words are combined into phrases and clauses, and the large patterns of sound, of the contours of intonation from phrase to phrase and sentence to sentence.

As part of the shape and structure, the ideas themselves have changed in emphasis. In the Renaissance, primary concerns were religion, education, and human relations. Increasingly in recent centuries, the critical essay on literature has developed, the interpretation of meaning through art, and along with it the essay of social interest—Thoreau's, James', Arnold's, Adams', Shaw's, Orwell's. But as we name these names we are carried back to More and Ascham again, and we see that certain basic ethical concerns persist, for man in his daily life, in his way of thought and belief, in his community.

If the essays gathered here make you like reading and writing prose, as I hope they will, where next will you turn for reading? I should hope, to modern prose-writers, who are not always essayists, but are more formally technical in their methods: in literary criticism to T. S. Eliot and I. A. Richards, to John Crowe Ransom, R. P. Blackmur, Allen Tate, Edward Sapir, Lionel Trilling. In science, to Edgar Anderson, Loren Eiseley, Albert Einstein, John Dollard, Robert Lynd, A. N. Whitehead, and the interpreters of Freud, Marx, and Darwin in our day. Good solid prose is increasing in our time, and the essay, the tentative personal attempt to develop an idea, is at the heart of it. In turn, then, we may look to the past great sources of our meditative prose—to the Greek historians, to Cicero, Seneca, St. Augustine, Boethius, the Bible, Montaigne, Pascal, Descartes, Voltaire, Kant and the German philosophers, and modern Europeans like Unamuno, Croce, Bergson, Jung, Sartre. The twentieth century is well dedicated to the clarification of its ideas. And like the one-act play, the short story, and the lyric, the essay in its personal intensity is characteristic of our time.

Note the specific limitations established for *Classic Essays in Eng-*

lish. That the essays be in English, not translation, is one. That they be well known and established for many readers in the present as well as the past is another. That they be integral units of thought is a third—thus allowing for chapters or sections of works not called "essays" by their authors. Every selection is printed without internal deletion, excepting Milton's *Areopagitica,* too long to include without omission of the part of the fourth section on difficulties. Finally, the selections were written to be read; they are not primarily rhetorical and oratorical. But rhetoric in the past, like technical research today, provided a matrix for the many assumptions and implications of the essay form.

Punctuation has been modernized, along with spelling, to the degree necessary to make the texts easily readable. Grammar is unchanged, so that its development may be accurately observed. Word usages differing from those discoverable in a modern dictionary are explained in the footnotes along with perhaps unfamiliar allusions.

Acknowledgment is due to various publishers for permission to include certain selections. Details will be found on the copyright page of this book.

Acknowledgment is also due to the selective perceptions and corrections of Mr. Michael Cooke.

And, for this second edition, to Mr. John Paul Graff.

J. M.
1965

Table of Contents

Notes on prose style

A style is an attitude, a set of values which underlies a set of habitual choices. A style of dress, a style of action, a style of speech, a style of writing—a stylus was a pen—all tell us something of what we want to know about the character and motive represented in the habitual choices. The *how,* with the *what,* is the message.

Is it useful to be aware of one's own style, or does such awareness interfere with being natural? My belief is that, once having become conscious of the possible choices and once having made the choices, one can be secure in them and they can become natural. Knowledge and conscious choice, in other words, support rather than oppose intuition, and give it flexibility as well as ease, sympathy as well as surety, a sense of alternatives as well as a sense of preferences.

The beginning essayist in prose is not apt to be very conscious of what he is doing, because he is not apt to know what the possibilities are. Or if he is excessively self-conscious, stumbling over the furniture, it may be because he has thought too much about his difficulties in writing, not enough about his purposes, strengths, and favorite ways of procedure.

So I propose to discuss some of the specific grammatical, and thus stylistic, alternatives in prose. A sentence has a ring to it, the sound of its character and construction. *Give me liberty, or give me death,* we say, and hear the two similar imperatives, the two dissimilar objects, joined by an alternative. Though for the structures we recognize these grammatical terms seem unduly weighty, just as the name *James W. Anderson, Attorney at Law* may seem weighty for someone usually called *Jim,* the greater formality may be useful for greater specificness of recognition, and for distinguishing one

Jim from another. The representative force of such aphorisms is limited by their unusual succinctness, and their re-enforcement by patterns of sound.

The usual sentence is more complex, yet less closely organized, moving along as a part of a sequence. At its simplest it predicates a subject, relates one concept to another: *The bird is yellow. The bird flies over the field. The bird sings a song.* As explicitly subordinate verb clauses: *The bird which is yellow flies over the field while he sings a song.* As qualification by adjectives: *The yellow bird, flying over the field, sings a song.* As connected phrasal material: *The yellow bird, in flight over the field, sings a song.* Differing proportions of the chief referential terms, nouns, adjectives, and verbs, and of their connectives, result from these differing choices. Of the basic subject, verb, and object, *bird, sings,* and *song,* even subject and object may be differently constructed; by pronoun and clause, for example: *He who flies sings what he feels.* There is, in other words, structural substitutability as well as the referential substitutability we call *synonym.* Only the verb cannot be replaced in structure, and thus, with its subject and object, provides the statement's stable center.

A masterly prose will employ all varieties of possibility, yet will maintain a main line of emphasis. So, for example, the prose of Sir Winston Churchill exemplifies all the alternatives noted here yet moves along in the basic moderation characteristic of its author. "No one pretends that democracy is perfect or all-wise. Indeed it has been said that democracy is the worst form of government except all those other forms that have been tried from time to time." (1947). The verbs and adjectives here work equally to give significance to the nouns, in forms explicitly connected and subordinated.

A more common, but still carefully subordinated way of speaking, is to be heard in the strong inner clauses of the following from 1943: "Some people's idea of [free speech] is that they are free to say what they like, but if anyone says anything back, that is an outrage." Under *idea is that* come successive verbs under *what, but,* and *if*—the activity of thought, in a dominance of verbs over adjectives which is characteristic of a majority of English prose writers.

The "curt" version of this predicative style is less subordinative. From 1915: "The truth is incontrovertible: Panic may resent it; ignorance may deride it; malice may distort it, but there it is." The free verb, unbound by connectives, is nevertheless related by the parallels of structure and function. Sentence by sentence, verb by verb, the curt style, fostered early by Seneca, and imitated by Elizabethan Senecans like Sidney and Lyly, scants the connectives of clauses and thus the complexity of subordination, though not so averse to phrasal modification.

Churchill indeed sometimes turns to phrasal pile-ups with the greatest zest, and provides, often in irony, the height of modification as alternative to predication. "I got into my bones the essential structure of the ordinary British sentence which is a noble thing." The adjectives here are dominant and thematic under the strongly modifying *bones* phrase. "Nothing is more dangerous in wartime than to live in the temperamental atmosphere of a Gallup Poll, always feeling one's pulse and taking one's temperature." Under the theme *dangerous,* the phrases of *atmosphere* and *Poll,* the adjectives of *feeling* and *taking* keep the sense of *dangerous* in suspension and continuity. So, even more emphatically, in 1944: "At the bottom of all the tributes paid to democracy is the little man, walking into the little booth, with a little pencil making a little cross on a little bit of paper—no amount of rhetoric or voluminous discussion can finally diminish the overwhelming importance of that point." The *little, little,* and *little* adjectives, *walking* and *making,* culminate in the final adjective *overwhelming.* Even in his most characteristic balanced form, Churchill may stress the epithet, as in 1945: "The inherent vice of Capitalism is the unequal sharing of blessings; the inherent value of Socialism is the equal sharing of miseries." Here is the classic matching of adjective to noun in both subject and predicate as these are joined by the single verb, with, in addition, the paralleling of phrase by phrase.

Of his own style, Churchill wrote, "I affected a combination of the styles of Macaulay and Gibbon, the staccato antithesis of the former and the rolling sentences and genitival endings of the latter; and I stuck in a bit of my own from time to time." But also, "Broadly speaking, the short words are best and the old words are best of all." (*Man of the Century.*) The elaborateness of the first combination is balanced by the simplicity of the second.

Churchill stands at the center of English prose style, both for past and for present. The strong active verb which he uses vigorously he supports with richly adjectival and with explicitly connective materials. Most writers make choices similarly varied, but not always with balanced emphasis. The dominant English style, indeed, is the predicative.

Note for example the following two passages, one written in the Renaissance, one recently. Note the direct independence of the many verbs in each.

> This is their sentence and opinion of virtue and pleasure. And they believe that by man's reason none can be found truer than this, unless any godlier be inspired into man from heaven. Wherein whether they believe well or no, neither the time doth suffer us to discuss, neither it is now necessary; for we have taken upon us to show and declare their lores and ordinances, and not to defend them. (Sir Thomas More, p. 3)

> It is hard to hear a new voice, as hard as it is to listen to an unknown language. We just don't listen. There is a new voice in the old American classics. The world has declined to hear it, and has blabbed about children's stories. (D. H. Lawrence, p. 373)

To hear, to listen, to decline to hear, to blab, these verbs provide the content, connected by a minimum of words like *as, and, about,* and modified very little. Little is assumed by Lawrence; much is stated. For More, the adjectives are equally few; the connectives more frequent—subordinative as with *that, than, unless, whether, neither,* coordinative as with *and;* but the strongest are the verbs *to be, to believe, to discuss, to show*—the process of thought and argument.

When strongly connected, predicative prose sounds as follows, again in an old and a new passage:

> Another man may be sick too, and sick to death, and this affliction may lie in his bowels, as gold in a mine, and be of no use to him; but this bell, that tells me of his affliction, digs out and applies that gold to me: if by this consideration of

another's danger I take mine own into contemplation, and so secure myself, by making my recourse to my God, who is our only security. (John Donne, p. 48)

Note the short frequent clauses linked by cumulative *ands.* there is an *and* series too in a passage by Shaw, plus a series of *by* and *that* and *how.*

Democracy, then, cannot be government by the people: it can only be government by consent of the governed. Unfortunately, when democratic statesmen propose to govern us by our own consent, they find that we don't want to be governed at all, and that we regard rates and taxes and rents and death duties as intolerable burdens. What we want to know is how little government we can get along with without being murdered in our beds. That question cannot be answered until we have explained what we mean by getting along. (George Bernard Shaw, p. 306)

These, like More's and Lawrence's, are styles guided by predicates, with minimal qualifications. For such "classical" or balanced writers as Sir Francis Bacon and T. S. Eliot, qualification goes along with predication in establishing balance.

The second fruit of friendship is healthful and sovereign for the understanding, as the first is for the affections. For friendship maketh indeed a fair day in the affections, from storm and tempests; but it maketh daylight in the understanding, out of darkness and confusion of thought. (Bacon, p. 18)

Yet if the only form of tradition, of handing down, consisted in following the ways of the immediate generation before us in blind or timid adherence to its successes, "tradition" should positively be discouraged. We have seen many such simple currents soon lost in the sand; and novelty is better than repetition. Tradition is a matter of much wider significance. It cannot be inherited, and if you want it you must obtain it by great labour. (Eliot, p. 382)

Note Eliot's *only, immediate, blind, timid, simple, better,* and others, explaining the *should, cannot, must,* of the verbs, as Bacon's *health-*

ful, sovereign, fair establishes the *maketh* and *maketh.* The structure seems more solid, more phrasally as more adjectively modified.

The extreme of qualification is to be seen in such an ancient-modern pair as Ascham and Ruskin:

> Thus experience of all fashions in youth, being in proof always dangerous, in issue seldom lucky, is a way indeed to overmuch knowledge, yet used commonly of such men, which be either carried by some curious affection of mind, or driven by some hard necessity of life to hazard the trial of over many perilous adventures. (Roger Ascham, p. 12)

Not only does almost every noun have its adjective here, but both are strong in relation to the verbs; with *of* and *in* and *by* phrases, and *either, or.* So too for Ruskin—the *or,* the many *of* phrases, and the persistent qualification of each noun, from *no frost-ploughed paths* to *joyful flowers* and *all the blessings of the earth.*

> No frost-ploughed, dust-encumbered paths of ancient glacier fret the soft Jura pastures; no splintered heaps of ruin break the fair ranks of her forest; no pale, defiled, or furious rivers rend their rude and changeful ways among her rocks. Patiently, eddy by eddy, the clear green streams wind along their well-known beds; and under the dark quietness of the undisturbed pines, there spring up, year by year, such company of joyful flowers as I know not the like of among all the blessings of the earth. (John Ruskin, p. 241)

No prolonged prose sequence could afford to use just one of these exemplified patterns. But with a natural play of variety, of stating, assuming, qualifying, subordinating, explaining, weighing, it is probable that for the sake of unity and progress there will be one prevailing thematic structural choice to carry the main tone and meaning. The paragraphs quoted, therefore, are not only representative of their authors' habits in general, but represent also in particular a recurrent unit of stylistic expression, a recognizable model of the way in which the author characteristically puts his ideas together. Graphically, for example, we may see the above by separating its working components into lines, somewhat as William Carlos Williams arranges his lines in what he considers to be the "American idiom."

No frost-ploughed, dust-encumbered paths
of ancient glacier
fret the soft Jura pastures;
no splintered heaps
of ruin
break the fair ranks
of her forest;
no pale, defiled, or furious rivers rend their rude and changeful
ways
Patiently, eddy among her rocks.
by eddy,
the clear green streams wind
along their well-known beds;
and
under the dark quietness
of the undisturbed pines,
there spring up,
year
by year,
such company
of joyful flowers
as I know not the like of
among all the blessings
of the earth.

Breaking the lines with each explicit connective, we see the power of qualification both at beginning and at end. In contrast, Lawrence's verbal style runs as follows, with fewer adjectives and connectives:

It is hard to hear a new voice,
as hard
as it is to listen
to an unknown language.
We just don't listen.
There is a new voice
in the old American classics.
The world has declined to hear it,
and has blabbed
about children's stories.

A reader may well feel a distinct taste for one choice or another; he may have an immediate sympathy for crisp predicative sequences on the one hand or cumulative adjectival structures on the other, for connections expressed by preposition and conjunction or left implicit. At least he will recognize the differences in pattern.

Part of the value may rise from the dexterity with which the form is treated, the fulfillment of possibilities in the choice. Part may rise from a judgment, beyond that of the skill and form itself, of the attitude carried in the style, the evident purpose to declare relations in coordinate sets, for example, in contrast to the constructing of a complex of more and more minor subordinations. Cicero was famed for supplying as much evidence as possible, especially in qualifying phrase and relative clause, before he arrived at his completed predication in the main verb. In his sentence, thought was to be taken as a *fait accompli.* It was considered the great virtue of Seneca, on the other hand, and later of Montaigne, that they seemed to carry the reader along with them in an incompleted process of thinking, with main verbs unpredictably supplemented by other main and other minor verbs, with statements possibly short and unmodified, possibly rambling and open-ended.

Often it is stated that one of these methods is preferable to another, more effective, more true to English; but inasmuch as lastingly effective English prose has been written in a number of different ways, it seems wise to recognize both the method and the purpose, as well as the limits of the reader's taste, before evaluating in any but an impressionistic fashion. The student who likes the inner sound of what he reads, and who wishes to achieve something like it, or who dislikes and wishes to avoid it, had best be able to discern just how it works.

In the pairs we have looked at, some readers may recognize, rather than a preference for one of the modes, a consistent preference for the modern, finding strangeness in all the early forms. Most of this strangeness is in vocabulary, in labels now out of use; but to some degree there is a difference between early and modern structures which we would do well to observe and define. Most simply, English sixteenth and seventeenth century prose was more predicative and connected; modern is more qualified and juxtaposed, in a reversed proportion. A defining trait of modern prose style in general then is its minimal subordination, its decrease in explicit connection, in phrase and clause structures. In the past, only a few, notably Sidney, Dryden, Swift, Johnson, Carlyle, scanted connectives as much as do most of the moderns from Shaw on. In the past, on the other hand, only a few, Ascham, Hobbes, Browne, Smith, Gibbon, relied on adjectives as strongly as do many moderns, from the group of De Quincey, Carlyle, Macaulay, Darwin, Ruskin in the nineteenth century to a majority of writers in the twentieth.

Like syntax and word-order, vocabulary too is open to choices which are related to time and to type of interest. What we want to talk about, what alternatives we select from a number of possibilities, are involved with our concerns and with the structural patterns we have in mind. Certain ideas and certain structures seem to go together. For example, and perhaps surprisingly, the scientific writer is usually not the logician but rather the observer, communicating more through adjectives and noun phrases than through verbs and clauses. His is the language of substance, concrete, descriptive, literal, as distinguished from the argumentative connections and abstractions of the civic philosopher and from the presented dilemmas of the artist. As a whole, the major vocabulary of the essayist has grown more concrete over the centuries, losing some of its key terms of value in favor of terms of sense, which in turn may be symbolic of value as the users of language emphasize new implications.

From literal to figurative is one range that a word may take: from *foot* of a person to *foot* of a mountain, a substituted or metaphoric use. To this, are related other substitutions, as of a foreign, archaic, or coined term. From concrete to abstract is another range: from *foot* to *extremity,* stressing one of the abstract characteristics of foot, a contrast for which the terms *image* and *symbol* as distinguished from *concept* are also used. From particular to general is another range, from *this foot* and *these feet,* plural, to *most* or *all feet* in general. A fourth range is from denotative or descriptive to connotative or associative. A fifth range is from neutral to evaluative, from *foot* as fact to *foot* as value as in "There's a foot for you!" These ranges do not necessarily run parallel; that is, the concrete may be more similar to the figurative than to the literal, the particular may be both an abstraction and a value. A sympathetic and understanding reading of a prose style will take account of the interplay between these possibilities.

For sound patterns too there are ranges of choice: from euphony to cacophony; from smooth to rough transitions; from little pause and stress, to much; and from a patterning almost as close as that of poetry, with symmetry in syllable, phrase, or clause, though not in measure, to a patterning of forms and intervals highly irregular.

Some suggestions about the study of style in historical perspective may also be in order. Not many years ago we were troubled to be told that an apparently solid table top was really a mass of swarming molecules, and that a human being was a subtle carbon compound. But we grew accustomed to accepting differences in levels, and came to consider at once the scientific and the everyday table, the concept and the use. Now we undertake to consider our own language also in these ways. We follow as scholars point out to us the complex underlying structures of phonemes, morphemes, and syntactic units, and try to create a grammar which will account for not just any but all possible sentences. At the same time, we look again at the surface of our language, able to note in relation to these deeper complexities the surface simplicities. Qualificative and connective sentences, for example, represent transformations of simpler "kernel" sentences. *The yellow bird sings* has combined *The bird is yellow* and *The bird sings.* The norms of prose practice work in patterns under which are to be seen the workings of a more theorizable grammar.

Here we have a pattern of structures—word, sentence, paragraph—each with its internal and external relations in implicit and explicit connection by agreement, order, or connective terms. For the word, its root and its affixes, derivational and inflectional; for the sentence, its subject-predicate focus and its adjuncts of qualification by word, phrase, or clause; for the paragraph or whole composition, its controlling theme-sentence and subordinate qualifying and substantiating sentences. As in speech these structures are distinguished by both stress and pause, so in print they are at least partialy distinguished by punctuation and spacing.

For example, in the word-structure, *unlikenesses,* the stressed root *like,* already qualified by its negative prefix *un,* its derivational noun-making suffix *-ness* and its pluralizing suffix *-es,* is given a boundary of space to distinguish it from its qualifiers, let us say *many extreme,* and from its predicate, let us say *demand recognition.* In turn, the sentence *Many extreme unlikenesses demand recognition.* is set off at either end by both space and punctuation, a capital and a period or semi-period; and a parenthetical extra phrase or clause would be set off by its own two marks, two commas, a capital and comma, or comma and period. In effect, a truism of Aristotle's, a functioning unit has a beginning, middle, and end. These are given graphic marking in suitable ways, including additional white space for new paragraph and new chapter.

In other words, in some simple ways, the page before us records the measures of the voice in grouping subordinate around dominant units in the chief structures of word, sentence, and paragraph. In each, the focus is on the relation of the dominant unit to its adjuncts. The simplest visible and audible relation, of each sentence's chief verb to its subject and complement, can then be seen to be amplified by simple modifying qualities in adjective and adverb, and then, with the guide of specific connectives and further punctuation, carried into phrasal and clausal elaborations.

As grammar provides a design of ordering, emphasizing, and linking its units of meaning to achieve relation in statement, and logic works toward a design of consistency between statements, so rhetoric works toward a design of effect between author and audience. And this rhetorical design includes, as all do to some degree, art as well as reason, the powers of sense as well as the powers of mind and feeling. So into rhetoric come all sorts of conscious questions of effect, in reference, in sequence, in emphasis: not only the grammar of compounding qualities in such a phrase as *smaller and briefer unlikenesses,* but the rhetorical impact of this order. Would *briefer and smaller* be a better order? Better for what? The questions of purpose and intent become important as part of effect. The traditional divisions of a prose composition, Introduction, Proposal, Demonstration, Conclusion, correspond to the forms, adjuncts, and connections of word and sentence.

Rhetoricians think of situation and purpose as a defining force. They distinguish showing, proving, and persuading: the first to make clear and plain; the second to argue a case, using all possible evidence on all sides; the third to move the hearer's belief and approval. Different purposes take different techniques; the achievement of clarity, for example, is more important to showing than to moving. To these purposes, poets and prose writers have added pleasure; they combine moving and instructing with the most delightful of sense impressions, so that the hearer of poetry may enjoy what he learns.

Questions of design, of aesthetic and effective pattern, have therefore been much discussed: the effects of series of terms, of balances and oppositions, of cumulative structures, of short incisive units or long involved suspensive ones. Questions of connection as well as of order: the logic of conjunction and disjunction, of *and . . . but;* the logic of alternative, *either . . . or;* the logic of implication, *if, therefore;* the ways to make explicit connections between statements. Questions, also, about individual words and sounds: differences and combinations between harsh and mellow sounds; differences between foreign and familiar words or figurative and literal uses of them.

Given all these choices, of ways to arrange in certain patterns for certain effects the units of sound, syllable, word, phrase, sentence, paragraph, which we distinguish in language, how do we ever get around to making a choice from the innumerable possibilities? In speaking and writing, as in daily life, we develop certain habits of combining materials, so that we do not have to think through each combination each time. Our habits make our style, for individual, for community, for whole culture.

Think then how an individual can develop a style of writing within his own world, like enough to his friends' that he can communicate with them, different enough so that he may call it his own: by being aware of the chief possibilities in his language, the combinations that will work pleasantly and effectively to get him where he wants to go.

Choose, in the light of purpose and situation, not only from among materials, whether you will talk about Greeks or Romans, about cats, felines, tigers, or dogs, but from among qualifying structures—simple qualifiers, or connected phrases and clauses, to support the main direction of what you undertake to assert or query. Certain habits of selection will characterize your style. For example,

Demetrius in Alexandria in the third century B.C. characterized styles not only by the rhetoric of purpose but, as we have done, by the rudimentary uses of certain grammatical constructions. The plain style, he said, is simple, using many active verbs and keeping its subjects spare. Its purposes include lucidity, clarity, familiarity, getting its work done crisply and well; so it uses few difficult compounds, coinages, or qualifications, avoids harsh sounds or odd orders, employs helpful connective terms and clear series with firm endings, and in every way tries to be natural, following the order of events themselves with moderation and repetition as in dialogue.

The eloquent style, in contrast, changes the natural order of materials in order to effect control over them even before predication. So the style may be called *passive* in translation of *pathos*, and in contrast to *active.* Subjects are tremendously amplified, as strong assumptions are made, without the activity of much predication, because inherent qualities rather than new relations are stressed. Sentences are lengthy, rounded, suspended, with a great deal of elaborately connected material. Words can be unusual, coined, figured; sounds can be mouth-filling, even harsh; and meanings can be implied, oblique, symbolic.

The modern student of prose may quickly praise plainness and condemn the eloquent, which he often calls "flowery," but after consideration may remember that purposes differ, and that if he wishes to move, to enhance, to persuade, some language of flowers, some structure of suspense and excitement, may be valuable in contrast to a plain naturalness.

Demetrius cut across this contrast with another, that between styles energetic on the one hand and polished on the other, between short, even harsh phrases, broken, loose, and spontaneous, as if under great stress, with a choice of terms symbolic like the eloquent, though not so elaborated, and without interconnected qualifying structures, in contrast to the polished, smoothly connected, aesthetically pleasant in reference and tone, which embellishes the familiar with charm and grace. Two centuries later, Dionysus of Halicarnassus characterized Pindar by this same contrast, his harmony natural, stately, spacious, articulated by pauses, rather than smoothly polished and joined by connectives; naturally off-balance, not rounded and symmetrical.

Note that this contrast is another version of the first, between an art of naturalness and an art of inventiveness; the first contrast grammatically stressing the choice between predication or qualification; the second, between implicit or explicit connection; these grammatical choices providing the structural basis for choices of reference, reason, and tone. Gradually the choices, in certain combinations, settled into three: plain, middle, and high; because, though the high could not easily descend or blend, the plain could easily be somewhat energetic, somewhat polished, even somewhat eloquent, and thus effect a middle style. In grammatical terms, the predicative style could be either implicitly or explicitly connected, abrupt or smooth; while the high qualifying style, because of its greater mass and extension, could not so easily get along with the abruptnesses of connectives merely implied. For the high style, the terms of reference are implicative of further qualities, rather than of further active relations. The gamut in choice between sparest and fullest materials of qualification is mediated by the choice along the way of sparest or fullest signals of relation. The sentence is a synthesis, a composition, an arrangement of sounds, references, and structures, put to a purpose of showing, weighing, moving, and pleasing along with these.

From the high style of Aeschylus and Demosthenes, to the smooth of Isocrates, to the moderate fullness of Cicero, and the intense brevity of the Stoics, classic prose tradition came into English with all its variations still possible in the new lanquage, so that More, Ascham, and Bacon all within one century could well disagree on what different styles would be appropriate even to similar subject-matters. Still today all three basic styles and their variations are useful, and are, indeed, still discernible by the measures of the most technical linguistic analysis, as beneath the differing surfaces of procedure may be seen the simple kernel forms for the plain style, the deeper and deeper levels of transforms for the high. Perhaps the lesser pertinence of eighteenth and nineteenth century forms of grammatical analysis to our purposes is explainable by their emphasis on the multiple interrelations of the parts of speech in a web of intermodification of forms, without attention to the clarifying main lines of function. In addition to the main function of grammatical structure, predication itself, we have only to consider degree of qualification, with degree of explicit connection as a further factor. So we are able to distinguish the main choices by others and put such choices to use ourselves.

Sentence-making, idea-making, has a strong ethical function, because it helps bring together and temper the extremes of the range, often unfortunately dichotomized, between objective and subjective, between community and individual. Forms of mechanization or of bureaucracy have tended to draw modern men toward the subjective and individual extremes of emotional superlatives unrelated to evidence, while fears of personal responsibility have drawn them to extremes of inert acceptance of evidence.

Statement of idea, in its implications of generality and its susceptibility of particular substantiation, shows how a man may take both firm and limited responsibility for his universe of subject matter. His predicate controls his subject; his adjectives and adverbs specify his assumptions; and his further materials, linked to the basic statement by explicit prepositional and conjunctive connectives, add the specifications of context, the *when, where, how, why,* to the basic *who* and *what.*

The process of statement-making thus develops two ethical powers: individual responsibility and, through awareness of one's own responsible choices, awareness of the like and unlike choices and responsibilities of others.

The English essay, the small trial of an idea, has been tried in many ways, with many tones and styles, in many variations upon the powers of the language, and with increasing emphasis upon some of these powers. For one who plans his own small trials in prose there is no better guide than the versatility of his predecessors.

For the reader over-accustomed to searching out cue words to respond to, rather than whole patterns of speech to comprehend, the way of reading here suggested may be useful in contrast: first to mark the main independent verbs, to see what they are saying about subject and object; then to note the single words and connected groups of words which qualify or parallel them.

For the explorer of ideas, both reader and writer, awareness of the patterns of idea-making may clarify and enrich the ideas themselves.

CLASSIC ESSAYS IN ENGLISH

Of pleasure

FROM *Utopia (1516)*
BY **Sir Thomas More** (1478-1535)

(The Utopians' Idea of Pleasure,
as Reported by Raphael Hythloday)

Pleasure they call every motion and state of the body or mind wherein man hath naturally delectation. Appetite they join to nature, and that not without a good cause. For like as not only the senses, but also right reason, coveteth whatsoever is naturally pleasant; so that it may be gotten without wrong or injury, not letting or debarring a greater pleasure, nor causing painful labor; even so those things that men by vain imagination do feign against nature to be pleasant (as though it lay in their power to change the things as they do the names of things), all such pleasures they believe to be of so small help and furtherance to felicity that they count them great let[1] and hindrance; because that, in whom they have once taken place,[2] all his mind they possess with a false opinion of pleasure; so that there is no place left for true and natural delectations. For there be many things which of their own nature contain no pleasantness, yea the most part of them much grief and sorrow; and yet, through the perverse and malicious flickering incitements of lewd and unhonest desires, be taken not only for special and sovereign pleasures, but also be counted among the chief causes of life.

[1] prevent or deprive [2] taken a fixed place

In this counterfeit kind of pleasure they put them that I spake of before; which, the better gown they have on, the better men they think themselves: in which thing they do twice err, for they be no less deceived in that they think their gown the better than they be in that they think themselves the better. For if you consider the profitable use of the garment, why should wool of a finer-spun thread be thought better than the wool of a coarse-spun thread? Yet they, as though the one did pass the other by nature and not by their mistaking, avaunce themselves and think the price of their own persons thereby greatly increased. And therefore the honor, which in a coarse gown they durst not have looked for, they require as it were of duty, for their finer gown's sake. And if they be passed by without reverence, they take it angrily and disdainfully.

And again, is it not a like madness to take a pride in vain and unprofitable honors? For what natural or true pleasure dost thou take of another man's bare head or bowed knees? Will this ease the pain of thy knees, or remedy the phrensy of thy head? In this image of counterfeit pleasure, they be of a marvellous madness, which for the opinion of nobility[3] rejoice much in their own conceit, because it was their fortune to come of such ancestors, whose stock of long time hath been counted rich (for now nobility is nothing else), specially rich in lands. And though their ancestors left them not one foot of land, or else they themselves have squandered it away, yet they think themselves not the less noble therefore of[4] one hair.

In this number also they count them that take pleasure and delight, as I said, in gems and precious stones, and think themselves almost gods if they chance to get an excellent one; specially of that kind which in that time of their own countrymen is had in highest estimation; for one kind of stone keepeth not his price still in all countries and at all times. Nor they buy them not[5] but taken out of the gold and bare; no, nor so neither, before they have made the seller to swear that he will warrant and assure it to be a true stone and no counterfeit gem. Such care they take lest a counterfeit stone should deceive their eyes in the stead of a right stone. But why shouldst thou not take even as much pleasure in beholding a coun-

[3] because they imagine themselves noble

[4] by

[5] double negatives used for emphasis

terfeit stone which thine eye cannot discern from a right stone? They should both be of a like value to thee, even as to a blind man. What shall I say of them that keep superfluous riches, to take delectation only in the beholding and not in the use or occupying thereof? Do they take true pleasure, or else be they deceived with false pleasure? Or of them that be in a contrary vice, hiding the gold which they shall never occupy, nor peradventure never see more; and, whiles they take care lest they shall lose it, do lose it indeed? For what is it else, when they hide it in the ground, taking it both from their own use and perchance from all other men's also? And yet thou, when thou hast hid thy treasure, as one out of all care hoppest for joy; the which treasure, if it should chance to be stolen and thou, ignorant of the theft, shouldst die ten years after; all that ten years' space that thou livedest after thy money was stolen, what matter was it to thee whether it had been taken away, or else safe as thou leftest it? Truly both ways like profit came to thee.

To these so foolish pleasures they join dicers, whose madness they know by hearsay and not by use; hunters also, and hawkers. For what pleasure is there, say they, in casting the dice upon a table; which thou hast done so often that if there were any pleasure in it, yet the oft use might make thee weary thereof? Or what delight can there be, and not rather displeasure, in hearing the barking and howling of dogs? Or what greater pleasure is there to be felt when a dog followeth an hare than when a dog followeth a dog? for one thing is done in both; that is to say, running; if thou hast pleasure therein. But if the hope of slaughter and the expectation of tearing in pieces the beast doth please thee, thou shouldst rather be moved with pity to see a silly innocent hare murdered of a dog, the weak of the stronger, the fearful of the fierce, the innocent of the cruel and unmerciful. Therefore all this exercise of hunting, as a thing unworthy to be used of free men, the Utopians have rejected to their butchers; to the which craft, as we said before, they appoint their bondmen. For they count hunting the lowest, vilest, and most abject part of butchery; and the other parts of it more profitable and more honest, as which do bring much more commodity; and do kill beasts only for necessity, whereas the hunter seeketh nothing but pleasure of the silly and woeful beast's slaughter and murder; the which pleasure in beholding death they think doth rise in the very beasts either of a cruel affection of mind or else to be changed in continuance of time into cruelty by long use of so cruel a pleasure. This therefore and all such like, which is innumerable, though the common sort of people doth take them for pleasures, yet they, seeing there is no natural pleasantness in them, do plainly determine them to have no affinity with true and right pleasure. For as touching that they do commonly move the sense with delectation (which seemeth to be a work of pleasure) this doth nothing diminish their opinion. For not the nature of the thing but their perverse and lewd custom is the cause hereof; which causeth them to accept bitter or sour things for sweet things, even as women with child, in their vitiate and corrupt taste, think pitch and tallow sweeter than any honey. Howbeit no man's judgement, depraved and corrupt either by sickness or by custom, can change the nature of pleasure more than it can do the nature of other things.

They make divers kinds of true pleasures; for some they attribute to the soul and some to the body. To the soul they give intelligence and that delectation that cometh of the contemplation of truth. Hereunto is joined the pleasant remembrance of the good life past and the assured hopes of a future happiness.

The pleasure of the body they divide into two parts. The first is when delectation is sensibly felt and perceived, which many times chanceth by the renewing and refreshing of those parts which our natural heat drieth up: this cometh by meat and drink, and sometimes whiles those things be voided whereof is in the body over-great abundance. Sometimes pleasure riseth, exhibiting to any member nothing that it desireth nor taking from it any pain that it feeleth, which for all that tickleth and moveth our senses with a certain secret efficacy, but with a manifest motion, and turneth them to it; as is that which cometh of music.

The second part of bodily pleasure they say is that which consisteth and resteth in the quiet and upright state of the body. And that truly is every man's own proper health, intermingled and disturbed with no grief. For this, if it be not letted nor assaulted with no grief, is delectable of itself, though it be moved with no external or outward pleasure. For though it be not so plain and manifest to the sense as the greedy lust[6] of eating and drinking, yet neverthe-

[6] pleasure

less many take it for the chiefest pleasure. All the Utopians grant it to be a right great pleasure, and, as you would say, the foundation and ground of all pleasures; as which even alone is able to make the state and condition of life delectable and pleasant; and, it being once taken away, there is no place left for any pleasure. For to be without grief, not having health, that they call unsensibility and not pleasure. The Utopians have long ago rejected and condemned the opinion of them which said that steadfast and quiet health (for this question also hath been diligently debated among them) ought not therefore to be counted a pleasure, because they say it cannot be presently and sensibly perceived and felt by some outward motion. But, of the contrary part, now they agree almost all in this, that health is a most sovereign pleasure. For seeing that in sickness, say they, is grief, which is a mortal enemy to pleasure, even as sickness is to health, why should not then pleasure be in the quietness of health? For they say it maketh nothing to this matter, whether you say that sickness is a grief, or that in sickness is grief, for all cometh to one purpose. For whether health be a pleasure itself or a necessary cause of pleasure, as fire is of heat, truly both ways it followeth, that they cannot be without pleasure that be in perfect health. Furthermore, whiles we eat, say they, then health, which began to be appaired, fighteth by the help of food against hunger; in the which fight whiles health by little and little getteth the upper hand, that same proceeding, and, as ye would say, that onwardness[7] to the wont[8] strength ministreth that pleasure whereby we be so refreshed. Health therefore, which in the conflict is joyful, shall it not be merry when it hath gotten the victory? But as soon as it hath recovered the pristinate strength, which thing only in all the fight it coveted, shall it incontinent be astonied? Nor shall it not know nor embrace the own wealth and goodness? For that it is said health cannot be felt, this, they think, is nothing true. For what man waking, say they, feeleth not himself in health but he that is not? Is there any man so possessed with stonish insensibility, or with the sleeping sickness, that he will not grant health to be acceptable to him and delectable? But what other thing is delectation than that which by another name is called pleasure?

They embrace [therefore] chiefly the pleasures of the mind; for

[7] approach [8] accustomed

them they count the chiefest and most principal of all. The chief part of them they think doth come of the exercise of virtue and conscience[9] of good life. Of these pleasures that the body ministreth they give the preeminence to health. For the delight of eating and drinking, and whatsoever hath any like pleasantness, they determine to be pleasures much to be desired, but no other ways than for health's sake. For such things of their own proper nature be not pleasant, but in that they resist sickness privily stealing on. Therefore, like as it is a wise man's part rather to avoid sickness than to wish for medicines, and rather to drive away and put to flight careful[10] griefs than to call for comfort, so it is much better not to need this kind of pleasure than in sealing the contrary grief to be eased of the same: the which kind of pleasure if any man take for his felicity, that man must needs grant that then he shall be in most felicity, if he live that life which is led in continual hunger, thirst, itching, eating, drinking, scratching, and rubbing; the which life how not only foul it is but also miserable and wretched, who perceiveth not? These doubtless be the basest pleasures of all, as unpure and unperfect; for they never come but accompanied with their contrary griefs, as with the pleasure of eating is joined hunger, and that after no very equal sort. For of these two the grief is both the more vehement, and also of longer continuance. For it riseth before the pleasure, and endeth not until the pleasure die with it.

Wherefore such pleasures they think not greatly to be set by, but in that they be necessary. Howbeit they have delight also in these, and thankfully knowledge the tender love of mother nature, which with most pleasant delectation allureth her children to that which of necessity they be driven often [to] use. For how wretched and miserable should our life be, if these daily griefs of hunger and thirst could not be driven away but with bitter potions and sour medicines, as the other diseases be wherewith we be seldomer troubled? But beauty, strength, nimbleness, these, as peculiar and pleasant gifts of nature, they make much of. But those pleasures which be received by the ears, the eyes, and the nose; which nature willeth to be proper and peculiar to man (for no other kind of living beasts doth behold the fairness and the beauty of the world, or is moved

[9] consciousness [10] full of care

with any respect of savours, but only for the diversity of meats, neither perceiveth the concordant and discordant distances of sounds and tunes) these pleasures, I say, they accept and allow as certain pleasant rejoicings of life. But in all things this cautel[11] they use, that a less pleasure hinder not a bigger, and that the pleasure be no cause of displeasure; which they think to follow of necessity, if the pleasure be unhonest. But yet to despise the comeliness of beauty, to waste the bodily strength, to turn nimbleness into sluggishness, to consume and make feeble the body with fasting, to do injury to health, and to reject the other pleasant motions of nature (unless a man neglect these his commodities whiles he doth with a fervent zeal procure the wealth of others, or the common profit, for the which pleasure forborne he is in hope of a greater pleasure of God): else for a vain shadow of virtue, for the wealth and profit of no man, to punish himself, or to the intent he may be able courageously to suffer adversity, which perchance shall never come to him: this to do they think it a point of extreme madness, and a token of a man cruelly-minded towards himself and unkind toward nature, as one so disdaining to be in her danger that he renounceth and refuseth all her benefits.

This is their sentence[12] and opinion of virtue and pleasure. And they believe that by man's reason none can be found truer than this, unless any godlier be inspired into man from heaven. Wherein whether they believe well or no, neither the time doth suffer us to discuss, neither it is now necessary; for we have taken upon us to show and declare their lores and ordinances,[13] and not to defend them.

[11]caution [12]proposition [13]attitudes and laws

☙ In 1516, when *Utopia* was first published in its original Latin version, there was much debate about morality, and there was much puritanical restriction of pleasure on the one hand as well as lawless excess on the other. Thomas More was a lawyer and scholar who rose to be Lord Chancellor under King Henry VIII, yet was beheaded by Henry for his fidelity to Catholic orthodoxy. Always he emphasized the "humanist" position of the use of natural reason to moderate extreme passion, the use of classical learning to moderate fanaticisms of the English Reformation.

Our brief selection on the goodness of pleasure is from Book II of *Utopia,* the first-written and more constructive of the two books. Raphael Hythloday, the "babbler of marvels," now retired from active life, meets More and tells him of the ideal "nowhere" island, of its government, finance, education, and religious toleration, all of these by implied contrast and comparison casting some light on England's own, though not all to be identified with More's own, ideals.

Though written originally in Latin, *Utopia* when it appeared in English translation in 1551 was one of the first solid prose texts in English. You may note the difference in its style of language from ours today: for example, the *-eth* verb-ending, and some unfamiliar uses of prepositions. But note also its lively and active developing of thought: *They call . . . they join . . . they believe . . . ,* and then the negative instances of the next four paragraphs, followed by the positive examples of the following five. As you reread "Of Pleasure," notice how directly and simply More proceeds.

Of learning and experience

FROM *The Schoolmaster (1570)*
BY **Roger Ascham** *(1515-1568)*

Learning teacheth more in one year than experience in twenty; and learning teacheth safely when experience maketh more miserable than wise. He hazardeth sore that waxeth wise by experience. An unhappy master he is that is made cunning[1] by many shipwrecks; a miserable merchant, that is neither rich nor wise but after some bankruptcies. It is costly wisdom that is bought by experience. We know by experience itself that it is a marvellous pain to find out but a short way by long wandering; and surely he that would prove wise by experience, he may be witty indeed, but even like a swift runner, that runneth fast out of his way, and upon the night, he knoweth not whither. And verily they be fewest of number that be happy or wise by unlearned[2] experience. And look well upon the former life of those few, whether your example be old or young, who without learning have gathered, by long experience, a little wisdom and some happiness; and when you do consider what mischief they have committed, what dangers they have escaped (and yet twenty for one do perish in the adventure), then think well with yourself whether ye would that your own son should come to wisdom and happiness by the way of such experience or no.

[1] knowledgeable [2] not gained by learning

It is a notable tale, that old Sir Roger Chamloe, sometime Chief Justice, would tell of himself. When he was Ancient in Inn of Court, certain young gentlemen were brought before him to be corrected for certain misorders. And one of the lustiest said: "Sir, we be young gentlemen, and wise men before us have proved all fashions, and yet those have done full well"; this they said because it was well known that Sir Roger had been a good fellow in his youth. But he answered them very wisely. "Indeed," saith he, "in youth I was as you are now; and I had twelve fellows like unto myself, but not one of them came to a good end. And therefore follow not my example in youth, but follow my council in age, if ever ye think to come to this place, or to these years, that I am come unto, lest ye meet either with poverty or Tyburn[3] in the way."

Thus experience of all fashions in youth, being in proof always dangerous, in issue seldom lucky, is a way indeed to overmuch knowledge, yet used commonly of such men, which be either carried by some curious affection of mind, or driven by some hard necessity of life to hazard the trial of over many perilous adventures.

Erasmus, the honour of learning of all our time, said wisely that experience is the common schoolhouse of fools and ill men. Men of wit and honesty be otherwise instructed, for there be that keep them out of fire, and yet was never burned; that beware of water, and yet was never nigh drowning; that hate harlots, and was never at the stews;[4] that abhor falsehood, and never break promises themselves.

But will ye see a fit similitude of this adventured experience? A father that doth let loose his son to all experiences is most like a fond[5] hunter that letteth slip a whelp to the whole herd. Twenty to one he shall fall upon a rascal[6] and let go the fair game. Men that hunt so be either ignorant persons, privy[7] stealers, or night walkers.[8]

Learning, therefore, ye wise fathers, and good bringing up, and not blind and dangerous experience, is the next and readiest way that must lead your children first to wisdom and then to worthiness, if ever ye purpose they shall come there.

[3] place of public execution
[4] brothel [5] foolish
[6] one of the rabble [7] secret
[8] worker by night, by stealth

And to say all in short, though I lack authority to give counsel, yet I lack not goodwill to wish that the youth in England, especially gentlemen—and, namely, nobility—should be by good bringing up so grounded in judgement of learning, so founded in love of honesty, as when they should be called forth to the execution of great affairs, in service of their prince and country, they might be able to use and to order all experiences, were they good, were they bad, and that according to the square, rule, and line of wisdom, learning, and virtue.

And I do not mean by all this my talk that young gentlemen should always be poring on a book, and by using good studies should leave honest pleasure and haunt no good pastime—I mean nothing less—for it is well known that I both like and love, and have always, and do yet still use, all exercises and pastimes that be fit for my nature and ability. And beside natural disposition, in judgement also I was never either stoic in doctrine or anabaptist in religion to mislike a merry, pleasant, and playful nature, if no outrage be committed against law, measure, and good order.

Therefore I would wish that, besides some good time fitly appointed and constantly kept, to increase by reading the knowledge of the tongues and learning, young gentlemen should use and delight in all courtly exercises and gentlemanlike pastimes.

Educated in classics at Cambridge, and tutor and secretary to Queen Mary and Queen Elizabeth, Ascham is nevertheless best known for his championing of simplicity, in his Protestant theories of religion, education, sport, and language. *The Schoolmaster* and his work on archery, *Toxophilus*, were written in English, marking the beginning, in the mid-sixteenth century, of serious composition in the native language. Ascham makes his main point with vivid qualification, much richer than More's. He contrasts the value of learning with that of experience both in quantity and in security. He gives examples, like that of the merchant, and analogies or comparisons, like that of the runner. He makes warnings—"Look well"—he addresses the reader directly as *you,* he gives an anecdote from Sir Roger and a quotation from his great humanist predecessor, Erasmus, he asks a question, he summarizes "in short," and finally he makes clear what he does not mean, in relation to what he does mean—all in all creating a succinct little essay section in his larger work.

Despite the clarity of sentence-structure and argument, some of the wording and order of words is now unfamiliar. For his sentence "He hazardeth sore that waxeth wise by experience," we would use different verbs, adverbs, and order: "He who grows wise by experience risks much."

Of friendship

FROM *The Essays, or Counsels, Civil and Moral,* XXVII (1625)
BY *Sir Francis Bacon (1561-1626)*

It had been hard for him that spake it to have put more truth and untruth together in few words, than in that speech, *Whosoever is delighted in solitude is either a wild beast or a god.* For it is most true that a natural and secret hatred and aversation towards society in any man, hath somewhat of the savage beast; but it is most untrue that it should have any character at all of the divine nature; except it proceed, not out of a pleasure in solitude, but out of a love and desire to sequester a man's self for a higher conversation: such as is found to have been falsely and feignedly in some of the heathen; as Epimenides the Candian, Numa the Roman, Empedocles the Sicilian, and Apollonius of Tyana; and truly and really in divers of the ancient hermits and holy fathers of the church. But little do men perceive what solitude is, and how far it extendeth. For a crowd is not company; and faces are but a gallery of pictures; and talk but a tinkling cymbal, where there is no love. The Latin adage meeteth with it a little: *Magna civitas, magna solitudo,*[1] because in a great town friends are scattered; so that there is not that fellowship, for the most part, which is in less neighbourhoods. But we may go further, and affirm most truly that it is a mere and miserable solitude to want true friends; without which the world is but a wilderness; and even in this sense also of solitude, whosoever in the

[1] a great town, a great solitude

frame of his nature and affections is unfit for friendship, he taketh it of the beast, and not from humanity.

A principal fruit of friendship is the ease and discharge of the fulness and swellings of the heart, which passions of all kinds do cause and induce. We know diseases of stoppings and suffocations are the most dangerous in the body; and it is not much otherwise in the mind; you may take sarza to open the liver, steel to open the spleen, flowers of sulphur for the lungs, castoreum for the brain; but no receipt[2] openeth the heart, but a true friend; to whom you may impart griefs, joys, fears, hopes, suspicions, counsels, and whatsoever lieth upon the heart to oppress it, in a kind of civil shrift or confession.

It is a strange thing to observe how high a rate great kings and monarchs do set upon this fruit of friendship whereof we speak: so great, as they purchase it many times at the hazard of their own safety and greatness. For princes, in regard of the distance of their fortune from that of their subjects and servants, cannot gather this fruit, except (to make themselves capable thereof) they raise some persons to be as it were companions and almost equals to themselves, which many times sorteth to[3] inconvenience. The modern languages give unto such persons the name of favourites, or *privadoes*;[4] as if it were matter of grace, or conversation. But the Roman name attaineth the true use and cause thereof, naming them *participes curarum*;[5] for it is that which tieth the knot. And we see plainly that this hath been done, not by weak and passionate princes only, but by the wisest and most politic that ever reigned; who have oftentimes joined to themselves some of their servants; whom both themselves have called friends, and allowed others likewise to call them in the same manner; using the word which is received between private men.

L. Sylla, when he commanded Rome, raised Pompey (after surnamed the Great) to that height, that Pompey vaunted himself for Sylla's over-match. For when he had carried the counsulship for a friend of his, against the pursuit of Sylla, and that Sylla did a little resent thereat, and began to speak great, Pompey turned upon him again, and in effect bade him be quiet; *for that more men adored the*

[2] prescription [3] results in [4] intimates [5] sharers of cares

sun rising than the sun setting. With Julius Caesar, Decimus Brutus had obtained that interest, as he set him down in his testament for heir in remainder after his nephew. And this was the man that had power with him to draw him forth to his death. For when Caesar would have discharged the senate, in regard of some ill presages, and specially a dream of Calpurnia; this man lifted him gently by the arm out of his chair, telling him he hoped he would not dismiss the senate till his wife had dreamt a better dream. And it seemeth his favour was so great, as Antonius, in a letter which is recited *verbatim* in one of Cicero's Philippics, calleth him *venefica,* witch; as if he had enchanted Caesar. Augustus raised Agrippa (though of mean birth) to that height, as when he consulted with Maecenas about the marriage of his daughter Julia, Maecenas took the liberty to tell him, *that he must either marry his daughter to Agrippa, or take away his life; there was no third way, he had made him so great.* With Tiberius Caesar, Sejanus had ascended to that height, as they two were termed and reckoned as a pair of friends. Tiberius in a letter to him saith, *haec pro amicitia nostra non occultavi;*[6] and the whole senate dedicated an altar to Friendship, as to a goddess, in respect of the great dearness of friendship between them two. The like or more was between Septimius Severus and Plautianus. For he forced his eldest son to marry the daughter of Plautianus; and would often maintain Plautianus in doing affronts to his son; and did write also in a letter to the senate, by these words: *I love the man so well, as I wish he may over-live me.* Now if these princes had been as a Trajan or a Marcus Aurelius, a man might have thought that this had proceeded of an abundant goodness of nature; but being men so wise, of such strength and severity of mind, and so extreme lovers of themselves, as all these were, it proveth most plainly that they found their own felicity (though as great as ever happened to mortal men) but as an half piece, except they mought have a friend to make it entire; and yet, which is more, they were princes that had wives, sons, nephews; and yet all these could not supply the comfort of friendship.

It is not to be forgotten what Commineus observeth of his first master, Duke Charles the Hardy; namely, that he would communi-

[6]These things, on account of our friendship, I have not hidden from you.

cate his secrets with none; and least of all, those secrets which troubled him most. Whereupon he goeth on and saith that towards his latter time *that closeness did impair and a little perish his understanding.* Surely Commineus mought have made the same judgment also, if it had pleased him, of his second master, Lewis the Eleventh, whose closeness was indeed his tormentor. The parable of Pythagoras is dark, but true; *Cor ne edito: Eat not the heart.* Certainly, if a man would give it a hard phrase, those that want friends to open themselves unto are cannibals of their own hearts. But one thing is most admirable (where-with I will conclude this first fruit of friendship), which is, that this communicating of a man's self to his friend works two contrary effects; for it redoubleth joys, and cutteth griefs in halfs. For there is no man that imparteth his joys to his friend, but he joyeth the more; and no man that imparteth his griefs to his friend, but he grieveth the less. So that it is in truth of operation upon a man's mind, of like virtue as the alchemists use to attribute to their stone for man's body; that it worketh all contrary effects, but still to the good and benefit of nature. But yet without praying in aid of alchemists, there is a manifest image of this in the ordinary course of nature. For in bodies, union strengtheneth and cherisheth any natural action; and on the other side weakeneth and dulleth any violent impression; and even so is it of minds.

The second fruit of friendship is healthful and sovereign for the understanding, as the first is for the affections. For friendship maketh indeed a fair day in the affections, from storm and tempests; but it maketh daylight in the understanding, out of darkness and confusion of thoughts. Neither is this to be understood only of faithful counsel, which a man receiveth from his friend; but before you come to that, certain it is that whosoever hath his mind fraught with many thoughts, his wits and understanding do clarify and break up, in the communicating and discoursing with another; he tosseth his thoughts more easily; he marshalleth them more orderly; he seeth how they look when they are turned into words: finally, he waxeth wiser than himself; and that more by an hour's discourse than by a day's meditation. It was well said by Themistocles to the king of Persia, *That speech was like cloth of Arras, opened and put abroad; whereby the imagery doth appear in figure; whereas in thoughts they lie but as in packs.* Neither is this second fruit of friendship, in opening the understanding, restrained only to such friends as are able to give a man counsel; (they indeed are best); but even without that, a man learneth of himself, and bringeth his own thoughts to light, and whetteth his wits as against a stone, which itself cuts not. In a word, a man were better relate himself to a statue or picture, than to suffer his thoughts to pass in smother.

Add now, to make this second fruit of friendship complete, that other point which lieth more open and falleth within vulgar observation; which is faithful counsel from a friend. Heraclitus saith well in one of his enigmas, *Dry light is ever the best.* And certain it is, that the light that a man receiveth by counsel from another, is drier and purer than that which cometh from his own understanding and judgment; which is ever infused and drenched in his affections and customs. So as there is as much difference between the counsel that a friend giveth, and that a man giveth himself, as there is between the counsel of a friend and of a flatterer. For there is no such flatterer as is a man's self; and there is no such remedy against flattery of a man's self, as the liberty of a friend. Counsel is of two sorts: the one concerning manners, the other concerning business. For the first, the best preservative to keep the mind in health is the faithful admonition of a friend. The calling of a man's self to a strict account is a medicine, sometime, too piercing and corrosive. Reading good books of morality is a little flat and dead. Observing our faults in others is sometimes unproper for our case. But the best receipt (best I say, to work, and best to take) is the admonition of a friend. It is a strange thing to behold what gross errors and extreme absurdities many (especially of the greater sort) do commit, for want of a friend to tell them of them; to the great damage both of their fame and fortune: for, as St. James saith, they are as men *that look sometimes into a glass, and presently forget their own shape and favour.* As for business, a man may think, if he will, that two eyes see no more than one; or that a gamester seeth always more than a looker-on; or that a man in anger is as wise as he that hath said over the four and twenty letters; or that a musket may be shot off as well upon the arm as upon a rest; and such other fond and high imaginations, to think himself all in all. But when all is done, the help of good counsel is that which setteth business straight. And if any man think that he will take counsel, but it shall be by pieces; asking counsel in one business of one man, and in another business of another man; it is well, (that is to say, better perhaps than if he asked none at all;) but he runneth two dangers: one, that he shall not be faithfully counselled; for it is a rare thing, except it be from a perfect and entire friend, to have counsel given, but such as shall be bowed and crooked to some ends which he hath that giveth it. The other, that he shall have counsel given, hurtful and unsafe, (though with good meaning,) and mixed partly of mischief and partly of remedy; even as if you would call a physician that is thought good for the cure of the disease you complain of, but is unacquainted with your body; and therefore may put you in way for a present cure, but overthroweth your health in some other kind; and so cure the disease and kill the patient. But a friend that is wholly acquainted with a man's estate will beware, by furthering any present business, how he dasheth upon other inconvenience. And therefore rest not upon scattered counsels, they will rather distract and mislead, than settle and direct.

After these two noble fruits of friendship (peace in the affections, and support of the judgment) followeth the last fruit; which is like the pomegranate, full of many kernels; I mean aid and bearing a part in all actions and occasions. Here the best way to represent to life the manifold use of friendship, is to cast and see how many things there are which a man cannot do himself; and then it will appear that it was a sparing speech of the ancients, to say, *that a friend is another himself;* for that a friend is far more than himself. Men have their time, and die many times in desire of some things which they principally take to heart; the bestowing of a child, the finishing of a work, or the like. If a man have a true friend, he may rest almost secure that the care of those things will continue after him. So that a man hath, as it were, two lives in his desires. A man hath a body, and that body is confined to a place; but where friendship is, all offices of life are as it were granted to him and his deputy. For he may exercise them by his friend. How many things are there which a man cannot, with any face or comeliness, say or do himself? A man can scarce allege his own merits with modesty, much less extol them; a man cannot sometimes brook to supplicate or beg; and a number of the like. But all these things are graceful in a friend's mouth, which are blushing in a man's own. So again, a man's person hath many proper relations which he cannot put off. A man cannot speak to his son but as a father; to his wife but as a husband; to his enemy but upon terms; whereas a friend may speak as the case requires, and not as it sorteth[7] with the person. But to enumerate these things were endless; I have given the rule, where a man cannot fitly play his own part; if he have not a friend, he may quit the stage.

[7] agrees

☙ The *Essays, or Counsels, Civil and Moral,* of Sir Francis Bacon represent a third step forward in the use of prose in English: they were consciously thought of as a new form, the essay, borrowed from the "essaies," or little attempts, little excursions, of Montaigne, in French, which John Florio had just recently translated into English. Bacon liked the form and began to use it, and it has been used ever since, for meditation, for philosophical argument, for humorous comment. Most of Bacon's essays concern problems of people and of public responsibility. Educated at Cambridge and in law at Gray's Inn, and anti-Catholic, he was one of the highest ranking officials in King James' court, Lord Chancellor, until an accusation that he had taken a bribe sent him into retirement. There he worked to complete a new system of philosophy to take the place of Aristotle's; there he, like Sir Thomas More, wrote a "Utopia," called "The New Atlantis," and there he revised the earlier essays, first published nearly thirty years before, and increased their number from ten to fifty-eight.

Much of his more monumental work was written first in Latin; but in his little "essays" he tried an intricate and complex English full of allusions, quotations, parentheses, and pithy remarks sounding almost like proverbs. You may note as you reread that he is neither so sharp in action as More nor so vivid in qualification as Ascham. He balances their powers by a strong sense of logical connection as in *more . . . than, for, but, except, such.* He develops the idea of two fruits of friendship as *idea*, more than as situation or quality. So we see the power of abstraction in his quotations and allusions.

How a gallant should behave himself in a play-house

FROM *The Gull's*[1] *Horn-Book*,[2] *Chapter VI (1609)*
BY *Thomas Dekker (c. 1572-1632)*

The theatre is your poets' royal exchange, upon which their muses (that are now turned to merchants) meeting, barter away that light commodity of words for a lighter ware than words, plaudities, and the breath of the great beast; which (like the threatenings of two cowards) vanish all into air. Players and their factors, who put away the stuff, and make the best of it they possibly can (as indeed 'tis their parts so to do), your gallant, your courtier, and your captain, had wont to be the soundest paymasters; and I think are still the surest chapmen; and these, by means that their heads are well stocked, deal upon this comical freight by the gross: when your groundling, and gallery-commoner buys his sport by the penny, and, like a haggler, is glad to utter it again by retailing.

Since then the place is so free in entertainment, allowing a stool as well to the farmer's son as to your templar:[3] that your stinkard has the selfsame liberty to be there in his tobacco fumes, which your sweet courtier hath: and that your carman and tinker claim as strong a voice in their suffrage, and sit to give judgment on the

[1] dupe or fool
[2] a parchment tablet for lessons or records, protected by a thin plate of horn
[3] a resident of one of the Inns of Court, a barrister or law student

play's life and death, as well as the proudest momus[4] among the tribes of critic: it is fit that he, whom the most tailors' bills do make room for, when he comes, should not be basely (like a viol) cased up in a corner.

Whether therefore the gatherers[5] of the public or private play-house stand to receive the afternoon's rent, let our gallant (having paid it) presently advance himself up to the throne of the stage. I mean not into the lord's room (which is now but the stage's suburbs): no, those boxes, by the iniquity of custom, conspiracy of waiting women and gentlemen ushers, that there sweat together, and the covetousness of shares, are contemptibly thrust into the rear, and much new satin is there damned, by being smothered to death in darkness. But on the very rushes where the comedy is to dance, yea, and under the state[6] of Cambises[7] himself must our feathered estridge, like a piece of ordnance, be planted, valiantly (because impudently) beating down the mewes and hisses of the opposed rascality.[8]

For do but cast up a reckoning, what large comings-in are pursed up[9] by sitting on the stage. First a conspicuous eminence is got; by which means, the best and most essential parts of a gallant (good clothes, a proportionable leg, white hand, the Persian lock, and a tolerable beard) are perfectly revealed.

By sitting on the stage, you have signed patent to engross the whole commodity of censure; may lawfully presume to be a girder; and stand at the helm to steer the passage of scenes; yet no man shall once offer to hinder you from obtaining the title of an insolent, overweening coxcomb.

By sitting on the stage, you may (without travelling for it) at the very next door ask whose play it is: and, by that quest of inquiry, the law warrants you to avoid much mistaking: if you know not the author, you may rail against him: and peradventure so behave yourself, that you may enforce the author to know you.

By sitting on the stage, if you be a knight, you may happily[10] get you a mistress: if a mere Fleet-street gentleman, a wife: but assure

[4] faultfinder, from Momus, god of censure and mockery [5] door-keeper
[6] canopy [7] the hero in a play, *Cambises King of Persia* [8] rabble
[9] what great advantage is secured (maintaining an economic metaphor)
[10] by chance

yourself, by continual residence, you are the first and principal man in election to begin the number of We Three.[11]

By spreading your body on the stage, and by being a justice in examining of plays, you shall put yourself into such true scenical authority, that some poet shall not dare to present his muse rudely upon your eyes, without having first unmasked her, rifled her, and discovered all her bare and most mystical parts before you at a tavern, when you most knightly shall, for his pains, pay for both their suppers.

By sitting on the stage, you may (with small cost) purchase the dear acquaintance of the boys: have a good stool for sixpence: at any time know what particular part any of the infants present: get your match lighted, examine the play-suits' lace, and perhaps win wagers upon laying 'tis copper, etc. And to conclude, whether you be a fool or a justice of peace, a cuckold, or a captain, a lord-mayor's son, or a dawcock, a knave, or an under-sheriff; of what stamp soever you be, current, or counterfeit, the stage, like time, will bring you to most perfect light and lay you open: neither are you to be hunted from thence, though the scarecrows in the yard hoot at you, hiss at you, spit at you, yea, throw dirt even in your teeth: 'tis most gentlemanlike patience to endure all this, and to laugh at the silly animals: but if the rabble, with a full throat, cry, "Away with the fool," you were worse than a madman to tarry by it: for the gentleman and the fool should never sit on the stage together.

Marry,[12] let this observation go hand in hand with the rest: or rather, like a country serving-man, some five yards before them. Present not yourself on the stage (especially at a new play) until the quaking prologue hath (by rubbing) got colour into his cheeks, and is ready to give the trumpets their cue, that he's upon point to enter: for then it is time, as though you were one of the properties, or that you dropped out of the hangings to creep from behind the arras, with your tripos or three-footed stool in one hand, and a teston[13] mounted between a forefinger and thumb in the other: for if you should bestow your person upon the vulgar, when the belly of the house is but half full, your apparel is quite eaten up, the

[11] a picture of two fools or asses thus inscribed

[12] exclamation, "by Mary" [13] coin

fashion lost, and the proportion of your body in more danger to be devoured than if it were served up in the counter amongst the poultry: avoid that as you would the bastome.[14] It shall crown you with rich commendation to laugh aloud in the midst of the most serious and saddest scene of the terriblest tragedy; and to let that clapper (your tongue) be tossed so high, that all the house may ring of it: your lords use it; your knights are apes to the lords, and do so too: your in-a-court-man is zany[15] to the knights, and (marry very scurvily) comes likewise limping after it: be thou a beagle to them all, and never lin[16] snuffing, till you have scented them: for talking and laughing (like a ploughman in a morris) you heap Pelion upon Ossa, glory upon glory: as first, all the eyes in the galleries will leave walking after the players, and only follow you: the simplest dolt in the house snatches up your name, and when he meets you in the streets, or that you fall into his hands in the middle of a watch, his word shall be taken for you: he'll cry "He's such a gallant," and you pass. Secondly, you publish your temperance to the world, in that you seem not to resort thither to taste vain pleasures with a hungry appetite: but only as a gentleman to spend a foolish hour or two, because you can do nothing else: thirdly, you mightily disrelish the audience, and disgrace the author: marry, you take up (though it be at the worst hand) a strong opinion of your own judgment, and enforce the poet to take pity of your weakness, and, by some dedicated sonnet, to bring you into a better paradise, only to stop your mouth.

If you can (either for love or money), provide yourself a lodging by the water side: for, above the convenience it brings to shun shoulder-clapping[17] and to ship away your cockatrice betimes in the morning, it adds a kind of state unto you, to be carried from thence to the stairs of your play-house: hate a sculler (remember that) worse than to be acquainted with one o' th' scullery. No, your oars are your only sea-crabs, board them, and take heed you never go twice together with one pair: often shifting is a great credit to gentlemen; and that dividing of your fare will make the poor water-snakes be ready to pull you in pieces to enjoy your custom: no matter whether upon landing, you have money or no: you may

[14] cudgel [15] ape [16] cease [17] by a constable, hence arrest

swim in twenty of their boats over the river upon ticket: marry, when silver comes in, remember to pay treble their fare, and it will make your flounder-catchers to send more thanks after you, when you do not draw, than when you do; for they know, it will be their own another day.

Before the play begins, fall to cards: you may win or lose (as fencers do in a prize) and beat one another by confederacy, yet share the money when you meet at supper: notwithstanding, to gull the ragamuffins that stand aloof gaping at you, throw the cards (having first torn four or five of them) round about the stage, just upon the third sound,[18] as though you had lost: it skills not if the four knaves lie on their backs, and outface the audience; there's none such fools as dare take exceptions at them, because, ere the play go off, better knaves than they will fall into the company.

Now sir, if the writer be a fellow that hath either epigrammed you, or hath had a flirt at your mistress, or hath brought either your feather, or your red beard, or your little legs, etc., on the stage, you shall disgrace him worse than by tossing him in a blanket, or giving him the bastinado in a tavern, if, in the middle of his play (be it pastoral or comedy, moral or tragedy), you rise with a screwed and discontented face from your stool to be gone: no matter whether the scenes be good or no; the better they are the worse do you distaste them: and, being on your feet, sneak not away like a coward, but salute all your gentle acquaintance, that are spread either on the rushes, or on stools about you, and draw what troop you can from the stage after you: the mimics are beholden to you, for allowing them elbow room: their poet cries, perhaps, "a pox go with you," but care not for that, there's no music without frets.

Marry, if either the company, or indisposition of the weather bind you to sit it out, my counsel is then that you turn plain ape, take up a rush, and tickle the earnest ears of your fellow gallants, to make other fools fall a-laughing: mew at passionate speeches, blare at merry, find fault with the music, whew at the children's action, whistle at the songs: and above all, curse the sharers, that whereas the same day you had bestowed forty shillings on an embroidered felt and feather (Scotch-fashion) for your mistress in the court, or

[18] equal to dimming the lights as the play is about to begin

your punk in the city, within two hours after, you encounter with the very same block[19] on the stage, when the haberdasher swore to you the impression was extant but that morning.

To conclude, hoard up the finest play-scraps you can get, upon which your lean wit may most savourly feed, for want of other stuff, when the Arcadian and Euphuised gentlewomen have their tongues sharpened to set upon you: that quality (next to your shuttlecock) is the only furniture to a courtier that's but a new beginner, and is but in his A B C of compliment. The next places that are filled, after the play-houses be emptied, are (or ought to be) taverns: into a tavern then let us next march, where the brains of one hogshead must be beaten out to make up another.

[19] style of hat

§ *The Gull's Horn-Book* (1609) is a sequence of satirical essays or recommendations in reverse. Thomas Dekker was a Londoner and a successful playwright; not college-educated, he was often irritated by the bad manners of foppish courtiers, and wrote these ironical instructions to them, saying the opposite of what he meant. He also wrote serious moral pamphlets and prose devotions; yet his best known work is the light comedy, *The Shoemaker's Holiday.*

His tone and style may be compared with those of Addison, Franklin, Swift, and Orwell.

Ecclesiastes

FROM *The Bible,* Authorized Version, King James Bible *(1611)*

Chapter 1

The words of the Preacher, the son of David, king in Jerusalem.
2 Vanity of vanities, saith the Preacher, vanity of vanities; all is
vanity.[1]
3 What profit hath a man of all his labour which he taketh under
the sun?
4 One generation passeth away, and another generation cometh:
but the earth abideth for ever.
5 The sun also ariseth, and the sun goeth down, and hasteth to
his place where he arose.
6 The wind goeth toward the south, and turneth about unto the
north; it whirleth about continually, and the wind returneth again
according to his circuits.
7 All the rivers run into the sea; yet the sea is not full; unto the
place from whence the rivers come, thither they return again.
8 All things are full of labour; man cannot utter it: the eye is not
satisfied with seeing, nor the ear filled with hearing.
9 The thing that hath been, it is that which shall be; and that
which is done is that which shall be done: and there is no new thing
under the sun.
10 Is there any thing whereof it may be said, See, this is new? it
hath been already of old time, which was before us.

[1] As used in the Bible, *vanity* is not restricted to its modern meaning of *prideful,* but suggests *worthlessness* or *futility* as *in vain.*

11 There is no remembrance of former things; neither shall
there be any remembrance of things that are to come with those
that shall come after.
12 ¶ I the Preacher was king over Israel in Jerusalem.
13 And I gave my heart to seek and search out by wisdom concerning all things that are done under heaven: this sore travail hath
God given to the sons of man to be exercised therewith.
14 I have seen all the works that are done under the sun; and,
behold, all is vanity and vexation of spirit.
15 That which is crooked cannot be made straight: and that
which is wanting cannot be numbered.
16 I communed with mine own heart, saying, Lo, I am come to
great estate, and have gotten more wisdom than all they that have
been before me in Jerusalem: yea, my heart had great experience of
wisdom and knowledge.
17 And I gave my heart to know wisdom, and to know madness
and folly: I perceived that this also is vexation of spirit.
18 For in much wisdom is much grief: and he that increaseth
knowledge increaseth sorrow.

Chapter 2

I said in mine heart, Go to now, I will prove thee with mirth,
therefore enjoy pleasure: and, behold, this also is vanity.
2 I said of laughter, It is mad: and of mirth, What doeth it?
3 I sought in mine heart to give myself unto wine, yet acquainting mine heart with wisdom: and to lay hold on folly, till I might see
what was that good for the sons of men, which they should do
under the heaven all the days of their life.
4 I made me great works; I builded me houses; I planted me
vineyards:
5 I made me gardens and orchards and I planted trees in them of
all kind of fruits:
6 I made me pools of water, to water therewith the wood that
bringeth forth trees:
7 I got me servants and maidens, and had servants born in my
house; also I had great possessions of great and small cattle above
all that were in Jerusalem before me:
8 I gathered me also silver and gold, and the peculiar treasure of

kings and of the provinces: I gat me men singers and women singers, and the delights of the sons of men, as musical instruments, and
that of all sorts.
9 So I was great, and increased more than all that were before
me in Jerusalem: also my wisdom remained with me.
10 And whatsoever mine eyes desired I kept not from them, I
withheld not my heart from any joy; for my heart rejoiced in all my
labour: and this was my portion of all my labour.
11 Then I looked on all the works that my hands had wrought,
and on the labour that I had laboured to do: and, behold, all was
vanity and vexation of spirit, and there was no profit under the sun.
12 ¶ And I turned myself to behold wisdom, and madness, and
folly: for what can the man do that cometh after the king? even that
which hath been already done.
13 Then I saw that wisdom excelleth folly, as far as light excelleth darkness.
14 The wise man's eyes are in his head; but the fool walketh in
darkness: and I myself perceived also that one event happeneth to
them all.
15 Then said I in my heart, As it happeneth to the fool, so it
happeneth even to me; and why was I then more wise? Then I said
in my heart, that this also is vanity.
16 For there is no remembrance of the wise more than of the
fool for ever; seeing that which now is in the days to come shall all
be forgotten. And how dieth the wise man? as the fool.
17 Therefore I hated life; because the work that is wrought
under the sun is grievous unto me: for all is vanity and vexation of
spirit.
18 ¶ Yea, I hated all my labour which I had taken under the sun:
because I should leave it unto the man that shall be after me.
19 And who knoweth whether he shall be a wise man or a fool?
yet shall he have rule over all my labour wherein I have laboured,
and wherein I have shewed myself wise under the sun. This is also
vanity.
20 Therefore I went about to cause my heart to despair of all the
labour which I took under the sun.
21 For there is a man whose labour is in wisdom, and in knowledge, and in equity; yet to a man that hath not laboured therein

shall he leave it for his portion. This also is vanity and a great evil.
22 For what hath man of all his labour, and of the vexation of his
heart, wherein he hath laboured under the sun?
23 For all his days are sorrows, and his travail grief; yea, his heart
taketh not rest in the night. This is also vanity.
24 ¶ There is nothing better for a man, than that he should eat
and drink, and that he should make his soul enjoy good in his
labour. This also I saw, that it was from the hand of God.
25 For who can eat, or who else can hasten hereunto, more than I?
26 For God giveth to a man that is good in his sight wisdom, and
knowledge, and joy: but to the sinner he giveth travail, to gather
and to heap up, that he may give to him that is good before God.
This also is vanity and vexation of spirit.

Chapter 3

To every thing there is a season, and a time to every purpose under
the heaven:
2 A time to be born, and a time to die; a time to plant, and a time
to pluck up that which is planted;
3 A time to kill, and a time to heal; a time to break down, and a
time to build up;
4 A time to weep, and a time to laugh; a time to mourn, and a
time to dance;
5 A time to cast away stones, and a time to gather stones together; a time to embrace, and a time to refrain from embracing;
6 A time to get, and a time to lose; a time to keep, and a time to
cast away;
7 A time to rend, and a time to sew; a time to keep silence, and a
time to speak;
8 A time to love, and a time to hate; a time of war, and a time of
peace.
9 What profit hath he that worketh in that wherein he labou-
reth?
10 I have seen the travail, which God hath given to the sons of
men to be exercised in it.
11 He hath made every thing beautiful in his time: also he hath
set the world in their heart, so that no man can find out the work
that God maketh from the beginning to the end.

12 I know that there is no good in them, but for a man to rejoice, and to do good in his life.
13 And also that every man should eat and drink, and enjoy the good of all his labour, it is the gift of God.
14 I know that, whatsoever God doeth, it shall be for ever: nothing can be put to it, nor any thing taken from it: and God doeth it, that men should fear before him.
15 That which hath been is now; and that which is to be hath already been; and God requireth that which is past.
16 ¶ And moreover I saw under the sun the place of judgment, that wickedness was there; and the place of righteousness, that iniquity was there.
17 I said in mine heart, God shall judge the righteous and the wicked: for there is a time there for every purpose and for every work.
18 I said in mine heart concerning the estate of the sons of men, that God might manifest them, and that they might see that they themselves are beasts.
19 For that which befalleth the sons of men befalleth beasts; even one thing befalleth them: as the one dieth, so dieth the other; yea, they have all one breath; so that a man hath no preeminence above a beast: for all is vanity.
20 All go unto one place; all are of the dust, and all turn to dust again.
21 Who knoweth the spirit of man that goeth upward, and the spirit of the beast that goeth downward to the earth?
22 Wherefore I perceive that there is nothing better, than that a man should rejoice in his own works; for that is his portion: for who shall bring him to see what shall be after him?

Chapter 4

So I returned, and considered all the oppressions that are done under the sun: and behold the tears of such as were oppressed, and they had no comforter; and on the side of their oppressors there was power; but they had no comforter.
2 Wherefore I praised the dead which are already dead more than the living which are yet alive.

3 Yea, better is he than both they, which hath not yet been, who
hath not seen the evil work that is done under the sun.
4 ¶ Again, I considered all travail, and every right work, that for
this a man is envied of his neighbour. This is also vanity and vexation of spirit.
5 The fool foldeth his hands together, and eateth his own flesh.
6 Better is an handful with quietness, than both the hands full
with travail and vexation of spirit.
7 ¶ Then I returned, and I saw vanity under the sun.
8 There is one alone, and there is not a second; yea, he hath
neither child nor brother: yet is there no end of all his labour;
neither is his eye satisfied with riches: neither saith he, For whom
do I labour, and bereave my soul of good? This is also vanity, yea, it
is a sore travail.
9 ¶ Two are better than one; because they have a good reward
for their labour.
10 For if they fall, the one will lift up his fellow: but woe to him
that is alone when he falleth; for he hath not another to help him
up.
11 Again, if two lie together, then they have heat: but how can
one be warm alone?
12 And if one prevail against him, two shall withstand him; and a
threefold cord is not quickly broken.
13 ¶ Better is a poor and a wise child than an old and foolish
king, who will no more be admonished.
14 For out of prison he cometh to reign; whereas also he that is
born in his kingdom becometh poor.
15 I considered all the living which walk under the sun, with the
second child that shall stand up in his stead.
16 There is no end of all the people, even of all that have been
before them: they also that come after shall not rejoice in him.
Surely this also is vanity and vexation of spirit.

Chapter 5

Keep thy foot when thou goest to the house of God, and be more
ready to hear, than to give the sacrifice of fools: for they consider
not that they do evil.

2 Be not rash with thy mouth, and let not thine heart be hasty to
utter any thing before God: for God is in heaven, and thou upon
earth: therefore let thy words be few.
3 For a dream cometh through the multitude of business; and a
fool's voice is known by multitude of words.
4 When thou vowest a vow unto God, defer not to pay it; for he
hath no pleasure in fools: pay that which thou hast vowed.
5 Better is it that thou shouldest not vow, than that thou shouldest vow and not pay.
6 Suffer not thy mouth to cause thy flesh to sin; neither say thou
before the angel, that it was an error: wherefore should God be
angry at thy voice, and destroy the work of thine hands?
7 For in the multitude of dreams and many words there are also
divers vanities: but fear thou God.
8 ¶ If thou seest the oppression of the poor, and violent pervert-
ing of judgment and justice in a province, marvel not at the matter:
for he that is higher than the highest regardeth; and there be higher
than they.
9 ¶ Moreover the profit of the earth is for all: the king himself is
served by the field.
10 He that loveth silver shall not be satisfied with silver; nor he
that loveth abundance with increase: this is also vanity.
11 When goods increase, they are increased that eat them: and
what good is there to the owners thereof, saving the beholding of
them with their eyes?
12 The sleep of a labouring man is sweet, whether he eat little or
much: but the abundance of the rich will not suffer him to sleep.
13 There is a sore evil which I have seen under the sun, namely,
riches kept for the owners thereof to their hurt.
14 But those riches perish by evil travail: and he begetteth a son,
and there is nothing in his hand.
15 As he came forth of his mother's womb, naked shall he return
to go as he came, and shall take nothing of his labour, which he may
carry away in his hand.
16 And this also is a sore evil, that in all points as he came, so
shall he go: and what profit hath he that hath laboured for the wind?
17 All his days also he eateth in darkness, and he hath much
sorrow and wrath with his sickness.

18 ¶ Behold that which I have seen: it is good and comely for
one to eat and to drink, and to enjoy the good of all his labour that
he taketh under the sun all the days of his life, which God giveth
him: for it is his portion.

19 Every man also to whom God hath given riches and wealth,
and hath given him power to eat thereof, and to take his portion,
and to rejoice in his labour; this is the gift of God.

20 For he shall not much remember the days of his life; because
God answereth him in the joy of his heart.

Chapter 6

There is an evil which I have seen under the sun, and it is common
among men:

2 A man to whom God hath given riches, wealth, and honour, so
that he wanteth nothing for his soul of all that he desireth, yet God
giveth him not power to eat thereof, but a stranger eateth it: this is
vanity, and it is an evil disease.

3 ¶ If a man beget an hundred children, and live many years, so
that the days of his years be many, and his soul be not filled with
good, and also that he have no burial; I say, that an untimely birth
is better than he.

4 For he cometh in with vanity, and departeth in darkness, and
his name shall be covered with darkness.

5 Moreover he hath not seen the sun, nor known any thing: this
hath more rest than the other.

6 ¶ Yea, though he live a thousand years twice told, yet hath he
seen no good: do not all go to one place?

7 All the labour of man is for his mouth, and yet the appetite is
not filled.

8 For what hath the wise more than the fool? what hath the poor,
that knoweth to walk before the living?

9 ¶ Better is the sight of the eyes than the wandering of the
desire: this is also vanity and vexation of spirit.

10 That which hath been is named already, and it is known that it
is man: neither may he contend with him that is mightier than he.

11 ¶ Seeing there be many things that increase vanity, what is
man the better?

12 For who knoweth what is good for man in this life, all the

days of his vain life which he spendeth as a shadow? for who can tell
a man what shall be after him under the sun?

Chapter 7

A good name is better than precious ointment; and the day of death
than the day of one's birth.
2 ¶ It is better to go to the house of mourning, than to go to the
house of feasting: for that is the end of all men; and the living will
lay it to his heart.
3 Sorrow is better than laughter: for by the sadness of the countenance the heart is made better.
4 The heart of the wise is in the house of mourning; but the
heart of fools is in the house of mirth.
5 It is better to hear the rebuke of the wise, than for a man to
hear the song of fools.
6 For as the crackling of thorns under a pot, so is the laughter of
the fool: this also is vanity.
7 ¶ Surely oppression maketh a wise man mad; and a gift destroyeth the heart.
8 Better is the end of a thing than the beginning thereof: and the
patient in spirit is better than the proud in spirit.
9 Be not hasty in thy spirit to be angry: for anger resteth in the
bosom of fools.
10 Say not thou, What is the cause that the former days were
better than these? for thou dost not enquire wisely concerning this.
11¶ Wisdom is good with an inheritance: and by it there is profit
to them that see the sun.
12 For wisdom is a defence, and money is a defence: but the
excellency of knowledge is, that wisdom giveth life to them that
have it.
13 Consider the work of God: for who can make that straight,
which he hath made crooked?
14 In the day of prosperity be joyful, but in the day of adversity
consider: God also hath set the one over against the other, to the
end that man should find nothing after him.
15 All things have I seen in the days of my vanity: there is a just
man that perisheth in his righteousness, and there is a wicked man
that prolongeth his life in his wickedness.

16 Be not righteous over much; neither make thyself over wise:
why shouldest thou destroy thyself?
17 Be not over much wicked, neither be thou foolish: why
shouldest thou die before thy time?
18 It is good that thou shouldest take hold of this; yea, also from
this withdraw not thine hand: for he that feareth God shall come-
forth of them all.
19 Wisdom strengtheneth the wise more than ten mighty men
which are in the city.
20 For there is not a just man upon earth, that doeth good, and
sinneth not.
21 Also take no heed unto all words that are spoken; lest thou
hear thy servant curse thee:
22 For oftentimes also thine own heart knoweth that thou thyself
likewise hast cursed others.
23 ¶ All this have I proved by wisdom: I said, I will be wise; but
it was far from me.
24 That which is far off, and exceeding deep, who can find it out?
25 I applied mine heart to know, and to search, and to seek out
wisdom, and the reason of things, and to know the wickedness of
folly, even of foolishness and madness:
26 And I find more bitter than death the woman, whose heart is
snares and nets, and her hands as bands: whoso pleaseth God shall
escape from her; but the sinner shall be taken by her.
27 Behold, this have I found, saith the preacher, counting one by
one, to find out the account:
28 Which yet my soul seeketh, but I find not: one man among a
thousand have I found; but a woman among all those have I not
found.
29 Lo, this only have I found, that God hath made man upright;
but they have sought out many inventions.

Chapter 8

Who is as the wise man? and who knoweth the interpretation of a
thing? a man's wisdom maketh his face to shine, and the boldness of
his face shall be changed.
2 I counsel thee to keep the king's commandment, and that in
regard of the oath of God.

3 Be not hasty to go out of his sight: stand not in an evil thing;
for he doeth whatsoever pleaseth him.
4 Where the word of a king is, there is power: and who may say
unto him, What doest thou?
5 Whoso keepeth the commandment shall feel no evil thing: and
a wise man's heart discerneth both time and judgment.
6 ¶ Because to every purpose there is time and judgment, therefore the misery of man is great upon him.
7 For he knoweth not that which shall be: for who can tell him
when it shall be?
8 There is no man that hath power over the spirit to retain the
spirit; neither hath he power in the day of death: and there is no
discharge in that war; neither shall wickedness deliver those that
are given to it.
9 All this have I seen, and applied my heart unto every work that
is done under the sun: there is a time wherein one man ruleth over
another to his own hurt.
10 And so I saw the wicked buried, who had come and gone
from the place of the holy, and they were forgotten in the city
where they had so done: this is also vanity.
11 Because sentence against an evil work is not executed
speedily, therefore the heart of the sons of men is fully set in them
to do evil.
12 ¶ Though a sinner do evil an hundred times, and his days be
prolonged, yet surely I know that it shall be well with them that fear
God, which fear before him:
13 But it shall not be well with the wicked, neither shall he
prolong his days, which are as a shadow; because he feareth not
before God.
14 There is a vanity which is done upon the earth; that there be
just men, unto whom it happeneth according to the work of the
wicked; again, there be wicked men, to whom it happeneth according to the work of the righteous: I said that this also is vanity.
15 Then I commended mirth, because a man hath no better
thing under the sun, than to eat, and to drink, and to be merry: for
that shall abide with him of his labour the days of his life, which
God giveth him under the sun.
16 ¶ When I applied mine heart to know wisdom, and to see the

business that is done upon the earth: (for also there is that neither
day nor night seeth sleep with his eyes:)
17 Then I beheld all the work of God, that a man cannot find out
the work that is done under the sun: because though a man labour
to seek it out, yet he shall not find it; yea farther; though a wise man
think to know it, yet shall he not be able to find it.

Chapter 9

For all this I considered in my heart even to declare all this, that the
righteous, and the wise, and their works, are in the hand of God: no
man knoweth either love or hatred by all that is before them.
2 All things come alike to all: there is one event to the righteous,
and to the wicked; to the good and to the clean, and to the unclean;
to him that sacrificeth, and to him that sacrificeth not: as is the good,
so is the sinner; and he that sweareth, as he that feareth an oath.
3 This is an evil among all things that are done under the sun,
that there is one event unto all: yea, also the heart of the sons of
men is full of evil, and madness is in their heart while they live, and
after that they go to the dead.
4 ¶ For to him that is joined to all the living there is hope: for a
living dog is better than a dead lion.
5 For the living know that they shall die: but the dead know not
any thing, neither have they any more a reward; for the memory of
them is forgotten.
6 Also their love, and their hatred, and their envy, is now perished; neither have they any more a portion for ever in any thing
that is done under the sun.
7 ¶ Go thy way, eat thy bread with joy, and drink thy wine with a
merry heart; for God now accepteth thy works.
8 Let thy garments be always white; and let thy head lack no
ointment.
9 Live joyfully with the wife whom thou lovest all the days of the
life of thy vanity, which he hath given thee under the sun, all the
days of thy vanity: for that is thy portion in this life, and in thy
labour which thou takest under the sun.
10 Whatsoever thy hand findeth to do, do it with thy might:
for there is no work, nor device, nor knowledge, nor wisdom, in
the grave, whither thou goest.

11 ¶ I returned, and saw under the sun, that the race is not to the swift, nor the battle to the strong, neither yet bread to the wise, nor yet riches to men of understanding, nor yet favour to men of skill; but time and chance happeneth to them all.

12 For man also knoweth not his time: as the fishes that are taken in an evil net, and as the birds that are caught in the snare; so are the sons of men snared in an evil time, when it falleth suddenly upon them.

13 ¶ This wisdom have I seen also under the sun, and it seemed great unto me:

14 There was a little city, and few men within it; and there came a great king against it, and besieged it, and built great bulwarks against it:

15 Now there was found in it a poor wise man, and he by his wisdom delivered the city; yet no man remembered that same poor man.

16 Then said I, Wisdom is better than strength: nevertheless the poor man's wisdom is despised, and his words are not heard.

17 The words of wise men are heard in quiet more than the cry of him that ruleth among fools.

18 Wisdom is better than weapons of war: but one sinner destroyeth much good.

Chapter 10

Dead flies cause the ointment of the apothecary to send forth a stinking savour: so doth a little folly him that is in reputation for wisdom and honour.

2 A wise man's heart is at his right hand; but a fool's heart at his left.

3 Yea also, when he that is a fool walketh by the way, his wisdom faileth him, and he saith to every one that he is a fool.

4 If the spirit of the ruler rise up against thee, leave not thy place; for yielding pacifieth great offences.

5 There is an evil which I have seen under the sun, as an error which proceedeth from the ruler:

6 Folly is set in great dignity, and the rich sit in low place.

7 I have seen servants upon horses, and princes walking as servants upon the earth.

8 He that diggeth a pit shall fall into it; and whoso breaketh an
hedge, a serpent shall bite him.
9 Whoso removeth stones shall be hurt therewith; and he that
cleaveth wood shall be endangered thereby.
10 If the iron be blunt, and he do not whet the edge, then must
he put to more strength: but wisdom is profitable to direct.
11 Surely the serpent will bite without enchantment; and a babbler is no better.
12 The words of a wise man's mouth are gracious; but the lips of
a fool will swallow up himself.
13 The beginning of the words of his mouth is foolishness: and
the end of his talk is mischievous madness.
14 A fool also is full of words: a man cannot tell what shall be;
and what shall be after him, who can tell him?
15 The labour of the foolish wearieth every one of them, because he knoweth not how to go to the city.
16 ¶ Woe to thee, O land, when thy king is a child, and thy
princes eat in the morning!
17 Blessed art thou, O land, when thy king is the son of nobles,
and thy princes eat in due season, for strength, and not for drunkenness!
18 ¶ By much slothfulness the building decayeth; and through
idleness of the hands the house droppeth through.
19 ¶ A feast is made for laughter, and wine maketh merry: but
money answereth all things.
20 ¶ Curse not the king, no not in thy thought; and curse not the
rich in thy bedchamber: for a bird of the air shall carry the voice,
and that which hath wings shall tell the matter.

Chapter 11

Cast thy bread upon the waters: for thou shalt find it after many
days.
2 Give a portion to seven, and also to eight; for thou knowest
not what evil shall be upon the earth.
3 If the clouds be full of rain, they empty themselves upon the
earth: and if the tree fall toward the south, or toward the north, in
the place where the tree falleth, there it shall be.

4 He that observeth the wind shall not sow; and he that regardeth the clouds shall not reap.

5 As thou knowest not what is the way of the spirit, nor how the bones do grow in the womb of her that is with child: even so thou knowest not the works of God who maketh all.

6 In the morning sow thy seed, and in the evening withhold not thine hand: for thou knowest not whether shall prosper, either this or that, or whether they both shall be alike good.

7 ¶ Truly the light is sweet, and a pleasant thing it is for the eyes to behold the sun:

8 But if a man live many years, and rejoice in them all; yet let him remember the days of darkness; for they shall be many. All that cometh is vanity.

9 ¶ Rejoice, O young man, in thy youth; and let thy heart cheer thee in the days of thy youth, and walk in the ways of thine heart, and in the sight of thine eyes: but know thou, that for all these things God will bring thee into judgment.

10 Therefore remove sorrow from thy heart, and put away evil from thy flesh: for childhood and youth are vanity.

Chapter 12

Remember now thy Creator in the days of thy youth, while the evil days come not, nor the years draw nigh, when thou shalt say, I have no pleasure in them;

2 While the sun, or the light, or the moon, or the stars, be not darkened, nor the clouds return after the rain:

3 In the day when the keepers of the house shall tremble, and the strong men shall bow themselves, and the grinders cease because they are few, and those that look out of the windows be darkened,

4 And the doors shall be shut in the streets, when the sound of the grinding is low, and he shall rise up at the voice of the bird, and all the daughters of musick shall be brought low;

5 Also when they shall be afraid of that which is high, and fears shall be in the way, and the almond tree shall flourish, and the grasshopper shall be a burden, and desire shall fail: because man goeth to his long home, and the mourners go about the streets:

6 Or ever the silver cord be loosed, or the golden bowl be bro-

ken, or the pitcher be broken at the fountain, or the wheel broken at the cistern.

7 Then shall the dust return to the earth as it was: and the spirit shall return unto God who gave it.

8 ¶ Vanity of vanities, saith the preacher; all is vanity.

9 And moreover, because the preacher was wise, he still taught the people knowledge; yea, he gave good heed, and sought out, and set in order many proverbs.

10 The preacher sought to find out acceptable words: and that which was written was upright, even words of truth.

11 The words of the wise are as goads, and as nails fastened by the masters of assemblies, which are given from one shepherd.

12 And further, by these, my son, be admonished: of making many books there is no end; and much study is a weariness of the flesh.

13 ¶Let us hear the conclusion of the whole matter: Fear God, and keep his commandments: for this is the whole duty of man.

14 For God shall bring every work into judgment, with every secret thing, whether it be good, or whether it be evil.

The Hebrew name of *Ecclesiastes* is *Koheleth,* meaning "the preacher," a term which applied to moralizers and wisdom-teachers as well as religious preachers. The author of the text, which was written around 225 B.C., was most likely a wisdom-teacher or a scribe, although he claimed to be "the son of David, King in Jerusalem," or Solomon, probably for dramatic purposes. A collection of aphorisms divided into twelve chapters, *Ecclesiastes* is notable for its strong strains of almost lyrical and unorthodox scepticism. For readers of the King James Bible in the seventeenth century, here was a model of an essay in meditation. Note, in contrast, the more classical tradition of Earle; the more personal of Donne.

Three meditations

FROM *Devotions upon Emergent Occasions (1624)*
BY ***John Donne*** *(1573-1631)*

XV. *I sleep not day nor night.*

Natural men have conceived a twofold use of sleep; that it is a refreshing of the body in this life; that it is a preparing of the soul for the next; that it is a feast, and it is the grace at that feast; that it is our recreation and cheers us, and it is our catechism and instructs us; we hope that we shall rise the stronger, and we lie down in a knowledge that we may rise no more. Sleep is an opiate which gives us rest, but such an opiate, as perchance, being under it, we shall wake no more. But though natural men, who have induced secondary and figurative considerations, have found out this second, this emblematical use of sleep, that it should be a representation of death, God, who wrought and perfected his work before nature began (for nature was but his apprentice, to learn in the first seven days, and now is his foreman, and works next under him), God, I say, intended sleep only for the refreshing of man by bodily rest, and not for a figure of death, for he intended not death itself then. But man having induced death upon himself, God hath taken man's creature, death, into his hand, and mended it; and whereas it hath in itself a fearful form and aspect, so that man is afraid of his own creature, God presents it to him in a familiar, in an assiduous, in an agreeable and acceptable form, in sleep; that so when he awakes from sleep, and says to himself, "Shall I be no otherwise when I am dead, than I was even now when I was asleep?" He may be ashamed of his waking dreams, and of his melancholy fancying out a horrid and an affrightful figure of that death which is so like sleep. As then we need sleep to live out our threescore and ten years, so we need death to live that life which we cannot outlive. And as death being our enemy, God allows us to defend ourselves against it (for we victual ourselves against death twice every day), as often as we eat, so God having so sweetened death unto us as he hath in sleep, we put ourselves into our enemy's hands once every day, so far as sleep is death; and sleep is as much death as meat is life. This then is the misery of my sickness, that death, as it is produced from me and is mine own creature, is now before mine eyes, but in that form in which God hath mollified it to us, and made it acceptable, in sleep I cannot see it. How many prisoners, who have even hollowed themselves their graves upon that earth on which they have lain long under heavy fetters, yet at this hour are asleep, though they be yet working upon their own graves by their own weight? He that hath seen his friend die to-day, or knows he shall see it to-morrow, yet will sink into a sleep between. I cannot, and oh, if I be entering now into eternity, where there shall be no more distinction of hours, why is it all my business now to tell clocks? Why is none of the heaviness of my heart dispensed into mine eye-lids, that they might fall as my heart doth? And why, since I have lost my delight in all objects, cannot I discontinue the faculty of seeing them by closing mine eyes in sleep? But why rather, being entering into that presence where I shall wake continually and never sleep more, do I not interpret my continual waking here, to be a parasceve[1] and a preparation to that?

XVI. *From the bells of the church adjoining, I am daily remembered[2] of my burial in the funerals of others.*

We have a convenient author, who writ a discourse of bells when he was prisoner in Turkey. How would he have enlarged himself if he had been my fellow-prisoner in this sick bed, so near to that steeple which never ceases, no more than the harmony of the spheres, but

[1] in Jewish religion, eve of the sabbath, day of preparation for an important occasion

[2] reminded

is more heard. When the Turks took Constantinople, they melted the bells into ordnance; I have heard both bells and ordnance; but never been so much affected with those as with these bells. I have lain near a steeple in which there are said to be more than thirty bells, and near another, where there is one so big, as that the clapper is said to weigh more than six hundred pounds, yet never so affected as here. Here the bells can scarce solemnize the funeral of any person, but that I knew him, or knew that he was my neighbour: we dwelt in houses near to one another before, but now he is gone into that house into which I must follow him. There is a way of correcting the children of great persons, that other children are corrected in their behalf, and in their names, and this works upon them who indeed had more deserved it. And when these bells tell me, that now one, and now another is buried, must not I acknowledge that they have the correction due to me, and paid the debt that I owe? There is a story of a bell in a monastery which, when any of the house was sick to death, rung always voluntarily, and they knew the inevitableness of the danger by that. It rung once when no man was sick, but the next day one of the house fell from the steeple and died, and the bell held the reputation of a prophet still. If these bells that warn to a funeral now, were appropriated to none, may not I, by the hour of the funeral, supply? How many men that stand at an execution, if they would ask, For what dies that man? should hear their own faults condemned, and see themselves executed by attorney? We scarce hear of any man preferred, but we think of ourselves that we might very well have been that man; why might not I have been that man that is carried to his grave now? Could I fit myself to stand or sit in any man's place, and not to lie in any man's grave? I may lack much of the good parts of the meanest, but I lack nothing of the mortality of the weakest; they may have acquired better abilities than I, but I was born to as many infirmities as they. To be an incumbent by lying down in a grave, to be a doctor by teaching mortification by example, by dying, though I may have seniors, others may be older than I, yet I have proceeded apace in a good university, and gone a great way in a little time, by the furtherance of a vehement fever, and whomsoever these bells bring to the ground to-day, if he and I had been compared yesterday, perchance I should have been thought likelier to come to this preferment then than he. God hath kept the power of death in his own hands, lest any man should bribe death. If man knew the gain of death, the ease of death, he would solicit, he would provoke death to assist him by any hand which he might use. But as when men see many of their own professions preferred, it ministers a hope that that may light upon them; so when these hourly bells tell me of so many funerals of men like me, it presents, if not a desire that it may, yet a comfort whensoever mine shall come.

XVII. *Now this bell tolling softly for another, says to me: Thou must die.*

Perchance he for whom this bell tolls may be so ill, as that he knows not it tolls for him; and perchance I may think myself so much better than I am, as that they who are about me, and see my state, may have caused it to toll for me, and I know not that. The church is Catholic, universal, so are all her actions; all that she does belongs to all. When she baptizes a child, that action concerns me; for that child is thereby connected to that body which is my head too, and ingrafted into that body whereof I am a member. And when she buries a man, that action concerns me: all mankind is of one author, and is one volume; when one man dies, one chapter is not torn out of the book, but translated into a better language; and every chapter must be so translated; God employs several translators; some pieces are translated by age, some by sickness, some by war, some by justice; but God's hand is in every translation, and his hand shall bind up all our scattered leaves again for that library where every book shall lie open to one another. As therefore the bell that rings to a sermon calls not upon the preacher only, but upon the congregation to come, so this bell calls us all, but how much more me, who am brought so near the door by this sickness. There was a contention as far as a suit (in which both piety and dignity, religion and estimation, were mingled), which of the religious orders should ring to prayers first in the morning; and it was determined, that they should ring first that rose earliest. If we understand aright the dignity of this bell that tolls for our evening prayer, we would be glad to make it ours by rising early, in that application, that it might be ours as well as his, whose indeed it is. The bell doth toll for him that thinks it doth; and though it intermit again, yet from that minute that that occasion wrought upon him, he is united to God. Who casts not up his eye to the sun when it rises? but who takes off his eye from a comet when that breaks out? Who bends not his ear to any bell which upon any occasion rings? but who can remove it from that bell which is passing a piece of himself out of this world? No man is an island, entire of itself; every man is a piece of the continent, a part of the main. If a clod be washed away by the sea, Europe is the less, as well as if a promontory were, as well as if a manor of thy friend's or of thine own were: any man's death diminishes me, because I am involved in mankind, and therefore never send to know for whom the bell tolls; it tolls for thee. Neither can we call this a begging of misery, or a borrowing of misery, as though we were not miserable enough of ourselves, but must fetch in more from the next house, in taking upon us the misery of our neighbours. Truly it were an excusable covetousness if we did, for affliction is a treasure, and scarce any man hath enough of it. No man hath affliction enough that is not matured and ripened by it, and made fit for God by that affliction. If a man carry treasure in bullion, or in a wedge of gold, and have none coined into current money, his treasure will not defray him as he travels. Tribulation is treasure in the nature of it, but it is not current money in the use of it, except we get nearer and nearer our home, heaven, by it. Another man may be sick too, and sick to death, and this affliction may lie in his bowels, as gold in a mine, and be of no use to him; but this bell, that tells me of his affliction, digs out and applies that gold to me: if by this consideration of another's danger I take mine own into contemplation, and so secure myself, by making my recourse to my God, who is our only security.

Son of an ironmonger in London, John Donne went to Cambridge and Oxford, planned to study law, was early a Catholic, finally took Anglican orders and became Dean of St. Paul's, where he preached to great urban and courtly congregations including King Charles I. He wrote complex, troubled, metaphysical poems, sermons, and meditations, like these *Devotions upon Emergent Occasions,* which trace the course of feeling and thought during a severe illness. How different from his friend Walton! Yet both give us the specific and speculative spirit of their world.

A conference

FROM *The Complete Angler,* Beginning of Chapter I *(1653)*
BY *Izaak Walton (1593-1683)*

A Conference betwixt an Angler [PISCATOR], a Falconer [AUCEPS], and a Hunter [VENATOR], each commending his Recreation

PISCATOR. You are well overtaken, Gentlemen! A good morning to you both! I have stretched my legs up Tottenham Hill to overtake you, hoping your business may occasion you towards Ware whither I am going this fine fresh May morning.

VENATOR. Sir, I, for my part, shall almost answer your hopes; for my purpose is to drink my morning's draught at the Thatched House in Hoddesden;[1] and I think not to rest till I come thither, where I have appointed a friend or two to meet me: but for this gentleman that you see with me, I know not how far he intends his journey; he came so lately into my company, that I have scarce had time to ask him the question.

AUCEPS. Sir, I shall by your favour bear you company as far as Theobalds,[2] and there leave you; for then I turn up to a friend's house, who mews a Hawk for me,[3] which I now long to see.

VENATOR. Sir, we are all so happy as to have a fine, fresh, cool

[1] now unknown; supposedly 17 miles from London, on the Ware road

[2] about 12 miles from London; built by Cecil, Lord Burleigh, who often entertained Elizabeth I there

[3] cages and cares for a hawk, during moulting season (from early March until August)

morning; and I hope we shall each be the happier in the others' company. And, Gentlemen, that I may not lose yours, I shall either abate or amend my pace to enjoy it, knowing that, as the Italians say, "Good company in a journey makes the way to seem the shorter."

AUCEPS. It may do so, Sir, with the help of good discourse, which, methinks, we may promise from you, that both look and speak so cheerfully: and for my part, I promise you, as an invitation to it, that I will be as free and open hearted as discretion will allow me to be with strangers.

VENATOR. And, Sir, I promise the like.

PISCATOR. I am right glad to hear your answers; and, in confidence you speak the truth, I shall put on a boldness to ask you, Sir, whether business or pleasure caused you to be so early up, and walk so fast? for this other gentleman hath declared he is going to see a hawk, that a friend mews for him.

VENATOR. Sir, mine is a mixture of both, a little business and more pleasure; for I intend this day to do all my business, and then bestow another day or two in hunting the Otter, which a friend, that I go to meet, tells me is much pleasanter than any other chase whatsoever: howsoever, I mean to try it; for to-morrow morning we shall meet a pack of Otter-dogs of noble Mr. Sadler's,[4] upon Amwell Hill, who will be there so early, that they intend to prevent the sunrising.

PISCATOR. Sir, my fortune has answered my desires, and my purpose is to bestow a day or two in helping to destroy some of those villanous vermin: for I hate them perfectly, because they love fish so well, or rather, because they destroy so much; indeed so much, that, in my judgment all men that keep Otter-dogs ought to have pensions from the King, to encourage them to destroy the very breed of those base Otters, they do so much mischief.

VENATOR. But what say you to the Foxes of the Nation, would not you as willingly have them destroyed? for doubtless they do as much mischief as Otters do.

[4]Ralph Sadler, grandson of Sir Ralph Sadler, who was Knight Banneret in the reigns of Henry VIII and Elizabeth I, favored hawking and hunting and was noted for his hospitality

PISCATOR. Oh, Sir, if they do, it is not so much to me and my fraternity, as those base vermin the Otters do.

AUCEPS. Why, Sir, I pray, of what fraternity are you, that you are so angry with the poor Otters?

PISCATOR. I am, Sir, a Brother of the Angle, and therefore an enemy to the Otter: for you are to note, that we Anglers all love one another, and therefore do I hate the Otter both for my own, and their sakes who are of my brotherhood.

VENATOR. And I am a lover of Hounds; I have followed many a pack of dogs many a mile, and heard many merry Huntsmen make sport and scoff at Anglers.

AUCEPS. And I profess myself a Falconer, and have heard many grave, serious men pity them, it is such a heavy, contemptible, dull recreation.

PISCATOR. You know, Gentlemen, it is an easy thing to scoff at any art or recreation; a little wit mixed with ill nature, confidence, and malice, will do it; but though they often venture boldly, yet they are often caught, even in their own trap, according to that of Lucian,[5] the father of the family of Scoffers:

> Lucian, well skilled in scoffing, this hath writ,
> Friend, that's your folly, which you think your wit:
> This you vent oft, void both of wit and fear,
> Meaning another, when yourself you jeer.

If to this you add what Solomon says of Scoffers,[6] that they are an abomination to mankind, let him that thinks fit scoff on, and be a Scoffer still; but I account them enemies to me and all that love Virtue and Angling.

And for you that have heard many grave, serious men pity Anglers; let me tell you, Sir, there be many men that are by others taken to be serious and grave men, whom we contemn and pity. Men that are taken to be grave, because nature hath made them of a sour complexion; money-getting men, men that spend all their time, first in getting, and next, in anxious care to keep it; men that are condemned to be rich, and then always busy or discontented:

[5] Greek satirist of the 2nd century A.D.

[6] "The scorner is an abomination to men" (Proverbs XXIV, 9)

for these poor rich-men, we Anglers pity them perfectly, and stand in no need to borrow their thoughts to think ourselves so happy. No, no, Sir, we enjoy a contentedness above the reach of such dispositions, and as the learned and ingenious Montaigne says,[7] like himself, freely, "When my Cat and I entertain each other with mutual apish tricks, as playing with a garter, who knows but that I make my Cat more sport than she makes me? Shall I conclude her to be simple, that has her time to begin or refuse, to play as freely as I myself have? Nay, who knows but that it is a defect of my not understanding her language, for doubtless Cats talk and reason with one another, that we agree no better: and who knows but that she pities me for being no wiser than to play with her, and laughs and censures my folly, for making sport for her, when we two play together?"

Thus freely speaks Montaigne concerning Cats; and I hope I may take as great a liberty to blame any man, and laugh at him too, let him be never so grave, that hath not heard what Anglers can say in the justification of their Art and Recreation; which I may again tell you, is so full of pleasure, that we need not borrow their thoughts, to think ourselves happy.

VENATOR. Sir, you have almost amazed me; for though I am no Scoffer, yet I have, I pray let me speak it without offence, always looked upon Anglers, as more patient, and more simple men, than I fear I shall find you to be.

PISCATOR. Sir, I hope you will not judge my earnestness to be impatience: and for my simplicity, if by that you mean a harmlessness, or that simplicity which was usually found in the primitive Christians, who were, as most Anglers are, quiet men, and followers of peace; men that were so simply wise, as not to sell their consciences to buy riches, and with them vexation and a fear to die; if you mean such simple men as lived in those times when there were fewer lawyers; when men might have had a lordship safely conveyed to them in a piece of parchment no bigger than your hand, though several sheets will not do it safely in this wiser age; I say, Sir, if you take us Anglers to be such simple men as I

[7] Michel Eyquem de Montaigne (1533-1592), French essayist; the passage here freely rendered is from *Apology for Raymond Sebond.*

have spoke of, then myself and those of my profession will be glad to be so understood: But if by simplicity you meant to express a general defect in those that profess and practice the excellent Art of Angling, I hope in time to disabuse you, and make the contrary appear so evidently, that if you will but have patience to hear me, I shall remove all the anticipations that discourse, or time, or prejudice, have possessed you with against that laudable and ancient Art; for I know it is worthy the knowledge and practice of a wise man.

☙ Izaak Walton was an ironmonger in London. He wrote biographies of John Donne, George Herbert, Richard Hooker, and others, many of whom were his friends; and he liked to fish and to write about fishing. Like Dekker, he was not educated formally in the classics at college, yet he was able to develop a clear and forthright prose style in English, showing the increased adaptability of the language in the century since Sir Thomas More. *The Complete Angler, or The Contemplative Man's Recreation* (1653) is in the form of a dialogue. Piscator, the fisherman, meditates on ways of catching and cooking, and thinking about, various sorts of fish, along the river Lea near London. The dialogue was continued somewhat more technically by Charles Cotton. Note that Walter Landor also uses dialogue form.

A sceptic in religion

FROM *Microcosmography (1628)*
BY *John Earle (1601?-1665)*

Is one that hangs in the balance with all sorts of opinions, whereof not one but stirs him and none sways him. A man guiltier of credulity than he is taken to be; for it is out of his belief of everything that he fully believes nothing. Each Religion scares him from its contrary: none persuades him to itself. He would be wholly a Christian but that he is something of an Atheist, and wholly an Atheist but that he is partly a Christian; and a perfect Heretic but that there are so many to distract him. He finds reason in all opinions, truth in none: indeed the least reason perplexes him, and the best will not satisfy him. He is at most a confused and wild Christian, not specialised by any form, but capable of all. He uses the land's Religion because it is next him, yet he sees not why he may not take the other, but he chooses this, not as better but because there is not a pin to choose. He finds doubts and scruples better than resolves them, and is always too hard for himself. His learning is too much for his brain and his judgement too little for his learning, and his over-opinion of both spoils all. Pity it was his mischance of being a scholar: for it does only distract and irregulate him and the world by him. He hammers much in general upon our opinion's uncertainty, and the possibility of erring makes him not venture on what is true. He is troubled at this naturalness of religion to countries, that Protestantism should be born so in England and Popery abroad, and that fortune and the stars should so much share in it. He likes not this connexion of the Commonweal and Divinity, and fears it may be an arch-practice of State. In our differences with Rome he is strangely unfixed, and a new man every new day, as his last discourse-book's meditations transport him. He could like the gray hairs of Popery did not some dotages[1] there stagger him; he would come to us sooner but our new name affrights him. He is taken with their miracles but doubts an imposture; he conceives of our doctrine better, but it seems too empty and naked. He cannot drive into his fancy the circumscription of Truth to our corner, and is as hardly persuaded to think their old legends true. He approves well of our Faith, and more of their Works, and is sometimes much affected at the zeal of Amsterdam.[2] His conscience interposes itself betwixt duellers, and whilst it would part both, is by both wounded. He will sometimes propend[3] much to us upon the reading a good writer, and at Bellarmine[4] recoils as far back again; and the Fathers[5] jostle him from one side to another. Now Socinus[6] and Vorstius[7] afresh torture him, and he agrees with none worse than himself. He puts his foot into heresies tenderly, as a cat in the water, and pulls it out again, and still something unanswered delays him, yet he bears away some parcel of each, and you may sooner pick all Religions out of him than one. He cannot think so many wise men should be in error, nor so many honest men out of the way, and his wonder is double when he sees these oppose one another. He hates authority as the tyrant of reason, and you cannot anger him worse than with a Father's *dixit*,[8] and yet that many are not persuaded with reason shall authorise his doubt. In sum, his whole life is a question, and his

[1] a folly or stupidity

[2] after Richard Bancroft's attack on puritanism, many English puritans went to the Low Countries to establish reform churches there

[3] incline

[4] Saint Robert Bellarmine (1542-1621), controversial Jesuit theologian

[5] early Christian writers

[6] Fausto Paulus Sozzini (1539-1604), Italian religious reformer who denied the Trinity and other traditional doctrines

[7] Conrad Vorst (1569-1622), German theologian whose *Tractatus Theologicus de Deo* was ordered burned in academic centers in England by James I

[8] usually *ipse dixit,* a dictum or dogmatic claim

salvation a greater, which death only concludes, and then he is resolved.

☙ Earle was educated in classics at Oxford, becoming a Fellow of Merton College in 1620 and taking his Doctorate of Divinity in 1642. He was made tutor of Charles II and accompanied him to exile in France, keeping active in court and ecclesiastical affairs. At the beginning of the Restoration, he became Bishop of Salisbury. Although he wrote some poetry, he is remembered for *Microcosmography,* which is subtitled *A Piece of the World Discovered in Essays and Characters.* The work consists of character sketches not unlike those of Theophrastus, neither descriptions of an individual nor abstracts of personal traits, but a concise delineation of a type in a brief essay form characteristic of the seventeenth century.

Conclusion

FROM *Hydriotaphia, or Urn-Burial (1658)*
BY *Sir Thomas Browne (1605-1682)*

Now since these dead bones have already out-lasted the living ones of Methuselah, and in a yard under ground, and thin walls of clay, outworn all the strong and specious buildings above it, and quietly rested under the drums and tramplings of three conquests: what prince can promise such diuturnity unto his reliques, or might not gladly say,

Sic ego componi versus in ossa velim?[1]

Time, which antiquates antiquities, and hath an art to make dust of all things, hath yet spared these minor monuments.

In vain we hope to be known by open and visible conservatories, when to be unknown was the means of their continuation, and obscurity their protection. If they died by violent hands, and were thrust into their urns, these bones become considerable, and some old philosophers would honor them, whose souls they conceived most pure, which were thus snatched from their bodies, and to retain a stronger propension unto them; whereas they weariedly left a languishing corpse, and with faint desires of re-union. If they fell by long and aged decay, yet wrapped up in the bundle of time, they fall into indistinction, and make but one blot with infants. If we begin to die when we live, and long life be but a prolongation of death, our life is a sad composition; we live with death, and die not

[1] thus should I wish to be buried when turned to bones

in a moment. How many pulses made up the life of Methuselah, were work for Archimedes:[2] common counters sum up the life of Moses his man. Our days become considerable, like petty sums, by minute accumulations; where numerous fractions make up but small round numbers; and our days of a span long, make not one little finger.

If the nearness of our last necessity brought a nearer conformity into it, there were a happiness in hoary hairs, and no calamity in half-senses. But the long habit of living indisposeth us for dying; when avarice makes us the sport of death, when even David grew politicly cruel and Solomon could hardly be said to be the wisest of men. But many are too early old, and before the date of age. Adversity stretcheth our days, misery makes Alcmena's nights,[3] and time hath no wings unto it. But the most tedious being is that which can unwish itself, content to be nothing, or never to have been, which was beyond the malcontent of Job, who cursed not the day of his life, but his nativity; content to have so far been, as to have a title to future being, although he had lived here but in an hidden state of life, and as it were an abortion.

What song the Syrens sang, or what name Achilles assumed when he hid himself among women, though puzzling questions, are not beyond all conjecture. What time the persons of these ossuaries[4] entered the famous nations of the dead, and slept with princes and counselors, might admit a wide solution. But who were the proprietaries of these bones, or what bodies these ashes made up, were a question above antiquarism; not to be resolved by man, nor easily perhaps by spirits, except we consult the provincial guardians, or tutelary observators. Had they made as good provision for their names, as they have done for their relics, they had not so grossly erred in the art of perpetuation. But to subsist in bones, and be but pyramidally extant, is a fallacy in duration. Vain ashes which in the oblivion of names, persons, times, and sexes, have found unto themselves a fruitless continuation, and only arise unto late posterity, as emblems of mortal vanities, antidotes against pride, vain-glory, and maddening vices. Pagan vain-glories which thought the world might last for ever, had encouragement for ambition; and, finding no

[2] Greek philosopher, here used to represent the best of thinkers

[3] one night as long as three [4] receptacles for bones

Atropos[5] unto the immortality of their names, were never damped with the necessity of oblivion. Even old ambitions had the advantage of ours, in the attempts of their vain-glories, who acting early, and before the probable meridian of time, have by this time found great accomplishment of their designs, whereby the ancient heroes have already out-lasted their monuments and mechanical preservations. But in this latter scene of time, we cannot expect such mummies unto our memories, when ambition may fear the prophecy of Elias, and Charles the Fifth can never hope to live within two Methuselahs of Hector.

And therefore, restless unquiet for the diuturnity of our memories unto present considerations seems a vanity almost out of date, and superannuated piece of folly. We cannot hope to live so long in our names, as some have done in their persons. One face of Janus holds no proportion unto the other. 'Tis too late to be ambitious. The great mutations of the world are acted, or time may be too short for our designs. To extend our memories by monuments, whose death we daily pray for, and whose duration we cannot hope, without injury to our expectations in the advent of the last day, were a contradiction to our beliefs. We whose generations are ordained in this setting part of time, are providentially taken off from such imaginations; and, being necessitated to eye the remaining particle of futurity, are naturally constituted unto thoughts of the next world, and cannot excusably decline the consideration of that duration, which maketh pyramids pillars of snow, and all that's past a moment.

Circles and right lines limit and close all bodies, and the mortal right-lined circle must conclude and shut up all. There is no antidote against the opium of time, which temporally considereth all things: our fathers find their graves in our short memories, and sadly tell us how we may be buried in our survivors. Gravestones tell truth scarce forty years. Generations pass while some trees stand, and old families last not three oaks. To be read by bare inscriptions like many in Gruter,[6] to hope for eternity by enigmatical epithets or first letters of our names, to be studied by antiquar-

[5] one of the Fates in Greek mythology, who was responsible for snipping the thread of life when each individual's skein had been unwound

[6] famous seventeenth-century philologist

ies, who we were, and have new names given us like many of the mummies, are cold consolations unto the students of perpetuity, even by everlasting languages.

To be content that times to come should only know there was such a man, not caring whether they knew more of him, was a frigid ambition in Cardan; disparaging his horoscopical inclination and judgment of himself. Who cares to subsist like Hippocrates' patients, or Achilles' horses in Homer, under naked nominations, without deserts and noble acts, which are the balsam of our memories, the *entelechia*[7] and soul of our subsistences? To be nameless in worthy deeds, exceeds an infamous history. The Canaanitish woman lives more happily without a name, than Herodias with one. And who had not rather been the good thief than Pilate?

But the iniquity of oblivion blindly scattereth her poppy, and deals with the memory of men without distinction to merit of perpetuity. Who can but pity the founder of the pyramids? Herostratus lives that burned the temple of Diana; he is almost lost that built it. Time hath spared the epitaph of Adrian's horse, confounded that of himself. In vain we compute our felicities by the advantage of our good names, since bad have equal durations, and Thersites is like to live as long as Agamemmon. Who knows whether the best of men be known, or whether there be not more remarkable persons forgot, than any that stand remembered in the known account of time? Without the favor of the everlasting register, the first man had been as unknown as the last, and Methuselah's long life had been his only chronicle.

Oblivion is not to be hired. The greater part must be content to be as though they had not been, to be found in the register of God, not in the record of man. Twenty-seven names make up the first story, and the recorded names ever since contain not one living century. The number of the dead long exceedeth all that shall live. The night of time far surpasseth the day, and who knows when was the equinox? Every hour adds unto that current arithmetic, which scarce stands one moment. And since death must be the *Lucina*[8] of life, and even Pagans could doubt, whether thus to live were to die;

[7] informing spirit, that which gives full expression and perfection to anything
[8] goddess who presided over childbirth, hence, midwife

since our longest sun sets at right descensions, and makes but winter arches, and therefore it cannot be long before we lie down in darkness, and have our light in ashes; since the brother of death daily haunts us with dying mementos, and time that grows old in itself, bids us hope no long duration; —diuturnity is a dream and folly of expectation.

Darkness and light divide the course of time, and oblivion shares with memory a great part even of our living beings; we slightly remember our felicities, and the smartest strokes of affliction leave but short smart upon us. Sense endureth no extremities, and sorrows destroy us or themselves. To weep into stones are fables. Afflictions induce callosities; miseries are slippery, or fall like snow upon us, which notwithstanding is no unhappy stupidity. To be ignorant of evils to come, and forgetful of evils past, is a merciful provision in nature, whereby we digest the mixture of our few and evil days, and, our delivered senses not relapsing into cutting remembrances, our sorrows are not kept raw by the edge of repetitions. A great part of antiquity contented their hopes of subsistency with a transmigration of their souls,—a good way to continue their memories, while having the advantage of plural successions, they could not but act something remarkable in such variety of beings, and enjoying the fame of their passed selves, make accumulation of glory unto their last durations. Others, rather than be lost in the uncomfortable night of nothing, were content to recede into the common being, and make one particle of the public soul of all things, which was no more than to return into their unknown and divine original again. Egyptian ingenuity was more unsatisfied, contriving their bodies in sweet consistencies, to attend the return of their souls. But all was vanity, feeding the wind and folly. The Egyptian mummies, which Cambyses or time hath spared, avarice now consumeth. Mummy is become merchandise, Mizraim cures wounds, and Pharaoh is sold for balsams.

In vain do individuals hope for immortality, or any patent from oblivion, in preservations below the moon; men have been deceived even in their flatteries above the sun, and studied conceits to perpetuate their names in heaven. The various cosmography of that Nimrod is lost in Orion, and Osyris in the Dog-star. While we look for incorruption in the heavens, we find they are but like the earth;

—durable in their main bodies, alterable in their parts; whereof, beside comets and new stars, perspectives begin to tell tales, and the spots that wander about the sun, with Phaeton's favor, would make clear conviction.

There is nothing strictly immortal, but immortality. Whatever hath no beginning, may be confident of no end (all others have a dependent being and within the reach of destruction); which is the peculiar of that necessary Essence that cannot destroy itself; and the highest strain of omnipotency, to be so powerfully constituted as not to suffer even from the power of itself. But the sufficiency of Christian immortality frustrates all earthly glory, and the quality of either state after death, makes a folly of posthumous memory. God who can only destroy our souls, and hath assured our resurrection, either of our bodies or names hath directly promised no duration. Wherein there is so much of chance, that the boldest expectants have found unhappy frustration; and to hold long subsistence, seems but a scape in oblivion. But man is a noble animal, splendid in ashes, and pompous[9] in the grave, solemnizing nativities and deaths with equal luster, nor omitting ceremonies of bravery in the infamy of his nature.

Life is a pure flame, and we live by an invisible sun within us. A small fire sufficeth for life, great flames seemed too little after death, while men vainly affected precious pyres, and to burn like Sardanapalus; but the wisdom of funeral laws found the folly of prodigal blazes, and reduced undoing fires unto the rule of sober obsequies, wherein few could be so mean as not to provide wood, pitch, a mourner, and an urn.

Five languages secured not the epitaph of Gordianus. The man of God lives longer without a tomb, than any by one, invisibly interred by angels, and adjudged to obscurity, though not without some marks directing human discovery. Enoch and Elias,[10] without either tomb or burial, in an anomalous state of being, are the great examples of perpetuity, in their long and living memory, in strict account being still on this side death, and having a late part yet to act upon this stage of earth. If in the decretory term of the world, we shall not all die but be changed, according to received translation, the last

[9] ceremonious [10] ascended alive into heaven, according to Biblical authority

day will make but few graves; at least quick resurrections will anticipate lasting sepultures. Some graves will be opened before they be quite closed, and Lazarus be no wonder. When many that feared to die, shall groan that they can die but once, the dismal state is the second and living death, when life puts despair on the damned; when men shall wish the coverings of mountains, not of monuments, and annihilations shall be courted.

While some have studied monuments, others have studiously declined them, and some have been so vainly boisterous, that they durst not acknowledge their graves; wherein Alaricus seems not subtle, who had a river turned to hide his bones at the bottom. Even Sylla, that thought himself safe in his urn, could not prevent revenging tongues, and stones thrown at his monument. Happy are they whom privacy makes innocent, who deal so with men in this world, that they are not afraid to meet them in the next; who, when they die, make no commotion among the dead, and are not touched with the poetical taunt of Isaiah.[11]

Pyramids, arches, obelisks, were but irregularities of vain-glory, and wild enormities of ancient magnanimity.[12] But the most magnanimous resolution rests in the Christian religion, which trampleth upon pride, and sits on the neck of ambition, humbly pursuing that infallible perpetuity, unto which all others must diminish their diameters, and be poorly seen in angles of contingency.

Pious spirits who passed their days in raptures of futurity, made little more of this world, than the world that was before it, while they lay obscure in the chaos of predomination, and night of their fore-beings. And if any have been so happy as truly to understand Christian annihilation, ecstasies, exolution,[13] liquefaction, transformation, the kiss of the spouse, gustation[14] of God, and ingression into the divine shadow, they have already had an handsome anticipation of heaven; the glory of the world is surely over, and the earth in ashes unto them.

To subsist in lasting monuments, to live in their productions, to

[11] Isaiah XIV – verse 10 or verses 16 and 17

[12] greatness of imagination or mind

[13] setting free, hence death, freedom from bonds of body and life

[14] taste, experience

exist in their names and predicament of chimaeras, was large satisfaction unto old expectations, and made one part of their Elysiums.[15] But all this is nothing in the metaphysics[16] of true belief. To live indeed, is to be again ourselves, which being not only an hope, but an evidence in noble believers, 'tis all one to lie in St. Innocents' churchyard, as in the sands of Egypt. Ready to be anything, in the ecstacy of being ever, and as content with six foot as the *moles*[17] of Adrianus.

—tabesne cadavera solvat,
An rogus, haud refert.[18]

[15] state or abode of the blessed, our heaven

[16] theoretical principles, essence of a thing [17] heap

[18] it matters not whether our bodies rot in the grave or are consumed by the funeral pyre

⁂ A physician-essayist and meditator on the frailty yet splendor of human forms, Sir Thomas Browne was educated at Oxford, practiced in Norwich, then wrote a book on the religion of a medical man, *Religio Medici,* and one on popular superstitions, *Vulgar Errors.* His *Urn-Burial* (1658) was inspired by the discovery of some ancient sepulchral urns in his native Norfolk and considers "with melancholy splendor," as a critic has said, burial customs in English and ancient history, and the question of immortality. The "Conclusion" is well known as an entity in itself, yet it is in some ways comparable to Pater's "Conclusion" to *The Renaissance.*

Areopagitica

(1644) BY ***John Milton*** *(1608-1674)*

> This is true Liberty, when free-born men,
> Having to advise the public, may speak free,
> Which he who can, and will, deserves high praise;
> Who neither can, nor will, may hold his peace:
> What can be juster in a State than this?
>
> Euripides, *Iketides*

A SPEECH FOR THE LIBERTY OF UNLICENSED PRINTING, TO THE PARLIAMENT OF ENGLAND (1644)

They, who to states and governors of the Commonwealth direct their speech, High Court of Parliament, or, wanting such access in a public good; I suppose them, as at the beginning of no mean endeavour, not a little altered and moved inwardly in their minds: some with doubt of what will be the success, others with fear of what will be the censure; some with hope, others with confidence of what they have to speak. And me perhaps each of these dispositions, as the subject was whereon I entered, may have at other times variously affected, and likely might in these foremost expressions now also disclose which of them swayed most, but that the very attempt of this address thus made, and the thought of whom it hath recourse to, hath got the power within me to a passion, far more welcome than incidental to a preface.

Which though I stay not to confess ere any ask, I shall be blameless, if it be not other than the joy and gratulation which it brings to all who wish and promote their country's liberty; whereof this whole discourse proposed will be a certain testimony, if not a trophy. For this is not the liberty which we can hope, that no grievance ever should arise in the Commonwealth—that let no man in this world expect; but when complaints are freely heard, deeply considered and speedily reformed, then is the utmost bound of civil liberty attained that wise men look for. To which if I now manifest by the very sound of this which I shall utter, that we are already in good part arrived, and yet from such a steep disadvantage of tyranny and superstition grounded into our principles as was beyond the manhood of a Roman recovery, it will be attributed first, as is most due, to the strong assistance of God our deliverer, next to your faithful guidance and undaunted wisdom, Lords and Commons of England. Neither is it in God's esteem the diminution of His glory, when honourable things are spoken of good men and worthy magistrates; which if I now first should begin to do, after so fair a progress of your laudable deeds, and such a long obligement upon the whole realm to your indefatigable virtues, I might be justly reckoned among the tardiest, and the unwillingest of them that praise ye.

Nevertheless there being three principal things, without which all praising is but courtship and flattery: First, when that only is praised which is solidly worth praise: next, when greatest likelihoods are brought that such things are truly and really in those persons to whom they are ascribed: the other, when he who praises, by showing that such his actual persuasion is of whom he writes, can demonstrate that he flatters not; the former two of these I have heretofore endeavoured, rescuing the employment from him who went about to impair your merits with a trivial and malignant encomium;[1] the latter as belonging chiefly to mine own acquittal, that whom I so extolled I did not flatter, hath been reserved opportunely to this occasion.

For he who freely magnifies what hath been nobly done, and fears not to declare as freely what might be done better, gives ye the best covenant of his fidelity; and that his loyalist affection and his hope waits on your proceedings. His highest praising is not

[1] formal expression of praise

flattery, and his plainest advice is a kind of praising. For though I should affirm and hold by argument, that it would fare better with truth, with learning and the Commonwealth, if one of your published Orders, which I should name, were called in; yet at the same time it could not but much redound to the lustre of your mild and equal government, whenas private persons are hereby animated to think ye better pleased with public advice, than other statists have been delighted heretofore with public flattery. And men will then see what difference there is between the magnanimity of a triennial Parliament, and that jealous haughtiness of prelates and Cabin Counsellors that usurped of late, whenas they shall observe ye in the midst of your victories and successes more gently brooking written exceptions against a voted Order than other Courts, which had produced nothing worth memory but the weak ostentation of wealth, would have endured the least signified dislike at any sudden Proclamation.

If I should thus far presume upon the meek demeanour of your civil and gentle greatness, Lords and Commons, as what your published Order hath directly said, that to gainsay, I might defend myself with ease, if any should accuse me of being new or insolent,[2] did they but know how much better I find ye esteem it to imitate the old and elegant humanity of Greece, than the barbaric pride of a Hunnish and Norwegian stateliness. And out of those ages, to whose polite wisdom and letters we owe that we are not yet Goths and Jutlanders,[3] I could name him who from his private house wrote that discourse to the Parliament of Athens, that persuades them to change the form of democraty which was then established. Such honour was done in those days to men who professed the study of wisdom and eloquence, not only in their own country, but in other lands, that cities and signiories[4] heard them gladly, and with great respect, if they had aught in public to admonish the state. Thus did Dion Prusaeus, a stranger and a private orator, counsel the Rhodians against a former edict; and I abound with other like examples, which to set here would be superfluous.

But if from the industry of a life wholly dedicated to studious

[2] newfangled, singular, not according to custom

[3] barbarians [4] democracies and oligarchies

labours, and those natural endowments haply not the worse for two and fifty degrees of northern latitude, so much must be derogated, as to count me not equal to any of those who had this privilege, I would obtain to be thought not so inferior, as yourselves are superior to the most of them who received their counsel: and how far you excel them, be assured, Lords and Commons, there can no greater testimony appear, than when your prudent spirit acknowledges and obeys the voice of reason from what quarter soever it be heard speaking; and renders ye as willing to repeal any Act of your own setting forth, as any set forth by your predecessors.

If ye be thus resolved, as it were injury to think ye were not, I know not what should withhold me from presenting ye with a fit instance wherein to show both that love of truth which ye eminently profess, and that uprightness of your judgment which is not wont to be partial to yourselves; by judging over again that order which ye have ordained to regulate Printing: — that no book, pamphlet, or paper shall be henceforth printed, unless the same be first approved and licensed by such, or at least one of such, as shall be thereto appointed. For that part which preserves justly every man's copy to himself, or provides for the poor, I touch not, only wish they be not made pretences to abuse and persecute honest and painful men, who offend not in either of these particulars. But that other clause of Licensing Books, which we thought had died with his brother quadragesimal and matrimonial[5] when the prelates expired, I shall now attend with such a homily, as shall lay before ye, first the inventors of it to be those whom ye will be loth to own; next what is to be thought in general of reading, whatever sort the books be; and that this Order avails nothing to the suppressing of scandalous, seditious, and libellous books, which were mainly intended to be suppressed. Last, that it will be primely to the discouragement of all learning, and the stop of Truth, not only by disexercising and blunting our abilities in what we know already, but by hindering and cropping the discovery that might be yet further made both in religious and civil Wisdom.

[5] licenses that were needed from Catholic Church authorities by those who wished to eat meat in Lent or get married. Both had been repealed under the Commonwealth, and Milton means the book license should be.

I deny not, but that it is of greatest concernment in the Church and Commonwealth, to have a vigilant eye how books demean themselves as well as men; and thereafter to confine, imprison, and do sharpest justice on them as malefactors. For books are not absolutely dead things, but do contain a potency of life in them to be as active as that soul was whose progeny they are; nay, they do preserve as in a vial the purest efficacy and extraction of that living intellect that bred them. I know they are as lively, and as vigorously productive, as those fabulous dragon's teeth; and being sown up and down, may chance to spring up armed men. And yet, on the other hand, unless wariness be used, as good almost kill a man as kill a good book. Who kills a man kills a reasonable creature, God's image; but he who destroys a good book, kills reason itself, kills the image of God, as it were in the eye. Many a man lives a burden to the earth; but a good book is the precious life-blood of a master spirit, embalmed and treasured up on purpose to a life beyond life. 'Tis true, no age can restore a life, whereof perhaps there is no great loss; and revolutions of ages do not oft recover the loss of a rejected truth, for the want of which whole nations fare the worse.

We should be wary therefore what persecution we raise against the living labours of public men, how we spill that seasoned life of man, preserved and stored up in books; since we see a kind of homicide may be thus committed, sometimes a martyrdom, and if it extend to the whole impression, a kind of massacre; whereof the execution ends not in the slaying of an elemental life, but strikes at that ethereal and fifth essence,[6] the breath of reason itself, slays an immortality rather than a life. But lest I should be condemned of introducing licence, while I oppose licensing, I refuse not the pains to be so much historical, as will serve to show what hath been done by ancient and famous commonwealths against this disorder, till the very time that this project of licensing crept out of the inquisition, was catched up by our prelates, and hath caught some of our presbyters.

In Athens, where books and wits were ever busier than in any other part of Greece, I find but only two sorts of writings which the magistrate cared to take notice of; those either blasphemous and

[6] very soul, quintessence

atheistical, or libellous. Thus the books of Protagoras were by the judges of Areopagus commanded to be burnt, and himself banished the territory for a discourse begun with his confessing not to know "whether there were gods, or whether not." And against defaming, it was agreed, that none should be traduced[7] by name, as was the manner of Vetus Comoedia, whereby we may guess how they censured libelling. And this course was quick enough, as Cicero writes, to quell both the desperate wits of other atheists, and the open way of defaming, as the event showed. Of other sects and opinions, though tending to voluptuousness, and the denying of Divine Providence, they took no heed.

Therefore we do not read that either Epicurus, or that libertine school of Cyrene,[8] or what the Cynic[9] impudence uttered, was ever questioned by the laws. Neither is it recorded that the writing of those old comedians were suppressed, though the acting of them were forbid; and that Plato commended the reading of Aristophanes, the loosest of them all, to his royal scholar Dionysius, is commonly known, and may be excused, if holy Chrysostom, as is reported, nightly studied so much the same author and had the art to cleanse a scurrilous vehemence into the style of a rousing sermon.

That other leading city of Greece, Lacedaemon, considering that Lycurgus their lawgiver was so addicted to elegant learning, as to have been the first that brought out of Ionia the scattered works of Homer, and sent the poet Thales from Crete to prepare and mollify the Spartan surliness with his smooth songs and odes, the better to plant among them law and civility, it is to be wondered how museless and unbookish they were, minding nought but the feats of war. There needed no licensing of books among them, for they disliked all but their own laconic apothegms, and took a slight occasion to chase Archilochus out of their city, perhaps for composing in a higher strain than their own soldierly ballads and roundels could reach to. Or if it were for his broad verses, they were not therein so cautious but they were as dissolute in their promiscuous conversing; whence Euripides affirms in *Andromache,* that their women were all unchaste. Thus much may give us light after what sort of books were prohibited among the Greeks.

[7] slandered [8] believers in practical hedonism

[9] philosophers who held in contempt the amenities of life

The Romans also, for many ages trained up only to a military roughness resembling most the Lacedaemonian guise, knew of learning little but what their twelve Tables, and the Pontific College with their augurs and flamens[10] taught them in religion and law, so unacquainted with other learning, that when Carneades and Critolaus, with the Stoic Diogenes coming ambassadors to Rome, took thereby occasion to give the city a taste of their philosophy, they were suspected for seducers[11] by no less a man than Cato the censor, who moved it in the Senate to dismiss them speedily, and to banish all such Attic babblers out of Italy. But Scipio and others of the noblest senators withstood him and his old Sabine austerity; honoured and admired the men; and the censor himself at last, in his old age, fell to the study of that whereof before he was so scrupulous.[12] And yet at the same time, Naevius and Plautus, the first Latin comedians, had filled the city with all the borrowed scenes of Menander and Philemon. Then began to be considered there also what was to be done to libellous books and authors; for Naevius was quickly cast into prison for his unbridled pen, and released by the tribunes upon his recantation; we read also that libels were burnt, and the makers punished by Augustus. The like severity, no doubt, was used if aught were impiously written against their esteemed gods. Except in these two points, how the world went in books, the magistrate kept no reckoning.

And therefore Lucretius without impeachment[13] versifies his Epicurism to Memmius and had the honour to be set forth the second time by Cicero, so great a father of the commonwealth; although himself disputes against that opinion in his own writings. Nor was the satirical sharpness or naked plainness of Lucilius, or Catullus, or Flaccus, by any order prohibited. And for matters of state, the story of Titus Livius, though it extolled that part which Pompey held, was not therefore suppressed by Octavius Caesar of the other faction. But that Naso[14] was by him banished in his old age, for the wanton poems of his youth, was but a mere covert of state over some secret cause: and besides, the books were neither banished nor called in. From hence we shall meet with little else but tyranny in the Roman empire, that we may not marvel, if not so

[10] in ancient Rome, priests of a particular god [11] subversives
[12] highly suspicious [13] hindrance [14] Ovid

often bad as good books were silenced. I shall therefore deem to have been large enough, in producing what among the ancients was punishable to write; save only which, all other arguments were free to treat on.

By this time the emperors were become Christians, whose discipline in this point I do not find to have been more severe than what was formerly in practice. The books of those whom they took to be grand heretics were examined, refuted, and condemned in the general Councils; and not till then were prohibited, or burnt, by authority of the emperor. As for the writings of heathen authors, unless they were plain invectives against Christianity, as those of Porphyrius and Proclus, they met with no interdict[15] that can be cited, till about the year 400, in a Carthaginian Council, wherein bishops themselves were forbid to read the books of Gentiles, but heresies they might read: while others long before them, on the contrary, scrupled more the books of heretics than of Gentiles. And that the primitive Councils and bishops were wont only to declare what books were not commendable, passing no further, but leaving it to each one's conscience to read or to lay by, till after the year 800, is observed already by Padre Paolo, the great unmasker of the Trentine Council.

After which time the Popes of Rome, engrossing[16] what they pleased of political rule into their own hands, extended their dominion over men's eyes, as they had before over their judgments, burning and prohibiting to be read what they fancied not; yet sparing in their censures, and the books not many which they so dealt with; till Martin V, by his bull, not only prohibited, but was the first that excommunicated the reading of heretical books; for about that time Wickliffe and Huss, growing terrible, were they who first drove the Papal Court to a stricter policy of prohibiting. Which course Leo X and his successors followed, until the Council of Trent and the Spanish Inquisition engendering together brought forth, or perfected, those Catalogues and expurging Indexes, that rake through the entrails of many an old good author, with a violation worse than any could be offered to his tomb. Nor did they stay in matters heretical, but any subject that was not to their palate,

[15] ban [16] seizing possession of or authority over

they either condemned in a Prohibition, or had it straight into the new Purgatory of an Index.[17]

To fill up the measure of encroachment, their last invention was to ordain that no book, pamphlet, or paper should be printed (as if St. Peter had bequeathed them the keys of the press also out of Paradise) unless it were approved and licensed under the hands of two or three glutton friars. For example:

> Let the Chancellor Cini be pleased to see if in this present work be contained aught that may withstand the printing.
>
> Vincent Rabbatta, Vicar of Florence.
>
> I have seen this present work, and find nothing athwart the Catholic faith and good manners: in witness whereof I have given, etc.
>
> Nicolo Cini, Chancellor of Florence.
>
> Attending the precedent relation, it is allowed that this present work of Davanzati may be printed.
>
> Vincent Rabbatta, etc.
>
> It may be printed, July 15.
>
> Friar Simon Mompei d'Amelia, Chancellor of the holy office in Florence.

Sure they have a conceit, if he of the bottomless pit had not long since broke prison, that this quadruple exorcism[18] would bar him down. I fear their next design will be to get into their custody the licensing of that which they say Claudius intended but went not through with. Vouchsafe to see another of their forms, the Roman stamp:

> Imprimatur, If it seem good to the reverend master of the holy Palace.
>
> Belcastro, Vicegerent.
>
> Imprimatur, Friar Nicolo Rodolphi, Master of the holy Palace.

Sometimes five Imprimaturs are seen together dialogue-wise in

[17] the index of forbidden books maintained by the Catholic Church

[18] casting out of devils

the piazza of one title-page, complimenting and ducking each to other with their shaven reverences,[19] whether the author, who stands by in perplexity at the foot of his epistle, shall to the press or to the sponge. These are the pretty responsories, these are the dear antiphonies,[20] that so bewitched of late our Prelates and their chaplains with the goodly echo they made; and besotted us to the gay imitation of a lordly Imprimatur, one from Lambeth House, another from the west end of Paul's; so apishly romanising, that the word of command still was set down in Latin; as if the learned grammatical pen that wrote it would cast no ink without Latin; or perhaps, as they thought, because no vulgar tongue was worthy to express the pure conceit of an Imprimatur; but rather, as I hope, for that our English, the language of men, ever famous and foremost in the achievements of liberty, will not easily find servile letters enow to spell such a dictatory presumption English.

And thus ye have the inventors and the original of book-licensing ripped up and drawn as lineally as any pedigree. We have it not, that can be heard of, from any ancient state, or polity or church; nor by any statute left us by our ancestors elder or later; nor from the modern custom of any reformed city or church abroad; but from the most anti-christian council and the most tyrannous inquisition that ever inquired. Till then books were ever as freely admitted into the world as any other birth; the issue of the brain was no more stifled than the issue of the womb: no envious Juno sat cross-legged over the nativity of any man's intellectual offspring; but if it proved a monster, who denies, but that it was justly burnt, or sunk into the sea? But that a book, in worse condition than a peccant soul, should be to stand before a jury ere it be born to the world, and undergo yet in darkness the judgment of Radamanth[21] and his colleagues, ere it can pass the ferry[22] backward into light, was never heard before, till that mysterious iniquity, provoked and troubled at the first entrance of Reformation, sought out new limbos and new hells wherein they might include our books also within the number of their damned. And this was the rare morsel so officiously snatched

[19] act of courtesy [20] musical terms indicating a chant and the answer to it
[21] one of the judges of the lower world, an inflexible judge
[22] over the river into death or oblivion in ancient mythology

up, and so ill-favouredly imitated by our inquisiturient[23] bishops, and the attendant minorities[24] their chaplains. That ye like not now these most certain authors of this licensing order, and that all sinister intention was far distant from your thoughts, when ye were importuned the passing it all men who know the integrity of your actions, and how ye honour Truth, will clear ye readily.

But some will say, What though the inventors were bad, the thing for all that may be good? It may be so; yet if that thing be no such deep invention, but obvious and easy for any man to light on, and yet best and wisest commonwealths through all ages and occasions have forborne to use it, and falsest seducers and oppressors of men were the first who took it up, and to no other purpose but to obstruct and hinder the first approach of Reformation; I am of those who believe it will be a harder alchymy than Lullius ever knew, to sublimate any good use out of such an invention. Yet this only is what I request to gain from this reason, that it may be held a dangerous and suspicious fruit, as certainly it deserves, for the tree that bore it, until I can dissect one by one the properties it has. But I have first to finish, as was propounded, what is to be thought in general of reading books, whatever sort they be, and whether be more the benefit or the harm that thence proceeds?

Not to insist upon the examples of Moses, Daniel, and Paul, who were skilful in all the learning of the Egyptians, Chaldeans, and Greeks, which could not probably be without reading their books of all sorts; in Paul especially, who thought it no defilement to insert into Holy Scripture the sentences of three Greek poets, and one of them a tragedian; the question was notwithstanding sometimes controverted among the primitive doctors, but with great odds on that side which affirmed it both lawful and profitable; as was then evidently perceived, when Julian the Apostate and subtlest enemy to our faith made a decree forbidding Christians the study of heathen learning: for, said he, they wound us with our own weapons, and with our own arts and sciences they overcome us. And indeed the Christians were put so to their shifts by this crafty

[23] eager to play the inquisitor

[24] subordinates, inferiors. Franciscans were called friars minor, or minorites, a rule of their order stating that *all* should be lesser brethren, no prior.

means, and so much in danger to decline into all ignorance, that the two Apollinarii[25] were fain, as a man may say, to coin all the seven liberal sciences[26] out of the Bible, reducing it into divers forms of orations, poems, dialogues, even to the calculating of a new Christian grammar. But, saith the historian Socrates, the providence of God provided better than the industry of Apollinarius and his son, by taking away that illiterate law with the life of him who devised it. So great an injury they then held it to be deprived of Hellenic learning; and thought it a persecution more undermining, and secretly decaying the Church, than the open cruelty of Decius or Diocletian.

And perhaps it was the same politic drift that the devil whipped St. Jerome in a Lenten dream, for reading Cicero; or else it was a phantasm bred by the fever which had then seized him. For had an angel been his discipliner, unless it were for dwelling too much upon Ciceronianisms, and had chastised the reading, not the vanity, it had been plainly partial; first to correct him for grave Cicero, and not for scurril Plautus, whom he confesses to have been reading, not long before; next to correct him only, and let so many more ancient fathers wax old in those pleasant and florid studies without the lash of such a tutoring apparition; insomuch that Basil teaches how some good use may be made of Margites, a sportful poem, not now extant, writ by Homer; and why not then of Morgante, an Italian romance much to the same purpose?

But if it be agreed we shall be tried by visions, there is a vision recorded by Eusebius, far ancienter than this tale of Jerome to the nun Eustochium, and, besides, has nothing of a fever in it. Dionysius Alexandrinus was about the year 240 a person of great name in the Church for piety and learning, who had wont to avail himself much against heretics by being conversant in their books; until a certain presbyter laid it scrupulously to his conscience, how he durst venture himself among those defiling volumes. The worthy man, loth to give offense, fell into a new debate with himself what was to be thought; when suddenly a vision sent from God (it is his

[25] father and son, learned men and skilled defenders of the Roman Catholic Church in the fourth century

[26] Grammar, Logic, Rhetoric, Arithmetic, Geometry, Astronomy, Music

own epistle that so avers it) confirmed him in these words: Read any books whatever come to thy hands, for thou art sufficient both to judge aright, and to examine each matter. To this revelation he assented the sooner, as he confesses, because it was answerable to that of the Apostle to the Thessalonians, Prove all things, hold fast that which is good. And he might have added another remarkable saying of the same author: To the pure, all things are pure; not only meats and drinks, but all kind of knowledge whether of good or evil; the knowledge cannot defile, nor consequently the books, if the will and conscience be not defiled.

For books are as meats and viands are; some of good, some of evil substance; and yet God, in that unapocryphal vision, said without exception, Rise, Peter, kill and eat, leaving the choice to each man's discretion. Wholesome meats to a vitiated stomach differ little or nothing from unwholesome; and best books to a naughty mind are not unappliable to occasions of evil. Bad meats will scarce breed good nourishment in the healthiest concoction; but herein the difference is of bad books, that they to a discreet and judicious reader serve in many respects to discover, to confute, to forewarn, and to illustrate. Whereof what better witness can ye expect I should produce, than one of your own now sitting in Parliament, the chief of learned men reputed in this land, Mr. Selden; whose volume of natural and national laws proves, not only by great authorities brought together, but by exquisite reasons and theorems almost mathematically demonstrative, that all opinions, yea errors, known, read, and collated, are of main service and assistance toward the speedy attainment of what is truest. I conceive, therefore, that when God did enlarge the universal diet of man's body, saving ever the rules of temperance, He then also, as before, left arbitrary the dieting and repasting of our minds; as wherein every mature man might have to exercise his own leading capacity.

How great a virtue is temperance, how much of moment through the whole life of man! Yet God commits the managing so great a trust, without particular law or prescription, wholly to the demeanour of every grown man. And therefore when he himself tabled the Jews from heaven, that omer, which was every man's daily portion of manna, is computed to have been more than might have well sufficed the heartiest feeder thrice as many meals. For those actions which enter into a man, rather than issue out of him, and therefore defile not, God uses not to captivate under a perpetual childbood of prescription, but trusts him with the gift of reason to be his own chooser; there were but little work left for preaching, if law and compulsion should grow so fast upon those things which heretofore were governed only by exhortation. Solomon informs us, that much reading is a weariness to the flesh; but neither he nor other inspired author tells us that such or such reading is unlawful: yet certainly had God thought good to limit us herein, it had been much more expedient to have told us what was unlawful than what was wearisome. As for the burning of those Ephesian books by St. Paul's converts; 'tis replied the books were magic, the Syriac so renders them. It was a private act, a voluntary act, and leaves us to a voluntary imitation: the men in remorse burnt those books which were their own: the magistrate by this example is not appointed: these men practised the books, another might perhaps have read them in some sort usefully.

Good and evil we know in the field of this world grow up together almost inseparably; and the knowledge of good is so involved and interwoven with the knowledge of evil, and in so many cunning resemblances hardly to be discerned, that those confused seeds which were imposed upon Psyche[27] as an incessant labour to cull out, and sort asunder, were not more intermixed. It was from out the rind of one apple tasted, that the knowledge of good and evil, as two twins cleaving together, leaped forth into the world. And perhaps this is that doom which Adam fell into of knowing good and evil, that is to say of knowing good by evil. As therefore the state of man now is; what wisdom can there be to choose, what continence to forbear without the knowledge of evil? He that can apprehend and consider vice with all her baits and seeming pleasures, and yet abstain, and yet distinguish, and yet prefer that which is truly better, he is the true wayfaring Christian.

I cannot praise a fugitive[28] and cloistered virtue, unexercised and unbreathed, that never sallies out and sees her adversary, but slinks out of the race, where that immortal garland is to be run for, not

[27] punished severely by Venus out of resentment of Cupid's love for Psyche
[28] fleeing from contact with everyday realities

without dust and heat. Assuredly we bring not innocence into the world, we bring impurity much rather; that which purifies us is trial, and trial is by what is contrary. That virtue therefore which is but a youngling in the contemplation of evil, and knows not the utmost that vice promises to her followers, and rejects it, is but a blank virtue, not a pure; her whiteness is but an excremental[29] whiteness. Which was the reason why our sage and serious poet Spenser, whom I dare be known to think a better teacher than Scotus or Aquinas, describing true temperance under the person of Guion, brings him in with his palmer through the cave of Mammon, and the bower of earthly bliss, that he might see and know, and yet abstain. Since therefore the knowledge and survey of vice is in this world so necessary to the constituting of human virtue, and the scanning of error to the confirmation of truth, how can we more safely, and with less danger, scout into the regions of sin and falsity than by reading all manner of tractates and hearing all manner of reason? And this is the benefit which may be had of books promiscuously read.

But of the harm that may result hence three kinds are usually reckoned. First, is feared the infection that may spread; but then all human learning and controversy in religious points must remove out of the world, yea the Bible itself; for that ofttimes relates blasphemy not nicely,[30] it describes the carnal sense of wicked men not unelegantly, it brings in holiest men passionately murmuring against Providence through all the arguments of Epicurus: in other great disputes it answers dubiously and darkly to the common reader. And ask a Talmudist what ails the modesty of his marginal Keri,[31] that Moses and all the prophets cannot persuade him to pronounce the textual Chetiv.[32] For these causes we all know the Bible itself put by the Papist into the first rank of prohibited books. The ancientest fathers must be next removed, as Clement of Alexandria, and that Eusebian book of Evangelic preparation, transmit-

[29] merely on the surface, superficial [30] judicious, discriminating [31] oral

[32] written. The Talmud is a sixth-century compilation of Jewish civil and canonical laws preserved in oral tradition, and it must be distinguished from the written law of the Pentateuch. Rabbinical commentators on Hebrew Scriptures, when a word needed to be altered, did not change the text as *written,* but put in the margin the word which was preferably to be *read.*

ting our ears through a hoard of heathenish obscenities to receive the Gospel. Who finds not that Irenaeus, Epiphanius, Jerome, and others discover more heresies than they well confute, and that oft for heresy which is the truer opinion?

Nor boots[33] it to say for these, and all the heathen writers of greatest infection, if it must be thought so, with whom is bound up the life of human learning, that they writ in an unknown tongue, so long as we are sure those languages are known as well to the worst of men who are both most able, and most diligent to instil the poison they suck, first into the courts of princes, acquainting them with the choicest delights and criticisms of sin.[34] as perhaps did that Petronius whom Nero called his Arbiter, the master of his revels; and the notorious ribald of Arezzo,[35] dreaded and yet dear to the Italian courtiers. I name not him for posterity's sake, whom Henry VIII named in merriment his Vicar of hell. By which compendious way all the contagion that foreign books can infuse will find a passage to the people far easier and shorter than an Indian voyage, though it could be sailed either by the north of Cataio eastward, or of Canada westward, while our Spanish licensing gags the English press never so severely.

But on the other side that infection which is from books of controversy in religion is more doubtful and dangerous to the learned than to the ignorant; and yet those books must be permitted untouched by the licenser. It will be hard to instance where any ignorant man hath been ever seduced by papistical book in English, unless it were commended and expounded to him by some of that clergy: and indeed all such tractates, whether false or true, are as the prophecy of Isaiah was to the eunuch, not to be understood without a guide. But of our priests and doctors how many have been corrupted by studying the comments of Jesuits and Sorbonists, and how fast they could transfuse that corruption into the people, our experience is both late and sad. It is not forgot, since the acute and distinct Arminius was perverted merely by the perusing of a nameless discourse written at Delft, which at first he took in hand to confute.

[33] profits [34] subtle varieties of sin, a unique usage of the word *criticism*

[35] Aretino (1492-1557), a writer of burlesques and satires, whose prospective victims, including great princes, saw fit to buy his silence

Seeing, therefore, that those books, and those in great abundance, which are likeliest to taint both life and doctrine, cannot be suppressed without the fall of learning and of all ability in disputation, and that these books of either sort are most and soonest catching to the learned, from whom to the common people whatever is heretical or dissolute may quickly be conveyed, and that evil manners are as perfectly learnt without books a thousand other ways which cannot be stopped, and evil doctrine not with books can propagate except a teacher guide, which he might also do without writing, and so beyond prohibiting, I am not able to unfold, how this cautelous enterprise of licensing can be exempted from the number of vain and impossible attempts. And he who were pleasantly disposed could not well avoid to liken it to the exploit of that gallant man who thought to pound[36] up the crows by shutting his park gate.

Besides another inconvenience, if learned men be the first receivers out of books and dispreaders both of vice and error, how shall the licensers themselves be confided in, unless we can confer upon them, or they assume to themselves above all others in the land, the grace of infallibility and uncorruptedness? And again, if it be true that a wise man, like a good refiner, can gather gold out of the drossiest volume, and that a fool will be a fool with the best book, yea or without book; there is no reason that we should deprive a wise man of any advantage to his wisdom, while we seek to restrain from a fool, that which being restrained will be no hindrance to his folly. For if there should be so much exactness always used to keep that from him which is unfit for his reading, we should in the judgment of Aristotle not only, but of Solomon and of our Saviour, not vouchsafe him good precepts, and by consequence not willingly admit him to good books, as being certain that a wise man will make better use of an idle pamphlet, than a fool will do of sacred Scripture.

'Tis next alleged we must not expose ourselves to temptations without necessity, and next to that, not employ our time in vain things. To both these objections one answer will serve, out of the grounds already laid, that to all men such books are not temptations, nor vanities, but useful drugs and materials wherewith to temper and compose effective and strong medicines, which man's

[36] impound, lock up

life cannot want.[37] The rest, as children and childish men, who have not the art to qualify and prepare these working minerals, well may be exhorted to forbear, but hindered forcibly they cannot be by all the licensing that Sainted Inquisition could ever yet contrive. Which is what I promised to deliver next, That this order of licensing conduces nothing to the end for which it was framed; and hath almost prevented[38] me by being clear already while thus much hath been explaining. See the ingenuity of Truth, who, when she gets a free and willing hand, opens herself faster than the pace of method and discourse can overtake her.

It was the task which I began with, to show that no nation, or well-instituted state, if they valued books at all, did ever use this way of licensing; and it might be answered that this is a piece of prudence lately discovered. To which I return, that as it was a thing slight and obvious to think on, so if it had been difficult to find out, there wanted not among them long since who suggested such a course; which they not following, leave us a pattern of their judgment that it was not the not knowing, but the not approving, which was the cause of their not using it.

Plato, a man of high authority, indeed, but least of all for his commonwealth, in the book of his Laws, which no city ever yet received, fed his fancy by making many edicts to his airy[39] burgomasters, which they who otherwise admire him wish had been rather buried and excused in the genial cups of an Academic night sitting. By which laws he seems to tolerate no kind of learning but by unalterable decree, consisting most of practical traditions, to the attainment whereof a library of smaller bulk than his own Dialogues would be abundant. And there also enacts, that no poet should so much as read to any private man what he had written, until the judges and law-keepers had seen it, and allowed it. But that Plato meant this law peculiarly to that commonwealth which he had imagined, and to no other is evident. Why was he not else a lawgiver to himself, but a transgressor, and to be expelled by his own magistrates; both for the wanton epigrams and dialogues which he made, and his perpetual reading of Sophron Mimus and Aristophanes, books of grossest infamy, and also for commending the

[37] do without [38] anticipated [39] imaginary

latter of them, though he were the malicious libeller of his chief friends, to be read by the tyrant Dionysius, who had little need of such trash to spend his time on? But that he knew this licensing of poems had reference and dependence to many other provisos there set down in his fancied republic, which in this world could have no place: and so neither he himself, nor any magistrate, or city ever imitated that course, which, taken apart from those other collateral injunctions, must needs be vain and fruitless. For if they fell upon one kind of strictness, unless their care were equal to regulate all other things of like aptness to corrupt the mind, that single endeavour they knew would be but a fond[40] labour; to shut and fortify one gate against corruption, and be necessitated to leave others round about wide open.

If we think to regulate printing, thereby to rectify manners, we must regulate all recreations and pastimes, all that is delightful to man. No music must be heard, no song be set or sung, but what is grave and Doric. There must be licensing dancers, that no gesture, motion, or deportment be taught our youth but what by their allowance shall be thought honest; for such Plato was provided of; it will ask more than the work of twenty licensers to examine all the lutes, the violins, and the guitars in every house; they must not be suffered to prattle as they do, but must be licensed what they may say. And who shall silence all the airs and madrigals that whisper softness in chambers? The windows also, and the balconies must be thought on; there are shrewd books, with dangerous frontispieces, set to sale; who shall prohibit them, shall twenty licensers? The villages also must have their visitors to inquire what lectures the bagpipe and the rebeck reads, even to the ballatry[41] and the gamut of every municipal fiddler, for these are the countryman's Arcadias, and his Monte Mayors.[42]

Next, what more national corruption, for which England hears ill

[40] foolish

[41] In 1634 William Laud, Archbishop of Canterbury, prompted Charles I to strengthen orders to the bishops that they exercise careful censorship over all lectures in their dioceses. Milton says that a comparable system of surveillance is now desired for the literature and poetry of every village so that inspectors will scrutinize even the bagpipe and fiddle accompaniment to rustic ballads.

[42] popular pastoral romances

abroad, than household gluttony: who shall be the rectors of our daily rioting? And what shall be done to inhibit the multitudes that frequent those houses where drunkenness is sold and harboured? Our garments also should be referred to the licensing of some more sober workmasters to see them cut into a less wanton garb. Who shall regulate all the mixed conversation of our youth, male and female together, as is the fashion of this country? Who shall still appoint what shall be discoursed, what presumed, and no further? Lastly, who shall forbid and separate all idle resort, all evil company? These things will be and must be; but how they shall be least hurtful, how least enticing, herein consists the grave and governing wisdom of a state.

To sequester out of the world into Atlantic and Utopian[43] polities which never can be drawn into use, will not mend our condition; but to ordain wisely as in this world of evil, in the midst whereof God hath placed us unavoidably. Nor is it Plato's licensing of books will do this, which necessarily pulls along with it so many other kinds of licensing, as will make us all both ridiculous and weary, and yet frustrate; but those unwritten, or at least unconstraining, laws of virtuous education, religious and civil nurture, which Plato there mentions as the bonds and ligaments of the commonwealth, the pillars and the sustainers of every written statute; these they be which will bear chief sway in such matters as these, when all licensing will be easily eluded. Impunity and remissness, for certain, are the bane of a commonwealth; but here the great art lies, to discern in what the law is to bid restraint and punishment, and in what things persuasion only is to work.

If every action, which is good or evil in man at ripe years, were to be under pittance and prescription and compulsion, what were virtue but a name, what praise could be then due to well-doing, what gramercy[44] to be sober, just, or continent? Many there be that complain of Divine Providence for suffering Adam to transgress; foolish tongues! When God gave him reason, He gave him freedom to choose, for reason is but choosing; he had been else a mere artificial Adam, such an Adam as he is in the motions.[45] We ourselves esteem not of that obedience, or love, or gift, which is of

[43] ideal, visionary [44] thanks
[45] in the puppet-shows

force: God therefore left him free, set before him a provoking object, ever almost in his eyes; herein consisted his merit, herein the right of his reward, the praise of his abstinence. Wherefore did He create passions within us, pleasures round about us, but that these rightly tempered are the very ingredients of virtue?

They are not skilful considerers of human things, who imagine to remove sin by removing the matter of sin; for, besides that it is a huge heap increasing under the very act of diminishing, though some part of it may for a time be withdrawn from some persons, it cannot from all, in such a universal thing as books are; and when this is done, yet the sin remains entire. Though ye take from a covetous man all his treasure, he has yet one jewel left, ye cannot bereave him of his covetousness. Banish all objects of lust, shut up all youth into the severest discipline that can be exercised in any hermitage, ye cannot make them chaste, that came not thither so: such great care and wisdom is required to the right managing of this point. Suppose we could expel sin by this means; look how much we thus expel of sin, so much we expel of virtue: for the matter of them both is the same; remove that, and ye remove them both alike.

This justifies the high providence of God, who, though He commands us temperance, justice, continence, yet pours out before us, even to a profuseness, all desirable things, and gives us minds that can wander beyond all limit and satiety. Why should we then affect a rigour contrary to the manner of God and of nature, by abridging or scanting those means, which books freely permitted are, both to the trial of virtue and the exercise of truth? It would be better done, to learn that the law must needs be frivolous, which goes to restrain things, uncertainly and yet equally working to good and to evil. And were I the chooser, a dram of well-doing should be preferred before many times as much the forcible hindrance of evil-doing. For God sure esteems the growth and completing of one virtuous person more than the restraint of ten vicious.

And albeit whatever thing we hear or see, sitting, walking, travelling, or conversing, may be fitly called our book, and is of the same effect that writings are, yet grant the thing to be prohibited were only books, it appears that this order hitherto is far insufficient to the end which it intends. Do we not see, not once or oftener but weekly, that continued court-libel[46] against the Parliament and City, printed, as the wet sheets can witness, and dispersed among us, for all that licensing can do? yet this is the prime service a man would think, wherein this Order should give proof of itself. If it were executed, you'll say. But certain, if execution be remiss or blindfold now, and in this particular, what will it be hereafter and in other books? If then the Order shall not be vain and frustrate, behold a new labour, Lords and Commons, ye must repeal and proscribe[47] all scandalous and unlicensed books already printed and divulged;[48] after ye have drawn them up into a list, that all may know which are condemned, and which not; and ordain that no foreign books be delivered out of custody, till they have been read over. This office will require the whole time of not a few overseers, and those no vulgar men. There be also books which are partly useful and excellent, partly culpable and pernicious; this work will ask as many more officials,[49] to make expurgations and expunctions, that the Commonwealth of Learning be not damnified. In fine, when the multitude of books increase upon their hands, ye must be fain to catalogue all those printers who are found frequently offending, and forbid the importation of their whole suspected typography. In a word, that this your Order may be exact and not deficient, ye must reform it perfectly according to the model of Trent and Seville,[50] which I know ye abhor to do.

Yet though ye should condescend to this, which God forbid, the Order still would be but fruitless and defective to that end whereto ye meant it. If to prevent sects and schisms, who is so unread or so uncatechised in story, that hath not heard of many sects refusing books as a hindrance, and preserving their doctrine unmixed for many ages, only by unwritten traditions? The Christian faith, for that was once a schism, is not unknown to have spread all over Asia, ere any Gospel or Epistle was seen in writing. If the amendment of manners be aimed at, look into Italy and Spain, whether those

[46] *Mercurius Aulicus* (Court Mercury), a periodical appearing weekly from 1643 to 1645, and occasionally afterwards, supported the cause of the King against the Parliament [47] ban [48] publish

[49] used technically, officers of Ecclesiastical Courts who saw to spiritual offenses

[50] The Council of Trent, with the Spanish Inquisition, is said above by Milton to be responsible for the establishment of the Index. Seville became the chief seat of the Holy Office in the time of Ferdinand and Isabella

places be one scruple the better, the honester, the wiser, the chaster, since all the inquisitional rigour that hath been executed upon books.

Another reason, whereby to make it plain that this Order will miss the end it seeks, consider by the quality which ought to be in every licenser. It cannot be denied but that he who is made judge to sit upon the birth or death of books, whether they may be wafted into this world or not, had need to be a man above the common measure, both studious, learned, and judicious; there may be else no mean mistakes in the censure of what is passable or not; which is also no mean injury. If he be of such worth as behoves him, there cannot be a more tedious and unpleasing journey-work, a greater loss of time levied upon his head, than to be made the perpetual reader of unchosen books and pamphlets, ofttimes huge volumes. There is no book that is acceptable unless at certain seasons; but to be enjoined the reading of that at all times, and in a hand scarce legible, whereof three pages would not down at any time in the fairest print, is an imposition which I cannot believe how he that values time and his own studies, or is but of a sensible nostril, should be able to endure. In this one thing I crave leave of the present licensers to be pardoned for so thinking; who doubtless took this office up, looking on it through their obedience to the Parliament, whose command perhaps made all things seem easy and unlaborious to them; but that this short trial hath wearied them out already, their own expressions and excuses to them who make so many journeys to solicit their licence are testimony enough. Seeing therefore those who now possess the employment by all evident signs wish themselves well rid of it; and that no man of worth, none that is not a plain unthrift of his own hours is ever likely to succeed them, except he mean to put himself to the salary of a press corrector; we may easily foresee what kind of licensers we are to expect hereafter, either ignorant, imperious, and remiss, or basely pecuniary. This is what I had to show, wherein this Order cannot conduce to that end whereof it bears the intention.

I lastly proceed from the no good it can do, to the manifest hurt it causes, in being first the greatest discouragement and affront that can be offered to learning, and to learned men.

* * *

We boast our light; but if we look not wisely on the Sun itself, it smites us into darkness. Who can discern those planets that are oft combust, and those stars of brightest magnitude that rise and set with the Sun, until the opposite motion of their orbs bring them to such a place in the firmament, where they may be seen evening or morning? The light which we have gained was given us, not to be ever staring on, but by it to discover onward things more remote from our knowledge. It is not the unfrocking of a priest, the unmitring of a bishop, and the removing him from off the presbyterian shoulders, that will make us a happy Nation. No, if other things as great in the Church, and in the rule of life both economical and political, be not looked into and reformed, we have looked so long upon the blaze that Zuinglius[51] and Calvin hath beaconed up to us, that we are stark blind. There be who perpetually complain of schisms and sects, and make it such a calamity that any man dissents from their maxims. 'Tis their own pride and ignorance which causes the disturbing, who neither will hear with meekness, nor can convince; yet all must be suppressed which is not found in their Syntagma.[52] They are the troublers, they are the dividers of unity, who neglect and permit not others to unite those dissevered pieces which are yet wanting to the body of Truth. To be still searching what we know not by what we know, still closing up truth to truth as we find it (for all her body is homogeneal and proportional), this is the golden rule in theology as well as in arithmetic, and makes up the best harmony in a Church; not the forced and outward union of cold and neutral, and inwardly divided minds.

Lords and Commons of England, consider what Nation it is whereof ye are, and whereof ye are the governors: a Nation not slow and dull, but of a quick, ingenious and piercing spirit, acute to invent, subtle and sinewy to discourse, not beneath the reach of any point, the highest that human capacity can soar to. Therefore the studies of Learning in her deepest sciences have been so ancient and so eminent among us, that writers of good antiquity and ablest judgment have been persuaded that even the school of Pythagoras and the Persian wisdom took beginning from the old philosophy of

[51] Zwingli, a religious reformer

[52] a regular, orderly collection of statements or propositions, a systematic treatise

this island. And that wise and civil Roman, Julius Agricola, who governed once here for Caesar, preferred the natural wits of Britain before the laboured studies of the French. Nor is it for nothing that the grave and frugal Transylvanian sends out yearly from as far as the mountainous borders of Russia, and beyond the Hercynian wilderness, not their youth, but their staid men, to learn our language and our theologic arts.

Yet that which is above all this, the favour and the love of Heaven, we have great argument to think in a peculiar manner propitious and propending towards us. Why else was this Nation chosen before any other, that out of her, as out of Sion, should be proclaimed and sounded forth the first tidings and trumpet of Reformation to all Europe? And had it not been the obstinate perverseness of our prelates against the divine and admirable spirit of Wickliff, to suppress him as a schismatic and innovator, perhaps neither the Bohemian Huss and Jerome, no nor the name of Luther or of Calvin, had been ever known: the glory of reforming all our neighbours had been completely ours. But now, as our obdurate clergy have with violence demeaned the matter, we are become hitherto the latest and backwardest scholars, of whom God offered to have made us the teachers. Now once again by all concurrence of signs, and by the general instinct of holy and devout men, as they daily and solemnly express their thoughts, God is decreeing to begin some new and great period in His Church, even to the reforming of Reformation itself: what does He then but reveal Himself to His servants, and as His manner is, first to His Englishmen? I say, as His manner is, first to us, though we mark not the method of His counsels, and are unworthy.

Behold now this vast City: a city of refuge, the mansion house of liberty, encompassed and surrounded with His protection; the shop of war hath not there more anvils and hammers waking, to fashion out the plates and instruments of armed Justice in defense of beleaguered Truth, than there be pens and heads there, sitting by their studious lamps, musing, searching, revolving new notions and ideas wherewith to present, as with their homage and their fealty, the approaching Reformation: others as fast reading, trying all things, assenting to the force of reason and convincement. What could a man require more from a Nation so pliant and so prone to seek after knowledge? What wants there to such a towardly and pregnant soil, but wise and faithful labourers, to make a knowing people, a Nation of Prophets of Sages, and of Worthies? We reckon more than five months yet to harvest; there need not be five weeks; had we but eyes to lift up, the fields are white already.

Where there is much desire to learn, there of necessity will be much arguing, much writing, many opinions; for opinion in good men is but knowledge in the making. Under these fantastic terrors of sect and schism, we wrong the earnest and zealous thirst after knowledge and understanding which God hath stirred up in this city. What some lament of, we rather should rejoice at, should rather praise this pious forwardness among men, to reassume the ill-reputed care of their Religion into their own hands again. A little generous prudence, a little forbearance of one another, and some grain of charity might win all these diligences to join, and unite in one general and brotherly search after Truth; could we but forego this prelatical tradition of crowding free consciences and Christian liberties into canons and precepts of men. I doubt not, if some great and worthy stranger should come among us, wise to discern the mould and temper of a people, and how to govern it, observing the high hopes and aims, the diligent alacrity of our extended thoughts and reasonings in the pursuance of truth and freedom, but that he would cry out as Pyrrhus did, admiring the Roman docility[53] and courage: If such were my Epirots,[54] I would not despair the greatest design that could be attempted, to make a Church or Kingdom happy.

Yet these are the men cried out against for schismatics and sectaries; as if, while the temple of the Lord was building, some cutting, some squaring the marble, others hewing the cedars, there should be a sort of irrational men who could not consider there must be many schisms and many dissections made in the quarry and in the timber, ere the house of God can be built. And when every stone is laid artfully together, it cannot be united into a continuity, it can but be contiguous in this world; neither can every piece of the building be of one form; nay rather the perfection consists in this, that, out of many moderate varieties and brotherly dissimilitudes that are

[53] readiness to learn [54] people who dwell inland

not vastly disproportional, arises the goodly and the graceful symmetry that commends the whole pile and structure.

Let us therefore be more considerate builders, more wise in spiritual architecture, when great reformation is expected. For now the time seems come, wherein Moses the great prophet may sit in heavn rejoicing to see that memorable and glorious wish of his fulfilled, when not only our seventy Elders, but all the Lord's people, are become prophets. No marvel then though some men, and some good men too perhaps, but young in goodness, as Joshua then was, envy them. They fret, and out of their own weakness are in agony, lest these divisions and subdivisions will undo us. The adversary again applauds, and waits the hour: When they have branched themselves out, saith he, small enough into parties and partitions, then will be our time. Fool! he sees not the firm root, out of which we all grow, though into branches: nor will be ware until he see our small divided maniples[55] cutting through at every angle of his ill-united and unwieldly brigade. And that we are to hope better of all these supposed sects and schisms, and that we shall not need that solicitude, honest perhaps though over-timorous of them that vex in this behalf, but shall laugh in the end at those malicious applauders of our differences, I have these reasons to persuade me.

First, when a City shall be as it were besieged and blocked about, her navigable river infested, inroads and incursions round, defiance and battle oft rumoured to be marching up even to her walls and suburb trenches, that then the people, or the greater part, more than at other times, wholly taken up with study of highest and most important matters to be reformed, should be disputing, reasoning, reading, inventing, discoursing, even to a rarity and admiration,[56] things not before discoursed or written of argues first a singular goodwill, contentedness and confidence in your prudent foresight and safe government, Lords and Commons; and from thence derives itself to a gallant bravery and well-grounded contempt of their enemies, as if there were no small number of as great spirits among us, as his was, who when Rome was nigh besieged by Hannibal, being in the city, bought that piece of ground at no cheap rate, whereon Hannibal himself encamped his own regiment.

[55] a small band of soldiers [56] a source of wonder by being rare

Next, it is a lively and cheerful presage of our happy success and victory. For as in a body, when the blood is fresh, the spirits pure and vigorous, not only to vital but to rational faculties, and those in the acutest and the pertest operations of wit and subtlety, it argues in what good plight and constitution the body is so when the cheerfulness of the people is so sprightly up, as that it has not only wherewith to guard well its own freedom and safety, but to spare, and to bestow upon the solidest and sublimest points of controversy and new invention, it betokens us not degenerated, nor drooping to a fatal decay, but casting off the old and wrinkled skin of corruption to outlive these pangs and wax young again, entering the glorious ways of truth and prosperous virtue, destined to become great and honourable in these latter ages. Methinks I see in my mind a noble and puissant nation rousing herself like a strong man after sleep, and shaking her invincible locks. Methinks I see her as an eagle mewing[57] her mighty youth,[58] and kindling her undazzled eyes at the full midday beam; purging and unscaling her long-abused sight at the fountain itself of heavenly radiance; while the whole noise of timorous and flocking birds, with those also that love the twilight, flutter about, amazed at what she means, and in their envious gabble would prognosticate a year of sects and schisms.

What would ye do then? should ye suppress all this flowery crop of knowledge and new light sprung up and yet springing daily in this city? should ye set an oligarchy of twenty engrossers over it, to bring a famine upon our minds again, when we shall know nothing but what is measured to us by their bushel? Believe it, Lords and Commons, they who counsel ye to such a suppressing do as good as bid ye suppress yourselves; and I will soon show how. If it be desired to know the immediate cause of all this free writing and free speaking, there cannot be assigned a truer than your own mild and free and humane government. It is the liberty, Lords and Commons, which your own valorous and happy counsels have purchased us, liberty which is the nurse of all great wits; this is that which hath rarefied and enlightened our spirits like the influence of heaven; this is that which hath enfranchised, enlarged and lifted up our apprehensions degrees above themselves.

[57] cast feathers [58] renew youth by throwing off old feathers

Ye cannot make us now less capable, less knowing, less eagerly pursuing of the truth, unless ye first make yourselves, that made us so, less the lovers, less the founders of our true liberty. We can grow ignorant again, brutish, formal[59] and slavish, as ye found us; but you then must first become that which ye cannot be, oppressive, arbitrary and tyrannous, as they were from whom ye have freed us. That our hearts are now more capacious, our thoughts more erected to the search and expectation of greatest and exactest things, is the issue of your own virtue propagated in us; ye cannot suppress that, unless ye reinforce an abrogated and merciless law, that fathers may despatch at will their own children. And who shall then stick closest to ye, and excite others? not he who takes up arms for coat and conduct,[60] and his four nobles of Danegelt.[61] Although I dispraise not the defence of just immunities, yet love my peace better, if that were all. Give me the liberty to know, to utter, and to argue freely according to conscience, above all liberties.

What would be best advised, then, if it be found so hurtful and so unequal to suppress opinions for the newness or the unsuitableness to a customary acceptance, will not be my task to say. I only shall repeat what I have learned from one of your own honourable number, a right noble and pious lord, who, had he not sacrificed his life and fortunes to the Church and Commonwealth, we had not now missed and bewailed a worthy and undoubted patron of this argument. Ye know him, I am sure; yet I for honour's sake, and may it be eternal to him, shall name him, the Lord Brook. He writing of Episcopacy and by the way of treating of sects and schisms, left ye his vote, or rather now the last words of his dying charge, which I know will ever be of dear and honoured regard with ye, so full of meekness and breathing charity, that next to His last testament, who bequeathed love and peace to His disciples, I cannot call to mind where I have read or heard words more mild and peaceful. He there exhorts us to hear with patience and humility those, however they be miscalled, that desire to live purely, in such a use of God's

[59] acting slavishly to set rules

[60] taxes to clothe and maintain new conscripts till they joined their corps

[61] annual tax in England in the eleventh century, supposed to provide funds for protecting the country against the Danes, continued after the Norman Conquest (1066) as a land tax

ordinances, as the best guidance of their conscience gives them, and to tolerate them, though in some disconformity to ourselves. The book itself will tell us more at large, being published to the world, and dedicated to the Parliament by him who, both for his life and for his death, deserves that what advice he left be not laid by without perusal.

And now the time in special is, by privilege to write and speak what may help to the further discussing of matters in agitation. The temple of Janus with his two controversial faces might now not unsignificantly be set open. And though all the winds of doctrine were let loose to play upon the earth, so Truth be in the field, we do injuriously, by licensing and prohibiting, to misdoubt her strength. Let her and Falsehood grapple; who ever knew Truth put to the worse, in a free and open encounter? Her confuting is the best and surest suppressing.[62] He who hears what praying there is for light and clearer knowledge to be sent down among us, would think of other matters to be constituted beyond the discipline of Geneva, framed and fabricked already to our hands. Yet when the new light which we beg for shines in upon us, there be who envy and oppose, if it come not first in at their casements. What a collusion is this, whenas we are exhorted by the wise man to use diligence, to seek for wisdom as for hidden treasures early and late, that another order shall enjoin us to know nothing but by statute? When a man hath been labouring the hardest labour in the deep mines of knowledge has furnished out his findings in all their equipage; drawn forth his reasons as it were a battle ranged; scattered and defeated all objections in his way; calls out his adversary into the plain, offers him the advantage of wind and sun, if he please, only that he may try the matter by dint of argument: for his opponents then to skulk, to lay ambushments, to keep a narrow bridge of licensing where the challenger should pass, though it be valour enough in soldiership, is but weakness and cowardice in the wars of Truth.

For who knows not that Truth is strong, next to the Almighty? She needs no policies, nor stratagems, nor licensings to make her victorious; those are the shifts and the defences that error uses

[62] the confuting (proving in error) of falsehood by truth is the best way of suppressing falsehood

against her power. Give her but room, and do not bind her when she sleeps, for then she speaks not true, as the old Proteus did, who spake oracles only when he was caught and bound, but then rather she turns herself into all shapes, except her own, and perhaps tunes her voice according to the time, as Micaiah did before Ahab, until she be adjured into her own likeness. Yet is it not impossible that she may have more shapes than one. What else is all that rank of things indifferent, wherein Truth may be on this side or on the other, without being unlike herself? What but a vain shadow else is the abolition of those ordinances, that hand-writing nailed to the cross? What great purchase is this Christian liberty which Paul so often boasts of? His doctrine is, that he who eats or eats not, regards a day or regards it not, may do either to the Lord. How many other things might be tolerated in peace, and left to conscience, had we but charity, and were it not the chief stronghold of our hypocrisy to be ever judging one another?

I fear yet this iron yoke of outward conformity hath left a slavish print upon our necks; the ghost of a linen decency yet haunts us. We stumble and are impatient at the least dividing of one visible congregation from another, though it be not in fundamentals; and through our forwardness to suppress, and our backwardness to recover any enthralled piece of truth out of the gripe of custom, we care not to keep truth separated from truth, which is the fiercest rent and disunion of all. We do not see that, while we still affect by all means a rigid external formality, we may as soon fall again into a gross conforming stupidity, a stark and dead congealment of wood and hay and stubble, forced and frozen together, which is more to the sudden degenerating of a Church than many subdichotomies of petty schisms.

Not that I can think well of every light separation, or that all in a Church is to be expected gold and silver and precious stones: it is not possible for man to sever the wheat from the tares, the good fish from the other fry; that must be the Angels' Ministry at the end of mortal things. Yet if all cannot be of one mind—as who looks they should be?—this doubtless is more wholesome, more prudent, and more Christian that many be tolerated, rather than all compelled. I mean not tolerated popery, and open superstition, which, as it extirpates all religions and civil supremacies, so itself should be extirpate, provided first that all charitable and compassionate means be used to win and regain the weak and the misled: that also which is impious or evil absolutely either against faith or manners no law can possibly permit, that intends not to unlaw itself: but those neighbouring differences, or rather indifferences, are what I speak of, whether in some point of doctrine or of discipline, which, though they may be many, yet need not interrupt the unity of Spirit, if we could but find among us the bond of peace.

In the meantime if any one would write, and bring his helpful hand to the slow-moving Reformation which we labour under, if Truth have spoken to him before others, or but seemed at least to speak, who hath so bejesuited[63] us that we should trouble that man with asking licence to do so worthy a deed? and not consider this, that if it come to prohibiting, there is not aught more likely to be prohibited than truth itself; whose first appearance to our eyes, bleared and dimmed with prejudice and custom, is more unsightly and unplausible than many errors, even as the person is of many a great man slight and contemptible to see to. And what do they tell us vainly of new opinions, when this very opinion of theirs, that none must be heard, but whom they like, is the worst and newest opinion of all others; and is the chief cause why sects and schisms do so much abound, and true knowledge is kept at distance from us; besides yet a greater danger which is in it?

For when God shakes a Kingdom with strong and healthful commotions to a general reforming, 'tis not untrue that many sectaries and false teachers are then busiest in seducing; but yet more true it is, that God then raises to His own work men of rare abilities, and more than common industry, not only to look back and revise what hath been taught heretofore, but to gain further and to go on some new enlightened steps in the discovery of truth. For such is the order of God's enlightening His Church, to dispense and deal out by degrees His beam, so as our earthly eyes may best sustain it.

Neither is God appointed and confined, where and out of what place these His chosen shall be first heard to speak; for He sees not as man sees, chooses not as man chooses, lest we should devote ourselves again to set places, and assemblies, and outward callings

[63] make subject to Jesuits, then most unpopular

of men; planting our faith one while in the old Convocation house, and another while in the Chapel at Westminster; when all the faith and religion that shall be there canonised is not sufficient without plain convincement, and the charity of patient instruction to supple the least bruise of conscience, to edify the meanest Christian, who desires to walk in the Spirit, and not in the letter of human trust, for all the number of voices that can be there made; no, though Harry VII himself there, with all his liege tombs about him, should lend them voices from the dead, to swell their number.

And if the men be erroneous who appear to be the leading schismatics, what withholds us but our sloth, our self-will, and distrust in the right cause, that we do not give them gentle meeting and gentle dismissions, that we debate not and examine the matter thoroughly with liberal and frequent audience; if not for their sakes, yet for our own? seeing no man who hath tasted learning, but will confess the many ways of profiting by those who, not contented with stale receipts, are able to manage and set forth new positions to the world. And were they but as the dust and cinders of our feet, so long as in that notion they may yet serve to polish and brighten the armoury of Truth, even for that respect they were not utterly to be cast away. But if they be of those whom God hath fitted for the special use of these times with eminent and ample gifts, and those perhaps neither among the Priests nor among the Pharisees, and we in the haste of a precipitant zeal shall make no distinction, but resolve to stop their mouths, because we fear they come with new and dangerous opinions, as we commonly forejudge them ere we understand them, no less than woe to us, while, thinking thus to defend the Gospel, we are found the persecutors.

There have been not a few since the beginning of this Parliament, both of the Presbytery and others, who by their unlicensed books, to the contempt of an Imprimatur, first broke that triple ice clung about our hearts, and taught the people to see day: I hope that none of those were the persuaders to renew upon us this bondage which they themselves have wrought so much good by contemning. But if neither the check that Moses gave to young Joshua, nor the countermand which our Saviour gave to young John, who was so ready to prohibit those whom he thought unlicensed, be not enough to admonish our Elders how unacceptable to God their testy mood of prohibiting is, if neither their own remembrance what evil hath abounded in the Church by this let of licensing, and what good they themselves have begun by transgressing it, be not enough, but that they will persuade and execute the most Dominican part of the Inquisition over us, and are already with one foot in the stirrup so active at suppressing, it would be no unequal distribution in the first place to suppress the suppressors themselves: whom the change of their condition hath puffed up, more than their late experience of harder times hath made wise.

And as for regulating the Press, let no man think to have the honour of advising ye better than yourselves have done in that Order published next before this, "that no book be Printed, unless the Printer's and the Author's name, or at least the Printer's, be registered." Those which otherwise come forth, if they be found mischievous and libellous, the fire and the executioner will be the timeliest and the most effectual remedy that man's prevention can use. For this authentic Spanish policy of licensing books, if I have said aught, will prove the most unlicensed book itself within a short while; and was the immediate image of a Star Chamber decree to that purpose made in those very times when that Court did the rest of those her pious works, for which she is now fallen from the stars with Lucifer. Whereby ye may guess what kind of state prudence, what love of the people, what care of Religion or good manners there was at the contriving, although with singular hypocrisy it pretended to bind books to their good behaviour. And how it got the upper hand of your precedent Order so well constituted before, if we may believe those men whose profession gives them cause to enquire most, it may be doubted there was in it the fraud of some old patentees and monopolisers in the trade of bookselling; who under pretence of the poor in their Company not to be defrauded, and the just retaining of each man his several copy, which God forbid should be gainsaid, brought divers glosing[64] colours[65] to the House, which were indeed but colours, and serving to no end except it be to exercise a superiority over their neighbours; men who do not therefore labour in an honest profession to which learning is indebted, that they should be made other men's vassals. Another

[64] flattering, deceiving [65] pretexts

end is thought was aimed at by some of them in procuring by petition this Order, that, having power in their hands, malignant books might the easier scape abroad, as the event shows.

But of these sophisms[66] and elenchs[67] of merchandise[68] I skill not. This I know, that errors in a good government and in a bad are equally almost incident; for what Magistrate may not be misinformed, and much the sooner, if Liberty of Printing be reduced into the power of a few? But to redress willingly and speedily what hath been erred, and in highest authority to esteem a plain advertisement[69] more than others have done a sumptuous bribe, is a virtue (honoured Lords and Commons) answerable to[70] your highest actions, and whereof none can participate but greatest and wisest men.

[66] fallacious argument [67] sophistry [68] crafty tricks of trade
[69] advice, instruction [70] in keeping with

As Milton's *Paradise Lost* is England's great Christian-heroic epic, so his *Areopagitica* is its epic of prose-argument. The Areopagus, the hill of Ares, was the meeting-place of the Upper Council in Athens. Milton addresses the Parliament in London as equally noble, reminding them that licensing or censoring of books is alien to the best traditions of both Greece and England; that such limitation of human thought for reader as for writer not only does no good but also does harm; and that they are governors whose decision should be worthy of a great free nation.

At Cambridge, Milton had begun to write poetry, and many years later, after he became blind, and after the Restoration of Charles II, published his greatest poems. It was in the years of political turmoil in between, from about 1640 to 1660, part of which time he was Latin Secretary to the Council of the Commonwealth, that he wrote the series of intense political and moral arguments on episcopacy, on divorce, on education, on the tenure of kings and magistrates, and on the freedom of the press, the *Areopagitica* (1645).

The historical occasion of the *Areopagitica* was as follows: The Order of Parliament (June 14, 1643) against which the *Areopagitica* was directed forbade the printing of Orders "of both or either House," Lords or Commons, except by command, forbade the printing or sale of any book without the approval and license of an official appointed by "either of the... Houses," reaffirmed the copyrights of the Stationers' Company and forbade, under pain of forfeiture "and such further punishment as shall be thought fit," the importing from overseas of books already published in England. It further sanctioned the searching out and breaking up of unlicensed presses, the confiscation of unlicensed books, the apprehension of "authors, printers and others" involved in publishing such books, and demanded punishment and a promise to amend their ways of the culprits. In these activities, the Order stated, "all Justices of the Peace, Captains, Constables and other officers" were to aid.

The *Areopagitica,* like the *Areopagitica* of Isocrates, a classic authority on the writing of orations, was written to be read, not to be spoken. It begins in the classic formal style with an *exordium,* an introduction to establish an understanding frame of mind, proceeds through four stages of argument, and ends with a *peroration* or stirring restatement. Of the four stages of argument, the first emphasizes historical experience. It begins with "But lest I be condemned." The second, "But I have first to finish," argues on the principle of moderation—the balance between the extremes argued by others. The third, "which is what I promised," gives the practical argument that limited licensing just does not work; the fourth, "I lastly proceed," talks about consequences—the harms and dangers of licensing. Part of the section on harms has been omitted here, as proportionally long for this text; the last argument on consequence is the strongest, beginning, "There is yet behind," and moving into the peroration on truth.

Thus the large sections of the thought. Within these, one may note details of Milton's prose style, the patterning of his sentences in classical fashion.

The action of an heroic poem

FROM Dedication of *The Aeneis (1697)*
BY ***John Dryden** (1631-1700)*

To the Most Honorable
JOHN,
Lord Marquess of Normanby, Earl of Mulgrave, etc.,
and Knight of the Most Noble Order of the Garter

A heroic poem, truly such, is undoubtedly the greatest work which the soul of man is capable to perform. The design of it is to form the mind to heroic virtue by example; 'tis conveyed in verse, that it may delight, while it instructs. The action of it is always one, entire, and great. The least and most trivial episodes, or under-actions, which are interwoven in it, are parts either necessary or convenient to carry on the main design; either so necessary, that, without them, the poem must be imperfect, or so convenient, that no others can be imagined more suitable to the place in which they are. There is nothing to be left void in a firm building; even the cavities ought not to be filled with rubbish which is of a perishable kind, destructive to the strength, but with brick or stone, though of less pieces, yet of the same nature, and fitted to the crannies. Even the least portions of them must be of the epic kind: all things must be grave, majestical, and sublime; nothing of a foreign nature, like the trifling novels,[1] which Ariosto,[2] and others, have inserted in their poems; by which the reader is misled into another sort of pleasure, opposite to that which is designed in an epic poem. One raises the soul, and hardens it to virtue; the other softens it again, and unbends it into vice. One conduces to the poet's aim, the completing of his work, which he is driving on, labouring and hastening in every line; the other slackens his pace, diverts him from his way, and locks him up like a knight-errant in an enchanted castle, when he should be pursuing his first adventure. Statius,[3] as Bossu[4] has well observed, was ambitious of trying his strength with his master Virgil,[5] as Virgil had before tried his with Homer. The Grecian gave the two Romans an example, in the games which were celebrated at the funerals of Patroclus.[6] Virgil imitated the invention of Homer, but changed the sports. But both the Greek and Latin poet took their occasions from the subject; though, to confess the truth, they were both ornamental, or, at best, convenient parts of it, rather than of necessity arising from it. Statius, who, through his whole poem, is noted for want of conduct and judgment, instead of staying, as he might have done, for the death of Capaneus, Hippomedon, Tydeus, or some other of his seven champions (who are heroes all alike), or more properly for the tragical end of the two brothers, whose exequies the next successor had leisure to perform when the siege was raised, and in the interval betwixt the poet's first action and his second—went out of his way, as it were on prepense malice to commit a fault. For he took his opportunity to kill a royal infant by the means of a serpent (that author of all evil), to make way for those funeral honours which he intended for him. Now, if this

[1] tales, or brief stories

[2] Lodovico Ariosto (1474-1533), Italian Renaissance poet, whose most famous work, *Orlando Furioso,* critics considered episodic, given to bringing in exciting stories that did not fit with the main theme

[3] (45-96 A.D.) the principal epic poet of the silver age of Latin literature, whose *Thebais,* the only one of his two epics completed, borrows from Virgil and is modeled after him

[4] René le Bossu (1631-1680) published a study of epic poetry in 1675

[5] Publius Virgilius Maro (70-19 B.C.), the greatest Latin epic poet of the Augustan or Golden Age, who modeled his *Aeneid* on Homer's works

[6] Greek warrior and friend of Achilles, in the Trojan War, mistaken for Achilles while wearing his armor and killed by Hector

innocent had been of any relation to his *Thebais;* if he had either furthered or hindered the taking of the town; the poet might have found some sorry excuse at least for detaining the reader from the promised siege. I can think of nothing to plead for him but what I verily believe he thought himself, which was, that as the funerals of Anchises were solemnised in Sicily, so those of Archemorus should be celebrated in Candy. For the last was an island, and a better than the first, because Jove was born there. On these terms, this Capaneus[7] of a poet engaged his two immortal predecessors; and his success was answerable to his enterprise.

If this economy must be observed in the minutest parts of an epic poem, which, to a common reader, seems to be detached from the body, and almost independent of it; what soul, though sent into the world with great advantages of Nature, cultivated with the liberal arts and sciences, conversant with histories of the dead, and enriched with observations on the living, can be sufficient to inform the whole body of so great a work? I touch here but transiently, without any strict method, on some few of those many rules of imitating nature which Aristotle drew from Homer's *Iliads* and *Odysseys,* and which he fitted to the drama; furnishing himself also with observations from the practice of the theatre, when it flourished under Æschylus, Euripides, and Sophocles. For the original of the stage was from the Epic Poem. Narration, doubtless, preceded acting, and gave laws to it: what at first was told artfully, was in process of time, represented gracefully to the sight and hearing. Those episodes of Homer, which were proper for the stage, the poets amplified each into an action; out of his limbs they formed their bodies; what he had contracted, they enlarged; out of one Hercules were made infinity of pigmies, yet all endued with human souls; for from him, their great creator, they have each of them the *divinœ particulam aurœ.*[8] They flowed from him at first, and are at last resolved into him. Nor were they only animated[9] by him, but their measure and symmetry was owing to him. His one, entire, and great action was copied by them according to the proportions of the

[7] one of the *Seven Against Thebes,* struck by lightning during the assault on the city, while he was busy boasting that not even the lightning of Zeus could frighten him away

[8] particle of the divine breath, *i.e.,* soul [9] literally, given a soul

drama. If he finished his orb within the year, it sufficed to teach them, that their action being less, and being also less diversified with incidents, their orb, of consequence, must be circumscribed in a less compass, which they reduced within the limits either of a natural or an artificial day;[10] so that, as he taught them to amplify what he had shortened, by the same rule, applied the contrary way, he taught them to shorten what he had amplified. Tragedy is the miniature of human life; an epic poem is the draught[11] at length. Here, my Lord, I must contract also; for, before I was aware, I was almost running into a long digression, to prove that there is no such absolute necessity that the time of a stage action should so strictly be confined to twenty-four hours as never to exceed them, for which Aristotle contends, and the Grecian stage has practised. Some longer space, on some occasions, I think, may be allowed, especially for the English theatre, which requires more variety of incidents than the French. Corneille[12] himself, after long practice, was inclined to think that the time allotted by the Ancients was too short to raise and finish a great action: and better a mechanic rule were stretched or broken, than a great beauty were omitted. To raise, and afterwards to calm the passions—to purge the soul from pride, by the examples of human miseries, which befall the greatest—in few words, to expel arrogance, and introduce compassion, are the great effects of tragedy. Great, I must confess, if they were altogether as true as they are pompous. But are habits to be introduced at three hours' warning? Are radical diseases so suddenly removed? A mountebank[13] may promise such a cure, but a skillful physician will not undertake it. An epic poem is not in so much haste: it works leisurely; the changes which it makes are slow; but the cure is likely to be more perfect. The effects of tragedy, as I said, are too violent to be lasting. If it be answered that, for this reason, tragedies are often to be seen, and the dose to be repeated, this is tacitly to confess that there is more virtue in one heroic poem than in many tragedies. A man is humbled one day, and his pride returns the next. Chymical medicines are observed to relieve of-

[10] obsolete expression, period during which the sun is above the horizon, sunrise to sunset [11] drawing, representation

[12] French dramatist of the seventeenth century [13] quack

tener than to cure: for 'tis the nature of spirits to make swift impressions, but not deep. Galenical[14] decoctions,[15] to which I may properly compare an epic poem, have more of body in them; they work by their substance and their weight. It is one reason of Aristotle's to prove that Tragedy is the more noble, because it turns in a shorter compass; the whole action being circumscribed within the space of four-and-twenty hours. He might prove as well that a mushroom is to be preferred before a peach, because it shoots up in the compass of a night. A chariot may be driven round the pillar in less space than a large machine, because the bulk is not so great. Is the Moon a more noble planet than Saturn, because she makes her revolution in less than thirty days, and he in less than thirty years? Both their orbs are in proportion to their several magnitudes; and consequently the quickness or slowness of their motion, and the time of their circumvolutions, is no argument of the greater or less perfection. And, besides, what virtue is there in a tragedy which is not contained in an epic poem, where pride is humbled, virtue rewarded, and vice punished; and those more amply treated than the narrowness of the drama can admit? The shining quality of an epic hero, his magnanimity, his constancy, his patience, his piety, or whatever characteristical virtue his poet gives him, raises first our admiration; we are naturally prone to imitate what we admire; and frequent acts produce a habit. If the hero's chief quality be vicious, as, for example, the choler[16] and obstinate desire of vengeance in Achilles, yet the moral is instructive: and, besides, we are informed in the very proposition of the *Iliads,* that this anger was pernicious; that it brought a thousand ills on the Grecian camp. The courage of Achilles is proposed to imitation, not his pride and disobedience to his general, nor his brutal cruelty to his dead enemy, nor the selling of his body to his father. We abhor these actions while we read them; and what we abhor we never imitate. The poet only shows them, like rocks or quicksands,[17] to be shunned.

[14] adjective from Galen, a famous Greek physician of the second century A.D.; used to describe a vegetable medicine

[15] liquor in which a substance has been boiled, to draw out certain elements for medicinal use

[16] anger, fierceness, wrathfulness

[17] as separate dangers, not in the same situation

By this example, the critics have concluded that it is not necessary the manners of the hero should be virtuous. They are poetically good, if they are of a piece: though where a character of perfect virtue is set before us, it is more lovely; for there the whole hero is to be imitated. This is the Æneas of our author; this is that idea of perfection in an epic poem which painters and statuaries have only in their minds, and which no hands are able to express. These are the beauties of a god in a human body. When the picture of Achilles is drawn in tragedy, he is taken with those warts, and moles, and hard features by those who represent him on the stage, or he is no more Achilles; for his creator, Homer, has so described him. Yet even thus he appears a perfect hero, though an imperfect character of virtue. Horace paints him after Homer, and delivers him to be copied on the stage with all those imperfections. Therefore they are either not faults in a heroic poem, or faults common to the drama. After all, on the whole merits of the cause, it must be acknowledged that the Epic Poem is more for the manners, and Tragedy for the passions. The passions, as I have said, are violent; and acute distempers require medicines of a strong and speedy operation. Ill habits of the mind are like chronical[18] diseases, to be corrected by degrees, and cured by alteratives;[19] wherein, though purges are sometimes necessary, yet diet, good air, and moderate exercise have the greatest part. The matter being thus stated, it will appear that both sorts of poetry are of use for their proper ends. The stage is more active; the Epic Poem works at greater leisure, yet is active too, when need requires; for dialogue is imitated by the drama from the more active parts of it. One puts off a fit, like the quinquina,[20] and relieves us only for a time; the other roots out the distemper, and gives a healthful habit. The sun enlightens and cheers us, dispels fogs, and warms the ground with his daily beams; but the corn is sowed, increases, is ripened, and is reaped for use in process of time, and in its proper season.

[18] chronic, lingering, long-continued, used of disease

[19] medicines which alter the processes of nutrition and reduce them gradually to healthy action

[20] Peruvian bark (also called Jesuits' bark), the bark of several species of cinchona, yielding quinine and other fever-combating alkaloids

☙ Today the essay in literary criticism is one of the most common kinds; John Dryden was our first great literary essayist. After his study at Cambridge he first wrote poems and plays, and it was as prefaces to these works and later to his translations of Juvenal, Virgil, Horace, Ovid, Chaucer, that his essays took shape, on such subjects as satire and dramatic poetry and heroic poetry, of which a portion follows. After Dryden, Addison, then Dr. Samuel Johnson, then Wordsworth and Coleridge, established the tradition of the literary essay, and in the past century it has grown to be a major form, with Hazlitt, Lamb, Arnold, Eliot, Woolf, Pound, Empson, and many younger writers using it. The famous English literary journals like *Blackwood's* have been succeeded by Eliot's *Criterion,* Spender's *Encounter,* and the *Southern Review, Sewanee, Kenyon, Hudson,* and other such reviews in America.

Of the beginning of political societies

FROM *Two Treatises on Government (1690)*
BY ***John Locke** (1632-1704)*

Men being, as has been said, by nature all free, equal, and independent, no one can be put out of this estate, and subjected to the political power of another, without his own consent, which is done by agreeing with other men to join and unite into a community for their comfortable, safe, and peaceable living one amongst another, in a secure enjoyment of their properties, and a greater security against any that are not of it. This any number of men may do, because it injures not the freedom of the rest; they are left as they were in the liberty of the state of nature. When any number of men have so consented to make one community or government, they are thereby presently incorporated, and makc one body politic, wherein the majority have a right to act and conclude[1] the rest.

For when any number of men have, by the consent of every individual, made a community, they have thereby made that community one body, with a power to act as one body, which is only the will and determination of the majority. For that which acts any community being only the consent of the individuals of it, and it being one body must move one way, it is necessary the body should move that way whither the greater force carries it, which is the consent of the majority; or else it is impossible it should act or

[1] bind, be an obligation on

continue one body, one community, which the consent of every individual that united into it agreed that it should; and so everyone is bound by that consent to be concluded by the majority. And therefore we see that in assemblies empowered to act by positive laws, where no number is set by that positive law which empowers them, the act of the majority passes for the act of the whole, and of course determines, as having by the law of nature and reason the power of the whole.

And thus every man, by consenting with others to make one body politic under one government, puts himself under an obligation to every one of that society, to submit to the determination of the majority, and to be concluded by it; or else this original compact, whereby he with others incorporates into one society, would signify nothing, and be no compact, if he be left free and under no other ties than he was in before in the state of nature. For what appearance would there be of any compact? What new engagement if he were no farther tied by any decrees of the society, than he himself thought fit, and did actually consent to? This would be still as great a liberty as he himself had before his compact, or anyone else in the state of nature hath, who may submit himself and consent to any acts of it if he thinks fit.

For if the consent of the majority shall not in reason be received as the act of the whole and conclude every individual, nothing but the consent of every individual can make anything to be the act of the whole, which considering the infirmities of health and avocations[2] of business, which in a number, though much less than that of a commonwealth, will necessarily keep many away from the public assembly, and the variety of opinions, and contrariety of interest, which unavoidably happen in all collections of men, 'tis next to impossible ever to be had. And therefore if the coming into society be upon such terms it will be only like Cato's coming into the theater, *tantum ut exiret.*[3] Such a constitution as this would make the mighty leviathan[4] of a shorter duration than the feeblest creatures, and not let it outlast the day it was born in; which cannot be

[2] employments [3] as much as if he went out

[4] originally, aquatic animal of enormous size, often mentioned in Hebrew poetry, used by Hobbes for the organism of political society

supposed till we can think that rational creatures should desire and constitute societies only to be dissolved. For where the majority cannot conclude the rest, there they cannot act as one body, and consequently will be immediately dissolved again.

Whosoever therefore out of a state of nature unite into a community must be understood to give up all the power necessary to the ends for which they unite into society, to the majority of the community, unless they expressly agreed in any number greater than the majority. And this is done by barely agreeing to unite into one political society, which is all the compact that is, or needs be, between the individuals that enter into or make up a commonwealth. And thus that which begins and actually constitutes any political society is nothing but the consent of any number of freemen capable of a majority to unite and incorporate into such a society. And this is that, and that only, which did or could give beginning to any lawful government in the world.

To this I find two objections made.

First: That there are no instances to be found in story of a company of men independent, and equal one amongst another, that met together and in this way began and set up a government.

Secondly: 'Tis impossible of right that men should do so, because all men being born under government, they are to submit to that, and are not at liberty to begin a new one.

To the first there is this to answer—That it is not at all to be wondered that history gives us but a very little account of men that lived together in the state of nature. The inconveniences of that condition, and the love and want of society, no sooner brought any number of them together, but they presently[5] united and incorporated if they designed to continue together. And if we may not suppose men ever to have been in the state of nature, because we hear not much of them in such a state, we may as well suppose the armies of Salmanasser of Xerxes were never children, because we hear little of them till they were men, and embodied[6] in armies. Government is everywhere antecedent to records, and letters seldom come in amongst a people, till a long continuation of civil society has, by other more necessary arts, provided for their safety,

[5] immediately [6] to unite, form in one body or company

ease, and plenty. And then they begin to look after the history of their founders, and search into their original,[7] when they have outlived the memory of it. For 'tis with commonwealths as with particular persons, they are commonly ignorant of their own birth and infancies. And if they know anything of their original, they are beholden for it to the accidental records that others have kept of it. And those that we have of the beginning of any polities in the world, excepting that of the Jews, where God Himself immediately interposed, and which favours not at all paternal dominion, are all either plain instances of such a beginning as I have mentioned, or at least have manifest footsteps of it.

He must show a strange inclination to deny evident matter of fact, when it agrees not with his hypothesis, who will not allow that the beginning of Rome and Venice were by the uniting together of several men, free and independent one of another, amongst whom there was no natural superiority or subjection. And if Josephus Acosta's[8] word may be taken, he tells us that in many parts of America,[9] there was no government at all. "There are great and apparent conjectures," says he, "that these men (speaking of those of Peru) for a long time had neither kings nor commonwealths, but lived in troops, as they do this day in Florida—the Cheriquanas, those of Brazil, and many other nations, which have no certain kings, but, as occasion is offered in peace or war, they choose their captains as they please." If it be said, that every man there was born subject to his father, or the head of his family, that the subjection due from a child to a father took not away his freedom of uniting into what political society he thought fit, has been already proved; but be that as it will, these men, it is evident, were actually free; and whatever superiority some politicians now would place in any of them, they themselves claimed it not; but, by consent, were all equal, till, by the same consent, they set rulers over themselves. So that their politic societies all began from a voluntary union, and the mutual agreement of men freely acting in the choice of their governors and forms of government.

[7] origins, beginning

[8] Jose de Acosta, Spanish Jesuit, historian and archaeologist, 1540-1600

[9] refers to both North and South America

And I hope those who went away from Sparta, with Palantus, mentioned by Justin,[10] will be allowed to have been freemen independent one of another, and to have set up a government over themselves by their own consent. Thus I have given several examples out of history of people, free and in the state of nature, that, being met together, incorporated and began a commonwealth. And if the want of such instances be an argument to prove that government were not nor could not be so begun, I suppose the contenders for paternal empire were better let it alone than urge it against natural liberty; for if they can give so many instances out of history of governments began upon paternal right, I think (though at least an argument from what has been to what should of right be of no great force) one might, without any great danger, yield them the cause.[11] But if I might advise them in the case, they would do well not to search too much into the original of governments as they have begun *de facto,* lest they should find at the foundation of most of them something very little favourable to the design they promote, and such a power as they contend for.

But, to conclude: reason being plain on our side that men are naturally free; and the examples of history showing that the governments of the world, that were begun in peace, had their beginning laid on that foundation, and were made by consent of the people; there can be little room for doubt, either where the right is, or what has been the opinion or practise of mankind about the first erecting of governments.

I will not deny that if we look back, as far as history will direct us, towards the original of commonwealths, we shall generally find them under the government and administration of one man. And I am also apt to believe that where a family was numerous enough to subsist by itself, and continued entire together, without mixing with others, as it often happens, where there is much land and few people, the government commonly began in the father. For the father having, by the law of nature, the same power, with every man else, to punish, as he thought fit, any offences against that law, might thereby punish his transgressing children, even when they were

[10] Roman historian, before the fifth century A.D.

[11] matter in dispute, affair to be decided

men, and out of their pupilage;[12] and they were very likely to submit to his punishment, and all join with him against the offender in their turns, giving him thereby power to execute his sentence against any transgression, and so, in effect, make him the law-maker and governor over all that remained in conjunction with his family. He was fittest to be trusted; paternal affection secured their property and interest under his care, and the custom of obeying him in their childhood made it easier to submit to him rather than any other. If, therefore, they must have one to rule them, as government is hardly to be avoided amongst men that live together, who so likely to be the man as he that was their common father, unless negligence, cruelty, or any other defect of mind or body, made him unfit for it. But when either the father died, and left his next heir – for want of age, wisdom, courage, or any other qualities – less fit for rule, or where several families met and consented to continue together, there, it is not to be doubted, but they used their natural freedom to set up him whom they judged the ablest and most likely to rule well over them. Conformable hereunto we find the people of America, who – living out of the reach of the conquering swords and spreading domination of the two great empires of Peru and Mexico – enjoyed their own natural freedom, though, *ceteris paribus,*[13] they commonly prefer the heir of their deceased king; yet, if they find him any way weak or incapable, they pass him by, and set up the stoutest and bravest man for their ruler.

Thus, though looking back as far as records give us any account of peopling the world, and the history of nations, we commonly find the government to be in one hand; yet it destroys not that which I affirm, viz.: that the beginning of politic society depends upon the consent of the individuals to join into, and make one society; who when they are thus incorporated, might set up what form of government they thought fit. But this having given occasion to men to mistake, and think that by nature government was monarchical, and belonged to the father, it may not be amiss here to consider why people in the beginning generally pitched upon this form, which, though perhaps the father's pre-eminence might in the first institution of some commonwealth give a rise to, and place in the begin-

[12] minority, condition of being a minor [13] other things being equal

ning, the power in one hand; yet it is plain that the reason that continued the form of government in a single person was not any regard or respect to paternal authority, since all petty monarchies, that is, almost all monarchies, near their original, have been commonly—at least upon occasion—elective.

First then, in the beginning of things, the father's government of the childhood of those sprung from him having accustomed them to the rule of one man, and taught them that where it was exercised with care and skill, with affection and love to those under it, it was sufficient to procure and preserve men all the political happiness they sought for in society, it was no wonder that they should pitch upon and naturally run into that form of government, which from their infancy they had been all accustomed to, and which, by experience, they had found both easy and safe. To which, if we add, that monarchy being simple and most obvious to men whom neither experience had instructed in forms of government, nor the ambition or insolence of empire had taught to beware of the encroachments of prerogative,[14] or the inconveniences of absolute power, which monarchy in succession was apt to lay claim to, and bring upon them; it was not at all strange that they should not much trouble themselves to think of methods of restraining any exorbitances of those to whom they had given the authority over them, and of balancing the power of government, by placing several parts of it in different hands. They had neither felt the oppression of tyrannical dominion, nor did the fashion of the age, nor their possessions or way of living (which afforded little matter for covetousness or ambition), give them any reason to apprehend or provide against it; and therefore it is no wonder they put themselves into such a frame of government as was not only, as I said, most obvious and simple, but also best suited to their present state and condition, which stood more in need of defence against foreign invasions and injuries than of multiplicity of laws, where there was but very little property; and wanted not a variety of rulers and abundance of officers to direct and look after their execution, where there were but few trespasses and few offenders. Since, then, those who liked one another so well as to join into society, cannot but be supposed to have some acquaintance and friendship together, and some trust

[14] intruding, as a usurper, especially by gradual stages, upon the rights of

one in another, they could not but have greater apprehensions of others than of one another; and therefore their first care and thought cannot but be supposed to be how to secure themselves against foreign force. It was natural for them to put themselves under a frame of government which might best serve to that end; and choose the wisest and bravest man to conduct them in their wars, and lead them out against their enemies, and in this chiefly be their ruler.

Thus we see that the kings of the Indians, in America, which is still a pattern of the first ages in Asia and Europe, whilst the inhabitants were too few for the country, and want of people and money gave men no temptation to enlarge their possessions of land or contest for wider extent of ground, are little more than generals of their armies; and though they command absolutely in war, yet at home, and in time of peace, they exercise very little dominion, and have but a very moderate sovereignty, the resolutions of peace and war being ordinarily either in the people or in a council, though the war itself, which admits not of pluralities of governors, naturally evolves the command into the king's sole authority.

And thus, in Israel itself, the chief business of their judges and first kings seems to have been to be captains in war and leaders of their armies, which (besides what is signified by "going out and in before the people," which was, to march forth to war and home again at the heads of their forces) appears plainly in the story of Jephtha. The Ammonites making war upon Israel, the Gileadites, in fear, send to Jephtha, a bastard of their family, whom they had cast off, and article[15] with him, if he will assist them against the Ammonites, to make him their ruler, which they do in these words: "And the people made him head and captain over them," which was as it seems, all one as to be judge. "And he judged Israel"—that is, was their captain-general—six years." So when Jotham upbraids the Shechemites with the obligation they had to Gideon, who had been their judge and ruler, he tells them: "He fought for you, and adventured his life for, and delivered you out of the hands of Midian." Nothing mentioned of him but what he did as a general, and, indeed, that is all is found in his history, or in any of the rest of the judges. And Abimelech particularly is called king, though at most he was but their

[15] negotiate, arrange by treaty

general. And when, being weary of the ill-conduct of Samuel's sons, the children of Israel desired a king, "like all the nations, to judge them, and to go out before them, and to fight their battles," God, granting their desire, says to Samuel, "I will send thee a man, and thou shalt anoint him to be captain over my people Israel, that he may save my people out of the hands of the Philistines." As if the only business of a king had been to lead out their armies and fight in their defence; and, accordingly, at his inauguration, pouring a vial of oil upon him, declares to Saul that "the Lord had anointed him to be captain over his inheritance." And therefore those who, after Saul's being solemnly chosen and saluted king by the tribes at Mizpah, were unwilling to have him their king, make no other objection but this, "How shall this man save us?" as if they should have said: "This man is unfit to be our King, not having skill and conduct enough in war to be able to defend us." And when God resolved to transfer the government to David, it is in these words: "But now thy kingdom shall not continue: the Lord hath sought him a man after His own heart, and the Lord hath commanded him to be captain over His people." As if the whole kingly authority were nothing else but to be their general; and therefore the tribes who had stuck to Saul's family, and opposed David's reign, when they came to Hebron with terms of submission to him, they tell him, amongst other arguments, they had to submit to him as to their king, that he was, in effect, their king in Saul's time, and therefore they had no reason but to receive him as their king now. "Also," say they, "in time past, when Saul was king over us, thou wast he that leddest out and broughtest in Israel, and the Lord said unto thee, thou shalt feed my people Israel, and thou shalt be a captain over Israel."

Thus, whether a family, by degrees, grew up into a commonwealth, and the fatherly authority being continued on to the elder son, everyone in his turn growing up under it tacitly submitted to it, and the easiness and equality of it not offending anyone, everyone acquiesced till time seemed to have confirmed it and settled a right of succession by prescription;[16] or whether several families, or the

[16] uninterrupted use, possession from time immemorial, possession or use for a period fixed by law as giving a title or right

descendants of several families, whom chance, neighbourhood, or business brought together, united into society; the need of a general whose conduct might defend them against their enemies in war, and the great confidence the innocence and sincerity of that poor but virtuous age, such as are almost all those which begin governments that ever come to last in the world, gave men one of another, made the first beginners of commonwealths generally put the rule into one man's hand, without any other express limitation or restraint but what the nature of the thing and the end of government required. It was given them for the public good and safety, and to those ends, in the infancies of commonwealths, they commonly used it; and unless they had done so, young societies could not have subsisted. Without such nursing fathers, without this care of the governors, all governments would have sunk under the weakness and infirmities of their infancy, the prince and the people had soon perished toghether.

But the golden age (through before vain ambition, and *amor sceleratus habendi,*[17] evil concupiscence had corrupted men's minds into a mistake of true power and honour) had more virtue, and consequently better governors, as well as less vicious subjects; and there was then no stretching prerogative on the one side to oppress the people, nor consequently, on the other, any dispute about privilege, to lesson or restrain the power of the magistrate; and so no contest betwixt rulers and people about governors or government. Yet, when ambition and luxury, in future ages, would retain and increase the power, without doing the business for which it was given, and aided by flattery, taught princes to have distinct and separate interests from their people, men found it necessary to examine more carefully the original and rights of government, and to find out ways to restrain the exorbitances and prevent the abuses of that power, which they having entrusted in another's hands, only for their own good, they found was made use of to hurt them.

Thus we may see how probable it is that people that were naturally free, and by their own consent either submitted to the government of their father, or united together out of different families to

[17] the wicked love of things (of owning things)

make a government, should generally put the rule into one man's hands, and choose to be under the conduct of a single person, without so much as by express conditions limiting or regulating his power, which they thought safe enough in his honesty and prudence, though they never dreamt of monarchy being *jure divino,*[18] which we never heard of among mankind till it was revealed to us by the divinity of this last age, nor ever allowed paternal power to have a right to dominion, or to be the foundation of all government. And thus much may suffice to show that, as far as we have any light from history, we have reason to conclude that all peaceful beginnings of government have been laid in the consent of the people. I say peaceful, because I shall have occasion in another place to speak of conquest, which some esteem a way of beginning of governments.

The other objection I find urged against the beginning of polities in the way I have mentioned is this, viz.: –

That all men being born under government, some or other, it is impossible any of them should ever be free and at liberty to unite together and begin a new one, or ever be able to erect a lawful government.

If this argument be good, I ask, how came so many lawful monarchies into the world? For if anybody, upon this supposition, can show me any one man, in any age of the world, free to begin a lawful monarchy, I will be found to show him ten other free men at liberty at the same time to unite and begin a new government under a regal, or any other form, it being demonstration that if anyone, born under the dominion of another, may be so free as to have a right to command others in a new and distinct empire, everyone that is born under the dominion of another may be so free too, and may become a ruler or subject of a distinct separate government. And so by this their own principle either all men, however born, are free, or else there is but one lawful prince, one lawful government in the world. And then they have nothing to do but barely to show us which that is; which, when they have done, I doubt not but all mankind will easily agree to pay obedience to him.

Though it be a sufficient answer to their objection to show that it

[18] by divine right

involves them in the same difficulties that it doth those they use it against, yet I shall endeavour to discover the weakness of this argument a little farther.

"All men," say they, "are born under government, and therefore they cannot be at liberty to begin a new one. Everyone is born a subject to his father, or his prince, and is therefore under the perpetual tie of subjection and allegiance." It is plain mankind never owned nor considered any such natural subjection that they were born in, to one or to the other that tied them without their own consents, to a subjection to them and their heirs.

For there are no examples so frequent in history, both sacred and profane, as those of men withdrawing themselves and their obedience from the jurisdiction they were born under, and the family or community they were bred up in, and setting up new governments in other places; from whence sprang all that number of petty commonwealths in the beginning of the ages, and which always multiplied, as long as there was room enough, till the stronger or more fortunate swallowed the weaker; and those great ones again breaking to pieces, dissolved into lesser dominions, all which are so many testimonies against paternal sovereignty, and plainly prove that it was not the natural right of the father descending to his heirs that made government in the beginning, since it was impossible upon that ground there should have been so many little kingdoms, but only one universal monarchy if men had not been at liberty to separate themselves from their families and their government, be it what it will, that was set up in it, and go and make distinct commonwealths and other governments as they thought fit.

This has been the practise of the world from its first beginning to this day; nor is it now any more hindrance to the freedom of mankind that they are born under constituted and ancient polities that have established laws and set forms of government, than if they were born in the woods amongst the unconfined inhabitants that run loose in them. For those who would persuade us that by being born under any government we are naturally subjects to it, and have no more any title or pretence to the freedom of the state of nature, have no other reason (bating[19] that of paternal power, which

[19] excepting

we have already answered) to produce for it, but only because our fathers or progenitors passed away their natural liberty, and thereby bound up themselves and their posterity to a perpetual subjection to the government which they themselves submitted to. It is true that whatever engagements or promises anyone made for himself, he is under the obligation of them, but cannot by any compact whatsoever bind his children or posterity. For his son when a man being altogether as free as his father, any act of the father can no more give away the liberty of the son than it can of anybody else. He may indeed annex such conditions to the land he enjoyed as a subject of any commonwealth as may oblige his son to be of that community, if he will enjoy those possessions which were his father's, because that estate being his father's property he may dispose or settle it as he pleases.

And this has generally given the occasion to the mistake in this matter, because commonwealths not permitting any part of their dominions to be dismembered, nor to be enjoyed by any but those of their community, the son cannot ordinarily enjoy the possessions of his father but under the same terms his father did: by becoming a member of the society; whereby he puts himself presently[20] under the government he finds there established as much as any other subject of that commonwealth. And thus the consent of freemen, born under government, which only makes them members of it, being given separately in their turns, as each comes to be of age, and not in a multitude together. People take no notice of it, and thinking it not done at all, or not necessary, conclude they are naturally subjects as they are men.

But it is plain governments themselves understand it otherwise; they claim no power over the son, because of that they had over the father; nor look on children as being their subjects by their father's being so. If a subject of England have a child by an English woman in France, whose subject is he? Not the King of England's, for he must have leave to be admitted to the privileges of it; nor the King of France's, for how then has his father a liberty to bring him away and breed him as he pleases? And whoever was judged as a traitor or deserter, if he left or warred against a country, for being barely

[20] at once, thereupon

born in it of parents that were aliens there? It is plain then by practise of governments themselves, as well as by the law of right reason, that a child is born a subject of no country or government. He is under his father's tuition and authority till he comes to age of discretion, and then he is a freeman, at liberty what government he will put himself under, what body politic he will unite himself to. For if an Englishman's son, born in France, be at liberty, and may do so, it is evident there is no tie upon him by his father's being a subject of that kingdom; nor is he bound up by any compact of his ancestors. And why then hath not his son by the same reason, the same liberty, though he be born anywhere else? Since the power that a father hath naturally over his children is the same wherever they be born, and the ties of natural obligations are not bounded by the positive limits of kingdoms and commonwealths.

Every man being, as has been shown, naturally free, and nothing being able to put him into subjection to any earthly power but only his own consent, it is to be considered what shall be understood to be sufficient declaration of a man's consent to make him subject to the laws of any government. There is a common distinction of an express and a tacit consent, which will concern our present case. Nobody doubts but an express consent of any man entering into any society makes him a perfect member of that society, a subject of that government. The difficulty is, what ought to be looked upon as tacit consent, and how far it binds, i.e., how far anyone shall be looked on to have consented, and thereby submitted to any government, where he has made no expressions of it at all. And to this I say that every man that hath any possession or enjoyment of any part of the dominions of any government doth hereby give his tacit consent, and is far forth obliged to obedience to the laws of that government during such enjoyment as anyone under it; whether this his possession be of land to him and his heirs for ever, or a lodging only for a week; or whether it be barely travelling freely on the highway; and in effect it reaches as far as the very being of anyone within the territories of that government.

To understand this the better, it is fit to consider that every man when he at first incorporates himself into any commonwealth, he, by his uniting himself thereunto, annexes also, and submits to the community those possessions which he has or shall acquire that do not already belong to any other government; for it would be a direct contradiction for anyone to enter into society with others for the securing and regulating of property, and yet to suppose his land, whose property is to be regulated by the laws of the society, should be exempt from the jurisdiction of that government to which he himself, and the property of the land, is a subject. By the same act, therefore, whereby anyone unites his person, which was before free, to any commonwealth, by the same he unites his possessions, which was before free, to it also; and they become, both of them, person and possession, subject to the government and dominion of that commonwealth as long as it hath a being. Whoever therefore from thenceforth by inheritance, purchases, permission, or otherwise, enjoys any part of the land so annexed to, and under the government of that commonwealth, must take it with the condition it is under, that is, of submitting to the government of the commonwealth under whose jurisdiction it is as far forth as any subject of it.

But since the government has a direct jurisdiction only over the land, and reaches the possessor of it (before he has actually incorporated himself in the society), only as he dwells upon, and enjoys that: the obligation anyone is under, by virtue of such enjoyment, to submit to the government, begins and ends with the enjoyment; so that whenever the owner, who has given nothing but such a tacit consent to the government, will by donation, sale, or otherwise, quit the said possession, he is at liberty to go and incorporate himself into any other commonwealth, or to agree with others to begin a new one *(in vacuis locis)*[21] in any part of the world they can find free and unpossessed. Whereas he that has once by actual agreement and any express declaration given his consent to be of any commonweal is perpetually and indispensably obliged to be and remain unalterably a subject to it, and can never be again in the liberty of the state of nature; unless, by any calamity, the government he was under comes to be dissolved, or else by some public acts cuts him off from being any longer a member of it.

But submitting to the laws of any country, living quietly and enjoying privileges and protection under them makes not a man a member of that society. This is only a local protection and homage

[21] in unoccupied, vacant places

due to and from all those who, not being in the state of war, come within the territories belonging to any government to all parts whereof the force of its law extends. But this no more makes a man a member of that society, a perpetual subject of that commonwealth, than it would make a man a subject to another in whose family he found it convenient to abide for some time; though whilst he continued in it he were obliged to comply with the laws, and submit to the government he found there. And thus we see, that foreigners by living all their lives under another government, and enjoying the privileges and protection of it, though they are bound even in conscience to submit to its administration as far forth as any denizen, yet do not thereby come to be subjects or members of that commonwealth. Nothing can make any man so, but his actually entering into it by positive engagement, and express promise and compact. This is that, which I think, concerning the beginning of political societies, and that consent which makes anyone a member of any commonwealth.

☙ Like Sir Thomas Browne, John Locke was a physician educated at Oxford. He was long resident there and later served as a commissioner under King William III. Unlike Browne's, his interests were analytical—psychological and political. His thought serves as a basis not only for our Constitution (his idea of contract in *Treatises of Government*) but also for our psychology of the conscious and subconscious mind (see his *Essay Concerning Human Understanding* and Ernest Tuveson's *The Imagination as a Means of Grace*).

A modest proposal

(1729) BY *Jonathan Swift (1667-1745)*

For Preventing the Children of the Poor People in Ireland
from Being a Burden to Their Parents or Country,
and for Making them Beneficial to the Public

It is a melancholy object to those who walk through this great town [Dublin] or travel in the country, when they see the streets, the roads, and cabin doors crowded with beggars of the female sex, followed by three, four, or six children, all in rags and importuning every passenger for an alms. These mothers, instead of being able to work for their honest livelihood, are forced to employ all their time in strolling to beg sustenance for their helpless infants, who, as they grow up, either turn thieves for want of work, or leave their dear native country to fight for the Pretender in Spain, or sell themselves to the Barbadoes.[1]

I think it is agreed by all parties that this prodigious number of children in the arms, or on the backs, or at the heels of their mothers, and frequently of their fathers, is in the present deplorable state of the kingdom a very great additional grievance; and, therefore, whoever could find out a fair, cheap, and easy method of making these children sound, useful members of the commonwealth, would deserve so well of the public as to have his statue set up for a preserver of the nation.

But my intention is very far from being confined to provide only

[1] as indentured slaves

for the children of professed[2] beggars; it is of a much greater extent, and shall take in the whole number of infants at a certain age who are born of parents in effect as little able to support them as those who demand our charity in the streets.

As to my own part, having turned my thoughts for many years upon this important subject, and maturely weighed the several schemes of our projectors,[3] I have always found them grossly mistaken in their computation. It is true, a child just dropped from its dam[4] may be supported by her milk for a solar year with little other nourishment, at most not above the value of two shillings, which the mother may certainly get, or the value in scraps, by her lawful occupation of begging; and it is exactly at one year old that I propose to provide for them in such a manner as instead of being a charge upon their parents or the parish, or wanting food[5] and raiment[6] for the rest of their lives, they shall, on the contrary, contribute to the feeding and partly to the clothing of many thousands.

There is likewise another great advantage in my scheme, that it will prevent those voluntary abortions, and that horrid practice of women murdering their bastard children, alas! too frequent among us! sacrificing the poor innocent babes, I doubt,[7] more to avoid the expense than the shame, which would move tears and pity in the most savage and inhuman breast.

The number of souls in this kingdom being usually reckoned one million and a half, of these, I calculate there may be about two hundred thousand couples whose wives are breeders; from which number I subtract thirty thousand couples, who are able to maintain their own children (although I apprehend[8] there cannot be so many, under the present distress of the kingdom); but this being granted, there will remain one hundred and seventy thousand breeders. I again subtract fifty thousand for those women who miscarry, or whose children die by accident or disease within the year. There

[2] self-acknowledged, as opposed to those who, without acting as beggars, live in identical conditions with them

[3] men noted for great ideas for bettering local or universal conditions of mankind; promoters, speculators

[4] a phrase commonly reserved for brute beasts, used by Swift to point up the condition of the people he is concerned with

[5] clothes [6] a Biblical echo [7] am afraid, fear

[8] both "fear" and "am aware"

only remain an hundred and twenty thousand children of poor parents annually born. The question therefore is, how this number shall be reared and provided for? which, as I have already said, under the present situation of affairs, is utterly impossible by all the methods hitherto proposed. For we can neither employ them in handicraft or agriculture; we neither build houses (I mean in the country) nor cultivate land; they can very seldom pick up a livelihood by stealing till they arrive at six years old, except where they are of towardly[9] parts,[10] although I confess they learn the rudiments much earlier, during which time, they can, however, be properly looked upon only as probationers, as I have been informed by a principal gentleman in the county of Cavan, who protested to me that he never knew above one or two instances under the age of six, even in a part of the kingdom so renowned for the quickest proficiency in that art.

I am assured by our merchants that a boy or girl before twelve years old is no saleable commodity, and even when they come to this age they will not yield above three pounds or three pounds and a half-crown at most on the exchange; which cannot turn to account either to the parents or the kingdom, the charge of nutriment and rags having been at least four times that value.

I shall now therefore humbly propose my own thoughts, which I hope will not be liable to the least objection.

I have been assured by a very knowing American[11] of my acquaintance in London, that a young healthy child well nursed is at a year old a most delicious, nourishing, and wholesome food whether stewed, roasted, baked, or boiled; and I make no doubt that it will equally serve in a fricassee or a ragout.

I do therefore humbly offer it to public consideration that of the hundred and twenty thousand children already computed, twenty thousand may be reserved for breed, whereof only one-fourth part to be males, which is more than we allow to sheep, black cattle or swine; and my reason is that these children are seldom the fruits of marriage, a circumstance not much regarded by our savages; therefore one male will be sufficient to serve four females. That the

[9] quick to learn, especially gifted in one way or another [10] talents, nature

[11] probably not an Indian; either a North or South American: Swift may be imputing savagery (cannibalism) to him and his country

remaining hundred thousand may, at a year old, be offered in sale to the persons of quality and fortune through the kingdom, always advising the mother to let them suck plentifully in the last month, so as to render them plump and fat for a good table. A child will make two dishes at an entertainment for friends, and when the family dines alone, the fore or hind quarter will make a reasonable dish, and seasoned with a little pepper or salt will be very good boiled on the fourth day, especially in winter.

I have reckoned upon a medium that a child just born will weigh twelve pounds, and in a solar year, if tolerably nursed, will increase to twenty-eight pounds.

I grant this food will be somewhat dear, and therefore very proper for landlords, who, as they have already devoured most of the parents, seem to have the best title to the children.

Infants' flesh will be in season throughout the year, but more plentiful in March, and a little before and after; for we are told by a grave author, an eminent French physician, that fish being a prolific diet, there are more children born in Roman Catholic countries about nine months after Lent than at any other season; therefore, reckoning a year after Lent, the markets will be more glutted than usual, because the number of popish infants is at least three to one in this kingdom, and therefore it will have one other collateral advantage, by lessening the number of papists among us.

I have already computed the charge of nursing a beggar's child (in which list I reckon all cottagers, laborers, and four-fifths of the farmers) to be about two shillings per annum, rags included; and I believe no gentleman would repine to give ten shillings for the carcass of a good fat child, which, as I have said, will make four dishes of excellent nutritive meat, when he has only some particular friend or his own family to dine with him. Thus the squire will learn to be a good landlord, and grow popular among his tenants; the mother will have eight shillings net profit, and be fit for work till she produces another child.

Those who are more thrifty (as I must confess the times require) may flay the carcass, the skin of which artificially dressed will make admirable gloves for ladies, and summer boots for fine gentlemen.

As to our city of Dublin, shambles[12] may be appointed for this

[12] slaughterhouse, abbatoir

purpose in the most convenient parts of it, and butchers, we may be assured, will not be wanting, although I rather recommend buying the children alive, and dressing them hot from the knife as we do roasting pigs.

A very worthy person, a true lover of his country, and whose virtues I highly esteem, was lately pleased, in discoursing on this matter, to offer a refinement upon my scheme. He said that many gentlemen of this kingdom, having of late destroyed their deer, he conceived that the want of venison[13] might be well supplied by the bodies of young lads and maidens, not exceeding fourteen years of age nor under twelve, so great a number of both sexes in every country being now ready to starve for want of work and service, and these to be disposed of by their parents, if alive, or otherwise by their nearest relations. But with due deference to so excellent a friend and so deserving a patriot, I cannot be altogether in his sentiments; for as to the males, my American acquaintance assured me from frequent experience that their flesh was generally tough and lean, like that of our school-boys, by continual exercise, and their taste disagreeable; and to fatten them would not answer the charge. Then as to the females, it would, I think, with humble submission, be a loss to the public, because they soon would become breeders themselves; and besides, it is not improbable that some scrupulous[14] people might be apt to censure such a practice (although indeed very unjustly) as a little bordering upon cruelty, which, I confess, has always been with me the strongest objection against any project, however so well intended.

But in order to justify my friend, he confessed that this expedient was put into his head by the famous Psalmanazar,[15] a native of the island Formosa, who came from thence to London above twenty years ago, and in conversation told my friend, that in his country when any young person happened to be put to death, the executioner sold the carcass to persons of quality as a prime dainty, and that in his time the body of a plump girl of fifteen, who was crucified for an attempt to poison the emperor, was sold to his imperial majesty's

[13] formerly applied to the flesh of many animals killed in hunting and used for food, not only deer

[14] overly sensitive

[15] famous impostor, posing as a Formosan

prime minister of state and other great mandarins of the court, in joints from the gibbet, at four hundred crowns. Neither indeed can I deny that if the same use were made of several plump young girls in this town, who, without one single groat[16] to their fortunes, cannot stir abroad without a chair,[17] and appear at the playhouse and assemblies in foreign fineries which they never will pay for, the kingdom would not be the worse.

Some persons of a desponding spirit are in great concern about that vast number of poor people, who are aged, diseased, or maimed, and I have been desired to employ my thoughts what course may be taken to ease the nation of so greivous an encumbrance. But I am not in the least pain upon that matter, because it is very well known that they are every day dying and rotting by cold, and famine, and filth, and vermin, as fast as can be reasonably expected. And as to the younger laborers, they are now in as hopeful a condition; they cannot get work, and consequently pine away for want of nourishment, to a degree that if at any time they are accidentally hired to common labor, they have not strength to perform it; and thus the country and themselves are happily delivered from the evils to come.

I have too long digressed, and therefore shall return to my subject. I think the advantages by the proposal which I have made are obvious, and many, as well as of the highest importance.

For first, as I have already observed, it would greatly lessen the number of papists, with whom we are yearly overrun, being the principal breeders of the nation as well as our most dangerous enemies; and who stay at home on purpose with a design to deliver the kingdom to the Pretender, hoping to take their advantage by the absence of so many good protestants, who have chosen rather to leave their country than stay at home and pay tithes against their conscience to an episcopal curate.

Secondly, The poorer tenants will have something valuable of their own, which by law may be made liable to distress, and help to pay their landlord's rent, their corn and cattle being already seized, and money a thing unknown.

[16] literally, four-pence, a paltry sum

[17] either a light vehicle drawn by one horse or an enclosed chair carried on poles by two men, hence, in luxury

Thirdly, Whereas the maintenance of an hundred thousand children, from two years old and upward, cannot be computed at less than ten shillings a-piece per annum, the nation's stock will be thereby increased fifty thousand pounds per annum, besides the profit of a new dish introduced to the tables of all gentlemen of fortune in the kingdom who have any refinement in taste. And the money will circulate among ourselves, the goods being entirely of our own growth and manufacture.

Fourthly, The constant breeders, besides the gain of eight shillings sterling per annum by the sale of their children, will be rid of the charge of maintaining them after the first year.

Fifthly, This food would likewise bring great custom to taverns, where the vintners will certainly be so prudent as to procure the best receipts[18] for dressing it to perfection, and consequently have their houses frequented by all the fine gentlemen, who justly value themselves upon their knowledge in good eating; and a skillful cook, who understands how to oblige his guests, will contrive to make it as expensive as they please.

Sixthly, This would be a great inducement to marriage, which all wise nations have either encouraged by rewards or enforced by laws and penalties. It would increase the care and tenderness of mothers toward their children, when they were sure of a settlement for life to the poor babes, provided in some sort by the public, to their annual profit instead of expense. We should see an honest emulation among the married women, which of them could bring the fattest child to the market. Men would become as fond of their wives during the time of their pregnancy as they are now of their mares in foal, their cows in calf, or sows whey they are ready to farrow; nor offer to beat or kick them (as is too frequent a practice) for fear of miscarriage.

Many other advantages might be enumerated. For instance, the addition of some thousand carcasses in our exportation of barreled beef, the propagation of swine's flesh, and improvement in the art of making good bacon, so much wanted among us by the great destruction of pigs, too frequent at our tables; which are in no way comparable in taste or magnificence to a well-grown, fat yearling child, which roasted whole will make a considerable figure at a lord

[18] recipes

mayor's feast, or any other public entertainment. But this and many others I omit, being studious of brevity.

Supposing that one thousand families in this city would be constant customers for infants' flesh, beside others who might have it at merry-meetings, particularly weddings and christenings, I compute that Dublin would take off annually about twenty thousand carcasses, and the rest of the kingdom (where probably they will be sold somewhat cheaper) the remaining eighty thousand.

I can think of no one objection that will possibly be raised against this proposal, unless it should be urged that the number of people will be thereby much lessened in the kingdom. This I freely own, and it was indeed one principal design in offering it to the world. I desire the reader will observe that I calculate my remedy for this one individual kingdom of Ireland, and for no other that ever was, is, or, I think, ever can be upon earth. Therefore let no man talk to me of other expedients:[19] of taxing our absentees at five shillings a pound; of using neither clothes nor household furniture, except what is of our own growth and manufacture; of utterly rejecting the materials and instruments that promote foreign luxury; of curing the expensiveness of pride, vanity, idleness, and gaming in our women; of introducing a vein of parsimony, prudence, and temperance; of learning to love our country, in the want of which we differ even from Laplanders and the inhabitants of Topinamboo; of quitting our animosities and factions, nor act any longer like the Jews, who were murdering one another at the very moment their city was taken; of being a little cautious not to sell our country and consciences for nothing; of teaching landlords to have at least one degree of mercy toward their tenants; lastly, of putting a spirit of honesty, industry, and skill into our shopkeepers, who, if a resolution could now be taken to buy only our native goods, would immediately unite to cheat and exact upon[20] us in the price, the measure, and the goodness, nor could ever yet be brought to make one fair proposal of just dealing, though often and earnestly invited to it.

Therefore, I repeat, let no man talk to me of these and the like

[19] These expedients give, in fact, part of the answer to Ireland's troubles, and it is because no use is made of them that Swift resorts to his satire

[20] force or oblige to make unjust payments

expedients, till he has at least some glimpse of hope that there will be ever some hearty and sincere attempt to put them in practice.

But as to myself, having been wearied out for many years with offering vain, idle, visionary thoughts, and at length utterly despairing of success, I fortunately fell upon this proposal, which, as it is wholly new, so it has something solid and real, of no expense and little trouble, full in our own power, and whereby we can incur no danger in disobliging England. For this kind of commodity will not bear exportation, the flesh being of too tender a consistence to admit a long continuance in salt, although perhaps I could name a country[21] which would be glad to eat up our whole nation without it.

After all, I am not so violently bent upon my own opinion as to reject any offer proposed by wise men, which shall be found equally innocent, cheap, easy, and effectual. But before something of that kind shall be advanced in contradiction to my scheme, and offering a better, I desire the author or authors will be pleased maturely to consider two points. First, as things now stand, how they will be able to find food and raiment for an hundred thousand useless mouths and backs. And secondly, there being a round million creatures in human figure throughout this kingdom, whose whole subsistence put into a common stock would leave them in debt two millions of pounds sterling, adding those who are beggars by profession to the bulk of farmers, cottagers, and laborers, with their wives and children, who are beggars in effect; I desire those politicians, who dislike my overture, and may perhaps be so bold as to attempt an answer, that they will first ask the parents of these mortals, whether they would not at this day think it a great happiness to have been sold for food at a year old in the manner I prescibe, and thereby have avoided such a perpetual scene of misfortunes as they have since gone through by the oppression of landlords, the impossibility of paying rent without money or trade, the want of common sustenance, with neither house nor clothes to cover them from the inclemencies of the weather, and the most inevitable prospect of entailing the like or greater miseries upon their breed for ever.

I profess, in the sincerity of my heart, that I have not the least

[21] England

personal interest in endeavoring to promote this necessary work, having no other motive than the public good of my country, by advancing our trade, providing for infants, relieving the poor, and giving some pleasure to the rich. I have no children by which I can propose to get a single penny; the youngest being nine years old, and my wife past child-bearing.

The fame of Jonathan Swift is based on his authorship of *Gulliver's Travels.* Gulliver, like the Gull of the *Gull's Horn-Book,* is a dupe, one who is gulled or fooled. Therefore, what he sees in his journeys is not always what we see through him. In the short piece, *A Modest Proposal,* Swift himself makes the ironic suggestions, saying what as a normal human being he cannot mean, yet logically following out some of the implications of actual human actions. Swift was Irish, a cousin of Dryden, became Dean of St. Patrick's in 1713, some years before his *Proposal,* wrote pamphlets for the English Tories, and was all his life a ferocious satirist of reason misused. What are the objects of satire now?

An academy for French diplomats

FROM *The Spectator (1712)*

BY ***Joseph Addison** (1672-1719)*

Tuesday, February 19.

Non tali auxilio, nec defensoribus istis Tempus eget—,—Virg.[1]

Our late news-papers being full of the project now on foot in the Court of France, for establishing a political academy, and I my self having received letters from several virtuosos among my foreign correspondents, which give some light into that affair, I intend to make it the subject of this day's speculation. A general account of this project may be met with in the *Daily Courant* of last Friday in the following words, translated in the *Gazette* of Amsterdam.

Paris, February 12. "'Tis confirmed that the King had resolv'd to establish a new academy for politicks, of which the Marquess de Torcy, Minister and Secretary of State, is to be protector. Six academicians are to be chosen, endow'd with proper talents, for beginning to form this academy, into which no person is to be admitted under twenty five years of age: they must likewise have each an estate of two thousand livres a year, either in possession, or to come to 'em by inheritance. The King will allow to each a pension of a thousand livres. They are likewise

[1]Time does not need such aid or such supporters (defenders, protectors)

to have able masters to teach 'em the necessary sciences,[2] and to instruct them in all the treaties of peace, alliance, and others which have been made in several ages past. These members are to meet twice a week at the *Louvre.* From this seminary[3] are to be chosen secretaries to ambassies, who by degrees may advance to higher employments."

Cardinal Richelieu's politicks made France the terror of Europe. The statesmen who have appeared in that nation of late years have on the contrary rendered it either the pity or the contempt of its neighbours. The Cardinal erected that famous academy which has carried all the parts of polite[4] learning to the greatest height. His chief design in that institution was to divert the men of genius from meddling with politicks, a province in which he did not care to have any one else interfere with him. On the contrary, the Marquess de Torcy seems resolved to make several young men in France as wise as himself, and is therefore taken up at present in establishing a nursery[5] of statesmen.

Some private letters add that there will also be erected a seminary of petticoat[6] politicians, who are to be brought up at the feet of Madam de Maintenon,[7] and to be dispatched into foreign Courts upon any emergencies of state; but as the news of this last project has not been yet confirmed, I shall take no farther notice of it.

Several of my readers may doubtless remember that upon the conclusion of the last war, which had been carried on so successfully by the enemy, their generals were many of them transformed into ambassadors; but the conduct of those who have commanded in the present war has, it seems, brought so little honor and advantage to their great monarch, that he is resolved to trust his affairs no longer in the hands of those military gentlemen.

The regulations of this new academy very much deserve our

[2] departments or branches of learning

[3] an institution for the training of persons destined for a particular profession

[4] literally polished, refined or scholarly

[5] place for training, with ironic connotations

[6] female, ironic usage

[7] (1635-1719), second wife of Louis XIV, noted for, among other things, her founding of a school for training of women

attention. The students are to have in possession, or reversion,[8] an estate of two thousand French livres per annum, which, as the present exchange runs, will amount to at least one hundred and twenty six pounds English. This, with the royal allowance of a thousand livres, will enable them to find themselves in coffee and snuff; not to mention news papers, pen and ink, wax[9] and wafers,[10] with the like necessaries for politicians.

A man must be at least five and twenty before he can be initiated into the misteries of this academy, tho' there is no question but many grave persons of a much more advanced age, who have been constant readers of the Paris Gazette, will be glad to begin the world anew, and enter themselves upon this list of politicians.

The society of these hopeful young gentlemen is to be under the direction of six professors, who, it seems, are to be speculative statesmen, and drawn out of the body of the Royal Academy. These six wise masters, according to my private letters, are to have the following parts allotted them.

The first is to instruct the students in *State Legerdemain,* as how to take off the impression of a seal, to split a wafer, to open a letter, to fold it up again, with other the like ingenious feats of dexterity and art. When the students have accomplished themselves in this part of their profession, they are to be delivered into the hands of their second instructor, who is a kind of *Posture-master.*

This artist is to teach them how to nod judiciously, to shrug up their shoulders in a dubious case, to connive with either eye, and in a word, the whole practice of *political grimace.*

The third is a sort of *Language Master,* who is to instruct them in the stile proper for a Foreign Minister in his ordinary discours. And to the end that this college of statesmen may be thoroughly practised in the political stile, they are to make use of it in their common conversations, before they are employed either in foreign or domestick affairs. If one of them asks another what o'clock it is, the other is to answer him indirectly, and, if possible, to turn off the question. If he is desired to change a *louis d'or,*[11] he must beg time to

[8] conditional upon the expiration of a grant or on the death of a person

[9] sealing wax

[10] a small disk of flour mixed with gum, or of gelatine, used for sealing letters

[11] gold coin

consider of it. If it be enquired of him whether the King is at *Versailles* or *Marly,* he must answer in a whisper. If he be asked the news of the late *Gazette,* or the subject of a proclamation, he is to reply that he has not yet read it: or if he does not care for explaining himself so far, he needs only draw his brow up in wrinkles, or elevate the left shoulder.

The fourth professor is to teach the whole art of political characters and hieroglyphicks; and to the end that they may be perfect also in this practice, they are not to send a note to one another (tho' it be but to borrow a Tacitus or a Machiavel)[12] which is not written in cypher.

Their fifth professor, it is thought, will be chosen out of the Society of Jesuits, and is to be well read in the controversies of probable doctrines, mental reservations, and the rights of the Princes. This learned man is to instruct them in the grammar, syntax, and construing part of *Treaty-latin:* how to distinguish between the spirit and the letter, and likewise demonstrate how the same form of words may lay an obligation upon any Prince in Europe different from that which it lays upon his most Christian Majesty. He is likewise to teach them the art of finding flaws, loop-holes, and evasions, in the most solemn compacts, and particularly a Great *rabbinical secret,* revived of late years by the fraternity of Jesuits, namely, that contradictory interpretations of the same article may both of them be true and valid.

When our statesmen are sufficiently improved by these several instructors, they are to receive their last polishing from one who is to act among them as *Master of the Ceremonies.* This gentleman is to give them lectures upon those important points of the *elbow-chair,* and the *stair-head;* to instruct them in the different situations of the right-hand, and to furnish them with bows and inclinations of all sizes, measures and proportions. In short, this professor is to give the society their *stiffening,* and infuse into their manners that beautiful political starch which may qualifie them for levees,[13] conferences, visits, and make them shine in what vulgar minds are apt to look upon as trifles.

[12] Niccolò Machiavelli (1469-1527), author of *The Prince* and famed for political subtlety and craft

[13] assembly or reception

I have not yet heard any further particulars which are apt to be observed in this society of unfledged statesmen; but I must confess, had I a son of five and twenty that shou'd take it into his head at that age to set up for a politician, I think I shou'd go near to disinherit him for a block-head. Besides, I should be apprehensive lest the same arts which are to enable him to negotiate between potentates might a little infect his ordinary behaviour between man and man. There is no question but these young Machiavels will, in a little time, turn their college upside-down with plots and stratagems, and lay as many schemes to circumvent one another in a frog or sallad, as they may hereafter put in practice to over-reach a neighbouring Prince or State.

We are told that the Spartans, tho' they punish'd theft in their young men, when it was discovered, looked upon it as honourable if it succeeded. Provided the conveyance[14] was clean and unsuspected, a youth might afterwards boast of it. This, say the historians, was to keep them sharp, and to hinder them from being imposed upon, either in their publick or private negociations. Whether any such relaxations of morality, such little *jeux d'esprit,*[15] ought not to be allowed in this intended seminary of politicians, I shall leave to the wisdom of their founder.

In the mean time we have fair warning given us by this doubty[16] body of statesmen; and as Sylla saw many Mariuses in Caesar, so I think we may discover many Torcys in this college of academicians. Whatever we think of our selves, I am afraid neither our Smyrna or St. James's will be a match for it. Our coffee-houses are, indeed, very good institutions, but whether or no these our British schools of politicks may furnish out as able envoys and secretaries as an academy that is set apart for that purpose will deserve our serious consideration; especially if we remember that our country is more famous for producing men of integrity than statesmen; and that, on the contrary, *French* truth and *British* policy make a conspicuous figure in Nothing, as the Earl of Rochester has very well observed in his admirable poem upon that barren subject.

[14] light-fingered carrying off, sly theft
[15] playfulness of spirit
[16] doughty, able or worthy or formidable

❧ From Lichfield, Oxford, travels on the continent, a secretaryship, and a post in Parliament, Joseph Addison, along with his friend Richard Steele, directed major energies toward essays for the Whig papers *The Tatler* and *The Spectator.* Note how the essay is becoming more informal, appearing in the new daily (except Sunday) one-sheet journals for perusal by ladies as well as gentlemen of fashion, and containing whimsical trivia as well as serious disquisitions on politics and literature, aiming, as *The Spectator* said, "to enliven morality with wit, and to temper wit with morality." Could our contemporary newspapers use essays effectively? Does a "column" serve the same purpose?

Rules by which a great empire may be reduced to a small one

(1773) BY ***Benjamin Franklin*** *(1706-1790)*

An ancient sage boasted, that, tho' he could not fiddle, he knew how to make a *great city* of a *little one.* The science that I, a modern simpleton, am about to communicate, is the very reverse.

I address myself to all ministers who have the management of extensive dominions, which from their very greatness are become troublesome to govern, because the multiplicity of their affairs leaves no time for *fiddling.*

I. In the first place, gentlemen, you are to consider, that a great empire, like a great cake, is most easily diminished at the edges. Turn your attention, therefore, first to your *remotest* provinces; that, as you get rid of them, the next may follow in order.

II. That the possibility of this separation may always exist, take special care the provinces are never incorporated with the mother country; that they do not enjoy the same common rights, the same privileges in commerce; and that they are governed by *severer* laws, all of *your enacting,* without allowing them any share in the choice of the legislators. By carefully making and preserving such distinctions, you will (to keep to my simile of the cake) act like a wise gingerbread-baker, who, to facilitate a division, cuts his dough half through in those places where, when baked, he would have it *broken to pieces.*

III. Those remote provinces have perhaps been acquired, purchased, or conquered, at the *sole expense* of the settlers, of their ancestors, without the aid of the mother country. If this should happen to increase her *strength,* by their growing numbers, ready to join in her wars; her *commerce,* by their growing demand for her manufactures; or her *naval power,* by greater employment for her ships and seamen, they may probably suppose some merit in this, and that it entitles them to some favour; you are therefore to *forget it all, or resent it,* as if they had done you injury. If they happen to be zealous whigs,[1] friends of liberty, nurtured in revolution principles, *remember all that* to their prejudice, and resolve to punish it; for such principles, after a revolution is thoroughly established, are of *no more use;* they are even *odious* and *abominable.*

IV. However peaceably your colonies have submitted to your government, shewn their affection to your interests, and patiently borne their grievances; you are to *suppose* them always inclined to revolt, and treat them accordingly. Quarter troops among them, who by their insolence may *provoke* the rising of mobs, and by their bullets and bayonets *suppress* them. By this means, like the husband who uses his wife ill *from suspicion*, you may in time convert your *suspicions* into *realities.*

V. Remote provinces must have *Governors* and *Judges,* to represent the Royal Person, and execute everywhere the delegated parts of his office and authority. You ministers now, that much of the strength of government depends on the *opinion* of the people; and much of that opinion on the *choice of rulers* placed immediately over them. If you send them wise and good men for governors, who study the interest of the colonists, and advance their prosperity, they will think their King wise and good, and that he wishes the welfare of his subjects. If you send them learned and upright men for Judges, they will think him a lover of justice. This may attach your provinces more to his government. You are therefore to be careful whom you recommend for those offices. If you can find prodigals, who have ruined their fortunes, broken gamesters or stockjobbers, these may do well as *governors;* for they will probably be rapacious, and provoke the people by their extortions. Wrangling proctors and pettifogging[2] lawyers, too, are not amiss;

[1] American colonists who supported the American Revolution, favoring democratic over monarchical government [2] mean and shifty

for they will be for ever disputing and quarrelling with their little parliaments. If withal they should be ignorant, wrong-headed, and insolent, so much the better. Attornies' clerks and Newgate[3] solicitors will do for *Chief Justices,* especially if they hold their places *during your pleasure;* and all will contribute to impress those ideas of your government, that are proper for a people *you would wish to renounce it.*

VI. To confirm these impressions, and strike them deeper, whenever the injured come to the capital with complaints of mal-administration, oppression, or injustice, punish such suitors with long delay, enormous expence, and a final judgment in favour of the oppressor. This will have an admirable effect every way. The trouble of future complaints will be prevented, and Governors and Judges will be encouraged to further acts of oppression and injustice; and thence the people may become more disaffected, and at length desperate.

VII. When such Governors have crammed their coffers, and made themselves so odious to the people that they can no longer remain among them, with safety to their person, *recall and reward* them with pensions. You may make them *baronets* too, if that respectable order should not think fit to resent it. All will contribute to encourage new governors in the same practice, and make the supreme government, *detestable.*

VIII. If, when you are engaged in war, your colonies should vie in liberal aids of men and money against the common enemy, upon your simple requisition, and give far beyond their abilities, reflect that a penny taken from them by your power is far more honourable to you, than a pound presented by their benevolence; despise therefore their voluntary grants, and resolve to harass them with novel taxes. They will probably complain to your parliaments, that they are taxed by a body in which they have no representative, and that this is contrary to common right. They will petition for redress. Let the Parliaments flout their claims, reject their petitions, refuse even to suffer the reading of them, and treat the petitioners with the utmost contempt. Nothing can have a better effect in producing

[3] a notorious London prison since pulled down, which better lawyers presumably would not frequent

the alienation proposed; for though many can forgive injuries, *none ever forgave contempt.*

IX. In laying these taxes, never regard the heavy burthens those remote people already undergo, in defending their own frontiers, supporting their own provincial governments, making new roads, building bridges, churches, and other public edifices, which in old countries have been done to your hands by your ancestors, but which occasion constant calls and demands on the purses of a new people. Forget the *restraints* you lay on their trade for *your* own benefit, and the advantage a *monopoly* of this trade gives your exacting merchants. Think nothing of the wealth those merchants and your manufacturers acquire by the colony commerce; their encreased ability thereby to pay taxes at home; their accumulating, in the price of their commodities, most of those taxes, and so levying them from their consuming customers; all this, and the employment and support of thousands of your poor by the colonists, you are *entirely to forget.* But remember to make your arbitrary tax more grievous to your provinces, by public declarations importing that your power of taxing them has *no limits;* so that when you take from them without their consent one shilling in the pound, you have a clear right to the other nineteen. This will probably weaken every idea of *security in their property,* and convince them, that under such a government they *have nothing they can call their own;* which can scarce fail of producing the *happiest consequences!*

X. Possibly, indeed, some of them might still comfort themselves, and say, "Though we have no property, we have yet *something* left that is valuable; we have constitutional *liberty,* both of person and of conscience. This King, these Lords, and these Commons, who it seems are too remote from us to know us, and feel for us, cannot take from us our *Habeas Corpus* right, or our right of trial *by a jury of our neighbours;* they cannot deprive us of the exercise of our religion, alter our ecclesiastical constitution, and compel us to be Papists, if they please, or Mahometans." To annihilate this comfort, begin by laws to perplex[4] their commerce with infinite regulations, impossible to be remembered and observed; ordain seizures of their property for every failure; take away the trial of such pro-

[4] tie up or make a tangle of

perty by Jury, and give it to arbitrary[5] Judges of your own appointing, and of the lowest characters in the country, whose salaries and emoluments[6] are to arise out of the duties[7] or condemnations,[8] and whose appointments are *during pleasure.* Then let there be a formal declaration of both Houses, that opposition to your edicts is *treason,* and that any person suspected of treason in the provinces may, according to some obsolete law, be seized and sent to the metropolis of the empire for trial; and pass an act, that those there charged with certain other offences, shall be sent away in chains from their friends and country to be tried in the same manner for felony. Then erect a new Court of Inquisition among them, accompanied by an armed force, with instructions to transport all such suspected persons; to be ruined by the expense, if they bring over evidences to prove their innocence, or be found guilty and hanged, if they cannot afford it. And, lest the people should think you cannot possibly go any farther, pass another solemn declaratory act, "that King, Lords, Commons had, hath, and of right ought to have, full power and authority to make statutes of sufficient force and validity to bind the unrepresented provinces IN ALL CASES WHATSOEVER." This will include *spiritual* with temporal, and, taken together, must operate wonderfully to your purpose; by convincing them, that they are at present under a power something like that spoken of in the scriptures, which can not only *kill their bodies,* but *damn their souls* to all eternity, by compelling them, if it pleases, *to worship the Devil.*

XI. To make your taxes more odious, and more likely to procure resistance, send from the capital a board of officers to superintend the collection, composed of the most *indiscreet, ill-bred,* and *insolent* you can find. Let these have large salaries out of the extorted revenue, and live in open, grating luxury upon the sweat and blood of the industrious; whom they are to worry continually with groundless and expensive prosecutions before the abovementioned arbitrary revenue Judges; *all at the cost of the party prosecuted,* tho' acquitted, because *the King is to pay no costs.* Let these men, *by your order,* be exempted from all the common taxes and burthens of the province, though they and their property are protected by its laws.

[5] of uncontrolled power or authority [6] profits or gain arising from an office
[7] payment due and enforced by law or custom [8] sentence or forfeiture

If any revenue officers are *suspected* of the least tenderness for the people, discard them. If others are justly complained of, protect and reward them. If any of the under officers behave so as to provoke the people to drub them, promote those to better offices: this will encourage others to procure for themselves such profitable drubbings, by multiplying and enlarging such provocations, and *all will work towards the end you aim at.*

XII. Another way to make your tax odious, is to misapply the produce of it. If it was originally appropriated for the *defence* of the provinces, the better support of government, and the administration of justice, where it may be *necessary,* then apply none of it to that *defence,* but bestow it where it is *not necessary,* in augmented salaries or pensions to every governor, who had distinguished himself by his enmity to the people, and by calumniating them to their sovereign. This will make them pay it more unwillingly, and be more apt to quarrel with those that collect it and those that imposed it, who will quarrel again with them, and all shall contribute to your *main purpose,* of making them *weary of your government.*

XIII. If the people of any province have been accustomed to support their own Governors and Judges to satisfactions you are to apprehend that such Governors and Judges may be thereby influenced to treat the people kindly, and do them justice. This is another reason for applying part of that revenue in larger salaries to such Governors and Judges, given, as their commissions are, *during your pleasure* only; forbidding them to take any salaries from their provinces; that thus the people may no longer hope any kindness from their Governors, or (in Crown cases) any justice from their Judges. And, as the money thus misapplied in one province is extorted from all, probably *all will resent the misapplication.*

XIV. If the parliaments of your provinces should dare to claim rights, or complain of your administration, order them to be harassed with *repeated dissolutions.* If the same men are continually returned by new elections, adjourn their meetings to some country village, where they cannot be accommodated, and there keep them *during pleasure;* for this, you know, is your PREROGATIVE; and an excellent one it is, as you may manage it to promote discontents among the people, diminish their respect, and *increase their disaffection.*

XV. Convert the brave, honest officers of your *navy* into pimping tide-waiters[9] and colony officers of the *customs.* Let those, who in time of war fought gallantly in defence of the commerce of their countrymen, in peace be taught to prey upon it. Let them learn to be corrupted by great and real smugglers; but (to show their diligence) scour with armed boats every bay, harbour, river, creek, cove, or nook throughout the coast of your colonies; stop and detain every coaster,[10] every wood-boat, every fisherman, tumble their cargoes and even their ballast inside out and upside down; and, if a penn'orth of pins is found un-entered, let the whole be seized and confiscated. Thus shall the trade of your colonists suffer more from their friends in time of peace, than it did from their enemies in war. Then let these boats' crews land upon every farm in their way, rob the orchards, steal the pigs and the poultry, and insult the inhabitants. If the injured and exasperated farmers, unable to procure other justice, should attack the aggressors, drub them, and burn their boats; you are to call this *high treason and rebellion,* order fleets and armies into their country, and threaten to carry all the offenders three thousand miles to be hanged, drawn, and quartered. *O! this will work admirably!*

XVI. If you are told of discontents in your colonies, never believe that they are general, or that you have given occasion for them; therefore do not think of applying any remedy, or of changing any offensive measure. Redress no grievance, lest they should be encouraged to demand the redress of some other grievance. Grant no request that is just and reasonable, lest they should make another that is unreasonable. Take all your informations of the state of the colonies from your Governors and officers in enmity with them. Encourage and reward these *leasing-makers;*[11] secrete their lying accusations, lest they should be confuted; but act upon them as the clearest evidence; and believe nothing you hear from the friends of the people: suppose all *their* complaints to be invented and promoted by a few factious demagogues,[12] whom if you could catch and hang, all would be quiet. Catch and hang a

[9] customs officers who boarded ships coming in with the tide

[10] vessel used to trade from port to port along the coast of a country

[11] liars who by slanders prejudice the relations between a king and subjects

[12] unprincipled popular orator, rabble-rouser

few of them accordingly; and the *blood of the Martyrs* shall *work miracles* in favour of your purpose.

XVII. If you see *rival nations* rejoicing at the prospect of your disunion with your provinces, and endeavouring to promote it; if they translate, publish, and applaud all the complaints of your discontented colonists, at the same time privately stimulating you to severer measures, let not that *alarm* or offend you. Why should it, since you all mean *the same thing?*

XVIII. If any colony should at their own charge erect a fortress to secure their port against the fleets of a foreign enemy, get your Governor to betray that fortress into your hands. Never think of paying what it costs the country, for that would look, at least, like some regard for justice; but turn it into a citadel to awe the inhabitants and curb their commerce. If they should have lodged in such fortress the very arms they bought and used to aid you in your conquests, seize them all; it will provoke like *ingratitude* added to *robbery.* One admirable effect of these operations will be, to discourage every other colony from erecting such defences, and so your enemies may more easily invade them; to the great disgrace of your government, and of course *the furtherance of your project.*

XIX. Send armies into their country under pretence of protecting the inhabitants; but, instead of garrisoning the forts on their frontiers with those troops, to prevent incursions, demolish those forts, and order the troops into the heart of the country, that the savages may be encouraged to attack the frontiers, and that the troops may be protected by the inhabitants. This will seem to proceed from your ill will or your ignorance, and contribute farther to produce and strengthen an opinion among them, *that you are no longer fit to govern them.*

XX. Lastly, invest the General of your army in the provinces, with great and unconstitutional powers, and free him from the controul of even your own Civil Governors. Let him have troops enow under his command with all the fortresses in his possession; and who knows but (like some provincial Generals in the Roman empire, and encouraged by the universal discontent you have produced) he may take it into his head to set up for himself? If he should, and you have carefully practised these few *excellent rules* of mine, take my word for it, all the provinces will immediately join him; and you will that day (if you have not done it sooner) get rid of the trouble of governing them, and all the *plagues* attending their *commerce* and connection from henceforth and for ever.

Q. E. D.

☙ We may think of Benjamin Franklin as the solid politician and diplomatic representative of the Colonies in Europe, and as the utterer of succinct wisdom in his *Autobiography* and *Poor Richard's Almanac.* He had also his own sense of humor and of absurdity, which may be compared with the sharper wit of Addison and Swift. He was the son of a candle-maker, and was self-educated, a printer, an inventor, a statesman, one of the authors of the Declaration of Independence. His square American courtliness is reflected in his prose. Might Thoreau have written on this same idea?

On biography

FROM *The Rambler (1750)*
BY ***Samuel Johnson*** *(1709-1784)*

—Quid sit pulchrum,[1] *quid turpe, quid utile, quid non,*
Planius et melius Chrysippo[2] *et Crantore*[3] *dicit.*
—Hor. Ep. 1. 2. 4.

Whose works the beautiful and base contain,
Of vice and virtue more instructive rules
Than all the sober sages of the schools.
—Francis.

All joy or sorrow for the happiness or calamities of others is produced by an act of the imagination that realizes the event however fictitious, or approximates it however remote, by placing us, for a time, in the condition of him whose fortune we contemplate; so that we feel, while the deception lasts, whatever motions[4] would be excited by the same good or evil happening to ourselves.

Our passions are therefore more strongly moved, in proportion as we can more readily adopt the pains or pleasure proposed to our minds, by recognising them as once our own, or considering them

[1] What may be beautiful, what base, what useful, what not, he states more plainly and better than Chrysippus and Crantor

[2] eminent Greek Stoic philosopher (280-207 B.C.), inventor of the logical argument called *sorites*

[3] philosopher of the Old Academy (about 325 B.C.), first commentator on Plato

[4] emotions, movements of feeling

as naturally incident to our state of life. It is not easy for the most artful writer to give us an interest in happiness or misery which we think ourselves never likely to feel, and with which we have never yet been made acquainted. Histories of the downfall of kingdoms, and revolutions of empires, are read with great tranquility; the imperial tragedy pleases common auditors[5] only by its pomp of ornament, and grandeur of ideas; and the man whose faculties have been engrossed by business, and whose heart never fluttered but at the rise or fall of the stocks, wonders how the attention can be seized, or the affection agitated, by a tale of love.

Those parallel circumstances and kindred images to which we readily conform our minds are, above all other writings, to be found in narratives of the lives of particular persons; and therefore no species of writing seems more worthy of cultivation than biography, since none can be more delightful or more useful, none can more certainly enchain the heart by irresistible interest, or more widely diffuse instruction to every diversity of condition.[6]

The general and rapid narratives of history, which involve a thousand fortunes in the business of a day, and complicate[7] innumerable incidents in one great transaction, afford few lessons applicable to private life, which derives its comforts and its wretchedness from the right or wrong management of things, which nothing but their frequency makes considerable—"Parva si non fiant quotidie,"[8] says Pliny—and which can have no place in those relations which never descend below the consultation of senates, the motions of armies, and the schemes of conspirators.

I have often thought that there has rarely passed a life of which a judicious and faithful narrative would not be useful. For, not only every man has, in the mighty mass of the world, great numbers in the same condition with himself, to whom his mistakes and miscarriages, escapes and expedients, would be of immediate and apparent use; but there is such an uniformity in the state of man, considered apart from adventitious[9] and separable decorations[10] and disguises, that there is scarce any possibility of good or ill, but is common to human kind. A great part of the time of those who are

[5] members of an audience [6] all sorts or classes of persons
[7] twist together, combine [8] negligible if they were not done every day
[9] not essential, casual [10] such as marks of honor, outward things

placed at the greatest distance by fortune, or by temper, must unavoidably pass in the same manner; and though, when the claims of nature are satisfied, caprice, and vanity, and accident, begin to produce discriminations[11] and peculiarities, yet the eye is not very heedful or quick which cannot discover the same causes still terminating their influence in the same effects, though sometimes accelerated, sometimes retarded, or perplexed[12] by multiplied combinations. We are all prompted by the same motives, all deceived by the same fallacies, all animated by hope, obstructed by danger, entangled by desire, and seduced by pleasure.

It is frequently objected to relations of particular lives, that they are not distinguished by any striking or wonderful vicissitudes. The scholar who passed his life among his books, the merchant who conducted only his own affairs, the priest whose sphere of action was not extended beyond that of his duty, are considered as no proper objects of public regard, however they might have excelled in their several[13] stations, whatever might have been their learning, integrity, and piety. But this notion arises from false measures[14] of excellence and dignity, and must be eradicated by considering that, in the esteem of uncorrupted reason, what is of most use is of most value.

It is, indeed, not improper to take honest advantages of prejudice,[15] and to gain attention by a celebrated name; but the business of the biographer is often to pass slightly over those performances and incidents which produce vulgar[16] greatness, to lead the thoughts into domestic privacies, and display the minute details of daily life, where exterior appendages are cast aside, and men excell each other only by prudence and by virtue. The account of Thuanus[17] is, with great propriety, said by its author to have been written that it might lay open to posterity the private and familiar character of that man, "cujus ingenium et candorem ex ipsius scriptis sunt olim semper miraturi" – "whose candour and genius will to the end of time be by his writings preserved in admiration."

There are many invisible circumstances which, whether we read

[11] distinguishing marks [12] made intricate or complicated

[13] individual, separate [14] ways of measuring

[15] judgment made beforehand; used without negative overtones [16] popular

[17] Jacques Auguste de Thou (1553-1617) French historian and statesman

as inquirers after natural or moral knowledge, whether we intend to enlarge our science,[18] or increase our virtue, are more important than public occurrences. Thus Sallust,[19] the great master of nature, has not forgot, in his account of Catiline,[20] to remark that "his walk was now quick, and again slow," as an indication of a mind revolving something with violent commotion. Thus the story of Melancthon[21] affords a striking lecture[22] on the value of time, by informing us that, when he made an appointment, he expected not only the hour, but the minute to be fixed, that the day might not run out in the idleness of suspense; and all the plans and enterprises of De Witt[23] are now of less importance to the world, than that part of his personal character which represents him as "careful of his health, and negligent of his life."

But biography has often been allotted to writers who seem very little acquainted with the nature of their task, or very negligent about the performance. They rarely afford any other account than might be collected from public papers, but imagine themselves writing a life when they exhibit a chronological series of actions or preferments;[24] and so little regard the manners or behaviour of their heroes, that more knowledge may be gained of a man's real character, by a short conversation with one of his servants, than from a formal and studied narrative, begun with his pedigree, and ended with his funeral.

If now and then they condescend to inform the world of particular facts, they are not always so happy as to select the most important. I know not well what advantage posterity can receive from the only circumstance by which Tickell[25] has distinguished Addison[26] from the rest of mankind, "the irregularity of his pulse"; nor can I think myself overpaid for the time spent in reading the life of Malherb[27] by being enabled to relate after the learned biographer, that Malherb had two predominant opinions: one, that the loose-

[18] knowledge [19] Caius Sallustius Crispus (c. 84-34 B.C.), Roman historian
[20] Lucius Sergius Catiline (c. 108-62 B.C.), Roman politician and conspirator
[21] religious reformer, *cf.* "Melancthon and Calvin" below [22] lesson or example
[23] Jan De Witt (1625-1672), murdered Dutch statesman
[24] advancement in position or status in life
[25] Thomas Tickell (1686-1740), English poet and elegist of Addison
[26] writer and statesman, *cf.* "Academy for French Diplomats" above
[27] Francois de Malherbe (1555-1628), celebrated French poet

ness of a single woman might destroy all her boast of ancient descent; the other, that the French beggars made use very improperly and barbarously of the phrase "noble gentleman," because either word included the sense of both.

There are, indeed, some natural reasons why these narratives are often written by such as were not likely to give much instruction or delight, and why most accounts of particular persons are barren and useless. If a life be delayed till interest and envy are at an end, we may hope for impartiality, but must expect little intelligence; for the incidents which give excellence to biography are of a volatile and evanescent kind, such as soon escape the memory, and are rarely transmitted by tradition. We know how few can portray a living acquaintance, except by his most prominent and observable particularities, and the grosser features of his mind; and it may be easily imagined how much of this little knowledge may be lost in imparting it, and how soon a succession of copies will lose all resemblance of the original.

If the biographer writes from personal knowledge, and makes haste to gratify the public curiosity, there is danger lest his interest, his fear, his gratitude, or his tenderness, overpower his fidelity, and tempt him to conceal, if not to invent. There are many who think it an act of piety to hide the faults or failings of their friends, even when they can no longer suffer by their detection; we therefore see whole ranks of characters adorned with uniform panegyric, and not to be known from one another, but by extrinsic and casual circumstances. "Let me remember," says Hale, "when I find myself inclined to pity a criminal, that there is likewise a pity due to the country." If we owe regard to the memory of the dead, there is yet more respect to be paid to knowledge, to virtue, and to truth.

Samuel Johnson was the son of a bookseller of Lichfield. After a few months at Oxford, poverty took him through a variety of work to a post as writer for the *Gentleman's Magazine* in London, to which he contributed biographies and discussions of political debates. In 1750 he started his own semi-weekly periodical, *The Rambler,* and then continued his dictionary, and his edition of Shakespeare. He is well known for his *Lives of the Poets, Rasselas,* and "The Vanity of Human Wishes." Noted friends were Garrick, Reynolds, Burke, Goldsmith, and Boswell who wrote his *Life,* with somewhat different principles of biography.

On tragedy

FROM *Four Dissertations (1757)*

BY *David Hume (1711-1776)*

It seems an unaccountable pleasure which the spectators of a well-written tragedy receive from sorrow, terror, anxiety, and other passions that are in themselves disagreeable and uneasy. The more they are touched and affected, the more are they delighted with the spectacle; and as soon as the uneasy passions cease to operate, the piece is at an end. One scene of full joy and contentment and security is the utmost that any composition of this kind can bear; and it is sure always to be the concluding one. If in the texture of the piece there be interwoven any scenes of satisfaction, they afford only faint gleams of pleasure, which are thrown in by way of variety, and in order to plunge the actors into deeper distress by means of that contrast and disappointment. The whole art of the poet is employed in rousing and supporting the compassion and indignation, the anxiety and resentment, of his audience. They are pleased in proportion as they are afflicted and never are so happy as when they employ tears, sobs, and cries, to give vent to their sorrow, and relieve their heart, swoln with the tenderest sympathy and compassion.

The few critics who have had some tincture of philosophy have remarked this singular phenomenon, and have endeavoured to account for it.

L'Abbe Dubos,[1] in his *Reflections on Poetry and Painting,* asserts,

[1]Jean Baptiste Dubos (1670-1740), French critic, also historian and diplomat

that nothing is in general so disagreeable to the mind as the languid, listless state of indolence into which it falls upon the removal of all passion and occupation. To get rid of this painful situation, it seeks every amusement and pursuit; business, gaming, shows, executions; whatever will rouse the passions and take its attention from itself. No matter what the passion is; let it be disagreeable, afflicting, melancholy, disordered; it is still better than that insipid languor which arises from perfect tranquility and repose.

It is impossible not to admit this account as being, at least in part, satisfactory. You may observe, when there are several tables of gaming, that all the company run to those where the deepest play is, even though they find not there the best players. The view, or, at least, imagination of high passions, arising from great loss or gain, affects the spectator by sympathy, gives him some touches of the same passions, and serves him for a momentary entertainment. It makes the time pass the easier with him, and is some relief to that oppression under which men commonly labour when left entirely to their own thoughts and meditations.

We find that common liars always magnify, in their narrations, all kinds of danger, pain, distress, sickness, deaths, murders, and cruelties, as well as joy, beauty, mirth, and magnificence. It is an absurd secret which they have for pleasing their company, fixing their attention, and attaching them to such marvellous relation by the passions and emotions which they excite.

There is, however, a difficulty in applying to the present subject, in its full extent, this solution, however ingenious and satisfactory it may appear. It is certain that the same object of distress, which pleases in a tragedy, were it really set before us, would give the most unfeigned uneasiness, though it be then the most effectual cure to languor and indolence. Monsieur Fontenelle[2] seems to have been sensible of this difficulty, and accordingly attempts another solution of the phenomenon, at least makes some addition to the theory above mentioned:

"Pleasure and pain," says he, "which are two sentiments so different in themselves, differ not so much in their cause. From the

[2]Bernard le Bovier de Fontenelle (1657-1757), French advocate, philosopher, poet, and writer

instance of tickling it appears, that the movement of pleasure, pushed a little too far, becomes pain, and that the movement of pain, a little moderate, becomes pleasure. Hence it proceeds, that there is such a thing as a sorrow, soft and agreeable: it is a pain weakened and diminished. The heart likes naturally to be moved and affected. Melancholy objects suit it, and even disastrous and sorrowful, provided they are softened by some circumstance. It is certain, that, on the theatre, the representation has almost the effect of reality; yet it has not altogether that effect. However we may be hurried away by the spectacle, whatever dominion the senses and imagination may usurp over the reason, there still lurks at the bottom a certain idea of falsehood in the whole of what we see. This idea, though weak and disguised, suffices to diminish the pain which we suffer from the misfortunes of those whom we love, and to reduce that affliction to such a pitch as converts it into a pleasure. We weep for the misfortune of a hero to whom we are attached. In the same instant we comfort ourselves by reflecting, that it is nothing but a fiction: and it is precisely that mixture of sentiments which composes an agreeable sorrow, and tears that delight us. But as that affliction which is caused by exterior and sensible objects is stronger than the consolation which arises from an internal reflection, they are the effects and symptoms of sorrow that ought to predominate in the composition."

This solution seems just and convincing: but perhaps it wants still some new addition, in order to make it answer fully the phenomenon which we here examine. All the passions, excited by eloquence, are agreeable in the highest degree, as well as those which are moved by painting and the theatre. The Epilogues of Cicero[3] are, on this account chiefly, the delight of every reader of taste; and it is difficult to read some of them without the deepest sympathy and sorrow. His merit as an orator, no doubt, depends much on his success in this particular. When he had raised tears in his judges and all his audience, they were then the most highly delighted, and expressed the greatest satisfaction with the pleader. The pathetic[4]

[3] Marcus Tullius Cicero (106-43 B.C.), famous orator, philosopher, and statesman of the Latin Golden Age [4] arousing pathos or sorrow

description of the butchery made by Verres[5] of the Sicilian captains, is a masterpiece of this kind; but I believe none will affirm, that the being present at a melancholy scene of that nature would afford any entertainment. Neither is the sorrow here softened by fiction; for the audience were convinced of the reality of every circumstance. What is it then which in this case raises a pleasure from the bosom of uneasiness, so to speak, and a pleasure which still retains all the features and outward symptoms of distress and sorrow?

I answer: this extraordinary effect proceeds from that very eloquence with which the melancholy scene is represented. The genius required to paint objects in a lively manner, the art employed in collecting all the pathetic circumstances, the judgment displayed in disposing them; the exercise, I say, of these noble talents, together with the force of expression, and beauty of oratorial[6] numbers,[7] diffuse the highest satisfaction on the audience, and excite the most delightful movements. By this means, the uneasiness of the melancholy passions is not only overpowered and effaced by something stronger of an opposite kind, but the whole impulse of those passions is converted into pleasure, and swells the delight which the eloquence raises in us. The same force of oratory, employed on an uninteresting subject, would not please half so much, or rather would appear altogether ridiculous; and the mind, being left in absolute calmness and indifference, would relish none of those beauties of imagination or expression, which, if joined to passion, give it such exquisite entertainment. The impulse or vehemence arising from sorrow, compassion, indignation, receives a new direction from the sentiments of beauty. The latter, being the predominant emotion, seize the whole mind, and convert the former into themselves, at least tincture them so strongly as totally to alter their nature. And the soul being at the same time roused by passion and charmed by eloquence, feels on the whole a strong movement, which is altogether delightful.

[5]Caius Verres (d. 43 B.C.), as governor plundered Sicily in addition to crimes cited here, went into voluntary exile after his trial at which Cicero was prosecuting attorney [6]pertaining to an orator or oratory [7]rhythm

The same principle takes place in tragedy; with this addition, that tragedy is an imitation, and imitation is always of itself agreeable. This circumstance serves still further to smooth the motions of passion, and convert the whole feeling into one uniform and strong enjoyment. Objects of the greatest terror and distress please in painting, and please more than the most beautiful objects that appear calm and indifferent.* The affection, rousing the mind, excites a large stock of spirit and vehemence; which is all transformed into pleasure by the force of the prevailing movement. It is thus the fiction of tragedy softens the passion, by an infusion of a new feeling, not merely by weakening or diminishing the sorrow. You may by degrees weaken a real sorrow, till it totally disappears; yet in none of its gradations will it ever give pleasure; except, perhaps, by accident, to a man sunk under lethargic indolence, whom it rouses from that languid state.

To confirm this theory, it will be sufficient to produce other instances, where the subordinate movement is converted into the predominant, and gives force to it, though of a different, and even sometimes though of a contrary nature.

Novelty naturally rouses the mind, and attracts our attention; and the movements which it causes are always converted into any passion belonging to the object, and join their force to it. Whether an event excite joy or sorrow, pride or shame, anger or good-will, it is sure to produce a stronger affection, when new or unusual. And though novelty of itself be agreeable, it fortifies the painful, as well as agreeable passions.

Had you any intention to move a person extremely by the narration of any event, the best method of increasing its effect would be artfully to delay informing him of it, and first to excite his curiosity and impatience before you let him into the secret. This is the artifice practiced by Iago in the famous scene of Shakespeare; and every spectator is sensible that Othello's jealousy acquires additional force from his preceding impatience, and that the subordinate passion is here readily transformed into the predominant one.

Difficulties increase passions of every kind; and by rousing our attention and exciting our active powers, they produce an emotion which nourishes the prevailing affection.

Parents commonly love that child most whose sickly infirm frame of body has occasioned them the greatest pains, trouble, and anxiety, in rearing him. The agreeable sentiment of affection here acquires force from sentiments of uneasiness.

Nothing endears so much a friend as sorrow for his death. The pleasure of his company has not so powerful an influence.

Jealousy is a painful passion; yet without some share of it, the agreeable affection of love has difficulty to subsist in its full force and violence. Absence is also a great source of complaint among lovers, and gives them the greatest uneasiness: yet nothing is more favourable to their mutual passion than short intervals of that kind. And if long intervals often prove fatal, it is only because, through time, men are accustomed to them, and they cease to give uneasiness. Jealousy and absence in love compose the *dolce peccante*[8] of the Italians, which they suppose so essential to all pleasure.

There is a fine observation of the elder Pliny, which illustrates the principle here insisted on: "It is very remarkable," says he, "that the last works of celebrated artists, which they left imperfect, are always the most prized, such as the IRIS of Aristides, the TYNDARIDES of Nicomachus, the MEDEA of Timomachus, and the VENUS of Apelles. These are valued even above their finished productions. The broken lineaments of the piece, and the half-formed idea of the painter, are carefully studied; and our very grief for that curious hand, which had been stopped by death, is an additional increase to our pleasure."

These instances (and many more might be collected) are sufficient to afford us some insight into the analogy of nature, and to show us, that the pleasure which poets, orators, and musicians give us, by exciting grief, sorrow, indignation, compassion, is not so extraordinary or paradoxical as it may at first sight appear. The force of imagination, the energy of expression, the power of numbers, the charms of imitation; all these are naturally, of themselves, delightful to the mind: and when the object presented lays also hold of some affection, the pleasure still rises upon us, by the conversion of this subordinate movement into that which is predominant. The passion, though perhaps naturally, and when excited by the simple appearance of a real object, it may be painful; yet is so

[8] sweet sinning

smoothed, and softened, and mollified, when raised by the finer arts, that it affords the highest entertainment.

To confirm this reasoning, we may observe, that if the movements of the imagination be not predominant above those of the passion, a contrary effect follows; and the former, being now subordinate, is converted into the latter, and still further increases the pain and affliction of the sufferer.

Who could ever think of it as a good expedient for comforting an afflicted parent, to exaggerate, with all the force of elocution, the irreparable loss which he has met with by the death of a favorite child? The more power of imagination and expression you here employ, the more you increase his despair and affliction.

The shame, confusion, and terror of Verres, no doubt, rose in proportion to the noble eloquence and vehemence of Cicero: so also did his pain and uneasiness. These former passions were too strong for the pleasure arising from the beauties of elocution; and operated, though from the same principle, yet in a contrary manner, to the sympathy, compassion, and indignation of the audience.

Lord Clarendon,[9] when he approaches towards the catastrophe of the royal party, supposes that his narration must then become infinitely disagreeable; and he hurries over the king's death without giving us one circumstance of it. He considers it as too horrid a scene to be contemplated with any satisfaction, or even without the utmost pain and aversion. He himself, as well as the readers of that age, were too deeply concerned in the events, and felt a pain from subjects which an historian and a reader of another age would regard as the most pathetic and most interesting, and, by consequence, the most agreeable.

An action, represented in tragedy, may be too bloody and atrocious. It may excite such movements of horror as will not soften into pleasure; and the greatest energy of expression, bestowed on descriptions of that nature, serves only to augment our uneasiness. Such is that action represented in the *Ambitious Step-mother,*[10] where a venerable old man, raised to the height of fury and despair, rushes against a pillar, and striking his head upon it, besmears it all

[9] Edward Hyde, Earl of . . . , a chief adviser to Charles I (who died by execution in 1649), statesman and historian

[10] by Nicholas Rowe, English playwright (1674-1718)

over with mingled brains and gore. The English theatre abounds too much with such shocking images.

Even the common sentiments of compassion require to be softened by some agreeable affection,[11] in order to give a thorough satisfaction to the audience. The mere suffering of plaintive virtue, under the triumphant tyranny and oppression of vice, forms a disagreeable spectacle, and is carefully avoided by all masters of the drama. In order to dismiss the audience with entire satisfaction and contentment, the virtue must either convert itself into a noble courageous despair, or the vice receive its proper punishment.

Most painters appear in this light to have been very unhappy in their subjects. As they wrought much for churches and convents, they have chiefly represented such horrible subjects as crucifixions and martyrdoms, where nothing appears but tortures, wounds, executions, and passive suffering, without any action or affection. When they turned their pencil from this ghastly mythology, they had commonly recourse to Ovid, whose fictions, though passionate and agreeable, are scarcely natural or probable enough for painting.

The same inversion of that principle which is here insisted on, displays itself in common life, as in the effects of oratory and poetry. Raise so the subordinate passion that it becomes the predominant, it swallows up that affection which it before nourished and increased. Too much jealousy extinguishes love; too much difficulty renders us indifferent; too much sickness and infirmity disgusts a selfish and unkind parent.

What so disagreeable as the dismal, gloomy, disastrous stories, with which melancholy people entertain their companions? The uneasy passion being there raised alone, unaccompanied with any spirit, genius, or eloquence, conveys a pure uneasiness, and is attended with nothing that can soften it into pleasure or satisfaction.

[11] state of mind or feeling

☙ The Scot David Hume wrote sceptical philosophical essays on human nature, morals, history, politics, and religion which were influential in France as well as in the British Isles. He was a friend of Rousseau and Adam Smith, a political secretary, and undersecretary of state before his retirement to Edinburgh. *On Tragedy* is the third of *Four Dissertations,* published in 1757.

Santayana's view of tragedy suggests a different attitude.

The greatness of Rome

FROM *The Decline and Fall of the Roman Empire (1781)*
BY **Edward Gibbon** *(1737-1794)*

The greatness of Rome (such is the language of the historian) was founded on the rare and almost incredible alliance of virtue and of fortune. The long period of her infancy was employed in a laborious struggle against the tribes of Italy, the neighbours and enemies of the rising city. In the strength and ardour of youth she sustained the storms of war, carried her victorious arms beyond the seas and the mountains, and brought home triumphal laurels from every country of the globe. At length, verging towards old age, and sometimes conquering by the terror only of her name, she sought the blessings of ease and tranquillity. The VENERABLE CITY, which had trampled on the necks of the fiercest nations, and established a system of laws, the perpetual guardians of justice and freedom, was content, like a wise and wealthy parent, to devolve on[1] the Caesars, her favourite sons, the care of governing her ample patrimony. A secure and profound peace, such as had been once enjoyed in the reign of Numa,[2] succeeded to[3] the tumults of a republic; while Rome was still adored as the queen of the earth, and the subject nations still reverenced the name of the people and the majesty of

[1] pass on to
[2] Numa Pompilius (715-672 B.C.), second (legendary) king of Rome
[3] followed

the senate. But this native splendour (continues Ammianus)[4] is degraded and sullied by the conduct of some nobles, who, unmindful of their own dignity and of that of their country, assume an unbounded license of vice and folly. They contend with each other in the empty vanity of titles and surnames, and curiously select or invent the most lofty and sonorous appellations—Reburrus or Fabunius, Pagonius or Tarrasius—which may impress the ears of the vulgar with astonishment and respect. From a vain ambition of perpetuating their memory, they affect to multiply their likeness in statues of bronze and marble; nor are they satisfied unless those statues are covered with plates of gold; an honourable distinction, first granted to Acilius the consul, after he had subdued by his arms and counsels the power of king Antiochus.[5] The ostentation of displaying, of magnifying perhaps, the rent-roll[6] of the estates which they possess in all the provinces, from the rising to the setting sun, provokes the just resentment of every man who recollects that their poor and invincible ancestors were not distinguished from the meanest of the soldiers by the delicacy of their food or the splendour of their apparel. But the modern nobles measure their rank and consequence according to the loftiness of their chariots, and the weighty magnificence of their dress. Their long robes of silk and purple[7] float in the wind; and as they are agitated, by art or accident, they occasionally discover[8] the under garments, the rich tunics, embroidered with the figures of various animals. Followed by a train of fifty servants, and tearing up the pavement, they move along the streets with the same impetuous speed as if they travelled with post-horses; and the example of the senators is boldly imitated by the matrons and ladies, whose covered carriages are continually driving round the immense space of the city and suburbs. Whenever these persons of high distinction condescend to visit the public baths, they assume, on their entrance, a tone of loud and insolent command, and appropriate to their own use the conveniences which were designed for the Roman people. If, in these

[4] Marcellinus Ammianus (c. 325-392 A.D.), last Roman historian of importance

[5] Antiochus III of Syria (c. 241-287 B.C.), called "the Great," fought the Romans

[6] register of lands and other property, with rents due from them; the sum of one's income from rents

[7] a color traditionally denoting high rank

[8] reveal, show

places of mixed and general resort,[9] they meet any of the infamous ministers of their pleasures, they express their affection by a tender embrace, while they proudly decline the salutations of their fellow-citizens, who are not permitted to aspire above the honour of kissing their hands or their knees. As soon as they have indulged themselves in the refreshment of the bath, they resume their rings and the other ensigns[10] of their dignity, select from their private wardrobe of the finest linen, such as might suffice for a dozen persons, the garments the most agreeable to their fancy, and maintain till their departure the same haughty demeanour, which perhaps might have been excused in the great Marcellus[11] after the conquest of Syracuse.[12] Sometimes indeed these heroes undertake more arduous achievements: they visit their estates in Italy, and procure themselves, by the toil of servile hands, the amusements of the chase. If at any time, but more especially on a hot day, they have courage to sail in their painted galleys from the Lucrine[13] lake to their elegant villas on the sea-coast of Puteoli[14] and Caieta,[15] they compare their own expeditions to the marches of Caesar[16] and Alexander.[17] Yet should a fly presume to settle on the silken folds of their gilded umbrellas, should a sunbeam penetrate through some unguarded and imperceptible chink, they deplore their intolerable hardships, and lament in affected language that they were not born in the land of the Cimmerians,[18] the regions of eternal darkness. In these journeys into the country the whole body of the household marches with their master. In the same manner as the cavalry and infantry, the heavy and the light armed troops, the advanced guard and the rear, are marshalled by the skill of their

[9] frequented by people of varying classes

[10] marks

[11] Marcus Claudius Marcellus (c. 268-208 B.C.), Roman general in the second Punic War

[12] a seaport in Southeast Sicily, where an ancient city was founded by the Carthaginians, and conquered by Marcellus in 212 B.C.

[13] a lake of Campania, Italy

[14] Pazzuoli, an ancient town of Campania

[15] Caiazzo, another ancient city of Campania; the total journey from the Lucrine to either Pazzouli or Caiazzo is quite slight

[16] Gaius Julius Caesar (c. 100-44 B.C.), Roman general, statesman, and historian, who led the armies of Rome to expansions of empire

[17] Alexander III of Macedon (356-323 B.C.), called "the Great," expanded the Greek empire

[18] a mythical western people said by Homer to dwell in perpetual darkness

military leaders, so the domestic officers, who bear a rod as an ensign of authority, distribute and arrange the numerous train of slaves and attendants. The baggage and wardrobe move in the front, and are immediately followed by a multitude of cooks and inferior ministers[19] employed in the service of the kitchens and of the table. The main body is composed of a promiscuous[20] crowd of slaves, increased by the accidental concourse of idle or dependent plebeians. The rear is closed by the favourite band of eunuchs, distributed from age to youth, according to the order of seniority. Their numbers and their deformity excite the horror of the indignant spectators, who are ready to execrate[21] the memory of Semiramis[22] for the cruel art which she invented of frustrating the purposes of nature, and of blasting in the bud the hopes of future generations. In the exercise of domestic jurisdiction the nobles of Rome express an exquisite sensibility for any personal injury, and a contemptuous indifference for the rest of the human species. When they have called for warm water, if a slave has been tardy in his obedience, he is instantly chastised with three hundred lashes; but should the same slave commit a wilful murder, the master will mildly observe that he is a worthless fellow, but that if he repeats the offence he shall not escape punishment. Hospitality was formerly the virtue of the Romans; and every stranger who could plead either merit or misfortune was relieved or rewarded by their generosity. At present, if a foreigner, perhaps of no contemptible rank, is introduced to one of the proud and wealthy senators, he is welcomed indeed in the first audience with such warm professions and such kind inquiries, that he retires enchanted with the affability of his illustrious friend, and full of regret that he had so long delayed his journey to Rome, the native seat of manners as well as of empire. Secure of a favourable reception, he repeats his visit the ensuing day, and is mortified by the discovery that his person, his name, and his country are already forgotten. If he still has resolution to persevere, he is gradually numbered in the train of dependents, and obtains the permission to pay his assiduous and unprofitable court to a haughty

[19] those who minister to the needs of others, servants

[20] indiscriminately mixed

[21] curse

[22] a famous Assyrian princess (c. 800 B.C.), whom legends credit with surpassing beauty, wisdom, or cruelty

patron, incapable of gratitude or friendship, who scarcely deigns to remark his presence, his departure, or his return. Whenever the rich prepare a solemn and popular entertainment, whenever they celebrate with profuse and pernicious luxury their private banquets, the choice of the guests is the subject of anxious deliberation. The modest, the sober, and the learned are seldom preferred;[23] and the nomenclators,[24] who are commonly swayed by interested motives, have the address to insert in the list of invitations the obscure names of the most worthless of mankind. But the frequent and familiar companions of the great are those parasites who practice the most useful of all arts, the art of flattery; who eagerly applaud each word and every action of their immortal patron; gaze with rapture on his marble columns and variegated pavements, and strenuously praise the pomp and elegance which he is taught to consider as a part of his personal merit. At the Roman tables the birds, the *squirrels,* or the fish, which appear of an uncommon size, are contemplated with curious attention; a pair of scales is accurately applied to ascertain their real weight; and, while the more rational guests are disgusted by the vain and tedious repetition, notaries are summoned to attest by an authentic record the truth of such a marvellous event. Another method of introduction into the houses and society of the great is derived from the profession of gaming, or as it is more politely styled, of play. The confederates are united by a strict and indissoluble bond of friendship, or rather of conspiracy; a superior degree of skill in the *Tesserarian* art (which may be interpreted the game of dice and tables) is a sure road to wealth and reputation. A master of that sublime science, who in a supper or assembly is placed below a magistrate, displays in his countenance the surprise and indignation which Cato[25] might be supposed to feel when he was refused the praetorship[26] by the votes of a capricious people. The acquisition of knowledge seldom engages the curiosity of the nobles, who abhor the fatigue and disdain the advantages of study; and the only books which they

[23] chosen, as a recognition of deserts

[24] ushers who assigned places at banquets

[25] Marcus Porcius Cato (95-46 B.C.), namesake and great grandson of Cato the Elder, philosopher and soldier; became praetor

[26] office of magistrate for the administration of justice

peruse are the Satires of Juvenal,[27] and the verbose and fabulous histories of Marius Maximus. The libraries which they have inherited from their fathers are secluded, like dreary sepulchres, from the light of day. But the costly instruments of the theatre, flutes, and enormous lyres, and hydraulic organs, are constructed for their use; and the harmony of vocal and instrumental music is incessantly repeated in the palaces of Rome. In those palaces sound is preferred to sense, and the care of the body to that of the mind. It is allowed as a salutary maxim, that the light and frivolous suspicion of a contagious malady is of sufficient weight to excuse the visits of the most intimate friends; and even the servants who are despatched to make the decent inquiries are not suffered to return home till they have undergone the ceremony of a previous ablution. Yet this selfish and unmanly delicacy occasionally yields to the more imperious passion of avarice. The prospect of gain will urge a rich and gouty senator as far as Spoleto;[28] every sentiment of arrogance and dignity is subdued by the hopes of an inheritance, or even of a legacy; and a wealthy childless citizen is the most powerful of the Romans. The art of obtaining the signature of a favourable testament, and sometimes of hastening the moment of its execution, is perfectly understood; and it has happened that in the same house, though in different apartments, a husband and a wife, with the laudable design of overreaching each other, have summoned their respective lawyers, to declare at the same time their mutual but contradictory intentions. The distress which follows and chastises extravagant luxury often reduces the great to the use of the most humiliating expedients. When they desire to borrow, they employ the base and supplicating style of the slave in the comedy; but when they are called upon to pay, they assume the royal and tragic declamation of the grandsons of Hercules. If the demand is repeated, they readily procure some trusty sycophant,[29] instructed to maintain a charge of poison, or magic, against the insolent creditor, who is seldom released from prison till he has signed a discharge of the whole debt. These vices, which degrade the moral character of the

[27] Decimus Junius Juvenalis (c. 60 - c. 140 A.D.), satirical poet

[28] a town in the province of Perugia, Italy, about ninety miles from Rome

[29] abject flatterer

Romans, are mixed with a puerile superstition that disgraces their understanding. They listen with confidence to the prediction of haruspices,[30] who pretend to read in the entrails of victims the signs of future greatness and prosperity; and there are many who do not presume either to bathe or to die, or to appear in public, till they have diligently consulted, according to the rules of astrology, the situation of Mercury and the aspect of the moon. It is singular enough that this vain credulity may often be discovered among the profane sceptics who impiously doubt or deny the existence of a celestial power.

In populous cities, which are the seat of commerce and manufactures, the middle ranks of inhabitants, who derive their subsistence from the dexterity or labour of their hands, are commonly the most prolific, the most useful, and, in that sense, the most respectable part of the community. But the plebeians of Rome, who disdained such sedentary and servile arts, had been oppressed from the earliest times by the weight of debt and usury, and the husbandman, during the term of his military service, was obliged to abandon the cultivation of his farm. The lands of Italy, which had been originally divided among the families of free and indigent proprietors, were insensibly purchased or usurped by the avarice of the nobles; and in the age which preceded the fall of the republic, it was computed that only two thousand citizens were possessed of any independent substance. Yet as long as the people bestowed by their suffrages the honours of the state, the command of the legions, and the administration of wealthy provinces, their conscious pride alleviated in some measure the hardships of poverty; and their wants were seasonably supplied by the ambitious liberality of the candidates, who aspired to secure a venal[31] majority in the thirty-five tribes, or the hundred and ninety-three centuries,[32] of Rome. But when the prodigal commons had imprudently alienated not only the *use,* but the *inheritance,* of power, they sunk, under the reign of the Caesars, into a vile and wretched populace, which must, in a few generations, have been totally extinguished, if it had not been continually recruited by the manumission[33] of slaves and the influx of strangers.

[30] plural of haruspex, minor priests who practiced divination, especially from entrails [31] corruptly mercenary [32] political divisions for voting

[33] setting free

As early as the time of Hadrian[34] it was the just complaint of the ingenuous natives that the capital had attracted the vices of the universe and the manners of the most opposite nations. The intemperance of the Gauls, the cunning and levity of the Greeks, the savage obstinacy of the Egyptians and Jews, the servile temper of the Asiatics, and the dissolute, effeminate prostitution of the Syrians, were mingled in the various multitude, which, under the proud and false denomination of Romans, presumed to despise their fellow-subjects, and even their sovereigns, who dwelt beyond the precincts of the ETERNAL CITY.

Yet the name of that city was still pronounced with respect: the frequent and capricious tumults of its inhabitants were indulged with impunity; and the successors of Constantine,[35] instead of crushing the last remains of the democracy by the strong arm of military power, embraced the mild policy of Augustus,[36] and studied to relieve the poverty and to amuse the idleness of an innumerable people. I. For the convenience of the lazy plebeians, the monthly distributions of corn were converted into a daily allowance of bread; a great number of ovens were constructed and maintained at the public expense; and at the appointed hour, each citizen, who was furnished with a ticket, ascended the flight of steps which had been assigned to his peculiar quarter or division, and received, either as a gift or at a very low price, a loaf of bread of the weight of three pounds for the use of his family. II. The forests of Lucania,[37] whose acorns fattened large droves of wild hogs, afforded, as a species of tribute, a plentiful supply of cheap and wholesome meat. During five months of the year a regular allowance of bacon was distributed to the poorer citizens; and the annual consumption of the capital, at a time when it was much declined from its former lustre, was ascertained, by an edict of Valentinian the Third,[38] at three millions six hundred and twenty-eight thousand pounds. III. In the manners of antiquity the use of oil was indispensable for the lamp as well as for the bath, and the annual tax which was imposed

[34] 76-138 A.D., Roman emperor 117-138

[35] called "the Great," 288?-337 A.D., Roman emperor 324-337

[36] Gaius Julius Caesar Octavianus, Augustus Caesar, 63 B.C. - 14 A.D., first Roman emperor, 27 B.C. - 14 A.D., reformer, patron of arts

[37] an ancient region in southern Italy, northwest of the Gulf of Taranto

[38] Roman emperor, lived from about 419-455 A.D.

on Africa for the benefit of Rome, amounted to the weight of three millions of pounds, to the measure, perhaps, of three hundred thousand English gallons. IV. The anxiety of Augustus to provide the metropolis with sufficient plenty of corn was not extended beyond that necessary article of human subsistence; and when the popular clamour accused the dearness and scarcity of wine, a proclamation was issued by the grave reformer to remind his subjects that no man could reasonably complain of thirst, since the aqueducts of Agrippa[39] had introduced into the city so many copious streams of pure and salubrious water. This rigid sobriety was insensibly relaxed; and, although the generous design of Aurelian[40] does not appear to have been executed in its full extent, the use of wine was allowed on very easy and liberal terms. The administration of the public cellars was delegated to a magistrate of honourable rank; and a considerable part of the vintage of Campania was reserved for the fortunate inhabitants of Rome.

The stupendous aqueducts, so justly celebrated by the praises of Augustus himself, replenished the *Thermoe,* or baths, which had been constructed in every part of the city with Imperial magnificence. The baths of Antoninus Caracalla, which were open, at stated hours, for the indiscriminate service of the senators and the people, contained above sixteen hundred seats of marble; and more than three thousand were reckoned in the baths of Diocletian. The walls of the lofty apartments were covered with curious mosaics, that imitated the art of the pencil in the elegance of design and the variety of colours. The Egyptian granite was beautifully encrusted with the precious green marble of Numidia; the perpetual stream of hot water was poured into the capacious basins through so many wide mouths of bright and massy silver; and the meanest Roman could purchase, with a small copper coin, the daily enjoyment of a scene of pomp and luxury which might excite the envy of the kings of Asia. From these stately palaces issued a swarm of dirty and ragged plebeians, without shoes and without a mantle; who loitered away whole days in the street or Forum to hear news and to hold disputes; who dissipated in extravagant gaming the

[39] Marcus Vipsanius Agrippa (63-12 B.C.), Roman, statesman, general, and engineer

[40] Lucius Domitius Aurelianus (c. 212-275 A.D.), Roman emperor 270-275

miserable pittance of their wives and children; and spent the hours of the night in obscure taverns and brothels in the indulgence of gross and vulgar sensuality.

But the most lively and splendid amusement of the idle multitude depended on the frequent exhibition of public games and spectacles. The piety of Christian princes had suppressed the inhuman combats of gladiators; but the Roman people still considered the Circus as their home, their temple, and the seat of the republic. The impatient crowd rushed at the dawn of day to secure their places, and there were many who passed a sleepless and anxious night in the adjacent porticos. From the morning to the evening, careless of the sun or of the rain, the spectators, who sometimes amounted to the number of four hundred thousand, remained in eager attention; their eyes fixed on the horses and charioteers, their minds agitated with hope and fear for the success of the *colours* which they espoused; and the happiness of Rome appeared to hang on the event of a race. The same immoderate ardour inspired their clamours and their applause as often as they were entertained with the hunting of wild beasts and the various modes of theatrical representation. These representations in modern capitals may deserve to be considered as a pure and elegant school of taste, and perhaps of virtue. But the Tragic and Comic Muse of the Romans, who seldom aspired beyond the imitation of Attic[41] genius, had been almost totally silent since the fall of the republic; and their place was unworthily occupied by licentious farce, effeminate music, and splendid pageantry. The pantomimes, who maintained their reputation from the age of Augustus to the sixth century, expressed, without the use of words, the various fables of the gods and heroes of antiquity; and the perfection of their art, which sometimes disarmed the gravity of the philosopher, always excited the applause and wonder of the people. The vast and magnificent theatres of Rome were filled by three thousand female dancers, and by three thousand singers, with the masters of the respective choruses. Such was the popular favour which they enjoyed, that, in a time of scarcity, when all strangers were banished from the city, the merit of contributing to the public pleasures exempted *them* from a law

[41] classical Greek

which was strictly executed against the professors[42] of the liberal arts.

It is said that the foolish curiosity of Elagabalus[43] attempted to discover, from the quantity of spiders' webs, the number of the inhabitants of Rome. A more rational method of inquiry might not have been undeserving of the attention of the wisest princes, who could easily have resolved a question so important for the Roman government and so interesting to succeeding ages. The births and deaths of the citizens were duly registered; and if any writer of antiquity had condescended to mention the annual amount, or the common average, we might now produce some satisfactory calculation which would destroy the extravagant assertions of critics, and perhaps confirm the modest and probable conjectures of philosophers. The most diligent researches have collected only the following circumstances, which, slight and imperfect as they are, may tend in some degree to illustrate the question of the populousness of ancient Rome. I. When the capital of the empire was besieged by the Goths,[44] the circuit of the walls was accurately measured by Ammonius, the mathematician, who found it equal to twenty-one miles. It should not be forgotten that the form of the city was almost that of a circle, the geometrical figure which is known to contain the largest space within any given circumference. II. The architect Vitruvius,[45] who flourished in the Augustan age, and whose evidence, on this occasion, has peculiar weight and authority, observes that the innumerable habitations of the Roman people would have spread themselves far beyond the narrow limits of the city; and that the want of ground, which was probably contracted on every side by gardens and villas, suggested the common, though inconvenient, practice of raising the houses to a considerable height in the air. But the loftiness of these buildings, which often consisted of hasty work and insufficient materials, was the cause of frequent and fatal accidents; and it was repeatedly enacted by Augustus, as

[42] those who profess or speak out their interest in support of something

[43] also Heliogabalus, c. 205-222 A.D., Roman emperor, 218-222

[44] Teutonic people who, in the 3rd to 5th centuries, invaded and settled in parts of the Roman Empire

[45] Marcus Vitruvius Pollio, Roman Architect, engineer, and author, lived in the first century, A.D.

well as by Nero,[46] that the height of private edifices within the walls of Rome should not exceed the measure of seventy feet from the ground. III. Juvenal laments, as it should seem from his own experience, the hardships of the poorer citizens, to whom he addresses the salutary advice of emigrating, without delay, from the smoke of Rome, since they might purchase in the little towns of Italy a cheerful, commodious dwelling at the same price which they annually paid for a dark and miserable lodging. House-rent was therefore immoderately dear: the rich acquired, at an enormous expense, the ground, which they covered with palaces and gardens; but the body of the Roman people was crowded into a narrow space; and the different floors and apartments of the same house were divided, as it is still the custom of Paris and other cities, among several families of plebeians. IV. The total number of houses in the fourteen regions of the city is accurately stated in the description of Rome composed under the reign of Theodosius,[47] and they amount to forty-eight thousand three hundred and eighty-two. The two classes of *domus*[48] and of *insulae,*[49] into which they are divided, include all the habitations of the capital, of every rank and condition, from the marble palaces of the Anicii, with a numerous establishment of freedmen and slaves, to the lofty and narrow lodging-house where the poet Codrus and his wife were permitted to hire a wretched garret immediately under the tiles. If we adopt the same average which, under similar circumstances, has been found applicable to Paris, and indifferently allow about twenty-five persons for each house, of every degree, we may fairly estimate the inhabitants of Rome at twelve hundred thousand; a number which cannot be thought excessive for the capital of a mighty empire, though it exceeds the populousness of the greatest cities of modern Europe.

Such was the state of Rome under the reign of Honorius,[50] at the time when the Gothic army formed the seige, or rather the blockade, of the city.

[46] 37-68 A.D., Roman emperor 54-68, notorious for his cruelty and corruption

[47] called "the Great," c. 346-395 A.D. emperor of the Eastern Roman Empire 379-395

[48] private residence

[49] houses for the poor, shared by several families

[50] Flavius Honorius 384-423 A.D. emperor of the Western Empire 395-423

At the age of thirty five, after years at Oxford and abroad, after "musing amid the ruins of the Capitol," Edward Gibbon settled down in London to write his epic history, *The Decline and Fall of the Roman Empire*—from Emperor Trajan to the subversion of the Empire; from Justinian to Charlemagne; and finally to the fall of Constantinople—the thirteen centuries of Christianity, the conquests of Germans and Mohammedans, and the Crusades.

Probably the best early prose in the European tradition was that of the Greek historians Herodotus and Thucydides and of the Roman Tacitus. Why was prose first well used in the writing of history?

Federalist Number X

FROM *The Federalist Papers (1787)*
BY *James Madison (1751-1836)*

Among the numerous advantages promised by a well constructed Union, none deserves to be more accurately developed than its tendency to break and control the violence of faction. The friend of popular governments, never finds himself so much alarmed for their character and fate, as when he contemplates their propensity to this dangerous vice. He will not fail, therefore, to set a due value on any plan which, without violating the principles to which he is attached, provides a proper cure for it. The instability, injustice, and confusion, introduced into the public councils, have, in truth, been the mortal diseases under which popular governments have everywhere perished; as they continue to be the favourite and fruitful topics from which the adversaries to liberty derive their most specious declamations. The valuable improvements made by the American constitutions on the popular models, both ancient and modern, cannot certainly be too much admired; but it would be an unwarrantable partiality, to contend that they have as effectually obviated the danger on this side, as was wished and expected. Complaints are everywhere heard from our most considerate and virtuous citizens, equally the friends of public and private faith, and of public and personal liberty, that our governments are too unstable; that the public good is disregarded in the conflicts of rival parties;

and that measures are too often decided, not according to the rules of justice, and the rights of the minor party, but by the superior force of an interested and overbearing majority. However anxiously we may wish that these complaints had no foundation, the evidence of known facts will not permit us to deny that they are in some degree true. It will be found, indeed, on a candid review of our situation, that some of the distresses under which we labour, have been erroneously charged on the operation of our governments; but it will be found, at the same time, that other causes will not alone account for many of our heaviest misfortunes; and, particularly, for that prevailing and increasing distrust of public engagements, and alarm for private rights, which are echoed from one end of the continent to the other. These must be chiefly, if not wholly, effects of the unsteadiness and injustice, with which a factious spirit has tainted our public administrations.

By a faction, I understand a number of citizens, whether amounting to a majority or minority of the whole, who are united and actuated by some common impulse of passion, or of interest, adverse to the rights of other citizens, or to the permanent and aggregate interests of the community.

There are two methods of curing the mischiefs of faction: The one, by removing its causes; the other, by controlling its effects.

There are again two methods of removing the causes of faction: The one, by destroying the liberty which is essential to its existence; the other, by giving to every citizen the same opinions, the same passions, and the same interests.

It could never be more truly said, that of the first remedy, that it was worse than the disease. Liberty is to faction what air is to fire, and aliment,[1] without which it instantly expires. But it could not be a less folly to abolish liberty, which is essential to political life because it nourishes faction, than it would be to wish the annihilation of air, which is essential to animal life, because it imparts to fire its destructive agency.

The second expedient is as impracticable, as the first would be unwise. As long as the reason of man continues fallible, and he is at liberty to exercise it, different opinions will be formed. As long as

[1] sustenance, support, here catalyst

the connection subsists between his reason and his self-love, his opinions and his passions will have a reciprocal influence on each other; and the former will be objects to which the latter will attach themselves. The diversity in the faculties of men, from which the rights of property originate, is not less an insuperable obstacle to an uniformity of interests. The protection of those faculties is the first object of government. From the protection of different and unequal faculties of acquiring property, the possession of different degrees and kinds of property immediately results; and from the influence of these on the sentiments and views of the respective proprietors, ensues a division of the society into different interests and parties.

The latent causes of faction are thus sown in the nature of man; and we see them everywhere brought into different degrees of activity, according to the different circumstances of civil society. A zeal for different opinions concerning religion, concerning government, and many other points, as well of speculation as of practice; an attachment to different leaders, ambitiously contending for pre-eminence and power; or to persons of other descriptions, whose fortunes have been interesting to the human passions, have, in turn, divided mankind into parties, inflamed them with mutual animosity, and rendered them much more disposed to vex and oppress each other, than to co-operate for their common good. So strong is this propensity of mankind, to fall into mutual animosities, that where no substantial occasion presents itself, the most frivolous and fanciful distinctions have been sufficient to kindle their unfriendly passions, and excite their most violent conflicts. But the most common and durable source of factions has been the various and unequal distribution of property. Those who hold, and those who are without property, have ever formed distinct interests in society. Those who are creditors, and those who are debtors, fall under a like discrimination. A landed interest, a manufacturing interest, a mercantile interest, a moneyed interest, with many lesser interests, grow up of necessity in civilized nations, and divide them into different classes, actuated[2] by different sentiments and views. The regulation of these various and interfering interests forms the

[2] influenced, quickened

principal task of modern legislation, and involves the spirit of party and faction in the necessary and ordinary operations of government.

No man is allowed to be a judge in his own cause; because his interest will certainly bias his judgment, and not improbably, corrupt his integrity. With equal, nay, with greater reason, a body of men are unfit to be both judges and parties at the same time; yet what are many of the most important acts of legislation, but so many judicial determinations, not indeed concerning the rights of single persons, but concerning the rights of large bodies of citizens? and what are the different classes of legislators, but advocates and parties to the causes which they determine? Is a law proposed concerning private debts? It is a question to which the creditors are parties on one side, and the debtors on the other. Justice ought to hold the balance between them. Yet the parties are, and must be, themselves the judges: and the most numerous party, or, in other words, the most powerful faction, must be expected to prevail. Shall domestic manufactures be encouraged, and in what degree, by restrictions on foreign manufactures? are questions which would be differently decided by the landed and the manufacturing classes; and probably by neither with a sole regard to justice and the public good. The apportionment of taxes, on the various descriptions of property, is an act which seems to require the most exact impartiality; yet there is, perhaps, no legislative act, in which greater opportunity and temptation are given to a predominant party, to trample on the rules of justice. Every shilling, with which they overburden the inferior number, is a shilling saved to their own pockets.

It is in vain to say, that enlightened statesmen will be able to adjust these clashing interests, and render them all subservient to the public good. Enlightened statesmen will not always be at the helm: nor, in many cases, can such an adjustment be made at all, without taking into view indirect and remote considerations, which will rarely prevail over the immediate interest which one party may find in disregarding the rights of another, or the good of the whole.

The inference to which we are brought is, that the *causes* of faction cannot be removed; and that relief is only to be sought in the means of controlling its *effects*.

If a faction consists of less than a majority, relief is supplied by the republican principle, which enables the majority to defeat its sinister views, by regular vote. It may clog the administration, it may convulse the society; but it will be unable to execute and mask its violence under the forms of the constitution. When a majority is included in a faction, the form of popular government, on the other hand, enables it to sacrifice to its ruling passion or interest, both the public good and the rights of other citizens. To secure the public good, and private rights, against the danger of such a faction, and at the same time to preserve the spirit and the form of popular government, is then the great object to which our inquiries are directed. Let me add, that it is the great desideratum,[3] by which alone this form of government can be rescued from the opprobrium[4] under which it has so long laboured, and be recommended to the esteem and adoption of mankind.

By what means is this object attainable? Evidently by one of two only. Either the existence of the same passion or interest in a majority, at the same time must be prevented; or the majority, having such coexistent passion or interest, must be rendered, by their number and local situation, unable to concert and carry into effect schemes of oppression. If the impulse and the opportunity be suffered to coincide, we well know, that neither moral nor religious motives can be relied on as an adequate control. They are not found to be such on the injustice and violence of individuals, and lose their efficacy in proportion to the number combined together; that is, in proportion as their efficacy becomes needful.

From this view of the subject, it may be concluded, that a pure democracy, by which I mean a society consisting of a small number of citizens, who assemble and administer the government in person, can admit of no cure from the mischiefs of faction. A common passion or interest will, in almost every case, be felt by a majority of the whole; a communication and concert, results from the form of government inself; and there is nothing to check the inducements to sacrifice the weaker party, or an obnoxious individual. Hence it is, that such democracies have ever been spectacles of turbulence and contention; have ever been found incompatible with personal

[3] goal or end, what is desired [4] ignominy

security, or the rights of property; and have, in general, been as short in their lives, as they have been violent in their deaths. Theoretic politicians, who have patronized this species of government, have erroneously supposed, that by reducing mankind to a perfect equality in their political rights, they would, at the same time, be perfectly equalized and assimilated in their possessions, their opinions, and their passions.

A republic, by which I mean a government in which the scheme of representation takes place, opens a different prospect, and promises the cure for which we are seeking. Let us examine the points in which it varies from pure democracy, and we shall comprehend both the nature of the cure and the efficacy which it must derive from the union.

The two great points of difference, between a democracy and a republic, are, first, the delegation of the government, in the latter, to a small number of citizens elected by the rest; secondly, the greater number of citizens, and greater sphere of country, over which the latter may be extended.

The effect of the first difference is, on the one hand, to refine and enlarge the public views, by passing them through the medium of a chosen body of citizens, whose wisdom may best discern the true interest of their country, and whose patriotism and love of justice, will be least likely to sacrifice it to temporary or partial considerations. Under such a regulation, it may well happen, that the public voice, pronounced by the representatives of the people, will be more consonant to the public good, than if pronounced by the people themselves, convened for the purpose. On the other hand, the effect may be inverted. Men of factious tempers, of local prejudices, or of sinister designs, may by intrigue, by corruption, or by other means, first obtain the suffrages, and then betray the interests of the people. The question resulting is, whether small or extensive republics are most favourable to the election of proper guardians of the public weal,[5] and it is clearly decided in favour of the latter by two obvious considerations.

In the first place, it is to be remarked, that however small the republic may be, the representatives must be raised to a certain

[5] state or nation

number, in order to guard against the cabals[6] of a few; and that however large it may be, they must be limited to a certain number, in order to guard against the confusion of a multitude. Hence, the number of representatives in the two cases not being in proportion to that of the constituents, and being proportionally greatest in the small republic, it follows that if the proportion of fit characters be not less in the large than in the small republic, the former will present a greater option, and consequently a greater probability of a fit choice.

In the next place, as each representative will be chosen by a greater number of citizens in the large than in the small republic, it will be more difficult for unworthy candidates to practice with success the vicious arts, by which elections are too often carried; and the suffrages of the people being more free, will be more likely to centre in men who possess the most attractive merit, and the most diffusive and established characters.

It must be confessed, that in this, as in most other cases, there is a mean, on both sides of which inconveniences will be found to lie. By enlarging too much the number of electors, you render the representative too little acquainted with all their local circumstances and lesser interests; as by reducing it too much, you render him unduly attached to these, and too little fit to comprehend and pursue great and national objects. The federal constitution forms a happy combination in this respect; the great and aggregate interests being referred to the national, the local, and particular to the state legislatures.

The other point of difference is, the greater number of citizens, and extent of territory, which may be brought within the compass of republican, than of democratic government; and it is this circumstance principally which renders factious combinations less to be dreaded in the former, than in the latter. The smaller the society, the fewer probably will be the distinct parties and interests composing it; the fewer the distinct parties and interests, the more frequently will a majority be found of the same party; and the smaller the number of individuals composing a majority, and the smaller the compass within which they are placed, the more easily

[6] secret factions, works of intrigue

will they concert and execute their plans of oppression. Extend the sphere, and you take in a greater variety of parties and interests; you make it less probable that a majority of the whole will have a common motive to invade the rights of other citizens; or if such a common motive exists, it will be more difficult for all who feel it to discover their own strength, and to act in unison with each other. Besides other impediments, it may be remarked, that where there is a consciousness of unjust or dishonourable purposes, communication is always checked by distrust, in proportion to the number whose concurrence is necessary.

Hence, it clearly appears, that the same advantage, which a republic has over a democracy, in controlling the effects of faction, is enjoyed by a large over a small republic—is enjoyed by the union over the states composing it. Does this advantage consist in the substitution of representatives, whose enlightened views and virtuous sentiments render them superior to local prejudices, and to schemes of injustice? It will not be denied, that the representation of the union will be most likely to possess these requisite endowments. Does it consist in the greater security afforded by a greater variety of parties, against the event of any one party being able to outnumber and oppress the rest? In an equal degree does the increased variety of parties, comprised within the union, increase this security. Does it, in fine, consist in the greater obstacles opposed to the concert and accomplishment of the secret wishes of an unjust and interested majority? Here, again, the extent of the union gives it the most palpable advantage.

The influence of factious leaders may kindle a flame within their particular states, but will be unable to spread a general conflagration through the other states; a religious sect may degenerate into a political faction in a part of the confederacy; but the variety of sects dispersed over the entire face of it, must secure the national councils against any danger from that source: a rage for paper money, for an abolition of debts, for an equal division of property, or for any other improper or wicked project, will be less apt to pervade the whole body of the union, than a particular member of it; in the same proportion as such a malady is more likely to taint a particular county or district, than an entire state,

In the extent and proper structure of the union, therefore, we behold a republican remedy for the diseases most incident to republican government. And according to the degree of pleasure and pride we feel in being republicans, ought to be our zeal in cherishing the spirit, and supporting the character of federalists.

PUBLIUS.

❧ Fourth President of the United States and an expert in constitutional history and theory, Madison is often called "the father of the Constitution." He joined Alexander Hamilton and John Jay in writing *The Federalist,* a series of 85 papers in reply to objections against the Constitution that had been passed at the Philadelphia convention in 1787. These papers appeared in the New York press between October 1787 and August 1788.

Melancthon and Calvin

FROM *Imaginary Conversations (1846)*
BY *Walter Savage Landor (1775-1864)*

CALVIN.[1] Are you sure, O Melancthon, that you yourself are among the elect?

MELANCTHON.[2] My dear brother, so please it God, I would rather be among the many.

CALVIN. Of the damned?

MELANCTHON. Alas! no. But I am inclined to believe that the many will be saved and will be happy, since Christ came into the world for the redemption of sinners.

CALVIN. Hath not our Saviour said explicitly that many are called, but few chosen?

MELANCTHON. Our Saviour?—hath he said it?

CALVIN. *Hath* he, forsooth! Where is your New Testament?

MELANCTHON. In my heart.

CALVIN. Without this page, however.

MELANCTHON. When we are wiser and more docile, that is, when we are above the jars and turmoils and disputations of the world, our Saviour will vouchsafe to interpret what, through the fumes of our intemperate vanity, is now indistinct or dark. He will plead for

[1]John Calvin, 1509-1564, born in France, theologian and leader of the Protestant Reformation in Geneva

[2]Phillip Melancthon (also Melanchthon), 1495-1560, German theologian and leader of the Lutheran Reformation

us before an inexorable judge. He came to remit the sins of man; not the sins of a few, but of many; not of many, but of all.

CALVIN. What! of the benighted heathen too? of the pagan? of the idolater?

MELANCTHON. I hope so; but I dare not say it.

CALVIN. You would include even the negligent, the indifferent, the sceptic, the unbeliever.

MELANCTHON. Pitying them for a want of happiness in a want of faith. They are my brethren; they are God's children. He will pardon the presumption of my wishes for their welfare; my sorrow that they have fallen, some through their blindness, others through their deafness, others through their terror, others through their anger peradventure at the loud denunciations of unforgiving man. If I would forgive a brother, may not he, who is immeasurably better and more merciful, have pity on a child? He came on earth to take our nature upon him: will he punish, will he reprehend us, for an attempt to take as much as may be of his upon ourselves?

CALVIN. There is no bearing any such fallacies.

MELANCTHON. Is it harder to bear these fallacies (as they appear to you, and perhaps are, for we all are fallible, and many even of our best thoughts are fallacies), is it harder, O my friend, to bear these, than to believe in the eternal punishment of the erroneous?

CALVIN. *Erroneous* indeed! Have they not the Book of Life,[3] now at last laid open before them, for their guidance?

MELANCTHON. No, indeed; they have only two or three places, dog-eared and bedaubed, which they are commanded to look into and study. These are so uninviting, that many close again the volume of salvation, clasp it tight, and throw it back in our faces. I would rather show a man green fields than gibbets: and if I called him to enter the service of a plenteous house and powerful master, he may not be rendered the more willing to enter it by my pointing out to him the stocks in the gateway, and telling him that nine-tenths of the household, however orderly, must occupy that position. The book of *good news* under your interpretation, tells people not only that they may go and be damned, but that unless they are lucky, they must inevitably.[4] Again it informs another set of inquir-

[3]Bible (a main belief of Calvinism is in the authority of Scripture)

[4]belief in predestination is another tenet of Calvinism

ers that if once they have been under what they feel to be the influence of grace, they never can relapse. All must go well who have once gone well and a name once written in the list of favorites can never be erased.

CALVIN. This is certain.

MELANCTHON. Let us hope then, and in holy confidence let us believe, that the book is large and voluminous; that it begins at an early date of man's existence; and that amid the agitation of inquiry, it comprehends the humble and submissive doubter. For doubt itself, between the richest patrimony and utter destitution, is quite sufficiently painful: and surely it is a hardship to be turned over into a criminal court for having lost in a civil one. But if all who have once gone right can never go astray, how happens it that so large a part of the angels fell off from their allegiance? They were purer and wiser than we are, and had the advantage of seeing God face to face. They were the ministers of his power; they knew its extent: yet they defied it. If we err, it is in relying too confidently on his mercies; not in questioning his omnipotence. If our hopes forsake us, if the bonds of sin bruise and corrode us, so that we can not walk upright, there is, in the midst of these calamities, no proof that we are utterly lost. Danger far greater is there in the presumption of an especial favour, which men incomparably better than ourselves can never have deserved. Let us pray, O Calvin, that we may hereafter be happier than our contentions and animosities will permit us to be at present; and that our opponents, whether now in the right or in the wrong, may come at last where all error ceases.

CALVIN. I am uncertain whether such a wish is rational: and I doubt more whether it is religious. God hath willed them to walk in their blindness. To hope against it, seems like repining at his unalterable decree; a weak indulgence in an unpermitted desire; an unholy entreaty of the heart that he will forego his vengeance, and abrogate the law that was from the beginning. Of one thing I am certain: we must lop off the unsound.

MELANCTHON. What a curse hath metaphor been to religion! It is the wedge that holds asunder the two great portions of the Christian world. We hear of nothing so commonly as fire and sword. And here indeed what was metaphor is converted into substance and applied to practice. The unsoundness of doctrine is not cut off nor cauterised; the professor is. The head falls on the scaffold, or fire surrounds the stake, because a doctrine is bloodless and incombustible. Fierce outrageous animals, for want of the man who has escaped them, lacerate and trample his cloak or bonnet. This, although the work of brutes, is not half so brutal as the practice of theologians, seizing the man himself, instead of bonnet or cloak.

CALVIN. We must leave such matters to the magistrate.

MELANCTHON. Let us instruct the magistrate in his duty; this is ours. Unless we can teach humanity, we may resign the charge of religion. For fifteen centuries, Christianity has been conveyed into many houses, in many cities, in many regions, but always through slender pipes; and never yet into any great reservoir in any part of the earth. Its principal ordinances have never been observed in the polity of any state whatever. Abstinence from spoliation, from oppression, from bloodshed, has never been inculcated by the chief priests of any. These two facts excite the doubts of many in regard to a divine origin and a divine protection. Wherefore it behoves us the more especially to preach forbearance. If the people are tolerant one toward another in the same country, they will become tolerant in time toward those whom rivers or seas have separated from them. For surely it is strange and wonderful that nations which are near enough for hostility should never be near enough for concord. This arises from bad government; and bad government arises from a negligent choice of counsellors by the prince, usually led or terrified by a corrupt, ambitious, wealthy (and therefore unchristian) priesthood. While their wealth lay beyond the visible horizon, they tarried at the cottage, instead of pricking on[5] for the palace.

CALVIN. By the grace and help of God we will turn them back again to their quiet and wholesome resting-place, before the people lay a rough hand upon the silk.

But you evaded my argument on predestination.

MELANCTHON. Our blessed Lord himself, in his last hours, ventured to express a wish before his heavenly Father, that the bitter cup might pass away from him. I humbly dare to implore that a cup much bitterer may be removed from the great body of mankind; a

[5] going (strictly, riding) rapidly

cup containing the poison of eternal punishment, where agony succeeds to agony, but never death.

CALVIN. I come armed with the Gospel.

MELANCTHON. Tremendous weapon! as we have seen it through many ages, if man wields it against man: but like the fabled spear of old mythology, endued with the faculty of healing the saddest wound its most violent wielder can inflict. Obscured and rusting with the blood upon it, let us hasten to take it up again, and apply it, as best we may, to its appointed uses.

The life of our Saviour is the simplest exposition of his words. Strife is what he both discountenanced and forbade. We ourselves are right-minded, each of us all: and others are right-minded in proportion as they agree with us, chiefly in matters which we insist are well worthy of our adherence, but which whosoever refuses to embrace displays a factious and unchristian spirit. These for the most part are matters which neither they nor we understand, and which, if we did understand them, would little profit us. The weak will be supported by the strong, if they can; if they can not, they are ready to be supported even by the weaker, and cry out against the strong, as arrogant or negligent, or deaf or blind; at last even their strength is questioned, and the more if, while there is fury all around them, they are quiet.

I remember no discussion on religion in which religion was not a sufferer by it, if mutual forbearance, and belief in another's good motives and intentions, are (as I must always think they are) its proper and necessary appurtenances.

CALVIN. Would you never make inquiries?

MELANCTHON. Yes; and as deep as possible; but into my own heart; for that belongs to me; and God hath entrusted it most especially to my own superintendence.

CALVIN. We must also keep others from going astray, by showing them the right road, and, if they are obstinate in resistance, then by coercing and chastising them through the magistrate.

MELANCTHON. It is sorrowful to dream that we are scourges in God's hand, and that he appoints for us no better work than lacerating one another. I am no enemy to inquiry, where I see abuses, and where I suspect falsehood. The Romanists, our great oppressors, think it presumptuous to search into things abstruse; and let us do them the justice to acknowledge that, if it is a fault, it is one which they never commit. But surely we are kept sufficiently in the dark by the infirmity of our nature: no need to creep into a corner and put our hands before our eyes. To throw away or turn aside from God's best gifts is verily a curious sign of obedience and submission. He not only hath given us a garden to walk in, but he hath planted it also for us, and he wills us to know the nature and properties of everything that grows up within it. Unless we look into them and handle them and register them, how shall we discover this to be salutary, that to be poisonous; this annual, that perennial?

CALVIN. Here we coincide; and I am pleased to find in you less apathy than I expected. It becomes us, moreover, to denounce God's vengeance on a sinful world.

MELANCTHON. Is it not better and pleasanter to show the wanderer by what course of life it may be avoided? is it not better and pleasanter to enlarge on God's promises of salvation, than to insist on his denunciations of wrath? is it not better and pleasanter to lead the wretched up to his mercy-seat, than to hurl them by thousands under his fiery chariot?

CALVIN. We have no option. By our heavenly Father many are called, but few are chosen.

MELANCTHON. There is scarcely a text in the Holy Scriptures to which there is not an opposite text, written in characters equally large and legible; and there has usually been a sword laid upon each. Even the weakest disputant is made so conceited by what he calls religion, as to think himself wiser than the wisest who thinks differently from him; and he becomes so ferocious by what he calls holding it fast, that he appears to me as if he held it fast much in the same manner as a terrier holds a rat, and you have about as much trouble in getting it from between his incisors. When at last it does come out, it is mangled, distorted, and extinct.

CALVIN. M. Melancthon! you have taken a very perverse view of the subject. Such language as yours would extinguish that zeal which is to enlighten the nations, and to consume the tares[6] by which they are overrun.

MELANCTHON. The tares and the corn are so intermingled

[6](in Biblical use) some injurious weed, perhaps the darnel

throughout the wide plain which our God hath given us to cultivate, that I would rather turn the patient and humble into it to weed it carefully, than a thresher who would thresh wheat and tare together before the grain is ripened, or who would carry fire into the furrows when it is.

CALVIN. Yet even the most gentle, and of the gentler sex, are inflamed with a holy zeal in the propagation of the faith.

MELANCTHON. I do not censure them for their earnestness in maintaining truth. We not only owe our birth to them, but also the better part of our education; and if we were not divided after their first lesson, we should continue to live in a widening circle of brothers and sisters all our lives. After our infancy and removal from home, the use of the rod is the principal thing we learn of our alien preceptors; and, catching their dictatorial language, we soon begin to exercise their instrument of enforcing it, and swing it right and left, even after we are paralysed by age, and until Death's hand strikes it out of ours. I am sorry you have cited the gentler part of the creation to appear before you, obliged as I am to bear witness that I myself have known a few specimens of the fair sex become a shade less fair, among the perplexities of religion. Indeed I am credibly informed that certain of them have lost their patience, running up and down in the dust where many roads diverge. This surely is not walking humbly with their God, not walking with him at all; for those who walk with him are always readier to hear *his* voice than their own, and to admit that it is more persuasive. But at last the zealot is so infatuated, by the serious mockeries he imitates and repeats, that he really takes his own voice for God's. Is it not wonderful that the words of eternal life should have hitherto produced only eternal litigation; and that in our progress heavenward, we should think it expedient to plant unthrifty thorns over bitter wells of blood in the wilderness we leave behind us?

CALVIN. It appears to me that you are inclined to tolerate even the rank idolatry of our persecutors. Shame! shame!

MELANCTHON. Greater shame if I tolerated it within my own dark heart, and waved before it the foul incense of self-love.

CALVIN. I do not understand you. What I do understand is this, and deny it at your peril – I mean at the peril of your salvation – that God is a jealous God; he himself declares it.

MELANCTHON. We are in the habit of considering the God of Nature as a jealous God, and idolatry as an enormous evil; an evil which is about to come back into the world, and to subdue or seduce once more our strongest and most sublime affections. Why do you lift up your eyes and hands?

CALVIN. An evil *about* to come back! *about* to come! Do we not find it in high places?

MELANCTHON. We do indeed, and always shall, while there are any high places upon earth. Thither will men creep, and there fall prostrate.

CALVIN. Against idolatry we still implore the Almighty that he will incline our hearts to keep his law.

MELANCTHON. The Jewish law; the Jewish idolatry. You fear the approach of this, and do not suspect the presence of a worse.

CALVIN. A worse than that which the living God hath denounced?

MELANCTHON. Even so.

CALVIN. Would it not offend, would it not wound to the quick, a more human creature, to be likened to a piece of metal or stone, a calf or monkey?

MELANCTHON. A mere human creature might be angry; because his influence among his neighbours arises in great measure from the light in which he appears to them; and this light does not emanate from himself, but may be thrown on him by any hand that is expert at mischief: beside, the likeness of such animals to him could never be suggested by reverence or esteem, nor be regarded as a type of any virtue. The mere human creature, such as human creatures for the most part are, would be angry; because he has nothing which he can oppose to ridicule but resentment.

CALVIN. I am in consternation at your lukewarmness. If you treat idolaters thus lightly, what hope can I entertain of discussing with you the doctrine of grace and predestination?

MELANCTHON. Entertain no such hope at all. Wherever I find in the Holy Scriptures a disputable doctrine, I interpret it as judges do, in favour of the culprit: such is man: the benevolent judge is God. But in regard to idolatry, I see more criminals who are guilty of it than you do. I go beyond the stone-quarry and the pasture, beyond the graven image and the ox-stall. If we bow before the distant image of good, while there exists within our reach one solitary object of substantial sorrow, which sorrow our efforts can remove, we are guilty (I pronounce it) of idolatry: we prefer the intangible effigy to the living form. Surely we neglect the service of our Maker if we neglect his children. He left us in the chamber with them, to take care of them, to feed them, to admonish them, and occasionally to amuse them: instead of which, after a warning not to run into the fire, we slam the door behind us in their faces, and run eagerly downstairs to dispute and quarrel with our fellows of the household who are about their business. The wickedness of idolatry does not consist in any inadequate representation of the Deity, for whether our hands or our hearts represent him, the representation is almost alike inadequate, Every man does what he hopes and believes will be most pleasing to his God; and God, in his wisdom and mercy, will not punish gratitude in its error.

CALVIN. How do you know that?

MELANCTHON. Because I know his loving-kindness, and experience it daily.

CALVIN. If men blindly and wilfully run into error when God hath shown the right way, he will visit it on their souls.

MELANCTHON. He will observe from the serenity of heaven, a serenity emanating from his presence, that there is scarcely any work of his creation on earth which hath not excited in some people or other remembrance, an admiration, a symbol, of his power. The evil of idolatry is this. Rival nations have raised up rival deities: war hath been denounced in the name of Heaven: men have been murdered for the love of God: and such impiety hath darkened all the regions of the world, that the Lord of all things hath been invoked by all simultaneously as the Lord of Hosts. This is the only invocation in which men of every creed are united: an invocation to which Satan, bent on the perdition of the human race, might have listened from the fallen angels.

CALVIN. We can not hope to purify men's hearts until we lead them away from the abomination of Babylon: nor will they be led away from it until we reduce the images to dust. So long as they stand, the eye will hanker after them, and the spirit be corrupt.

MELANCTHON. And long afterward, I sadly fear.

We attribute to the weakest of men the appellations and powers of Deity: we fall down before them: we call the impious and cruel by the title of *gracious* and *most religious:* and, even in the house of God himself, and before his very altar, we split his Divine Majesty asunder, and offer the largest part to the most corrupt and most corrupting of his creatures.

CALVIN. Not *we*, M. Melancthon. I will preach, I will exist, in no land of such abomination.

MELANCTHON. So far, well: but religion demands more. Our reformers knock off the head from Jupiter: thunderbolt and sceptre stand. The attractive, the impressive, the august, they would annihilate, leaving men nothing but their sordid fears of vindictive punishment, and their impious doubts of our Saviour's promises.

CALVIN. We should teach men to retain for ever the fear of God before their eyes, never to cease from the apprehension[7] of his wrath, to be well aware that he often afflicts when he is farthest from wrath, and that such infliction is a benefit bestowed by him.

MELANCTHON. What! If only a few are to be saved when the infliction is over?

CALVIN. It becometh not us to repine at the number of vessels which the supremely wise Artificer forms, breaks, and casts away, or at the paucity it pleaseth him to preserve. The ways of Providence are inscrutable.

MELANCTHON. Some of them are, and some of them are not; and in these it seems to be his design that we should see and adore his wisdom. We fancy that all our inflictions are sent us directly and immediately from above: sometimes we think it in piety and contrition, but oftener in moroseness and discontent. It would, however, be well if we attempted to trace the causes of them. We should probably find their origin in some region of the heart which we never had well explored, or in which we had secretly deposited our worst indulgences. The clouds that intercept the heavens from us come not from the heavens, but from the earth.

Why should we scribble our own devices over the Book of God, erasing the plainest words, and rendering the Holy Scriptures a a worthless palimpsest?[8]

[7] recognition, and also fear

[8] from which writing has been erased to make room for another text

☙§ Walter Savage Landor of Warwickshire, Oxford, Bath, and Italy, wrote poetry and essays throughout his life, with especial interest, like Browning's, in historical attitudes dramatically expressed. Hence his use of the conversation or dialogue form, quite different from Walton's, for example, in that actual historical points of view are being imaginatively recreated.

Plato's philosophical dialogues provide a basis for this tradition. What are their essential characteristics?

On familiar style

FROM *Table Talk (1821-22)*

BY *William Hazlitt (1778-1830)*

It is not easy to write a familiar style. Many people mistake a familiar for a vulgar[1] style, and suppose that to write without affectation is to write at random. On the contrary, there is nothing that requires more precision, and, if I may so say, purity of expression, than the style I am speaking of. It utterly rejects not only all unmeaning pomp, but all low, cant[2] phrases, and loose, unconnected, *slipshod* allusions. It is not to take the first word that offers, but the best word in common use; it is not to throw words together in any combinations we please, but to follow and avail ourselves of the true idiom of the language. To write a genuine familiar or truly English style, is to write as any one would speak in common conversation, who had a thorough command and choice of words, or who could discourse with ease, force, and perspicuity,[3] setting aside all pedantic and oratorical flourishes. Or to give another illustration, to write naturally is the same thing in regard to common conversation, as to read naturally is in regard to common speech. It does not follow that it is an easy thing to give the true accent and inflection to the words you utter, because you do not attempt to rise above the level of ordinary life and colloquial speaking. You do not assume indeed the solemnity of the pulpit, or the tone of stage-

[1] marked by want of good taste and training

[2] peculiar to a special class, party, profession, or other group, not in general use

[3] clarity

declamation: neither are you at liberty to gabble on at a venture, without emphasis or discretion, or to resort to vulgar dialect or clownish pronunciation. You must steer a middle course. You are tied down to a given and appropriate articulation, which is determined by the habitual associations between sense and sound, and which you can only hit by entering into the author's meaning, as you must find the proper words and style to express yourself by fixing your thoughts on the subject you have to write about. Any one may mouth out a passage with a theatrical cadence, or get upon stilts to tell his thoughts: but to write or speak with propriety and simplicity is a more difficult task. Thus it is easy to affect a pompous style, to use a word twice as big as the thing you want to express: it is not so easy to pitch upon the very word that exactly fits it. Out of eight or ten words equally common, equally intelligible, with nearly equal pretensions, it is a matter of some nicety[4] and discrimination to pick out the very one, the preferableness of which is scarcely perceptible, but decisive. The reason why I object to Dr. Johnson's style is, that there is no discrimination, no variety in it. He uses none but "tall, opaque words,"[5] taken from the "first row of the rubric":[6] —words with the greatest number of syllables, or Latin phrases with merely English terminations. If a fine style depended on this sort of arbitrary pretension, it would be fair to judge of an author's elegance by the measurement of his words, and the substitution of foreign circumlocutions (with no precise associations) for the mother-tongue. How simple it is to be dignified without ease, to be pompous without meaning! Surely, it is but a mechanical rule for avoiding what is low to be always pedantic and affected. It is clear you cannot use a vulgar English word, if you never use a common English word at all. A fine tact is shewn in adhering to those which are perfectly common, and yet never falling into any expressions which are debased by disgusting circumstances, or which owe their signification and point to technical or professional allusions. A truly natural or familiar style can never be quaint or vulgar, for this reason, that it is of universal force and applicability, and that quaint-

[4] fineness of judgment

[5] quoted from Bk. 3 of *Tristram Shandy,* by Laurence Sterne

[6] part of manuscript or book printed in red or otherwise set off from the rest

ness and vulgarity arise out of the immediate connection of certain words with coarse and disagreeable, or with confined ideas. The last form what we understand by *cant* or *slang* phrases.—To give an example of what is not very clear in the general statement. I should say that the phrase *To cut with a knife,* or *To cut a piece of wood,* is perfectly free from vulgarity, because it is perfectly common: but to *cut an acquaintance*[7] is not quite unexceptionable, because it is not perfectly common or intelligible, and has hardly yet escaped out of the limits of slang phraseology. I should hardly therefore use the word in this sense without putting it in italics as a license of expression, to be received *cum grano salis.*[8] All provincial or bye-phrases come under the same mark of reprobation—all such as the writer transfers to the page from his fireside or a particular *coterie,* or that he invents for his own sole use and convenience. I conceive that words are like money, not the worse for being common, but that it is the stamp of custom alone that gives them circulation or value. I am fastidious in this respect, and would almost as soon coin the currency of the realm as counterfeit the King's English. I never invented or gave a new and unauthorized meaning to any word but one single one (the term *impersonal* applied to feelings) and that was in an abstruse metaphysical discussion to express a very difficult distinction. I have been (I know) loudly accused of revelling in vulgarisms and broken English. I cannot speak to that point: but so far I plead guilty to the determined use of acknowledged idioms and common elliptical expressions. I am not sure that the critics in question know the one from the other, that is, can distinguish any medium between formal pedantry and the most barbarous solecism.[9] As an author, I endeavour to employ plain words and popular modes of construction, as were I[10] a chapman[11] and dealer, I should common weights and measures.[12]

The proper force of words lies not in the words themselves, but in their application. A word may be a fine-sounding word of an unusual length, and very imposing from its learning and novelty, and yet in the connection in which it is introduced, may be quite

[7] still not in standard usage, though now more generally clear
[8] with a grain of salt [9] violation of standard usage [10] as if I were
[11] pedlar [12] I should *employ* . . . , an example of Hazlitt's use of ellipsis

pointless and irrelevant. It is not pomp or pretension, but the adaptation of the expression to the idea that clenches a writer's meaning:—as it is not the size or glossiness of the materials, but their being fitted each to its place, that gives strength to the arch; or as the pegs and nails are as necessary to the support of the building as the large timbers, and more so than the mere shewy, unsubstantial ornaments. I hate any thing that occupies more space than it is worth. I hate to see a load of band-boxes go along the street, and I hate to see a parcel of big words without any thing in them. A person who does not deliberately dispose of all his thoughts alike in cumbrous draperies and flimsy disguises, may strike out twenty varieties of familiar everyday language, each coming somewhat nearer to the feeling he wants to convey, and at last not hit upon that particular and only one, which may be said to be identical with the exact impression in his mind. This would seem to shew that Mr. Cobbett[13] is hardly right in saying that the first word that occurs is always the best. It may be a very good one; and yet a better may present itself on reflection or from time to time. It should be suggested naturally, however, and spontaneously, from a fresh and lively conception of the subject. We seldom succeed by trying at improvement, or by merely substituting one word for another that we are not satisfied with, as we cannot recollect the name of a place or person by merely plaguing ourselves about it. We wander farther from the point by persisting in a wrong scent, but it starts up accidentally in the memory when we least expected it, by touching some link in the chain of previous association.

There are those who hoard up and make a cautious display of nothing but rich and rare phraseology;—ancient medals, obscure coins, and Spanish pieces of eight.[14] They are very curious to inspect; but I myself would neither offer nor take them in the course of exchange. A sprinkling of archaisms is not amiss; but a tissue of obsolete expressions is more fit *for keep than wear.* I do not say I would not use any phrase that had been brought into fashion before the middle or the end of the last century; but I should be shy of

[13] William Cobbett, 1763-1835, English journalist and reformer, wrote *A Grammar of the English Language*

[14] obsolete Spanish or Spanish-American silver dollar, equal to eight reals

using any that had not been employed by any approved author during the whole of that time. Words, like clothes, get old-fashioned, or mean and ridiculous, when they have been for some time laid aside. Mr. Lamb is the only imitator of old English style I can read with pleasure; and he is so thoroughly imbued with the spirit of his authors, that the idea of imitation is almost done away. There is an inward unction, a marrowy vein both in the thought and feeling, an intuition, deep and lively, of his subject, that carries off any quaintness or awkwardness arising from an antiquated style and dress. The matter is completely his own, though the manner is assumed. Perhaps his ideas are altogether so marked and individual, as to require their point and pungency to be neutralised by the affectation of a singular but traditional form of conveyance. Tricked out in the prevailing costume, they would probably seem more startling and out of the way. The old English authors, Burton,[15] Fuller,[16] Coryate,[17] Sir Thomas Browne,[18] are a kind of mediators between us and the more eccentric and whimsical modern, reconciling us to his peculiarities. I do not, however, know how far this is the case or not, till he condescends to write like one of us. I must confess that what I like best of his papers under the signature of Elia (still I do not presume, amidst such excellence, to decide what is most excellent) is the account of *Mrs. Battle's Opinions on Whist,* which is also the most free from obsolete allusions and turns of expressions—

A well of native English undefiled.[19]

To those acquainted with his admired prototypes, these *Essays* of the ingenious and highly gifted author have the same sort of charm and relish, that Erasmus's[20] *Colloquies* or a fine piece of modern Latin have to the classical scholar. Certainly, I do not know

[15] Robert Burton, 1577-1640 scholar and clergyman, *The Anatomy of Melancholy*

[16] Thomas Fuller, 1608-1661, English clergyman and historian, wrote *The History of the Worthies of England*

[17] Thomas Coryate, c. 1577-1617, a genial eccentric, wrote *Coryats Crudities Hastily Gobbled Up in Five Months Travels*

[18] cf. "Urn Burial" above [19] from Bk. IV, Spenser's *Faerie Queene*

[20] Desiderus Erasmus, born Gerhard Gerhards, c. 1466-1536, Dutch humanist, theologian

any borrowed pencil that has more power or felicity of execution than the one of which I have here been speaking.

It is as easy to write a gaudy style without ideas, as it is to spread a pallet of shewy colours, or to smear in a flaunting transparency. "What do you read?" – "Words, words, words." – "What is the matter?"[21] – *"Nothing,"* it might be answered. The florid style is the reverse of the familiar. The last is employed as an unvarnished medium to convey ideas; the first is resorted to as a spangled veil to conceal the want of them. When there is nothing to be set down but words, it costs little to have them fine. Look through the dictionary, and cull out a *florilegium,*[22] rival the *tulipomania.*[23] *Rouge* high enough, and never mind the natural complexion. The vulgar, who are not in the secret, will admire the look of preternatural health and vigour; and the fashionable, who regard only appearances, will be delighted with the imposition. Keep to your sounding generalities, your tinkling phrases, and all will be well. Swell out an unmeaning truism to a perfect tympany of style. A thought, a distinction is the rock on which all this brittle cargo of verbiage splits at once. Such writers have merely *verbal* imaginations, that retain nothing but words. Or their puny thoughts have dragon-wings, all green and gold. They soar far above the vulgar failing of the *Sermo humi obrepens*[24] – their most ordinary speech is never short of an hyperbole, splendid, imposing, vague, incomprehensible, magniloquent, a cento[25] of sounding common-places. If some of us, whose "ambition is more lowly," pry a little too narrowly into nooks and corners to pick up a number of "unconsidered trifles," they never once direct their eyes or lift their hands to seize on any but the most gorgeous, tarnished, thread-bare patch-work set of phrases, the left-off finery of poetic extravagance, transmitted down through successive generations of barren pretenders. If they criticise actors and actresses, a huddled phantasmagoria of feather, spangles, floods of light, and oceans of sound float before their morbid sense, which they paint in the style of Ancient Pistol. Not a glimpse can you get of the merits or defects of the performers: they are hidden

[21] content or gist [22] divination by means of flowers

[23] craze for growing or getting tulips, such as arose in Holland in 1634

[24] talk creeping on the ground

[25] patchwork, a work made up of parts from other works

in a profusion of barbarous epithets and wilful rhodomontade.[26] Our hypercritics are not thinking of these little fantoccini beings—[27]

That strut and fret their hour upon the stage—[28]

but of tall phantoms of words, abstractions, *genera* and *species*, sweeping clauses, periods that unite the Poles, forced alliterations, astounding antitheses—

And on their pens[29] *Fustian*[30] sits plumed.

If they describe kings and queens, it is an Eastern pageant. The Coronation at either House is nothing to it. We get at four repeated images—a curtain, a throne, a sceptre, and a foot-stool. These are with them the wardrobe of a lofty imagination; and they turn their servile strains to servile uses. Do we read a description of pictures? It is not a reflection of tones and hues which "nature's own sweet and cunning hand laid on," but piles of precious stones, rubies, pearls, emeralds, Golconda's[31] mines, and all the blazonry of art. Such persons are in fact besotted with words, and their brains are turned with the glittering, but empty and sterile phantoms of things. Personifications, capital letter, seas of sunbeams, visions of glory, shining inscriptions, the figures of a transparency, Britannia with her shield, or Hope leaning on an anchor, make up their stock in trade. They may be considered as *hieroglyphical*[32] writers. Images stand out in their minds isolated and important merely in themselves, without any ground-work of feeling—there is no context in their imaginations. Words affect them in the same way, by the mere sound, that is, by their possible, not by their actual application to the subject in hand. They are fascinated by first appearances, and have no sense of consequences. Nothing more is meant by them than meets the ear: they understand or feel nothing more than meets their eye. The web and texture of the universe, and of the heart of man, is a mystery to them: they have no faculty that strikes a chord in unison with it. They cannot get beyond the daubings of

[26] also rodomontade, pretentious talk [27] puppets

[28] Act V, sc. v of *Macbeth* [29] Bk. V of *Paradise Lost*

[30] literally, thick, coarse cloth, and hence bombastic talk or writing

[31] an ancient city in Hyderabad, India, famous for diamond cutting

[32] extremely hard to understand owing to lack of clarity of symbols used

fancy, the varnish of sentiment. Objects are not linked to feelings, words to things, but images revolve in splendid mockery, words represent themselves in their strange rhapsodies. The categories of such a mind are pride and ignorance—pride in outside show, to which they sacrifice every thing, and ignorance of the true worth and hidden structure both of words and things. With a sovereign contempt for what is familiar and natural, they are the slaves of vulgar affection—of a routine of high-flown phrases. Scorning to imitate realities, they are unable to invent any thing, to strike out one original idea. They are not copyists of nature, it is true; but they are the poorest of all plagiarists, the plagiarists of words. All is far-fetched, dear-bought, artificial, oriental[33] in subject and allusion: all is mechanical, conventional, vapid, formal, pedantic in style and execution. They startle and confound the understanding of the reader, by the remoteness and obscurity of their illustrations: they soothe the ear by the monotony of the same everlasting round of circuitous metaphors. They are the *mock-school* in poetry and prose. They flounder about between fustian in expression, and bathos in sentiment. They tantalise the fancy but never reach the head nor touch the heart. Their Temple of Fame is like a shadowy structure raised by Dulness to Vanity, or like Cowper's[34] description of the Empress of Russia's palace of ice, as "worthless as in shew 'twas glittering"—

It smiled, and it was cold!

[33] highly elaborate

[34] William Cowper, 1731-1800, English poet, wrote *The Task,* from which Hazlitt quotes

☙ Son of a Unitarian minister in an English village, William Hazlitt wrote for various liberal papers, including the *Edinburgh Review,* on art, on literature, and on topics like journeys and fights. Essay-writing was his life. His two wives and his friends, like Lamb, were literary. The essay in this book is from *Table Talk* (1821). Does it describe a style "familiar" also today?

Levana and our ladies of sorrow

FROM *Suspira de Profundis (1852)*

BY *Thomas De Quincey (1785-1859)*

Oftentimes at Oxford I saw Levana in my dreams. I knew her by her Roman symbols. Who is Levana? Reader, that do not pretend to have leisure for very much scholarship, you will not be angry with me for telling you. Levana was the Roman goddess that performed for the new-born infant the earliest office of ennobling kindness—typical, by its mode, of that grandeur which belongs to man everywhere, and of that benignity in powers invisible which even in pagan worlds sometimes descends to sustain it. At the very moment of birth, just as the infant tasted for the first time the atmosphere of our troubled planet, it was laid on the ground. But immediately, lest so grand a creature should grovel there for more than one instant, either the paternal hand, as proxy for the goddess Levana, or some near kinsman, as proxy for the father, raised it upright, bade it look erect as the king of all this world, and presented its forehead to the stars, saying, perhaps, in his heart, "Behold what is greater than yourselves!" This symbolic act represented the function of Levana. And that mysterious lady, who never revealed her face (except to me in dreams), but always acted by delegation, had her name for the Latin verb (as still it is the Italian verb) *levare,* to raise aloft.

This is the explanation of Levana, and hence it has risen that some people have understood by Levana the tutelary power that controls the education of the nursery. She, that would not suffer at his birth even a prefigurative or mimic degradation for her awful ward, far less could be supposed to suffer the real degradation attaching to the non-development of his powers. She therefore watches over human education. Now, the word *educo,* with the penultimate short, was derived (by a process often exemplified in the crystallisation of languages) from the word *educo,* with the penultimate long. Whatever *educes* or develops, *educates.* By the education of Levana, therefore, is meant—not the poor machinery that moves by spelling-books and grammars, but by that mighty system of central forces hidden in the deep bosom of human life, which by passion, by strife, by temptation, by the energies of resistance, works for ever upon children—resting not day or night, any more than the mighty wheel of the day and night themselves, whose moments, like restless spokes, are glimmering for ever as they revolve.

If, then, *these* are the ministries by which Levana works, how profoundly must she reverence the agencies of grief. But you, reader, think that children generally are not liable to grief such as mine. There are two senses in the word *generally*—the sense of Euclid, where it means *universally* (or in the whole extent of the *genus*), and a foolish sense of this word, where it means *usually.* Now, I am far from saying that children universally are capable of grief like mine. But there are more than you ever heard of who die of grief in this island of ours. I will tell you a common case. The rules of Eton require that a boy on the *foundation* should be there twelve years: he is superannuated at eighteen, consequently he must come at six. Children torn away from mothers and sisters at that age not unfrequently die. I speak of what I know. The complaint is not entered by the registrar as grief; but *that* it is. Grief of that sort, and at that age, has killed more than have ever been counted amongst its martyrs.

Therefore it is that Levana often communes with the powers that shake man's heart: therefore it is that she dotes on grief. "These ladies," said I softly to myself, on seeing the ministers with whom Levana was conversing, "these are the Sorrows; and they are three in number, as the *Graces*[1] are three, who dress man's life with

[1] Aglaia (brilliance), Euphrosyne (joy), and Thalia (bloom), presided over all beauty and charm in nature and humanity

beauty; the *Parcae*[2] are three, who weave the dark arras of man's life in their mysterious loom always with colours sad in part, sometimes angry with tragic crimson and black; the *Furies*[3] are three, who visit with retribution called from the other side of the grave offences that walk upon this; and once even the *Muses*[4] were but three, who fit the harp, the trumpet, or the lute, to the great burdens of man's impassioned creations. These are the Sorrows, all three of whom I know." The last words I say *now;* but in Oxford I said, "One of whom I know, and the others too surely I *shall* know." For already, in my fervent youth, I saw (dimly relieved upon the dark background of my dreams) the imperfect lineaments of the awful sisters. These sisters—by what name shall we call them?

If I say simply, "The Sorrows," there will be a chance of mistaking the term; it might be understood of individual sorrow—separate cases of sorrow—whereas I want a term expressing the mighty abstractions that incarnate themselves in all individual sufferings of man's heart; and I wish to have these abstractions presented as impersonations, that is, as clothed with human attributes of life, and with functions pointing to flesh. Let us call them, therefore, *Our Ladies of Sorrow.* I know them thoroughly, and have walked in all their kingdoms. Three sisters they are, of one mysterious household; and their paths are wide apart; but of their dominion there is no end. Them I saw often conversing with Levana, and sometimes about myself. Do they talk, then? Oh, no! Mighty phantoms like these disdain the infirmities of language. They may utter voices through the organs of man when they dwell in human hearts, but amongst themselves is no voice nor sound; eternal silence reigns in *their* kingdoms. *They* spoke not as they talked with Levana. *They* whispered not. *They* sang not. Though oftentimes methought they *might* have sung; for I upon earth had heard their mysteries oftentimes deciphered by harp and timbrel,[5] by dulcimer[6] and organ. Like God, whose servants they are, they utter their pleasure, not by sounds that perish, or by words that go astray, but by signs in

[2] the Fates, Clotho, Lachesis, and Atropos, who spun, measured, and snipped off, respectively, the thread of a human life

[3] Alecto, Megaera, and Tisiphone, the avenging deities of classical mythology

[4] the sisters (ultimately nine in number) who presided over the various arts and sciences in Greek mythology [5] tambourine [6] type of zither or of guitar

heaven, by changes on earth, by pulses in secret rivers, heraldries painted on darkness, and hieroglyphics written on the tablets of the brain. *They* wheeled in mazes; *I* spelled[7] the steps. *They* telegraphed from afar; *I* read the signals. *They* conspired together; and on the mirrors of darkness *my* eye traced the plots. *Theirs* were the symbols; *mine* are the words.

What is it the sisters are? What is it that they do? Let me describe their form, and their presence: if form it were that still fluctuated in its outline, or presence it were that for ever advanced to the front, or for ever receded amongst shades.

The eldest of the three is named *Mater Lachrymarum,* Our Lady of Tears. She it is that night and day raves and moans, calling for vanished faces. She stood in Rama, where a voice was heard of lamentation—Rachel[8] weeping for her children, and refusing to be comforted. She it was that stood in Bethlehem on the night when Herod's sword swept its nurseries of Innocents, and the little feet were stiffened for ever, which, heard at times as they tottered along floors overhead, woke pulses of love in household hearts that were not unmarked in heaven. Her eyes are sweet and subtle, wild and sleepy by turns; oftentimes rising to the clouds, oftentimes challenging the heavens. She wears a diadem round her head. And I knew by childish memories that she could go abroad upon the winds, when she heard the sobbing of litanies or the thundering of organs, and when she beheld the mustering of summer clouds. This sister, the eldest, it is that carries keys more than papal at her girdle, which open every cottage and every palace. She, to my knowledge, sat all last summer by the bedside of the blind beggar, him that so often and so gladly I talked with, whose pious daughter, eight years old, with the sunny countenance, resisted the temptations of play and village mirth to travel all day long on dusty roads with her afflicted father. For this did God send her a great reward. In the springtime of the year, and whilst yet her own Spring was budding. He recalled her to Himself. But her blind father mourns for ever over *her;* still he dreams at midnight that the little guiding

[7] spell out, interpret with difficulty

[8] in the Bible, the favorite of the two wives of Jacob, mother of Joseph and Benjamin

hand is locked within his own; and still he wakens to a darkness that is *now* within a second and a deeper darkness. This *Mater Lachrymarum* also has been sitting all this winter of 1844-5 within the bedchamber of the Czar, bringing before his eyes a daughter (not less pious) that vanished to God not less suddenly, and left behind her a darkness not less profound. By the power of the keys it is that Our Lady of Tears glides a ghostly intruder into the chambers of sleepless men, sleepless women, sleepless children, from Ganges to Nile, from Nile to Mississippi. And her, because she is the first-born of her house, and has the widest empire, let us honour with the title of "Madonna."

The second sister is called *Mater Suspiriorum,* Our Lady of Sighs. She never scales the clouds, nor walks abroad upon the winds. She wears no diadem. And her eyes, if they were ever seen, would be neither sweet nor subtle; no man could read their story; they would be found filled with perishing dreams, and with wrecks of forgotten delirium. But she raises not her eyes; her head, on which sits a dilapidated turban, droops for ever, for ever fastens on the dust. She weeps not. She groans not. But she sighs inaudibly at intervals. Her sister, Madonna, is oftentimes stormy and frantic, raging in the highest against heaven, and demanding back her darlings. But Our Lady of Sighs never clamours, never defies, dreams not of rebellious aspirations. She is humble to abjectness. Hers is the meekness that belongs to the hopeless. Murmur she may, but it is in her sleep. Whisper she may, but it is to herself in the twilight. Mutter she does at times, but it is in solitary places that are desolate as she is desolate, in ruined cities, and when the sun has gone down to his rest. This sister is the visitor of the Pariah,[9] of the Jew, of the bondsman to the oar in Mediterranean galleys, and of the English criminal in Norfolk Island,[10] blotted out from the books of remembrance in sweet far-off England, of the baffled penitent reverting his eyes for ever upon a solitary grave, which to him seems the altar overthrown of some past and bloody sacrifice, on which altar no oblations[11] can now be availing, whether towards pardon that he

[9] member of oppressed social class in Indian caste system, outcast

[10] off Australia, whither criminals used to be transported from England

[11] offerings

might implore, or towards reparation that he might attempt. Every slave that at noonday looks up to the tropical sun with timid reproach, as he points with one hand to the earth, our general mother, but for *him* a stepmother, as he points with the other hand to the Bible, our general teacher, but against *him* sealed and sequestered;[12] every woman sitting in darkness, without love to shelter her head, or hope to illumine her solitude, because the heaven-born instincts kindling in her nature germs of holy affections, which God implanted in her womanly bosom, having been stifled by social necessities, now burn sullenly to waste, like sepulchral lamps amongst the ancients; every nun defrauded of her unreturning Maytime[13] by wicked kinsmen,[14] whom God will judge; every captive in every dungeon; all that are betrayed, and all that are rejected outcasts by traditionary law, and children of *hereditary* disgrace—all these walk with Our Lady of Sighs. She also carries a key; but she needs it little. For her kingdom is chiefly amongst the tents of Shem,[15] and the houseless vagrant of every clime. Yet in the very highest walks of man she finds chapels of her own; and even in glorious England there are some that, to the world, carry their heads as proudly as the reindeer, who yet secretly have received her mark upon their foreheads.

But the third sister, who is also the youngest!—Hush, whisper whilst we talk of *her!* Her kingdom is not large, or else no flesh should live; but within that kingdom all power is hers. Her head, turreted[16] like that of Cybele,[17] rises almost beyond the reach of sight. She droops not, and her eyes rising so high *might* be hidden by distance; but, being what they are, they cannot be hidden; through the treble veil of crape which she wears, the fierce light of blazing misery, that rests not for matins[18] or for vespers,[19] for noon of day or noon of night, for ebbing or for flowing tide, may be read from the very ground. She is the defier of God. She is also the mother of lunacies, and the suggestress of suicides. Deep lie the

[12] set apart, removed [13] youth

[14] who forced young ladies under their jurisdiction to enter convents

[15] in the Bible, eldest of Noah's three sons, and traditional ancestor of the Semitic people [16] having whorls that form a conical spiral

[17] in Phrygian mythology, the goddess of nature [18] morning prayers

[19] evening prayers

roots of her power; but narrow is the nation that she rules. For she can approach only those in whom a profound nature has been upheaved by central convulsions; in whom the heart trembles and the brain rocks under conspiracies of tempest from without and tempest from within. Madonna moves with uncertain steps, fast or slow, but still with tragic grace. Our Lady of Sighs creeps timidly and stealthily. But this youngest sister moves with incalculable motions, bounding, and with a tiger's leaps. She carries no key; for, though coming rarely amongst men, she storms all doors at which she is permitted to enter at all. And *her* name is *Mater Tenebrarum*—Our Lady of Darkness.

These were the *Semnai Theai,* or Sublime Goddesses; these were the *Eumenides*[20] or Gracious Ladies (so called by antiquity in shuddering propitiation), of my Oxford dreams. Madonna spoke. She spoke by her mysterious hand. Touching my head, she beckoned to Our Lady of Sighs; and *what* she spoke, translated out of the signs which (except in dreams) no man reads, was this:

"Lo! here is he whom in childhood I dedicated to my altars. This is he that once I made my darling. Him I led astray, him I beguiled, and from heaven I stole away his young heart to mine. Through me did he become idolatrous: and through me it was, by languishing desires, that he worshipped the worm, and prayed to the wormy grave. Holy was the grave to him; lovely was its darkness; saintly its corruption. Him, this young idolater, I have seasoned for thee, dear gentle Sister of Sighs! Do thou take him now to *thy* heart, and season him for our dreadful sister. And thou"—turning to the *Mater Tenebrarum,* she said—"wicked sister, that temptest and hatest, do thou take him from *her.* See that thy sceptre lie heavy on his head. Suffer not woman and her tenderness to sit near him in his darkness. Banish the frailties of hope, wither the relentings of love, scorch the fountains of tears, curse him as only thou canst curse. So shall he be accomplished in the furnace, so shall he see the things that ought *not* to be seen, sights that are abominable, and secrets that are unutterable. So shall he read elder truths, sad truths, grand truths, fearful truths. So shall he rise again *before* he dies, and so shall our commission be accomplished which from God we had—to

[20] Furies

plague his heart until we had unfolded the capacities of his spirit."

☙§ For Thomas De Quincey, too, the essay in periodical writing was his major career. He left Oxford without a degree, to write for *Blackwood's* on opium-eating, on murder, on drama, on dreams, in what is often called a "poetic" or "ornate" or "impassioned" prose, which he consciously tried to restore from the days of Sir Thomas Browne.

Labour

FROM *Past and Present,* Chapter XI *(1843)*
BY *Thomas Carlyle (1795-1881)*

For there is a perennial nobleness, and even sacredness, in Work. Were he never so benighted, forgetful of his high calling, there is always hope in a man that actually and earnestly works: in Idleness alone is there perpetual despair. Work, never so Mammonish,[1] mean, *is* in communication with Nature; the real desire to get Work done will itself lead one more and more to truth, to Nature's appointments and regulations, which are truth.

The latest Gospel in this world is, Know thy work and do it. "Know thyself": long enough has that poor "self" of thine tormented thee; thou wilt never get to "know" it, I believe! Think it not thy business, this of knowing thyself; thou art an unknowable individual: know what thou canst work at; and work at it, like a Hercules! That will be thy better plan.

It has been written, "an endless significance lies in Work"; a man perfects himself by working. Foul jungles are cleared away, fair seed fields rise instead, and stately cities; and withal the man himself first ceases to be a jungle and foul unwholesome desert thereby. Consider how, even in the meanest sorts of Labour, the whole soul of a man is composed into a kind of real harmony, the instant he sets himself to work! Doubt, Desire, Sorrow, Remorse, Indignation, Despair itself, all these like helldogs lie beleaguering the soul of the poor dayworker, as of every man: but he bends himself with

[1] in sympathy with Mammon, false god of riches and greed

free valour against his task, and all these are stilled, all these shrink murmuring far off into their caves. The man is now a man. The blessed glow of Labour in him, is it not as purifying fire, wherein all poison is burnt up, and of sour smoke itself there is made bright blessed flame!

Destiny, on the whole, has no other way of cultivating us. A formless Chaos,[2] once set it *revolving*, grows round and ever rounder; ranges itself, by mere force of gravity, into strata, spherical courses; is no longer a Chaos, but a round compacted World. What would become of the Earth, did she cease to revolve? In the poor old Earth, so long as she revolves, all inequalities, irregularities disperse themselves; all irregularities are incessantly becoming regular. Hast thou looked on the Potter's wheel,—one of the venerablest objects; old as the Prophet Ezechiel[3] and far older? Rude lumps of clay, how they spin themselves up, by mere quick whirling, into beautiful circular dishes. And fancy the most assiduous Potter, but without his wheel; reduced to make dishes, or rather amorphous botches, by mere kneading and baking! Even such a Potter were Destiny, with a human soul that would rest and lie at ease, that would not work and spin! Of an idle unrevolving man the kindest Destiny, like the most assiduous Potter without wheel, can bake and knead nothing other than a botch; let her spend on him what expensive colouring, what gilding and enamelling she will, he is but a botch. Not a dish; no, a bulging, kneaded, crooked, shambling, squint-cornered,[4] amorphous botch—a mere enamelled vessel of dishonour! Let the idle think of this.

Blessed is he who has found his work; let him ask no other blessedness. He has a work, a life-purpose; he has found it, and will follow it! How, as a free-flowing channel, dug and torn by noble force through the sour mud-swamp of one's existence, like an ever-deepening river there, it runs and flows;—draining-off the sour festering water, gradually from the root of the remotest grass-blade; making, instead of pestilential swamp, a green fruitful meadow with its clear-flowing stream. How blessed for the meadow itself, let the

[2] formless matter and infinite space, supposed to have existed before the ordered universe

[3] also Ezekiel, Hebrew prophetic writer who lived in the 6th century B.C.

[4] misshapen

stream and *its* value be great or small! Labour is Life: from the inmost heart of the Worker rises his god-given Force, the sacred celestial Life-essence breathed into him by Almighty God; from his inmost heart awakens him to all nobleness,—to all knowledge, "self-knowledge" and much else, so soon as Work fitly begins. Knowledge? The knowledge that will hold good in working, cleave thou to that; for Nature herself accredits that, says Yea to that. Properly thou hast no other knowledge but what thou hast got by working: the rest is yet all a hypothesis of knowledge; a thing to be argued of in schools, a thing floating in the clouds, in endless logic-vortices, till we try it and fix it. "Doubt, of whatever kind, can be ended by Action alone."

And again, hast thou valued Patience, Courage, Perseverance, Openness to light; readiness to own thyself mistaken, to do better next time? All these, all virtues, in wrestling with the dim brute Powers of Fact, in ordering of thy fellows in such wrestle, there and elsewhere not at all, thou wilt continually learn. Set down a brave Sir Christopher[5] in the middle of black ruined Stone-heaps, of foolish unarchitectural Bishops, redtape Officials, idle Nell-Gwyn[6] Defenders of the Faith; and see whether he will ever raise a Paul's Cathedral[7] out of all that, yea or no! Rough, rude, contradictory are all things and persons, from the mutinous masons and Irish hodmen, up to the idle Nell-Gwyn Defenders, to blustering redtape Officials, foolish unarchitectural Bishops. All these things and persons are there not for Christopher's sake and his Cathedral's; they are there for their own sake mainly! Christopher will have to conquer and constrain all these,—if he be able. All these are against him. Equitable Nature herself, who carries her mathematics and architectonics not on the face of her, but deep in the hidden heart of her,—Nature herself is but partially for him; will be wholly against him, if he constrain her not! His very money, where is it to come from? The pious munificence of England lies far-scattered, distant, unable to speak, and say, "I am here";—must be spoken to before it can speak. Pious munificence, and all help, is so silent,

[5] Sir Christopher Wren (1632-1723), famous English architect

[6] Nell (Eleanor) Gwyn (1650-1687), English actress and mistress of Charles II, hence meretricious

[7] St. Paul's Cathedral, in London, for which Sir Christopher Wren is best known

invisible like the gods; impediment, contradictions manifold are so loud and near! O brave Sir Christopher, trust thou in those notwithstanding, and front all these; understand all these; by valiant patience, noble effort, insight, by man's strength, vanquish and compel all these,—and, on the whole, strike down[8] victoriously the last topstone of that Paul's Edifice; thy monument for certain[9] centuries, the stamp "Great Man" impressed very legibly on Portland-stone there!—

Yes, all manner of help, and pious response from Men or Nature, is always what we call silent; cannot speak or come to light, till it be seen, till it be spoken to. Every noble work is at first "impossible." In very truth, for every noble work the possibilities will lie diffused through Immensity; inarticulate, undiscoverable except to faith. Like Gideon[10] thou shalt spread out thy fleece at the door of thy tent; see whether under the wide arch of Heaven there be any bounteous moisture, or none. Thy heart and life-purpose shall be as a miraculous Gideon's fleece, spread out in silent appeal to Heaven: and from the kind Immensities,[11] what from the poor unkind Localities and town and country Parishes there never could, blessed dew-moisture to suffice thee shall have fallen![12]

Work is of a religious nature:—work is of a *brave* nature; which it is the aim of all religion to be. All work of man is as the swimmer's: a waste ocean threatens to devour him; if he front it not bravely, it will keep its word. By incessant wise defiance of it, rebuke and buffet of it, behold how it loyally supports him, bears him as its conqueror along. "It is so," says Goethe, "with all things that man undertakes in this world."

Brave Sea-captain, Norse Sea-king,—Columbus, my hero, royalest Sea-king of all! it is no friendly environment this of thine, in the waste deep waters; around thee mutinous discouraged souls, behind thee disgrace and ruin, before thee the unpenetrated veil of Night. Brother, these wild water-mountains, bounding from their deep bases (ten miles deep, I am told), are not entirely there on thy behalf! Meseems *they* have other work than floating thee forward:

[8] set firmly in place [9] sure to come about

[10] in the Bible, a hero and, for forty years, a judge of Israel

[11] heavenly expanses

[12] dew, as we have since learnt, does not fall but forms by condensation

—and the huge Winds, that sweep from Ursa Major to the Tropics and Equators, dancing their giant-waltz through the kingdoms of Chaos and Immensity, they care little about filling rightly or filling wrongly the small shoulder-of-mutton sails in this cockle-skiff of thine! Thou art not among articulate-speaking friends, my brother: thou art among immeasurable dumb monsters, tumbling, howling wide as the world here. Secret, far off, invisible to all hearts but thine, there lies a help in them: see how thou wilt get at that. Patiently thou wilt wait till the mad Southwester spend itself, saving thy self by dextrous science of defence, the while: valiantly, with swift decisions, wilt thou strike in, when the favouring East, the Possible, springs up. Mutiny of men thou wilt sternly repress; weakness, despondency, thou wilt cheerily encourage: thou wilt swallow down complaint, unreason, weariness, weakness of others and thyself;—how much wilt thou swallow down! There shall be a depth of Silence in thee, deeper than this Sea, which is but ten miles deep: a Silence unsoundable; known to God only. Thou shalt be a Great Man. Yes, my World-Soldier, thou of the World Marine-service,—thou wilt have to be *greater* than this tumultuous unmeasured World here round thee is: thou, in thy strong soul, as with wrestler's arms, shalt embrace it, harness it down; and make it bear thee on,—to new Americas, or whither God wills!

☙ From poverty in Scotland, from the University of Edinburgh, from his wife's farm at Craigenputtock and from Chelsea, Thomas Carlyle began writing by translating German, continued with work for the *London Magazine,* the *Edinburgh Review, Fraser's,* and other magazines, lectured on heroic medievalism, and wrote studies of the French Revolution and Frederick the Great. Volumes of his letters to Emerson, to Mill and others have been collected. His interest was in the power of intense hard-working individual leadership, as opposed to the rationalist views of Locke and the "enlightenment."

On self-reliance

FROM *Self-Reliance (1841)*
BY ***Ralph Waldo Emerson** (1803-1882)*

It is easy to see that a greater self-reliance must work a revolution in all the offices and relations of men; in their religion; in their education; in their pursuits; their modes of living; their association; in their property; in their speculative views.

1. In what prayers do men allow themselves! That which they call a holy office is not so much as brave and manly. Prayer looks abroad and asks for some foreign addition to come through some foreign virtue, and loses itself in endless mazes of natural and supernatural, and mediatorial[1] and miraculous. Prayer that craves a particular commodity, anything less than all good, is vicious. Prayer is the contemplation of the facts of life from the highest point of view. It is the soliloquy of a beholding and jubilant soul. It is the spirit of God pronouncing his works good. But prayer as a means to effect a private end is meanness and theft. It supposes dualism and not unity in nature and consciousness. As soon as the man is at one with God, he will not beg. He will then see prayer in all action. The prayer of the farmer kneeling in his field to weed it, the prayer of the rower kneeling with the stroke of his oar, are true prayers heard throughout nature, though for cheap ends. Caratach, in Fletcher's[2]

[1] meditating, seeking favors from a high person for a lower one, from God for man
[2] John Fletcher (1579-1625), English dramatist, collaborated with Francis Beaumont

Bonduca, when admonished to inquire the mind of the god Andate, replies,—

> His hidden meaning lies in our endeavors
> Our valors are our best gods.

Another sort of false prayers are our regrets. Discontent is the want of self-reliance: it is infirmity of will. Regret calamities if you can thereby help the sufferer; if not, attend your own work and already the evil begins to be repaired. Our sympathy is just as base. We come to them who weep foolishly and sit down and cry for company, instead of imparting to them truth and health in rough electric shocks, putting them once more in communication with their own reason. The secret of fortune is joy in our hands. Welcome evermore to gods and men is the self-helping man. For him all doors are flung wide; him all tongues greet, all honors crown, all eyes follow with desire. Our love goes out to him and embraces him because he did not need it. We solicitously and apologetically caress and celebrate him because he held on his way and scorned our disapprobation. The gods love him because men hated him. "To the persevering mortal," said Zoroaster,[3] the blessed Immortals are swift."

As men's prayers are a disease of the will, so are their creeds a disease of the intellect. They say with those foolish Israelites, "Let not God speak to us, lest we die. Speak thou, speak any man with us, and we will obey." Everywhere I am hindered of meeting God in my brother, because he has shut his own temple doors and recites fables merely of his brother's, or his brother's brother's God. Every new mind is a new classification. If it prove a mind of uncommon activity and power, a Locke,[4] a Lavoisier,[5] a Hutton,[6] a Bentham,[7] a Fourier,[8] it imposes its classification on other men, and lo! a new system. In proportion to the depth of the thought and so to the

[3]also Zarathustra, founder of the pre-Islamic Persian religion, Zoroastrianism, which held to belief in an afterlife and in a ceaseless struggle between good and evil 7th century B.C. [4]John Locke, *cf.* "Political Societies" above [5]Antoine Laurent Lavoisier (1734-1794) French chemist founder of modern chemistry

[6]James Hutton (1726-1797), Scottish geologist and natural philosopher, wrote *Theory of the Earth*

[7]Jeremy Bentham (1748-1832), English philosopher and political scientist [8]François Marie Charles Fourier (1772-1837), French socialist and reformer

number of the objects it touches and brings within reach of the pupil, is his complacency. But chiefly is this apparent in creeds and churches, which are also classifications of some powerful mind acting on the elemental thought of duty and man's relation to the Highest. Such is Calvinism, Quakerism, Swedenborgism.[9] The pupil takes the same delight in subordinating everything to the new terminology as a girl who has just learned botany in seeing a new earth and new seasons thereby. It will happen for a time that the pupil will find his intellectual power has grown by the study of his master's mind. But in all unbalanced minds the classification is idolized, passes for the end and not for a speedily exhaustible means, so that the walls of the system blend to their eye in the remote horizon with the walls of the universe; the luminaries of heaven seem to them hung on the arch their master built. They cannot imagine how you aliens have any right to see—how you can see; "It must be somehow that you stole the light from us." They do not yet perceive that light, unsystematic, indomitable, will break into any cabin, even into theirs. Let them chirp awhile and call it their own. If they are honest and do well, presently their neat new pinfold will be too strait and low, will crack, will lean, will rot and vanish, and the immortal light, all young and joyful, million-orbed, million-colored, will beam over the universe as on the first morning.

2. It is for want of self-culture that the superstition of Travelling, whose idols are Italy, England, Egypt, retains its fascination for all educated Americans. They who made England, Italy, or Greece venerable in the imagination, did so by sticking fast where they were, like an axis of the earth. In manly hours we feel that duty is our place. The soul is no traveller; the wise man stays at home, and when his necessities, his duties, on any occasion call him from his house, or into foreign lands, he is at home still and shall make men sensible by the expression of his countenance that he goes, the missionary of wisdom and virtue, and visits cities and men like a sovereign and not like an interloper or a valet.

I have no churlish objection to the circumnavigation of the globe for the purposes of art, of study, and benevolence, so that the man is first domesticated, or does not go abroad with the hope of finding

[9]religious system based on the doctrines of Emanuel Swedenborg (1688-1772), Swedish scientist, and mystic, who claimed Scriptural revelations from God

somewhat greater than he knows. He who travels to be amused, or to get somewhat which he does not carry, travels away from himself, and grows old even in youth among old things. In Thebes,[10] in Palmyra,[11] his will and mind have become old and dilapidated as they. He carries ruins to ruins.

Travelling is a fool's paradise. Our first journeys discover to us the indifference of places. At home I dream that at Naples, at Rome, I can be intoxicated with beauty and lose my sadness. I pack my trunk, embrace my friends, embark on the sea, and at last wake up in Naples, and there beside me is the stern fact, the sad self, unrelenting, identical, that I fled from. I seek the Vatican and palaces. I affect to be intoxicated with sights and suggestions, but I am not intoxicated. My giant goes with me wherever I go.

3. But the rage of travelling is a symptom of a deeper unsoundness affecting the whole intellectual action. The intellect is vagabond, and our system of education fosters restlessness. Our minds travel when our bodies are forced to stay at home. We imitate; and what is imitation but the travelling of the mind? Our houses are built with foreign taste; our shelves are garnished with foreign ornaments; our opinions, our tastes, our faculties, lean, and follow the Past and the Distant. The soul created the arts wherever they have flourished. It was in his own mind that the artist sought his model. It was an application of his own thought to the thing to be done and the conditions to be observed. And why need we copy the Doric[12] or the Gothic[13] model? Beauty, convenience, grandeur of thought and quaint expression are as near to us as to any, and if the American artist will study with hope and love the precise thing to be done by him, considering the climate, the soil, the length of the day, the wants of the people, the habit and form of the government, he will create a house in which all these will find themselves fitted, and tastes and sentiment will be satisfied also.

Insist on yourself; never imitate. Your own gift you can present every moment with the cumulative force of a whole life's cultivation; but of the adopted talent of another you have only an extemporaneous half possession. That which each can do best, none but his Maker can teach him. No man yet knows what it is, nor can, till

[10] a city in ancient Greece [11] ancient city in Syria

[12] style marked by simplicity of form [13] style marked by elaborateness

that person has exhibited it. Where is the master who could have taught Shakespeare? Where is the master who could have instructed Franklin, or Washington, or Bacon, or Newton? Every great man is a unique. The Scipionism of Scipio[14] is precisely that part he could not borrow. Shakespeare will never be made by the study of Shakespeare. Do that which is assigned you, and you cannot hope too much or dare too much. There is at this moment for you an utterance brave and grand as that of the colossal chisel of Phidias,[15] or trowel of the Egyptians, or the pen of Moses or Dante, but different from all these. Not possibly will the soul, all rich, all eloquent, with thousand-cloven tongue,[16] deign to repeat itself; but if you can hear what these patriarchs say, surely you can reply to them in the same pitch of voice; for the ear and the tongue are two organs of one nature. Abide in the simple and noble regions of thy life, obey thy heart, and thou shalt reproduce the Foreworld again.

4. As our Religion, our Education, our Art look abroad, so does our spirit of society. All men plume themselves on the improvement of society, and no man improves.

Society never advances. It recedes as fast on one side as it gains on the other. It undergoes continual changes; it is barbarous, it is civilized, it is christianized, it is rich, it is scientific; but this change is not amelioration. For everything that is given something is taken. Society acquires new arts and loses old instincts. What a contrast between the well-clad, reading, writing, thinking American, with a watch, a pencil, and a bill of exchange in his pocket, and the naked New Zealander, whose property is a club, a spear, a mat, and an undivided twentieth of a shed to sleep under! But compare the health of the two men and you shall see that the white man has lost his aboriginal strength. If the traveller tells us truly, strike the savage with a broad-axe and in a day or two the flesh shall unite and heal as if you struck the blow into soft pitch, and the same blow shall send the white to his grave.

The civilized man has built a coach, but has lost the use of his feet. He is supported on crutches, but lacks so much support of

[14] leader of the "Scipionic circle," Scipio Aemilianus Africanus, Publius Cornelius the younger (c. 185-129 B.C.)

[15] famous Greek sculptor, lived 5th century B.C.

[16] having innumerable forks; used in a complimentary sense

muscle. He has a fine Geneva watch, but he fails of the skill to tell the hour by the sun. A Greenwich[17] nautical almanac he has, and so being sure of the information when he wants it, the man in the street does not know a star in the sky. The solstice he does not observe; the equinox he knows as little; and the whole bright calendar of the year is without a dial in his mind. His note-books impair his memory; his libraries overload his wit; the insurance-office increases the number of accidents; and it may be a question whether machinery does not encumber; whether we have not lost by refinement some energy, by a Christianity, entrenched in establishments and forms, some vigor of wild virtue. For every Stoic was a Stoic; but in Christendom where is the Christian?

There is no more deviation in the moral standard than in the standard of height or bulk. No greater men are now than ever were. A singular equality may be observed between the great men of the first and of the last ages; nor can all the science, art, religion, and philosophy of the nineteenth century avail to educate greater men than Plutarch's heroes, three or four and twenty centuries ago. Not in time is the race progressive. Phocion,[18] Socrates,[19] Anaxagoras,[20] Diogenes,[21] are great men, but they leave no class. He who is really of their class will not be called by their name, but will be his own man, and in his turn the founder of a sect. The arts and inventions of each period are only its costume and do not invigorate men. The harm of the improved machinery may compensate its good. Hudson[22] and Bering[23] accomplished so much in their fishing-boats as to astonish Parry[24] and Franklin, whose equipment exhausted the resources of science and art. Galileo,[25] with an opera-glass, discovered a more splendid series of celestial phenomena than

[17] a borough in London, formerly the site of an astronomical observatory

[18] Athenian statesman general (c. 402-317 B.C.)

[19] Athenian idealist philosopher and teacher (c. 470-399 B.C.)

[20] Greek philosopher and geometrician (c. 500-428 B.C.), advanced the theory of atoms

[21] Greek Cynic philosopher (c. 412-323 B.C.), lived in a tub to show his austerity, and searched with a lantern for an honest man

[22] Henry Hudson (died 1611), English navigator and explorer, discovered river and bay named after him [23] Vitus Bering (1680-1741) Danish navigator for whom Bering Straits were named

[24] Sir William Edward Parry (1790-1855), English arctic explorer

[25] Italian astronomer and physicist (1554-1642)

any one since. Columbus found the New World in an undecked boat. It is curious to see the periodical disuse and perishing of means and machinery which were introduced with loud laudation a few years or centuries before. The great genius returns to essential man. We reckoned the improvements of the art of war among the triumphs of science, and yet Napoleon conquered Europe by the bivouac, which consisted of falling back on naked valor and disencumbering it of all aids. The Emperor held it impossible to make a perfect army, says Las Cases[26] "without abolishing our arms, magazines, commissaries and carriages, until, in imitation of the Roman custom, the soldier should receive his supply of corn, grind it in his hand-mill, and bake his bread himself."

Society is a wave. The wave moves onward, but the water of which it is composed does not. The same particle does not rise from the valley to the ridge. Its unity is only phenomenal. The persons who make up a nation to-day, next year die, and their experience dies with them.

And so the reliance on Property, including the reliance on governments which protect it, is the want of self-reliance. Men have looked away from themselves and at things so long that they have come to esteem the religious, learned and civil institutions as guards of property, and they deprecate assaults on these, because they feel them to be assaults on property. They measure their esteem of each other by what each has, and not by what each is. But a cultivated man becomes ashamed of his property, out of new respect for his nature. Especially he hates what he has if he sees that it is accidental,—came to him by inheritance, or gift, or crime; then he feels that it is not having; it does not belong to him, has no root in him, and merely lies there because no revolution or no robber takes it away. But that which a man is, does always by necessity acquire; and what the man acquires, is living property, which does not wait the beck of rulers, or mobs, or revolutions, or fire, or storm, or bankruptcies, but perpetually renews itself wherever the man breathes. "Thy lot or portion of life," said the Caliph[27] Ali,[28] is seeking after thee; therefore be at rest from seeking after it." Our depend-

[26] Comte Emmanuel Augustin Dieudonne de Las Cases (1766-1842), historian, companion of Napoleon at St. Helena, 1815-1816

[27] title of Mohammed's successors as secular and religious heads of Islam

[28] son-in-law of Mohammed, fourth caliph of Islam (600-661 A.D.)

ence on these foreign goods leads us to our slavish respect for numbers. The political parties meet in numberous conventions; the greater the concourse and with each new uproar of announcement, The delegation from Essex! The Democrats from New Hampshire! The Whigs of Maine! the young patriot feels himself stronger than before by a new thousand of eyes and arms. In like manner the reformers summon conventions and vote and resolve in multitude. Not so, O friends! will the God deign to enter and inhabit you, but by a method precisely the reverse. It is only as a man puts off all foreign support and stands alone that I see him to be strong and to prevail. He is weaker by every recruit to his banner. Is not a man better than a town? Ask nothing of men, and, in the endless mutation, thou only firm column must presently appear the upholder of all that surrounds thee. He who knows that power is inborn, that he is weak because he has looked for good out of him and elsewhere, and, so perceiving, throws himself unhesitatingly on his thought, instantly rights himself, stands in the erect position, commands his limbs, works miracles; just as a man who stands on his feet is stronger than a man who stands on his head.

So use all that is called Fortune. Most men gamble with her, and gain all, and lose all, as her wheel rolls. But do thou leave as unlawful these winnings, and deal with Cause and Effect, the chancellors of God. In the Will work and acquire, and thou hast chained the wheel of Chance, and shall sit hereafter out of fear from her rotations. A political victory, a rise of rents, the recovery of your sick or the return of your absent friend, or some other favorable event raises your spirits, and you think good days are preparing for you. Do not believe it. Nothing can bring you peace but yourself. Nothing can bring you peace but the triumph of principles.

☙ Educated for the ministry at Harvard, Ralph Waldo Emerson later gave up his Boston pastorate, traveled in England and Europe, and settled in Concord to write—on nature and the transcendental over-soul. He lectured widely, contributed to James Russell Lowell's *Atlantic Monthly,* participated in anti-slavery campaigns, and kept a journal of his musings. His force of belief, like Carlyle's, was in the presence of duty in the individual person, even in the individual object. The transcendental tradition in American thought prospered especially on the lecture circuit and at Chautauqua meetings.

Worms and the soil

FROM *The Formation of Vegetable Mould, Through the Action of Worms, with Observations on Their Habits (1881)*

BY *Charles Darwin (1809-1882)*

Worms have played a more important part in the history of the world than most persons would at first suppose. In almost all humid countries they are extraordinarily numerous, and for their size possess great muscular power. In many parts of England a weight of more than ten tons of dry earth annually passes through their bodies and is brought to the surface on each acre of land; so that the whole superficial bed of vegetable mould passes through their bodies in the course of every few years. From the collapsing of the old burrows the mould is in constant though slow movement, and the particles composing it are thus rubbed together. By these means fresh surfaces are continually exposed to the action of the carbonic acid in the soil, and of the humus-acids[1] which appear to be still more efficient in the decomposition of rocks. The generation of the humus-acids is probably hastened during the digestion of the many half-decayed leaves which worms consume. Thus the particles of earth, forming the superficial mould, are subjected to conditions eminently favorable for their decomposition and disintegration. Moreover, the particles of the softer rocks suffer some amount of

[1] acids in the humus, a brown or black substance resulting from the partial decay of leaves and other vegetable matter

mechanical trituration[2] in the muscular gizzards of worms, in which small stones serve as mill-stones.

The finely levigated[3] castings,[4] when brought to the surface in a moist condition, flow during rainy weather down any moderate slope; and the smaller particles are washed far down even a gently inclined surface. Castings when dry often crumple into small pellets and these are apt to roll down any sloping surface. Where the land is quite level and is covered with herbage, and where the climate is humid so that much dust cannot be blown away, it appears at first sight impossible that there should be any appreciable amount of subaerial[5] denudation; but worm castings are blown, especially whilst moist and viscid, in one uniform direction by the prevalent winds which are accompanied by rain. By these several means the superficial mould is prevented from accumulating to a great thickness; and a thick bed of mould checks in many ways the disintegration of the underlying rocks and fragments of rock.

The removal of worm castings by the above means leads to results which are far from insignificant. It has been shown that a layer of earth, two tenths of an inch in thickness, is in many places annually brought to the surface per acre; and if a small part of this amount flows, or rolls, or is washed, even for a short distance down every inclined surface, or is repeatedly blown in one direction, a great effect will be produced in the course of ages. It was found by measurements and calculations that on a surface with a mean inclination of 9°26′, two and four tenths cubic inches of earth which had been ejected by worms crossed, in the course of a year, a horizontal line one yard in length; so that 240 cubic inches would cross a line 100 yards in length. This latter amount in a damp state would weigh 11½ pounds. Thus a considerable weight of earth is continually moving down each side of every valley, and will in time reach its bed. Finally this earth will be transported by the streams flowing in the valleys into the ocean, the great receptacle for all matter denuded from the land. It is known from the amount of sediment annually delivered into the sea by the Mississippi, that its enor-

[2] rubbing or grinding into very fine particles or powder

[3] ground to a fine, smooth powder [4] things thrown off or ejected

[5] beneath the air, hence on the surface

mous drainage-area must on an average be lowered .00263 of an inch each year; and this would suffice in four and a half million years to lower the whole drainage-area to the level of the seashore. So that, if a small fraction of the layer of fine earth, two tenths of an inch in thinkness, which is annually brought to the surface by worms, is carried away, a great result cannot fail to be produced within a period which no geologist considers extremely long.

Archaeologists ought to be grateful to worms, as they protect and preserve for an indefinitely long period every object not liable to decay, which is dropped on the surface of the land, by burying it beneath their castings. Thus, also, many elegant and curious tessellated[6] pavements and other ancient remains have been preserved; though no doubt the worms have in these cases been largely aided by earth washed and blown from the adjoining land, especially when cultivated. The old tessellated pavements have, however, often suffered by having subsided unequally from being unequally undermined by the worms. Even old massive walls may be undermined and subside; and no building is in this respect safe, unless the foundations lie six or seven feet beneath the surface, at a depth at which worms cannot work. It is probable that many monoliths[7] and some old walls have fallen down from having been undermined by worms.

Worms prepare the ground in an excellent manner for the growth of fibrous-rooted plants and for seedlings of all kinds. They periodically expose the mould to the air, and sift it so that no stones larger than the particles which they can swallow are left in it. They mingle the whole intimately together, like a gardener who prepares fine soil for his choicest plants. In this state it is well fitted to retain moisture and to absorb all soluble substances, as well as for the process of nitrification.[8] The bones of dead animals, the harder parts of insects, the shells of land-molluscs, leaves, twigs, etc., are before long all buried beneath the accumulated castings of worms, and are thus brought in a more or less decayed state within reach of the roots of plants. Worms likewise drag an infinite number of dead

[6] laid out in a mosaic pattern of small, square blocks

[7] in architecture, single large blocks of stone

[8] impregnation of soil with nitrates, which serve as fertilizers

leaves and other parts of plants into their burrows, partly for the sake of plugging them up and partly as food.

The leaves which are dragged into the burrows as food, after being torn into the finest shreds, partially digested, and saturated with the intestinal and urinary secretions, are commingled with much earth. This earth forms the dark colored, rich humus which almost everywhere covers the surface of the land with a fairly well-defined layer or mantle. Von Hensen placed two worms in a vessel eighteen inches in diameter, which was filled with sand, on which fallen leaves were strewed; and these were soon dragged into their burrows to a depth of three inches. After about six weeks an almost uniform layer of sand four tenths of an inch in thickness was converted into humus by having passed through the alimentary canals of these two worms. It is believed by some people that worm burrows, which often penetrate the ground almost perpendicularly to a depth of five or six feet, materially aid in its drainage; notwithstanding that the viscid castings piled over the mouths of the burrows prevent or check the rainwater directly entering them. They allow the air to penetrate deeply into the ground. They also greatly facilitate the downward passage of roots of moderate size; and these will be nourished by the humus with which the burrows are lined. Many seeds owe their germination to having been covered by castings; and others buried to a considerable depth beneath accumulated castings lie dormant, until at some future time they are accidentally uncovered and germinate.

Worms are poorly provided with sense-organs, for they cannot be said to see, although they can just distinguish between light and darkness; they are completely deaf, and have only a feeble power of smell; the sense of touch alone is well developed. They can therefore learn little about the outside world, and it is surprising that they should exhibit some skill in lining their burrows with their castings and with leaves, and in the case of some species in piling up their castings into tower-like constructions. But it is far more surprising that they should apparently exhibit some degree of intelligence instead of a mere blind instinctive impulse, in their manner of plugging up the mouths of their burrows. They act in nearly the same manner as would a man, who had to close a cylindrical tube with different kinds of leaves, petioles,[9] triangles of paper, etc., for they commonly seize such objects by their pointed ends. But with thin objects a certain number are drawn in by their broader ends. They do not act in the same unvarying manner in all cases, as do most of the lower animals; for instance, they do not drag in leaves by their foot-stalks, unless the basal part of the blade is as narrow as the apex, or narrower than it.

When we behold a wide, turf-covered expanse, we should remember that its smoothness, on which so much of its beauty depends, is mainly due to all the inequalities having been slowly leveled by worms. It is a marvelous reflection that the whole of the superficial mould over any such expanse has passed, and will again pass, every few years through the bodies of worms. The plough is one of the most ancient and most valuable of man's inventions; but long before he existed the land was in fact regularly ploughed, and still continues to be thus ploughed by earth-worms. It may be doubted whether there are many other animals which have played so important a part in the history of the world, as have these lowly organized creatures. Some other animals, however, still more lowly organized, namely corals, have done far more conspicuous work in having constructed innumerable reefs and islands in the great oceans; but these are almost confined to the tropical zones.

[9] the stalks to which leaves are attached

Grandson of the botanist Erasmus Darwin, Charles Darwin embarked, after education at Edinburgh and Oxford, on the voyage of the "Beagle" to South America, his first experience in the field of geology and natural history, reports on which he published during the 1840's. His *On the Origin of Species by Means of Natural Selection* came a decade later in 1859. After his theory of evolution had been supported by other scholars, he continued to write for another twenty years on plants, animals, and men. Note the presentative quality of his style.

Conclusion

FROM *Walden, or Life in the Woods (1854)*

BY ***Henry David Thoreau*** *(1817-1862)*

To the sick the doctors wisely recommend a change of air and scenery. Thank Heaven, here is not all the world. The buckeye does not grow in New England, and the mockingbird is rarely heard here. The wild goose is more of a cosmopolite than we; he breaks his fast in Canada, takes a luncheon in the Ohio, and plumes himself for the night in a southern bayou. Even the bison, to some extent, keeps pace with the seasons, cropping the pastures of the Colorado only till a greener and sweeter grass awaits him by the Yellowstone. Yet we think that if rail fences are pulled down, and stone walls piled up on our farms, bounds are henceforth set to our lives and our fates decided. If you are chosen town clerk, forsooth, you cannot go to Tierra del Fuego this summer; but you may go to the land of infernal fire nevertheless. The universe is wider than our views of it.

Yet we should oftener look over the taffel[1] of our craft, like curious passengers, and not make the voyage like stupid sailors picking oakum. The other side of the globe is but the home of our correspondent. Our voyaging is only great-circle sailing, and the doctors prescribe for diseases of the skin merely. One hastens to southern Africa to chase the giraffe; but surely that is not the game he would be after. How long, pray, would a man hunt giraffes if he

[1] taffrail, the rail across the stern of a vessel

could? Snipes and woodcocks also may afford rare sport; but I trust it would be nobler game to shoot one's self.—

> Direct your eye right inward, and you'll find
> A thousand regions in your mind
> Yet undiscovered. Travel them, and be
> Expert in home-cosmography.

What does Africa,—what does the West stand for? Is not our own interior white on the chart? black though it may prove, like the coast, when discovered. Is it the source of the Nile, or the Niger, or the Mississippi, or a Northwest Passage around this continent, that we would find? Are these the problems which most concern mankind? Is Franklin[2] the only man who is lost, that his wife should be so earnest to find him? Does Mr. Grinnell[3] know where he himself is? Be rather the Mungo Park,[4] the Lewis and Clark[5] and Frobisher,[6] of your own streams and oceans; explore your own higher latitudes,—with shiploads of preserved meats to support you, if they be necessary; and pile the empty cans sky-high for a sign. Were preserved meats invented to preserve meat merely? Nay, be a Columbus to whole new continents and worlds within you, opening new channels, not of trade, but of thought. Every man is the lord of a realm beside which the earthly empire of the Czar is but a petty state, a hummock[7] left by the ice. Yet some can be patriotic who have no *self*-respect, and sacrifice the greater to the less. They love the soil which makes their graves, but have no sympathy with the spirit which may still animate their clay. Patriotism is a maggot in their heads. What was the meaning of that South-Sea Exploring Expedition, with all its parade and expense, but an indirect recognition of the fact that there are continents and seas in the moral world

[2] Sir John Franklin (1786-1847), explorer

[3] Henry Grinnell (1799-1874), American merchant who in 1850 fitted out an expedition to go in search of Sir John Franklin; the expedition found an unknown body of land, now named after Grinnell, but did not find Sir John, lost seeking the Northwest Passage [4] Scotsman (1771-c. 1806), African explorer

[5] Meriwether Lewis (1774-1809) and William Clark (or Clarke) (1770-1838), commanded an exploring expedition from St. Louis to the Columbia, 1804-1806

[6] Sir Martin Frobisher (died 1594), English navigator who, seeking the Northwest Passage found the bay that now bears his name

[7] a ridge, as on a floe of ice

to which every man is an isthmus or an inlet, yet unexplored by him, but that it is easier to sail many thousand miles through cold and storm and cannibals, in a government ship, with five hundred men and boys to assist one, than it is to explore the private sea, the Atlantic and Pacific Ocean of one's being alone.—

> Erret, et extremos alter scrutetur Iberos.
> Plus habet hic vitae, plus habet ille viae.[8]

Let them wander and scrutinize the outlandish Australians. I have more of God, they more of the road.

It is not worth the while to go round the world to count the cats in Zanzibar.[9] Yet do this even till you can do better, and you may perhaps find some "Symmes' Hole"[10] by which to get at the inside at last. England and France, Spain and Portugal, Gold Coast[11] and Slave Coast[12] all front on this private sea; but no bark from them has ventured out of sight of land, though it is without doubt the direct way to India. If you would learn to speak all tongues and conform to the customs of all nations, if you would travel farther than all travellers, be naturalized in all climes, and cause the Sphinx to dash her head against a stone, even obey the precept of the old philosopher, and Explore thyself. Herein are demanded the eye and the nerve. Only the defeated and deserters go to the wars, cowards that run away and enlist. Start now on that farthest western way, which does not pause at the Mississippi or the Pacific, nor conduct toward a worn-out China or Japan, but leads on direct, a tangent to this sphere, summer and winter, day and night, sun down, moon down, and at last earth down too.

It is said that Mirabeau[13] took to highway robbery "to ascertain what degree of resolution was necessary in order to place one's self in formal opposition to the most sacred laws of society." He de-

[8]literally, let a man wander and scrutinize furthest Iberia. While he has more of travel, another has more of life. From Claudian's "Old Man of Verona."

[9]island off the eastern coast of Africa

[10]in 1818 Capt. John Cleves Symmes of St. Louis argued that the earth was open at the poles and habitable in the center [11]modern Ghana [12]modern Nigeria

[13]Gabriel Honoré Riquetti, Comte de Mirabeau (1749-1791), the greatest orator of the French Revolution

clared that "a soldier who fights in the ranks does not require half so much courage as a foot-pad,"—"that honor and religion have never stood in the way of a well-considered and a firm resolve." This was manly, as the world goes; and yet it was idle, if not desperate. A saner man would have found himself often enough "in formal opposition" to what are deemed "the most sacred laws of society," through obedience to yet more sacred laws, and so have tested his resolution without going out of his way. It is not for a man to put himself in such an attitude to society, but to maintain himself in whatever attitude he find himself through obedience to the laws of his being, which will never be one of opposition to a just government, if he should chance to meet with such.

I left the woods for as good a reason as I went there. Perhaps it seemed to me that I had several more lives to live, and could not spare more time for that one. It is remarkable how easily and insensibly we fall into a particular route, and make a beaten track for ourselves. I had not lived there a week before my feet wore a path from my door to the pond-side; and though it is five or six years since I trod it, it is still quite distinct. It is true, I fear, that others may have fallen into it, and so helped to keep it open. The surface of the earth is soft and impressible by the feet of men; and so with the paths which the mind travels. How worn and dusty, then, must be the highways of the world, how deep the ruts of tradition and conformity! I did not wish to take a cabin passage, but rather to go before the mast and on the deck of the world, for there I could best see the moonlight amid the mountains. I do not wish to go below now.

I learned this, at least, by my experiment: that if one advances confidently in the direction of his dreams, and endeavors to live the life which he has imagined, he will meet with a success unexpected in common hours. He will put some things behind, will pass an invisible boundary; new, universal, and more liberal laws will begin to establish themselves around and within him; or the old laws be expanded, and interpreted in his favor in a more liberal sense, and he will live with the license of a higher order of beings. In proportion as he simplifies his life, the laws of the universe will appear less complex, and solitude will not be solitude, nor poverty poverty, nor weakness weakness. If you have built castles in the air, your work need not be lost; that is where they should be. Now put the foundations under them.

It is a ridiculous demand which England and America make, that you shall speak so that they can understand you. Neither men nor toadstools grow so. As if that were important, and there were not enough to understand you without them. As if Nature could support but one order of understandings, could not sustain birds as well as quadrupeds, flying as well as creeping things, and *hush* and *whoa,* which Bright can understand, were the best English. As if there were safety in stupidity alone. I fear chiefly lest my expression may not be *extra-vagant*[14] enough, may not wander far enough beyond the narrow limits of my daily experience, so as to be adequate to the truth of which I have been convinced. *Extra vagance!* it depends on how you are yarded. The migrating buffalo, which seeks new pastures in another latitude, is not extravagant like the cow which kicks over the pail, leaps the cowyard fence, and runs after her calf, in milking time. I desire to speak somewhere *without* bounds; like a man in a waking moment, to men in their waking moments; for I am convinced that I cannot exaggerate enough even to lay the foundation of a true expression. Who that has heard a strain of music feared then lest he should speak extravagantly any more forever? In view of the future or possible, we should live quite laxly and undefined in front, our outlines dim and misty on that side; as our shadows reveal an insensible perspiration toward the sun. The volatile truth of our words should continually betray the inadequacy of the residual statement. Their truth is instantly *translated;* its literal monument alone remains. The words which express our faith and piety are not definite; yet they are significant and fragrant like frankincense to superior natures.

Why level downward to our dullest perception always, and praise that as common sense? The commonest sense is the sense of men asleep, which they express by snoring. Sometimes we are inclined to class those who are once-and-a-half-witted with the half-witted, because we appreciate only a third part of their wit. Some would find fault with the morning red, if they ever got up early enough. "They pretend," as I hear, "that the verses of Kabir[15] have four

[14] Latin in root, means literally wandering outside (boundaries)

[15] Hindu religious reformer

different senses; illusion, spirit, intellect, and the esoteric doctrine of the Vedas";[16] but in this part of the world it is considered a ground for complaint if a man's writings admit of more than one interpretation. While England endeavors to cure the potato-rot, will not any endeavor to cure the brain-rot, which prevails so much more widely and fatally?

I do not suppose that I have attained to obscurity, but I should be proud if no more fatal fault were found with my pages on this score than was found with the Walden ice. Southern customers objected to its blue color, which is the evidence of its purity, as if it were muddy, and preferred the Cambridge ice, which is white, but tastes of weeds. The purity men love is like the mists which envelop the earth, and not like the azure ether beyond.

Some are dinning in our ears that we Americans, and moderns generally, are intellectual dwarfs compared with the ancients, or even the Elizabethan men. But what is that to the purpose? A living dog is better than a dead lion. Shall a man go and hang himself because he belongs to the race of pygmies, and not be the biggest pygmy that he can? Let every one mind his own business, and endeavor to be what he was made.

Why should we be in such desperate haste to succeed and in such desperate enterprises? If a man does not keep pace with his companions, perhaps it is because he hears a different drummer. Let him step to the music which he hears, however measured or far away. It is not important that he should mature as soon as an apple tree or an oak. Shall he turn his spring into summer? If the condition of things which we were made for is not yet, what were any reality which we can substitute? We will not be shipwrecked on a vain reality. Shall we with pains erect a heaven of blue glass over ourselves, though when it is done we shall be sure to gaze still at the true ethereal heaven far above, as if the former were not?

There was an artist in the city of Kouroo who was disposed to strive after perfection. One day it came into his mind to make a staff. Having considered that in an imperfect work time is an ingredient, but into a perfect work time does not enter, he said to himself, it shall be perfect in all respects, though I should do nothing else in

[16] Hindu sacred literature

my life. He proceeded instantly to the forest for wood, being resolved that it should not be made of unsuitable material; and as he searched for and rejected stick after stick, his friends gradually deserted him, for they grew old in their works and died, but he grew not older by a moment. His singleness of purpose and resolution, and his elevated piety, endowed him, without his knowledge, with perennial youth. As he made no compromise with Time, Time kept out of the way, and only sighed at a distance because he could not overcome him. Before he had found a stick in all respects suitable the city of Kouroo was a hoary ruin, and he sat on one of its mounds to peel the stick. Before he had given it the proper shape the dynasty of the Candahars was at an end, and with the point of the stick he wrote the name of the last of that race in the sand, and then resumed his work. By the time he had smoothed and polished the staff Kalpa[17] was no longer the pole-star; and ere he had put on the ferule and the head adorned with precious stones, Brahma had awoke and slumbered many times. But why do I stay to mention these things? When the finishing stroke was put to his work, it suddenly expanded before the eyes of the astonished artist into the fairest of all the creations of Brahma. He had made a new system in making a staff, a world with full and fair proportions; in which, though the old cities and dynasties had passed away, fairer and more glorious ones had taken their places. And now he saw by the heap of shavings still fresh at his feet, that, for him and his work, the former lapse of time had been an illusion, and that no more time had elapsed than is required for a single scintillation from the brain of Brahma to fall on and inflame the tinder of a mortal brain. The material was pure, and his art was pure; how could the result be other than wonderful?

No face which we can give to a matter will stead us so well at last as the truth. This alone wears well. For the most part, we are not where we are, but in a false position. Through an infirmity of our natures, we suppose a case, and put ourselves into it, and hence are in two cases at the same time, and it is doubly difficult to get out. In sane moments we regard only the facts, the case that is. Say what you have to say, not what you ought. Any truth is better than make-

[17] Sanskrit day of Brahma, over four billion years

believe. Tom Hyde, the tinker, standing on the gallows, was asked if he had anything to say. "Tell the tailors," said he, "to remember to make a knot in their thread before they take the first stitch." His companion's prayer is forgotten.

However mean your life is, meet it and live it; do not shun it and call it hard names. It is not so bad as you are. It looks poorest when you are richest. The faultfinder will find faults even in paradise. Love your life, poor as it is. You may perhaps have some pleasant, thrilling, glorious hours, even in a poor-house. The setting sun is reflected from the windows of the almshouse as brightly as from the rich man's abode; the snow melts before its door as early in the spring. I do not see but a quiet mind may live as contentedly there, and have as cheering thoughts, as in a palace. The town's poor seem to me often to live the most independent lives of any. Maybe they are simply great enough to receive without misgiving. Most think that they are above being supported by the town; but it oftener happens that they are not above supporting themselves by dishonest means, which should be more disreputable. Cultivate poverty like a garden herb, like sage. Do not trouble yourself much to get new things, whether clothes or friends. Turn the old; return to them. Things do not change; we change. Sell your clothes and keep your thoughts. God will see that you do not want society. If I were confined to a corner of a garret all my days, like a spider, the world would be just as large to me while I had my thoughts about me. The philosopher said: "From an army of three divisions one can take away its general, and put it in disorder; from the man the most abject and vulgar one cannot take away his thought." Do not seek so anxiously to be developed, to subject yourself to many influences to be played on; it is all dissipation. Humility like darkness reveals the heavenly lights. The shadows of poverty and meanness gather around us, "and lo! creation widens to our view." We are often reminded that if there were bestowed on us the wealth of Croesus,[18] our aims must still be the same, and our means essentially the same. Moreover, if you are restricted in your range by poverty, if you cannot buy books and newspapers, for instance, you are but confined to the most significant and vital experiences; you

[18] rich king of Lydia, 6th century B.C.

are compelled to deal with the material which yields the most sugar and the most starch. It is life near the bone where it is sweetest. You are defended from being a trifler. No man loses ever on a lower level by magnanimity on a higher. Superfluous wealth can buy superfluities only. Money is not required to buy one necessary of the soul.

I live in the angle of a leaden wall, into whose composition was poured a little alloy of bell-metal. Often, in the repose of my mid-day, there reaches my ears a confused *tintinnabulum*[19] from without. It is the noise of my contemporaries. My neighbors tell me of their adventures with famous gentlemen and ladies, what notabilities they met at the dinner-table; but I am no more interested in such things than in the contents of the Daily Times. The interest and the conversation are about costume and manners chiefly; but a goose is a goose still, dress it as you will. They tell me of California and Texas, of England and the Indies, of the Hon. Mr. —— of Georgia or of Massachusetts, all transient and fleeting phenomena, till I am ready to leap from their court-yard like the Mameluke bey. I delight to come to my bearings,—not walk in procession with pomp and parade, in a conspicuous place, but to walk even with the Builder of the universe, if I may,—not to live in this restless, nervous, bustling, trivial Nineteenth Century, but stand or sit thoughtfully while it goes by. What are men celebrating? They are all on a committee of arrangements, and hourly expect a speech from somebody. God is only the president of the day, and Webster[20] is his orator. I love to weigh, to settle, to gravitate toward that which most strongly and rightfully attracts me;—not hang by the beam of the scale and try to weigh less,—not suppose a case, but take the case that is; to travel the only path I can, and that on which no power can resist me. It affords me no satisfaction to commence to spring an arch before I have got a solid foundation. Let us not play at kittly-benders.[21] There is a solid bottom everywhere. We read that the traveller asked the boy if the swamp before him had a hard bottom. The boy replied that it had. But presently the traveller's horse sank in up to the girths, and he observed to the boy, "I thought you said

[19] jingling or ringing sound hence simply noise [20] Daniel Webster (1782-1852) American statesman, orator and lawyer [21] precarious skimming

that this bog had a hard bottom." "So it has," answered the latter, "but you have not got half way to it yet." So it is with the bogs and quicksands of society; but he is an old boy that knows it. Only what is thought, said, or done at a certain rare coincidence is good. I would not be one of those who will foolishly drive a nail into mere lath and plastering; such a deed would keep me awake nights. Give me a hammer, and let me feel for the furring.[22] Do not depend on the putty. Drive a nail home and clinch it so faithfully that you can wake up in the night and think of your work with satisfaction,—a work at which you would not be ashamed to invoke the Muse. So will help you God, and so only. Every nail driven should be as another rivet in the machine of the universe, you carrying on the work.

Rather than love, than money, than fame, give me truth. I sat at a table where were rich food and wine in abundance, and obsequious attendance, but sincerity and truth were not; and I went away hungry from the inhospitable board. The hospitality was as cold as the ices. I thought that there was no need of ice to freeze them. They talked to me of the age of the wine and the fame of the vintage; but I thought of an older, a newer, and a purer wine, of a more glorious vintage, which they had not got, and could not buy. The style, the house and grounds and "entertainment" pass for nothing with me. I called on the king, but he made me wait in his hall, and conducted like a man incapacitated for hospitality. There was a man in my neighborhood who lived in a hollow tree. His manners were truly regal. I should have done better had I called on him.

How long shall we sit in our porticoes practising idle and musty virtues, which any work would make impertinent? As if one were to begin the day with long-suffering, and hire a man to hoe his potatoes; and in the afternoon go forth to practise Christian meekness and charity with goodness aforethought! Consider the China[23] pride and stagnant self-complacency of mankind. This generation inclines a little to congratulate itself on being the last of an illustrious line; and in Boston and London and Paris and Rome, thinking of its long descent, it speaks of its progress in art and science and

[22] thin strips of wood or metal placed under plaster to create air spaces

[23] made of earthenware, hence fragile

literature with satisfaction. There are the Records of the Philosophical Societies, and the public Eulogies of *Great Men!* It is the good Adam contemplating his own virtue. "Yes, we have done great deeds, and sung divine songs, which shall never die,"—that is, as long as *we* can remember them. The learned societies and great men of Assyria,[24]—where are they? What youthful philosophers and experimentalists we are! There is not one of my readers who has yet lived a whole human life. These may be but the spring months in the life of the race. If we have had the seven-years' itch, we have not seen the seventeen-year locust yet in Concord. We are acquainted with a mere pellicle of the globe on which we live. Most have not delved six feet beneath the suface, nor leaped as many above it. We know not where we are. Beside, we are sound asleep nearly half our time. Yet we esteem ourselves wise, and have an established order on the surface. Truly, we are deep thinkers, we are ambitious spirits! As I stand over the insect crawling amid the pine needles on the forest floor, and endeavoring to conceal itself from my sight, and ask myself why it will cherish those humble thoughts, and hide its head from me who might, perhaps, be its benefactor, and impart to its race some cheering information, I am reminded of the greater Benefactor and Intelligence that stands over me the human insect.

There is an incessant influx of novelty into the world and yet we tolerate incredible dulness. I need only suggest what kind of sermons are still listened to in the most enlightened countries. There are such words as joy and sorrow, but they are only the burden of a psalm, sung with a nasal twang, while we believe in the ordinary and mean. We think that we can change our clothes only. It is said that the British Empire is very large and respectable, and that the United States are a first-rate power. We do not believe that a tide rises and falls behind every man which can float the British Empire like a chip, if he should ever harbor it in his mind. Who knows what sort of seventeen-year locust will next come out of the ground? The government of the world I live in was not framed, like that of Britain, in after-dinner conversations over the wine.

The life in us is like the water in the river. It may rise this year

[24]an ancient Asiatic state of impressive power

higher than man has ever known it, and flood the parched uplands; even this may be the eventful year, which will drown out all our muskrats. It was not always dry land where we dwell. I see far inland the banks which the stream anciently washed, before science began to record its freshets. Every one has heard the story which has gone the round of New England, of a strong and beautiful bug which came out of the dry leaf of an old table of apple-tree wood, which had stood in a farmer's kitchen for sixty years, first in Connecticut, and afterward in Massachusetts,—from an egg deposited in the living tree many years earlier still, as appeared by counting the annual layers beyond it; which was heard gnawing out for several weeks, hatched perchance by the heat of an urn. Who does not feel his faith in a resurrection and immortality strengthened by hearing of this? Who knows what beautiful and winged life, whose egg has been buried for ages under many concentric layers of woodenness in the dead dry life of society, deposited at first in the alburnum[25] of the green and living tree, which has been gradually converted into the semblance of its well-seasoned tomb,—heard perchance gnawing out now for years by the astonished family of man, as they sat round the festive board,—may unexpectedly come forth from amidst society's most trivial and handselled[26] furniture, to enjoy its perfect summer life at last!

I do not say that John or Jonathan will realize all this; but such is the character of that morrow which mere lapse of time can never make to dawn. The light which puts out our eyes is darkness to us. Only that day dawns to which we are awake. There is more day to dawn. The sun is but a morning star.

[25] the soft, light-colored, young wood between the inner bark and the heartwood

[26] new, newfangled, a handsel being the first use or specimen of something regarded as an indication of what is to follow

The author of *Walden,* too, was educated at Harvard and wrote, carpentered, meditated in Concord, a friend of Emerson. Henry David Thoreau was a rebel against taxes, slavery, puritanism, conventionality, supporting individual sensibility against traditional generality. Franklin and Thoreau were characteristic American individuals, and their styles offer striking contrasts.

The lamp of memory

FROM *Seven Lamps of Architecture (1849)*

BY *John Ruskin (1819-1900)*

Among the hours of his life to which the writer looks back with peculiar gratitude, as having been marked by more than ordinary fulness of joy or clearness of teaching, is one passed, now some years ago, near time of sunset, among the broken masses of pine forest which skirt the course of the Ain,[1] above the village of Champagnole, in the Jura. It is a spot which has all the solemnity, with none of the savageness, of the Alps; where there is a sense of a great power beginning to be manifested in the earth, and of a deep and majestic concord in the rise of the long low lines of piny hills; the first utterance of those mighty mountain symphonies, soon to be more loudly lifted and wildly broken along the battlements of the Alps. But their strength is as yet restrained; and the far reaching ridges of pastoral mountain succeed each other, like the long and sighing swell which moves over quiet water from some far-off stormy sea. And there is a deep tenderness pervading that vast monotony. The destructive forces and the stern expression of the central ranges are alike withdrawn. No frost-ploughed, dust-encumbered paths of ancient glacier fret the soft Jura[2] pastures; no splintered heaps of ruin break the fair ranks of her forest; no pale,

[1] a tributary to the river Rhone, in France

[2] a chain of mountains in eastern France, and western and northern Switzerland

defiled, or furious rivers rend their rude and changeful ways among her rocks. Patiently, eddy by eddy, the clear green streams wind along their well-known beds; and under the dark quietness of the undisturbed pines, there spring up, year by year, such company of joyful flowers as I know not the like of among all the blessings of the earth. It was spring time, too; and all were coming forth in clusters crowded for very love; there was room enough for all, but they crushed their leaves into all manner of strange shapes only to be nearer each other. There was the wood anemone,[3] star after star, closing every now and then into nebulae;[4] and there was the oxalis,[5] troop by troop, like virginal processions of[6] the Mois de Marie,[7] the dark vertical clefts in the limestone choked up with them as with heavy snow, and touched with ivy on the edges—ivy as light and lovely as the vine; and, ever and anon, a blue gush of violets, and cowslip bells in sunny places; and in the more open ground, the vetch,[8] and comfrey,[9] and mezereon,[10] and the small sapphire buds of the Polygala Alpina,[11] and the wild strawberry, just a blossom or two all showered amidst the golden softness of deep, warm, amber-coloured moss. I came out presently on the edge of the ravine: the solemn murmur of its waters rose suddenly from beneath, mixed with the singing of the thrushes among the pine boughs; and, on the opposite side of the valley, walled all along as it was by grey cliffs of limestone, there was a hawk sailing slowly off their brow, touching them nearly with his wings, and with the shadows of the pines flickering upon his plumage from above; but with the fall of a hundred fathoms under his breast, and the curling pools of the green river gliding and glittering dizzily beneath him, their foam globes moving with him as he flew. It would be difficult to conceive a scene less dependent upon any other interest than that of its own secluded and serious beauty; but the writer well remembers the

[3] any number of related plants with airy, white flowers, cup-shaped or star-shaped

[4] literally clouds, hence light, misty patches

[5] numerous related plants with cloverlike leaves and a variety of colors

[6] May Day processions [7] Month of Mary

[8] any of a number of short, leafy, climbing or trailing plants of the pea family

[9] any of a group of European plants of the borage family, with rough, hairy leaves

[10] a small European shrub with clusters of fragrant, purplish flowers

[11] polygala of the Alpine variety, a plant with yellow or rosy-purple, irregular flowers and small pods

sudden blankness and chill which were cast upon it when he endeavoured, in order more strictly to arrive at the sources of its impressiveness, to imagine it, for a moments, a scene in some aboriginal forest of the New Continent. The flowers in an instant lost their lights, the river its music; the hills became oppressively desolate; a heaviness in the boughs of the darkened forest showed how much of their former power had been dependent upon a life which was not theirs, how much of the glory of the imperishable, or continually renewed, creation is reflected from things more precious in their memories than it, in its renewing. Those ever springing flowers and ever flowing streams had been dyed by the deep colours of human endurance, valour, and virtue; and the crests of the sable hills that rose against the evening sky received a deep worship, because their far shadows fell eastward over the iron wall of Joux,[12] and the four-square keep of Granson.[13]

It is as the centralization and protectress of this sacred influence, that Architecture is to be regarded by us with the most serious thought. We may live without her, and worship without her, but we cannot remember without her. How cold is all history, how lifeless all imagery, compared to that which the living nation writes, and the uncorrupted marble bears! – how many pages of doubtful record might we not often spare, for a few stones left one upon another! The ambition of the old Babel builders was well directed for this world: there are but two strong conquerors of the forgetfulness of men. Poetry and Architecture; and the latter in some sort includes the former, and is mightier in its reality: it is well to have, not only what men have thought and felt, but what their hands have handled, and their strength wrought, and their eyes beheld, all the days of their life. The age of Homer is surrounded with darkness, his very personality with doubt. Not so that of Pericles:[14] and the day is coming when we shall confess that we have learned more of Greece out of the crumbled fragments of her sculpture than even from her sweet singers or soldier historians. And if indeed there be any profit in our knowledge of the past, or any joy in the thought of being

[12] Fort de Joux, a fortress in Doubs, France

[13] also Grandson, a village in Vaud, Switzerland

[14] Athenian statesman and orator (c. 495-429 B.C.), the principal minister of Athens from 444, encouraged art and literature

remembered hereafter, which can give strength to present exertion, or patience to present endurance, there are two duties respecting national architecture whose importance it is impossible to overrate: the first, to render the architecture of the day, historical; and the second, to preserve, as the most precious of inheritances, that of past ages.

It is in the first of these two directions that Memory may truly be said to be the Sixth Lamp of Architecture; for it is in becoming memorial or monumental that a true perfection is attained by civil and domestic buildings; and this partly as they are, with such a view, built in a more stable manner, and partly as their decorations are consequently animated by a metaphorical or historical meaning.

As regards domestic buildings, there must always be a certain limitation to views of this kind in the power, as well as in the hearts, of men; still I cannot but think it an evil sign of people when their houses are built to last for one generation only. There is a sanctity in a good man's house which cannot be renewed in every tenement that rises on its ruins: and I believe that good men would generally feel this; and that having spent their lives happily and honourably, they would be grieved, at the close of them, to think that the place of their earthly abode, which had seen, and seemed almost to sympathize in, all their honour, their gladness, or their suffering,—that this, with all the record it bare of them, and of all material things that they had loved and ruled over, and set the stamp of themselves upon—was to be swept away, as soon as there was room made for them in the grave; that no respect was to be shown to it, no affection felt for it, no good to be drawn from it by their children; that though there was a monument in the church, there was no warm monument in the hearth and house to them; that all that they ever treasured was despised, and the places that had sheltered and comforted them were dragged down to the dust. I say that a good man would fear this; and that, far more, a good son, a noble descendant, would fear doing it to his father's house. I say that if men lived like men indeed, their houses would be temples—temples which we should hardly dare to injure, and in which it would make us holy to be permitted to live; and there must be a strange dissolution of natural affection, a strange unthankfulness for all that homes have given and parents taught, a strange consciousness that we have been unfaithful to our fathers' honour, or that our own lives are not such as would make our dwellings sacred to our children, when each man would fain build to himself, and build for the little revolution of his own life only. And I look upon those pitiful concretions of lime and clay which spring up, in mildewed forwardness, out of the kneaded fields about our capital – upon those thin, tottering, foundationless shells of splintered wood and imitated stone – upon those gloomy rows of formalized minuteness, alike without difference and without fellowship, as solitary as similar – not merely with the careless disgust of an offended eye, not merely with sorrow for a desecrated landscape, but with a painful foreboding that the roots of our national greatness must be deeply cankered[15] when they are thus loosely struck[16] in their native ground; that those comfortless and unhonoured dwellings are the signs of a great and spreading spirit of popular discontent; that they mark the time when every man's aim is to be in some more elevated sphere than his natural one, and every man's past life is his habitual scorn; when men build in the hope of leaving the places they have built, and live in the hope of forgetting the years that they have lived; when the comfort, the peace, the religion of home have ceased to be felt; and the crowded tenements of a struggling and restless population differ only from the tents of the Arab or the Gipsy by their less healthy openness to the air of heaven, and less happy choice of their spot of earth; by their sacrifice of liberty without the gain of rest, and of stability without the luxury of change.

This is not slight, no consequenceless evil; it is ominous, infectious, and fecund of other fault and misfortune. When men do not love their hearths, nor reverence their thresholds, it is a sign that they have dishonored both, and that they have never acknowledged the true universality of that Christian worship which was indeed to supersede the idolatry, but not the piety, of the pagan. Our God is a household God, as well as a heavenly one; He has an altar in every man's dwelling; let men look to it when they rend it lightly and pour out its ashes.[17] It is not a question of mere ocular delight, it is

[15] diseased (of trees), decayed [16] fixed, holding firm (of roots)

[17] the household gods of ancient Rome, called Penates or Lares, were often domiciled in the family hearth, and so cleaning out the hearth, pouring out the ashes, would signify eviction of the gods

no question of intellectual pride, or of cultivated and critical fancy, how, and with what aspect of durability and of completeness, the domestic buildings of a nation shall be raised. It is one of those moral duties, not with more impunity to be neglected because the perception of them depends on a finely toned and balanced conscientiousness, to build our dwellings with care, and patience, and fondness, and diligent completion, and with a view to their duration at least for such a period as, in the ordinary course of national revolutions, might be supposed likely to extend to the entire alteration of the direction of local interests. This at the least; but it would be better if, in every possible instance, men built their own houses on a scale commensurate rather with their condition at the commencement, than their attainments at the termination, of their worldly career; and built them to stand as long as human work at its strongest can be hoped to stand; recording to their children what they had been, and from what, if so it had been permitted them, they had risen. And when houses are thus built, we may have that true domestic architecture, the beginning of all other, which does not disdain to treat with respect and thoughtfulness the small habitation as well as the large, and which invests with the dignity of contented manhood the narrowness of worldly circumstance.

☙§ In his early twenties John Ruskin published anonymously his first volume on "Modern Painters," after education at Oxford and travel in Europe. One of his main concerns was the relation of art to nature, in both painting and architecture; another, the defense of the new views and technique of Turner, Millais, and the Pre-Raphaelites. After 1860 he turned to educational and economic reform, as in *Sesame and Lilies, Ethics of the Dust,* and *Fors Clavigera.* Later he became a professor of art at Oxford. His autobiography *Praeterita* is incomplete, but is interesting as one of the first to try to convey in prose, like Pater's *Child in the House,* the atmosphere and sensations of childhood.

On literature and science

FROM *Literature and Science (1885)*
BY *Matthew Arnold (1822-1888)*

Practical people talk with a smile of Plato and of his absolute ideas; and it is impossible to deny that Plato's ideas do often seem unpractical and impracticable, and especially when one views them in connection with the life of a great work-a-day world like the United States. The necessary staple of the life of such a world Plato regards with disdain; handicraft and trade and the working professions he regards with disdain; but what becomes of the life of an industrial modern community if you take handicraft and trade and the working professions out of it? The base mechanic arts and handicrafts, says Plato, bring about a natural weakness in the principle of excellence in a man, so that he cannot govern the ignoble growths in him, but nurses them, and cannot understand fostering any other. Those who exercise such arts and trades, as they have their bodies, he says, marred by their vulgar businesses, so they have their souls, too, bowed and broken by them. And if one of these uncomely people has a mind to seek self-culture and philosophy, Plato compares him to a bald little tinker, who has scraped together money, and has got his release from service, and has had a bath, and bought a new coat, and is rigged out like a bridegroom about to marry the daughter of his master who has fallen into poor and helpless estate.

Nor do the working professions fare any better than trade at the hands of Plato. He draws for us an inimitable picture of the working lawyer, and of his life of bondage; he shows how this bondage from his youth up has stunted and warped him, and made him small and crooked of soul, encompassing him with difficulties which he is not man enough to rely on justice and truth as means to encounter, but has recourse, for help out of them, to falsehood and wrong. And so, says Plato, this poor creature is bent and broken, and grows up from boy to man without a particle of soundess in him, although exceedingly smart and clever in his own esteem.

One cannot refuse to admire the artist who draws these pictures. But we say to ourselves that his ideas show the influence of a primitive and obsolete order of things, when the warrior caste and the priestly caste were alone in honour, and the humble work of the world was done by slaves. We have now changed all that; the modern majority consists in work, as Emerson declares; and in work, we may add, principally of such plain and dusty kind as the work of cultivators of the ground, handicraftsmen, men of trade and business, men of the working professions. Above all is this true in a great industrious community such as that of the United States.

Now education, many people go on to say, is still mainly governed by the ideas of men like Plato, who lived when the warrior caste and the priestly or philosophical class were alone in honour, and the really useful part of the community were slaves. It is an education fitted for persons of leisure in such a community. This education passed from Greece and Rome to the feudal communities of Europe, where also the warrior caste and the priestly caste were alone held in honour, and where the really useful and working part of the community, though not nominally slaves as in the pagan world, were practically not much better off than slaves, and not more seriously regarded. And how absurd it is, people end by saying, to inflict this education upon an industrious modern community, where very few indeed are persons of leisure, and the mass to be considered has not leisure, but is bound, for its own great good, and for the great good of the world at large, to plain labour and to industrial pursuits, and the education in question tends necessarily to make men dissatisfied with these pursuits and unfitted for them!

That is what is said. So far I must defend Plato, as to plead that his view of education and studies is in the general, as it seems to me, sound enough, and fitted for all sorts and conditions of men, whatever their pursuits may be. "An intelligent man," says Plato, "will prize those studies which result in his soul getting soberness, righteousness, and wisdom, and will less value the others." I cannot consider *that* a bad description of the aim of education, and of the motives which should govern us in the choice of studies, whether we are preparing ourselves for a hereditary seat in the English House of Lords or for the pork trade in Chicago.

Still I admit that Plato's world was not ours, that his scorn of trade and handicraft is fantastic, that he had no conception of a great industrial community such as that of the United States, and that such a community must and will shape its education to suit its own needs. If the usual education handed down to it from the past does not suit it, it will certainly before long drop this and try another. The usual education in the past has been mainly literary. The question is whether the studies which were long supposed to be the best for all of us are practically the best now; whether others are not better. The tyranny of the past, many think, weighs on us injuriously in the predominance given to letters in education. The question is raised whether, to meet the needs of our modern life, the predominance ought not now to pass from letters to science; and naturally the question is nowhere raised with more energy than here in the United States. The design of abasing what is called "mere literary instruction and education," and of exalting what is called "sound, extensive, and practical scientific knowledge," is, in this intensely modern world of the United States, even more perhaps than in Europe, a very popular design, and makes great and rapid progress.

I am going to ask whether the present movement for ousting letters from their old predominance in education, and for transferring the predominance in education to the natural sciences, whether this brisk and flourishing movement ought to prevail, and whether it is likely that in the end it really will prevail. An objection may be raised which I will anticipate. My own studies have been almost wholly in letters, and my visits to the field of the natural sciences have been very slight and inadequate, although those sciences have always strongly moved my curiosity. A man of letters, it will perhaps be said, is not competent to discuss the comparative merits of letters and natural science as means of education. To this objection I reply, first of all, that his incompetence, if he attempts the discussion but is really incompetent for it, will be abundantly visible; nobody will be taken in; he will have plenty of sharp observers and critics to save mankind from that danger. But the line I am going to follow is, as you will soon discover, so extremely simple, that perhaps it may be followed without failure even by one who for a more ambitious line of discussion would be quite incompetent.

Some of you may possibly remember a phrase of mine which has been the object of a good deal of comment; an observation to the effect that in our culture, the aim being *to know ourselves and the world,* we have, as the means to this end, *to know the best which has been thought and said in the world.* A man of science, who is also an excellent writer and the very prince of debaters, Professor Huxley,[1] in a discourse at the opening of Sir Josiah Mason's college[2] at Birmingham, laying hold of this phrase, expanded it by quoting some more words of mine, which are these: "The civilized world is to be regarded as now being, for intellectual and spiritual purposes, one great confederation, bound to a joint action and working to a common result; and whose members have for their proper outfit a knowledge of Greek, Roman, and Eastern antiquity, and of one another. Special local and temporary advantages being put out of account, that modern nation will in the intellectual and spiritual sphere make most progress, which most thoroughly carries out this programme."

Now on my phrase, thus enlarged, Professor Huxley remarks that when I speak of the above-mentioned knowledge as enabling us to know ourselves and the world, I assert *literature* to contain the materials which suffice for thus making us know ourselves and the world. But it is not by any means clear, says he, that after having learnt all which ancient and modern literatures have to tell us, we have laid a sufficiently broad and deep foundation for that criticism of life, that knowledge of ourselves and the world, which consti-

[1]Thomas Henry Huxley (1825-1895), celebrated English biologist and a chief exponent of science over literature in education. (The speech which Arnold freely quotes is published as an essay entitled "Science and Culture")

[2]named after its founder; in 1880 one of the first science institutions in England

tutes culture. On the contrary, Professor Huxley declares that he finds himself "wholly unable to admit that either nations or individuals will really advance, if their outfit draws nothing from the stores of physical science. An army without weapons of precision, and with no particular base of operations, might more hopefully enter upon a campaign on the Rhine, than a man, devoid of a knowledge of what physical science has done in the last century, upon a criticism of life."

This shows how needful it is for those who are to discuss any matter together, to have a common understanding as to the sense of the terms they employ,—how needful, and how difficult. What Professor Huxley says, implies just the reproach which is so often brought against the study of *belles lettres,*[3] as they are called: that the study is an elegant one, but slight and ineffectual; a smattering of Greek and Latin and other ornamental things, of little use for anyone whose object is to get at truth, and to be a practical man. So, too, M. Renan[4] talks of the "superficial Humanism" of a school-course which treats us as if we were all going to be poets, writers, preachers, orators, and he opposes this humanism to positive science, or the critical search after truth. And there is always a tendency in those who are remonstrating against the predominance of letters in education, to understand by letters *belles lettres,* and by *belles lettres* a superficial humanism, the opposite of science or true knowledge.

But when we talk of knowing Greek and Roman antiquity, for instance, which is the knowledge people have called the humanities, I for my part mean a knowledge which is something more than a superficial humanism, mainly decorative. "I call all teaching *scientific,*" says Wolf, the critic of Homer, "which is systematically laid out and followed up to its original sources. For example: a knowledge of classical antiquity is scientific when the remains of classical antiquity are correctly studied in the original languages." There can be no doubt that Wolf[5] is perfectly right; that all learning is scientific which is systematically laid out and followed up to its original sources, and that a genuine humanism is scientific.

[3]literature as a fine art, but with negative overtones, as Arnold's own gloss indicates [4]Joseph Ernest Renan (1823-1892), French philologist and historian

[5]Friedrich August Wolf (1759-1824), German classical scholar, regarded as the founder of scientific classical philology

When I speak of knowing Greek and Roman antiquity, therefore, as a help to knowing ourselves and the world, I mean more than a knowledge of so much vocabulary, so much grammar, so many portions of authors in the Greek and Latin languages, I mean knowing the Greeks and Romans, and their life and genius, and what they were and did in the world; what we get from them, and what is its value. That, at least, is the ideal; and when we talk of endeavouring to know Greek and Roman antiquity, as a help to knowing ourselves and the world, we mean endeavouring so to know them as to satisfy this ideal, however much we may still fall short of it.

The same also as to knowing our own and other modern nations, with the like aim of getting to understand ourselves and the world. To know the best that has been thought and said by the modern nations, is to know, says Professor Huxley, "only what modern *literatures* have to tell us; it is the criticism of life contained in modern literature." And yet "the distinctive character of our times," he urges, "lies in the vast and constantly increasing part which is played by natural knowledge." And how, therefore, can a man, devoid of knowledge of what physical science has done in the last century, enter hopefully upon a criticism of modern life?

Let us, I say, be agreed about the meaning of the terms we are using. I talk of knowing the best which has been thought and uttered in the world; Professor Huxley says this means knowing *literature.* Literature is a lagre word; it may mean everything written with letters or printed in a book. Euclid's *Elements* and Newton's *Principia* are thus literature. All knowledge that reaches us through books is literature. But by literature Professor Huxley means *belles lettres.* He means to make me say, that knowing the best which has been thought and said by the modern nations is knowing their *belles lettres* and no more. And this is no sufficient equipment, he argues, for a criticism of modern life. But as I do not mean, by knowing ancient Rome, knowing merely more or less of Latin *belles lettres,* and taking no account of Rome's military, and political, and legal, and administrative work in the world; and as, by knowing ancient Greece, I understand knowing her as the giver of Greek art, and the guide to a free and right use of reason and to scientific method, and the founder of our mathematics and physics and astronomy and biology,—I understand knowing her as all this, and not merely knowing certain Greek poems, and histories, and treatises, and speeches,—so as to the knowledge of modern nations also. By knowing modern nations, I mean not merely knowing their *belles lettres,* but knowing also what has been done by such men as Copernicus, Galileo, Newton, Darwin. "Our ancestors learned," says Professor Huxley, "that the earth is the centre of the visible universe, and that man is the cynosure of things terrestrial; and more especially was it inculcated that the course of nature had no fixed order, but that it could be, and constantly was, altered." But for us now, continues Professor Huxley, "the notions of the beginning and the end of the world entertained by our forefathers are no longer credible. It is very certain that the earth is not the chief body in the material universe, and that the world is not subordinated to man's use. It is even more certain that nature is the expression of a definite order, with which nothing interferes." "And yet," he cries, "the purely classical education advocated by the representatives of the humanists in our day gives no inkling of all this!"

In due place and time I will just touch upon that vexed question of classical education; but at present the question is as to what is meant by knowing the best which modern nations have thought and said. It is not knowing their *belles lettres* merely which is meant. To know Italian *belles lettres* is not to know Italy, and to know English *belles lettres* is not to know England. Into knowing Italy and England there comes a great deal more, Galileo and Newton amongst it. The reproach of being a superficial humanism, a tincture of *belles lettres,* may attach rightly enough to some other disciplines; but to the particular discipline recommended when I proposed knowing the best that has been thought and said in the world, it does not apply. In that best I certainly include what in modern times has been thought and said by the great observers and knowers of nature.

There is, therefore, really no question between Professor Huxley and me as to whether knowing the great results of the modern scientific study of nature is not required as a part of our culture, as well as knowing the products of literature and art. But to follow the processes by which those results are reached, ought, say the friends of physical science, to be made the staple of education for the bulk of mankind. And here there does arise a question between those whom Professor Huxley calls with playful sarcasm "the Levites[6] of culture," and those whom the poor humanist is sometimes apt to regard as its Nebuchadnezzars.[7]

The great results of the scientific investigation of nature we are agreed upon knowing, but how much of our study are we bound to give to the processes by which those results are reached? The results have their visible bearing on human life. But all the processes, too, all the items of fact, by which those results are reached and established, are interesting. All knowledge is interesting to a wise man, and the knowledge of nature is interesting to all men. It is very interesting to know, that, from the albuminous white of the egg, the chick in the egg gets the materials for its flesh, bones, blood, and feathers; while, from the fatty yolk of the egg, it gets the heat and energy which enable it at length to break its shell and begin the world. It is less interesting, perhaps, but still it is interesting, to know that when a taper burns, the wax is converted into carbonic acid and water. Moreover, it is quite true that the habit of dealing with facts, which is given by the study of nature, is, as the friends of physical science praise it for being, an excellent discipline. The appeal, in the study of nature, is constantly to observation and experiment; not only is it said that the thing is so, but we can be made to see that it is so. Not only does a man tell us that when a taper burns the wax is converted into carbonic acid and water, as a man may tell us, if he likes, that Charon[8] is punting his ferry-boat on the river Styx,[9] or that Victor Hugo[10] is a sublime poet, or Mr. Gladstone[11] the most admirable of statesmen; but we are made to see that the conversion into carbonic acid and water does actually

[6] assistants to the priests in the tabernacle and temple service of the Jews

[7] King of Babylonia (605-562 B.C.), one of the greatest monarchs of the ancient world, among other cultural improvements saw to the construction of the "hanging gardens of Babylon," and of great canals and walls, and the restoration of many temples

[8] in Greek mythology, ferryman who transported the souls of the dead, provided their bodies had been duly buried, over the rivers of the lower world

[9] river of the lower world or Underworld

[10] French poet (1802-1885), recognized leader of the Romantic school in France

[11] William Ewart Gladstone (1809-1898), eminent English statesman, financier, and orator, Prime Minister of England 1868-74, 1880-85, 1886, 1892-94

happen. This reality of natural knowledge it is, which makes the friends of physical science contrast it, as a knowledge of things, with the humanist's knowledge, which is, say they, a knowledge of words. And hence Professor Huxley is moved to lay it down that, "for the purpose of attaining real culture, an exclusively scientific education is at least as effectual as an exclusively literary education." And a certain President of the Section for Mechanical Science in the British Association is, in Scripture phrase, "very bold," and declares that if a man, in his mental training, "has substituted literature and history for natural science, he has chosen the less useful alternative." But whether we go these lengths or not, we must all admit that in natural science the habit gained of dealing with facts is a most valuable discipline, and that every one should have some experience of it.

More than this, however, is demanded by the reformers. It is proposed to make the training in natural science the main part of education, for the great majority of mankind at any rate. And here, I confess, I part company with the friends of physical science, with whom up to this point I have been agreeing. In differing from them, however, I wish to proceed with the utmost caution and diffidence. The smallness of my own acquaintance with the disciplines of natural science is ever before my mind, and I am fearful of doing these disciplines an injustice. The ability and pugnacity of the partisans of natural science make them formidable persons to contradict. The tone of tentative inquiry, which befits a being of dim faculties and bounded knowledge, is the tone I would wish to take and not to depart from. At present it seems to me, that those who are for giving to natural knowledge, as they call it, the chief place in the education of the majority of mankind, leave one important thing out of their account: the constitution of human nature. But I put this forward on the strength of some facts not at all recondite, very far from it; facts capable of being stated in the simplest possible fashion, and to which, if I so state them, the man of science will, I am sure, be willing to allow their due weight.

Deny the facts altogether, I think, he hardly can. He can hardly deny, that when we set ourselves to enumerate the powers which go to the building up of human life, and say that they are the power of conduct, the power of intellect and knowledge, the power of beauty, and the power of social life and manners,—he can hardly deny that this scheme, though drawn in rough and plain lines enough, and not pretending to scientific exactness, does yet give a fairly true representation of the matter. Human nature is built up by these powers; we have the need for them all. When we have rightly met and adjusted the claims of them all, we shall then be in a fair way for getting soberness and righteousness, with wisdom. This is evident enough, and the friends of physical science would admit it.

But perhaps they may not have sufficiently observed another thing: namely, that the several powers just mentioned are not isolated, but there is, in the generality of mankind, a perpetual tendency to relate them one to another in divers ways. With one such way of relating them I am particularly concerned now. Following our instinct for intellect and knowledge, we acquire pieces of knowledge; and presently, in the generality of men, there arises the desire to relate these pieces of knowledge to our sense for conduct, to our sense for beauty—and there is weariness and dissatisfaction if the desire is balked. Now in this desire lies, I think, the strength of that hold which letters have upon us.

All knowledge is, as I said just now, interesting; and even items of knowledge which from the nature of the case cannot well be related, but must stand isolated in our thoughts, have their interest. Even lists of exceptions have their interest. If we are studying Greek accents, it is interesting to know that *pais* and *pas,* and some other monosyllables of the same form of declension, do not take the circumflex upon the last syllable of the genitive plural, but vary, in this respect, from the common rule. If we are studying physiology, it is interesting to know that the pulmonary artery carries dark blood and the pulmonary vein carries bright blood, departing in this respect from the common rule for the division of labour between the veins and the arteries. But every one knows how we seek naturally to combine the pieces of our knowledge together, to bring them under general rules, to relate them to principles; and how unsatisfactory and tiresome it would be to go on forever learning lists of exceptions, or accumulating items of fact which must stand isolated.

Well, that same need of relating our knowledge, which operates here within the sphere of our knowledge itself, we shall find operating, also, outside that sphere. We experience, as we go on learning and knowing,—the vast majority of us experience,—the need of relating what we have learned and known to the sense which we have in us for conduct, to the sense which we have in us for beauty.

A certain Greek prophetess of Mantineia[12] in Arcadia,[13] Diotima[14] by name, once explained to the philosopher Socrates that love, and impulse, and bent of all kinds, is, in fact, nothing else but the desire in men that good should forever be present to them. This desire for good, Diotima assured Socrates, is our fundamental desire, of which fundamental desire every impulse in us is only some one particular form. And therefore this fundamental desire it is, I suppose,—this desire in men that good should be forever present to them,—which acts in us when we feel the impulse for relating our knowledge to our sense for conduct and to our sense for beauty. At any rate, with men in general the instinct exists. Such is human nature. And the instinct, it will be admitted, is innocent, and human nature is preserved by our following the lead of its innocent instincts. Therefore, in seeking to gratify this instinct in question, we are following the instinct of self-preservation in humanity.

[12]or Mantinera, in ancient geography a city about forty miles from Corinth

[13]in ancient geography, a region in the heart of the Peloponnesus

[14]priestess and prophetess of Mantinea, the reputed teacher of Socrates, mentioned in Plato's "Symposium," probably is a fictitious person

Matthew Arnold worked all his life in education in England. His father had been a noted head of Rugby School; he himself was educated at Rugby and Oxford, and then became an inspector of schools and later the first professor of English poetry at Oxford. He wrote mostly poetry before 1860, mostly prose after—including *Essays in Criticism* and *Culture and Anarchy,* and his report *Schools and Universities on the Continent.*

How to tell a story

FROM *How to Tell a Story, and Other Essays (1898)*
BY *Mark Twain (1835-1910)*

The Humorous Story—An American Development.
Its Difference from Comic and Witty Stories.

I do not claim that I can tell a story as it ought to be told. I only claim to know how a story ought to be told, for I have been almost daily in the company of the most expert story-tellers for many years.

There are several kinds of stories, but only one difficult kind—the humorous. I will talk mainly about that one. The humorous story is American, the comic story is English, the witty story is French. The humorous story depends for its effect upon the *manner* of the telling; the comic story and the witty story upon the *matter.*

The humorous story may be spun out to great length, and may wander around as much as it pleases, and arrive nowhere in particular; but the comic and witty stories must be brief and end with a point. The humorous story bubbles gently along, the others burst.

The humorous story is strictly a work of art—high and delicate art—and only an artist can tell it; but no art is necessary in telling the comic and the witty story; anybody can do it. The art of telling a humorous story—understand, I mean by word of mouth, not print—was created in America, and has remained at home.

The humorous story is told gravely; the teller does his best to conceal the fact that he even dimly suspects that there is anything funny about it; but the teller of the comic story tells you beforehand that it is one of the funniest things he has ever heard, then tells it with eager delight, and is the first person to laugh when he gets through. And sometimes, if he has had good success, he is so glad and happy that he will repeat the "nub" of it and glance around from face to face, collecting applause, and then repeat it again. It is a pathetic thing to see.

Very often of course, the rambling and disjointed humorous story finishes with a nub, point, snapper,[1] or whatever you like to call it. Then the listener must be alert, for in many cases the teller will divert attention from that nub by dropping it in a carefully casual and indifferent way, with the pretense that he does not know it is a nub.

Artemus Ward[2] used that trick a good deal; then when the belated audience presently caught the joke he would look up with innocent surprise, as if wondering what they had found to laugh at. Dan Setchell[3] used it before him, Nye[4] and Riley[5] and others use it to-day.

But the teller of the comic story does not slur the nub; he shouts it at you—every time. And when he prints it, in England, France, Germany, and Italy, he italicizes it, puts some whooping exclamation-points after it, and sometimes explains it in a parenthesis. All of which is very depressing, and makes one want to renounce joking and lead a better life.

Let me set down an instance of the comic method, using an anecdote which has been popular all over the world for twelve or fifteen hundred years. The teller tells it this way:

The Wounded Soldier

In the course of a certain battle a soldier whose leg had been shot off appealed to another soldier who was hurrying by to carry him to

[1] word or phrase giving a pointed finish to something, by analogy with the cracker at a whip's end [2] pen name of Charles Farrar Brown (1834-1867), American humorist [3] American actor of mid-nineteenth century

[4] Edgar Wilson Nye (1850-1896), American journalist, humorous writer, and lecturer [5] James Whitcomb Riley (1849-1916), American poet and lecturer

the rear, informing him at the same time of the loss which he had sustained; whereupon the generous son of Mars, shouldering the unfortunate, prodeeded to carry out his desire. The bullets and cannonballs were flying in all directions, and presently one of the latter took the wounded man's head off—without, however, his deliverer being aware of it. In no long time he was hailed by an officer, who said:

"Where are you going with that carcass?"

"To the rear, sir—he's lost his leg!"

"His leg, forsooth?" responded the astonished officer; "you mean his head, you booby."

Whereupon the soldier dispossessed himself of his burden, and stood looking down upon it in great perplexity. At length he said:

"It is true, sir, just as you have said," Then after a pause he added, *"But he* TOLD *me* IT WAS HIS LEG ! ! ! !"

Here the narrator bursts into explosion after explosion of thunderous horse-laughter, repeating that nub from time to time through his gasping and shriekings and suffocatings.

It takes only a minute and a half to tell that in its comic-story form; and isn't worth the telling, after all. Put into the humorous-story form it takes ten minutes, and is about the funniest thing I have ever listened to—as James Whitcomb Riley tells it.

He tells it in the character of a dull-witted old farmer who has just heard it for the first time, thinks it is unspeakably funny, and is trying to repeat it to a neighbor. But he can't remember it; so he gets all mixed up and wanders helplessly round and round, putting in tedious details that don't belong in the tale and only retard it; taking them out conscientiously and putting in others that are just as useless; making minor mistakes now and then and stopping to correct them and explain how he came to make them; remembering things which he forgot to put in in their proper place and going back to put them in there; stopping his narrative a good while in order to try to recall the name of the soldier that was hurt, and finally remembering that the soldier's name was not mentioned, and remarking placidly that the name is of no real importance, anyway—better, or course, if one knew it, but not essential, after all—and so on, and so on, and so on.

The teller is innocent and happy and pleased with himself and has to stop every little while to hold himself in and keep from laughing outright; and does hold in, but his body quakes in a jelly-like way with interior chuckles; and at the end of the ten minutes the audience have laughed until they are exhausted, and the tears are running down their faces.

The simplicity and innocence and sincerity and unconsciousness of the old farmer are perfectly simulated, and the result is a performance which is thoroughly charming and delicious. This is art—and fine and beautiful, and only a master can compass it; but a machine could tell the other story.

To string incongruities and absurdities together in a wandering and sometimes purposeless way, and seem innocently unaware that they are absurdities, is the basis of the American art, if my position is correct. Another feature is the slurring of the point. A third is the dropping of a studied remark apparently without knowing it, as if one were thinking aloud. The fourth and last is the pause.

Artemus Ward dealt in numbers three and four a good deal. He would begin to tell with great animation something which he seemed to think was wonderful; then lose confidence, and after an apparently absent-minded pause add an incongruous remark in a soliloquizing way; and that was the remark intended to explode the mine—and it did.

For instance, he would say eagerly, excitedly, "I once knew a man in New Zealand who hadn't a tooth in his head"—here his animation would die out; a silent, reflective pause would follow, then he would say dreamily, and as if to himself, "and yet that man could beat a drum better than any man I ever saw."

The pause is an exceedingly important feature in any kind of story, and a frequently recurring feature, too. It is a dainty thing, and delicate, and also uncertain and treacherous; for it must be exactly the right length—no more and no less—or it fails of its purpose and makes trouble. If the pause is too short[6] the impressive point is passed, and the audience have had time to divine that a surprise is intended—and then you can't surprise them, of course.

On the platform I used to tell a negro ghost story that had a pause

[6] sic! The sense calls for "long."

in front of the snapper on the end, and that pause was the most important thing in the whole story. If I got it the right length precisely, I could spring the finishing ejaculation with effect enough to make some impressible girl deliver a startled little yelp and jump out of her seat—and that was what I was after. This story was called "The Golden Arm," and was told in this fashion. You can practice with it yourself—and mind you look out for the pause and get it right.

The Golden Arm

Once 'pon a time dey wuz a monsus[7] mean man, en he live 'way out in de prairie all 'lone by hisself, 'cep'n he had a wife. En bimeby she died, en he tuck en toted[8] her way out dah in de prairie en buried her. Well, she had a golden arm—all solid gold, fum de shoulder down. He wuz pow'ful mean—pow'ful; en dat night he couldn't sleep, caze he want dat golden arm so bad.

When it come midnight, he couldn't stan' it no mo'; so he git up, he did, en tuck his lantern en shoved out thoo de storm en dug her up en got de golden arm; en he bent his head down 'gin de win', en plowed en plowed en plowed thoo de snow. Den all on a sudden he stop (make a considerable pause here, and look startled, and take a listening attitude) en say: "My *lan'*, what's dat!"

En he listen—en listen—en de win' say (set your teeth together and imitate the wailing and wheezing singsong of the wind), "Bzzz-z-zzz"—en den, way back yonder whah de grave is, he hear a *voice*! —he hear a voice all mix' up in de win'—can't hardly tell 'em 'part—"Bzzz-zzz—W-h-o—g-o-t—m-y—g-o-l-d-e-n *arm?—zzz-zzz* —W-h-o g-o-t m-y g-o-l-d-e-n *arm?*" (You must begin to shiver violently now.)

En he begin to shiver en shake, en say, "Oh, my! *Oh,* my lan'!" en de win' blow de lantern out, en de snow en sleet blow in his face en mos' choke him, en he start a-plowin' knee-deep towards home mos' dead, he so sk'yerd—en pooty soon he hear de voice agin, en (pause) it 'us comin' *after* him! "Bzzz—zzz—W-h-o—g-o-t—m-y—g-o-l-d-e-n—*arm?*"

[7] monstrously [8] carried, a dialectal phrase

When he git to de pasture he hear it agin—closter now, en *a-comin'*!—a-comin' back dah in de dark en de storm—(repeat the wind and the voice). When he git to de house he rush up-stairs en jump in de bed en kiver up, head and years,[9] en lay dah shiverin' en shakin'—en den way out dah he hear it *agin*! en a-*comin*! En bimeby he hear (pause—awed, listening attitude)—pat—pat—pat— *hit's a-comin' up-stairs*! Den he hear de latch, en he know it's in de room!

Den pooty soon he know it's a-*stannin' by de bed*! (Pause.) Den—he know it's a-*bendin' down over him*—en he cain't skasely git his breath! Den—den—he seem to feel someth'n *c-o-l-d,* right down 'most agin his head! (Pause.)

Den de voice say, *right at his year*—"W-h-o—g-o-t—m-y—g-o-l-d-e-n *arm?*" (you must wail it out very plaintively and accusingly; then you stare steadily and impressively into the face of the farthest-gone[10] auditor—a girl, preferably—and let that awe-inspiring pause begin to build itself in the deep hush. When it has reached exactly the right length, jump suddenly at that girl and yell, "*You've* got it!"

If you've got the *pause* right, she'll fetch a dear little yelp and spring right out of her shoes. But you *must* get the pause right; and you will find it the most troublesome and aggravating and uncertain thing you ever undertook.

[9] ears

[10] farthest away, and probably also the one farthest away who seems most impressed or "gone"

Mark Twain is the nom de plume of Samuel Langhorne Clemens, who was at various times a journeyman printer, steamboat pilot on the Mississippi, Confederate soldier, miner, journalist, novelist, travel writer, publisher, comic lecturer and satirist. Our selection shows his humorously irreverent attitude toward European tradition and manners, and the realism and neat use of native American idiom for which he is noted. Among his chief book-length works are *The Innocents Abroad, A Connecticut Yankee in King Arthur's Court, Life on the Mississippi, The Adventures of Tom Sawyer, and The Adventures of Huckleberry Finn.*

The dynamo and the virgin

FROM *The Education of Henry Adams (1907)*
BY *Henry Adams (1838-1918)*

Until the Great Exposition[1] of 1900 closed its doors in November, Adams haunted it, aching to absorb knowledge, and helpless to find it. He would have liked to know how much of it could have been grasped by the best-informed man in the world. While he was thus meditating chaos, Langley[2] came by, and showed it to him. At Langley's behest, the Exhibition dropped its superfluous rags and stripped itself to the skin, for Langley knew what to study, and why, and how; while Adams might as well have stood outside in the night, staring at the Milky Way. Yet Langley said nothing new, and taught nothing that one might not have learned from Lord Bacon, three hundred years before; but though one should have known the "Advancement of Science"[3] as well as one knew the "Comedy of Errors," the literary knowledge counted for nothing until some teacher should show how to apply it. Bacon took a vast deal of trouble in teaching King James I and his subjects, American or other, towards the year 1620, that true science was the development or economy of forces; yet an elderly American[4] in 1900 knew neither the formula nor the forces; or even so much as to say to

[1] Exhibition of Arts and Science held in the Palais du Trocadero in Paris from 1878-1900 [2] Samuel Pierpont Langley (1834-1906), American astronomer [3] more commonly "Advancement of Learning," by Francis Bacon [4] the author

himself that his historical business in the Exposition concerned only the economies or developments of force since 1893, when he began the study at Chicago.

Nothing in education is so astonishing as the amount of ignorance it accumulates in the form of inert facts. Adams had looked at most of the accumulations of art in the storehouses called Art Museums; yet he did not know how to look at the art exhibits of 1900. He had studied Karl Marx and his doctrines of history with profound attention, yet he could not apply them at Paris. Langley, with the ease of a great master of experiment, threw out of the field every exhibit that did not reveal a new application of force, and naturally threw out, to begin with, almost the whole art exhibit. Equally, he ignored almost the whole industrial exhibit. He led his pupil directly to the forces. His chief interest was in new motors to make his airship feasible, and he taught Adams the astonishing complexities of the new Daimler motor, and of the automobile, which, since 1893, had become a nightmare at a hundred kilometres an hour, almost as destructive as the electric tram which was only ten years older; and threatening to become as terrible as the locomotive steam-engine itself, which was almost exactly Adams's own age.

Then he showed his scholar the great hall of dynamos, and explained how little he knew about electricity or force of any kind, even of his own special sun, which spouted heat in inconceivable volume, but which, as far as he knew, might spout less or more, at any time, for all the certainty he felt in it. To him, the dynamo itself was but an ingenious channel for conveying somewhere the heat latent in a few tons of poor coal hidden in a dirty engine-house carefully kept out of sight; but to Adams the dynamo became a symbol of infinity. As he grew accustomed to the great gallery of machines, he began to feel the forty-foot dynamos as a moral force, much as the early Christians felt the Cross. The planet itself seemed less impressive, in its old-fashioned, deliberate, annual or daily revolution, than this huge wheel, revolving within arm's-length at some vertiginous[5] speed, and barely murmuring—scarcely humming an audible warning to stand a hair's-breadth further for re-

[5] dizzy

spect of power—while it would not wake the baby lying close against its frame. Before the end, one began to pray to it; inherited instinct taught the natural expression of man before silent and infinite force. Among the thousand symbols of ultimate energy, the dynamo was not so human as some, but it was the most expressive.

Yet the dynamo, next to the steam-engine, was the most familiar of exhibits. For Adam's objects its value lay chiefly in its occult mechanism. Between the dynamo in the gallery of machines and the engine-house outside, the break of continuity amounted to abysmal fracture for a historian's objects. No more relation could he discover between the steam and the electric current than between the Cross and the Cathedral. The forces were interchangeable if not reversible, but he could see only an absolute *fiat* in electricity as in faith. Langley could not help him. Indeed, Langley seemed to be worried by the same trouble, for he constantly repeated that the new forces were anarchical, and specially that he was not responsible for the new rays, that were little short of parricidal in their wicked spirit towards science. His own rays, with which he had doubled the solar spectrum, were altogether harmless and beneficent; but Radium denied its God—or, what was to Langley the same thing, denied the truths of his Science. The force was wholly new.

A historian who asked only to learn enough to be as futile as Langley or Kelvin,[6] made rapid progress under this teaching, and mixed himself up in the tangle of ideas until he achieved a sort of Paradise of ignorance vastly consoling to his fatigued senses. He wrapped himself in vibrations and rays which were new, and he would have hugged Marconi and Branley[7] had he met them, as he hugged the dynamo; while he lost his arithmetic in trying to figure out the equation between the discoveries and the economies of force. The economies, like the discoveries, were absolute, supersensual,[8] occult; incapable of expression in horse-power. What mathematical equivalent could he suggest as the value of a Branle

[6] Sir William Thomson, Baron Kelvin (1824-1907), British mathematician and physicist

[7] Edouard Branley (born 1846), French physicist who invented a coherer or radio-conductor making possible wireless telegraphy

[8] above what pertains to the senses

coherer? Frozen air, or the electric furnace, had some scale of measurement, no doubt, if somebody could invent a thermometer adequate to the purpose; but X-rays had played no part whatever in man's consciousness, and the atom itself had figured only as a fiction of thought. In these seven years man had translated himself into a new universe which had no common scale of measurement with the old. He had entered a supersensual world, in which he could measure nothing except by chance collisions of movements imperceptible to his senses, perhaps even imperceptible to his instruments, but perceptible to each other, and so to some known ray at the end of the scale. Langley seemed prepared for anything, even for an indeterminable number of universes interfused—physics stark mad in metaphysics.

Historians undertake to arrange sequences,—called stories, or histories—assuming in silence a relation of cause and effect. These assumptions, hidden in the depths of dusty libraries, have been astounding, but commonly unconscious and childlike; so much so, that if any captious critic were to drag them to light, historians would probably reply, with one voice, that they had never supposed themselves required to know what they were talking about. Adams, for one, had toiled in vain to find out what he meant. He had even published a dozen volumes of American history for no other purpose than to satisfy himself whether, by the severest process of stating, with the least possible comment, such facts as seemed sure, in such order as seemed rigorously consequent,[9] he could fix for a familiar moment a necessary sequence of human movement. The result had satisfied him as little as at Harvard College. Where he saw sequence, other men saw something quite different, and no one saw the same unit of measure. He cared little about his experiments and less about his statesmen, who seemed to him quite as ignorant as himself and, as a rule, no more honest; but he insisted on a relation of sequence, and if he could not reach it by one method, he would try as many methods as science knew. Satisfied that the sequence of men led to nothing and that the sequence of their society could lead no further, while the mere sequence of time was artificial, and the sequence of thought was chaos, he turned at last to

[9] following in a logical chain

the sequence of force; and thus it happened that, after ten years' pursuit, he found himself lying in the Gallery of Machines at the Great Exposition of 1900, his historical neck broken by the sudden irruption of forces totally new.

Since no one else showed much concern, an elderly person without other cares had no need to betray alarm. The year 1900 was not the first to upset school-masters. Copernicus and Galileo had broken many professional necks about 1600; Columbus had stood the world on its head towards 1500; but the nearest approach to the revolution of 1900 was that of 310, when Constantine[10] set up the Cross. The rays that Langley disowned, as well as those which he fathered, were occult, supersensual, irrational; they were a revelation of mysterious energy like that of the Cross; they were what, in terms of mediaeval science, were called immediate modes of the divine substance.

The historian was thus reduced to his last resources. Clearly if he was bound to reduce all these forces to a common value, this common value could have no measure but that of their attraction on his own mind. He must treat them as they had been felt; as convertible, reversible, interchangeable attraction on thought. He made up his mind to venture it; he would risk translating rays into faith. Such a reversible process would vastly amuse a chemist, but the chemist could not deny that he, or some of his fellow physicists, could feel the force of both. When Adams was a boy in Boston, the best chemist in the place had probably never heard of Venus except by way of scandal, or of the Virgin except as idolatry; neither had he heard of dynamos or automobiles or radium; yet his mind was ready to feel the force of all, though the rays were unborn and the women were dead.

Here opened another totally new education, which promised to be by far the most hazardous of all. The knife-edge along which he must crawl, like Sir Lancelot in the twelfth century, divided two kingdoms of force which had nothing in common but attraction. They were as different as a magnet is from gravitation, supposing one knew what a magnet was, or gravitation, or love. The force of

[10] Constantine the Great (c. 274-337 A.D.), Roman emperor who made Christianity the state religion

the Virgin was still felt at Lourdes, and seemed to be as potent as X-rays; but in America neither Venus nor Virgin ever had value as force—at most as sentiment. No American had ever been truly afraid of either.

The problem in dynamics gravely perplexed an American historian. The Woman had once been supreme; in France she still seemed potent, not merely as a sentiment, but as a force. Why was she unknown in America? For evidently America was ashamed of her, and she was ashamed of herself, otherwise they would not have strewn fig-leaves so profusely all over her. When she was a true force, she was ignorant of fig-leaves, but the monthly-magazine-made American female had not a feature that would have been recognized by Adam. The trait was notorious, and often humorous, but any one brought up among Puritans, knew that sex was sin. In any previous age, sex was strength. Neither art nor beauty was needed. Every one, even among Puritans, knew that neither Diana of the Ephesians nor any of the Oriental goddesses was worshipped for her beauty. She was goddess because of her force; she was the animated dynamo; she was reproduction—the greatest and most mysterious of all energies; all she needed was to be fecund. Singularly enough, not one of Adams's many schools of education had ever drawn his attention to the opening lines of Lucretius,[11] though they were perhaps the finest in all Latin literature, where the poet invoked Venus exactly as Dante invoked the Virgin:—

> Quae quoniam rerum naturam *sola* gubernas.[12]

The Venus of Epicurean philosophy survived in the Virgin of the Schools:—

> Donna, sei tanto grande, e tanto vali,
> Che qual vuol grazia, e a te non ricorre,
> Sua disianza vuol volar senz' ali.[13]

All this was to American thought as though it had never existed.

[11] Titus Lucretius Carus (c. 96-55 B.C.), Roman philosophical poet

[12] Since you alone govern the nature of things: from Bk. 1 of *De Rerum Natura*

[13] Lady, you are so great and so worthy, that (if) anyone seeks favor, and does not have recourse to you, his desire wishes to fly without wings: from Canto XXXIII of the "Paradise," in Dante's *Divina Commedia*

The true American knew something of the facts, but nothing of the feelings; he read the letter, but he never felt the law. Before this historical chasm, a mind like that of Adams felt itself helpless; he turned from the Virgin to the Dynamo as though he were a Branle coherer. On one side, at the Louvre and at Chartres, as he knew by the record of work actually done and still before his eyes, was the highest energy ever known to man, the creator of four-fifths of his noblest art, exercising vastly more attraction over the human mind than all the steam-engines and dynamos ever dreamed of; and yet this energy was unknown to the American mind. An American Virgin would never dare command; an American Venus would never dare exist.

The question, which to any plain American of the nineteenth century seemed as remote as it did to Adams, drew him almost violently to study, once it was posed; and on this point Langleys were as useless as though they were Herbert Spencers[14] or dynamos. The idea survived only as art. There one turned as naturally as though the artist were himself a woman. Adams began to ponder, asking himself whether he knew of any American artist who had ever insisted on the power of sex, as every classic had always done; but he could think only of Walt Whitman; Bret Harte,[15] as far as the magazines would let him venture; and one or two painters, for the flesh-tones. All the rest had used sex for sentiment, never for force; to them, Eve was a tender flower, and Herodias[16] an unfeminine horror. American art, like the American language and American education, was as far as possible sexless. Society regarded this victory over sex as its greatest triumph, and the historian readily admitted it, since the moral issue, for the moment, did not concern one who was studying the relations of unmoral force. He cared nothing for the sex of the dynamo until he could measure its energy.

Vaguely seeking a clue, he wandered through the art exhibit, and, in his stroll, stopped almost every day before St. Gauden's[17] Gen-

[14] English philosopher (1820-1902), founder of the synthetic philosophy

[15] Francis Bret Harte (1839-1902), American poet and novelist

[16] sister of Herod Agrippa I, wife of Herod Philip, and afterward second wife of Philip's half-brother, Herod Antipas

[17] Augustus St. Gaudens (1848-1907), American sculptor

eral Sherman, which had been given the central post of honor. St. Gaudens himself was in Paris, putting on the work his usual interminable last touches, and listening to the usual contradictory suggestions of brother sculptors. Of all the American artists who gave to American art whatever life it breathed in the seventies, St. Gaudens was perhaps the most sympathetic, but certainly the most inarticulate. General Grant or Don Cameron[18] had scarcely less instinct of rhetoric than he. All the others—the Hunts,[19] Richardson,[20] John La Farge,[21] Stanford White[22]—were exuberant; only St. Gaudens could never discuss or dilate on an emotion, or suggest artistic arguments for giving to his work the forms that he felt. He never laid down the law, or affected the despot, or became brutalized like Whistler[23] by the brutalities of his world. He required no incense; he was no egoist; his simplicity of thought was excessive; he could not imitate, or give any form but his own to the creations of his hand. No one felt more strongly than he the strength of other men, but the idea that they could affect him never stirred an image in his mind.

This summer his health was poor and his spirits were low. For such a temper, Adams was not the best companion, since his own gaiety was not *folle;* but he risked going now and then to the studio on Mont Parnasse to draw him out for a stroll in the Bois de Boulogne, or dinner as pleased his moods, and in return St. Gaudens sometimes let Adams go about in his company.

Once St. Gaudens took him down to Amiens, with a party of Frenchmen, to see the cathedral. Not until they found themselves actually studying the sculpture of the western portal, did it dawn on Adams's mind that, for his purposes, St. Gaudens on that spot had more interest to him than the cathedral itself. Great men before great monuments express great truths, provided they are not taken too solemnly. Adams never tired of quoting the supreme phrase of

[18] James Donald Cameron (1833-1918), American politician

[19] William Morris Hunt (1824-1879), American painter, and Richard Morris Hunt (1827-1895), American architect

[20] Henry Hobson Richardson (1838-1886), American architect

[21] John La Farge (1835-1910), American painter, worker in stained glass, and writer [22] American architect (1853-1896)

[23] James Abbott MacNeill Whistler (1834-1903), American painter, and etcher

his idol Gibbon, before the Gothic cathedrals: "I darted a contemptuous look on the stately monuments of superstition." Even in the footnotes of his history, Gibbon had never inserted a bit of humor more human than this, and one would have paid largely for a photograph of the fat little historian, on the background of Notre Dame of Amiens, trying to persuade his readers—perhaps himself—that he was darting a contemptuous look on the stately monument, for which he felt in fact the respect which every man of his vast study and active mind always feels before objects worthy of it; but besides the humor, one felt also the relation. Gibbon ignored the Virgin, because in 1789 religious monuments were out of fashion. In 1900 his remark sounded fresh and simple as the green fields to ears that had heard a hundred years of other remarks, mostly no more fresh and certainly less simple. Without malice, one might find it more instructive than a whole lecture of Ruskin. One sees what one brings, and at that moment Gibbon brought the French Revolution. Ruskin brought reaction against the Revolution. St. Gaudens had passed beyond all. He liked the stately monuments much more than he liked Gibbon or Ruskin; he loved their dignity; their unity; their scale; their lines; their lights and shadows; their decorative sculpture; but he was even less conscious than they of the force that created it all—the Virgin, the Woman—by whose genius "the stately monuments of superstition" were built, through which she was expressed. He would have seen more meaning in Isis[24] with the cow's horns, at Edfoo,[25] who expressed the same thought. The art remained, but the energy was lost even upon the artist.

Yet in mind and person St. Gaudens was a survival of the 1500's; he bore the stamp of the Renaissance, and should have carried an image of the Virgin round his neck, or stuck in his hat, like Louis XI.[26] In mere time he was a lost soul that had strayed by chance into the twentieth century, and forgotten where it came from. He writhed and cursed at his ignorance, much as Adams did at his own, but in the opposite sense. St. Gaudens was a child of Benvenuto Cellini, smothered in an American cradle. Adams was a quintes-

[24] in Egyptian mythology, the chief female deity

[25] Edfu, a town in upper Egypt

[26] King of France 1226-1270

sence of Boston, devoured by curiosity to think like Benvenuto. St. Gauden's art was starved from birth, and Adams's instinct was blighted from babyhood. Each had but half of a nature, and when they came together before the Virgin of Amiens they ought both to have felt in her the force that made them one; but it was not so. To Adams she became more than ever a channel of force; to St. Gaudens she remained as before a channel of taste.

For a symbol of power, St. Gaudens instinctively perferred the horse, as was plain in his horse and Victory of the Sherman monument. Doubtless Sherman also felt it so. The attitude was so American that, for at least forty years, Adams had never realized that any other could be in sound taste. How many years had he taken to admit a notion of what Michel Angelo and Rubens were driving at? He could not say; but he knew that only since 1895 had he begun to feel the Virgin or Venus as force, and not everywhere even so. At Chartres—perhaps at Lourdes—possibly at Cnidos[27] if one could still find there the divinely naked Aphrodite of Praxiteles[28]—but otherwise one must look for force to the goddesses of Indian mythology. The idea died out long ago in the German and English stock. St. Gaudens at Amiens was hardly less sensitive to the force of the female energy than Matthew Arnold at the Grande Chartreuse.[29] Neither of them felt goddesses as power—only as reflected emotion, human expression, beauty, purity, taste, scarcely even as sympathy. They felt a railway train as power; yet they, and all other artists, constantly complained that the power embodied in a railway train could never be embodied in art. All the steam in the world could not, like the Virgin, build Chartres.

Yet in mechanics, whatever the mechanicians might think, both energies acted as interchangeable forces on man, and by action on man all known force may be measured. Indeed, few men of science measured force in any other way. After once admitting that a straight line was the shortest distance between two points, no serious mathematician cared to deny anything that suited his convenience, and rejected no symbol, unproved or unproveable, that

[27] an ancient city of Caria, in Asia Minor

[28] Greek sculptor, born at Athens about the end of the 5th century B.C.

[29] the leading Carthusian monastery, near Grenoble, France, which inspired a poem by Arnold

helped him to accomplish work. The symbol was force, as a compass needle or a triangle was force, as the mechanist might prove by losing it, and nothing could be gained by ignoring their value. Symbol or energy, the Virgin had acted as the greatest force the Western world ever felt, and had drawn man's activities to herself more strongly than any other power, natural or supernatural, had ever done; the historian's business was to follow the track of the energy; to find where it came from and where it went to; its complex source and shifting channels; its values, equivalents, conversions. It could scarcely be more complex than radium; it could hardly be deflected, diverted, polarized, absorbed more perplexingly than other radiant matter. Adams knew nothing about any of them, but as a mathematical problem of influence on human progress, though all were occult, all reacted on his mind, and he rather inclined to think the Virgin easiest to handle.

The pursuit turned out to be long and tortuous, leading at last into the vast forests of scholastic[30] science. From Zeno[31] to Descartes,[32] hand in hand with Thomas Aquinas,[33] Montaigne,[34] and Pascal,[35] one stumbled as stupidly as though one were still a German student of 1860. Only with the instinct of despair could one force one's self into this old thicket of ignorance after having been repulsed at a score of entrances more promising and more popular. Thus far, no path had led anywhere, unless perhaps to an exceedingly modest living. Forty-five years of study had proved to be quite futile for the pursuit of power; one controlled no more force in 1900 than in 1850, although the amount of force controlled by society had enormously increased. The secret of education still hid itself somewhere behind ignorance, and one fumbled over it as feebly as ever. In such labyrinths, the staff is a force almost more necessary than the legs; the pen becomes a sort of blind-man's dog, to keep him from falling into the gutters. The pen works for itself,

[30] theological and philosophical teaching prevalent in the middle ages, based chiefly on the authority of the church fathers and of Aristotle and his commentators

[31] Greek philosopher, lived in the 5th century B.C.

[32] René Descartes (1596-1650), French philosopher, founder of Cartesianism and of modern philosophy

[33] famous Italian theologian and scholastic philosopher (c. 1225-1274)

[34] Michel Eyquem de Montaigne (1533 - c. 1592), celebrated French essayist

[35] Blaise Pascal (1623-1662), French geometrician, philosopher, and writer

and acts like a hand, modelling the plastic material over and over again to the form that suits it best. The form is never arbitrary, but is a sort of growth like crystallization, as any artist knows too well; for often the pencil or pen runs into side-paths and shapelessness, loses its relations, stops or is bogged. Then it has to return on its trail, and recover, if it can, its line of force. The result of a year's work depends more on what is struck out than on what is left in; on the sequence of the main lines of thought, than on their play or variety. Compelled once more to lean heavily on this support, Adams covered more thousands of pages with figures as formal as though they were algebra, laboriously striking out, altering, burning, experimenting, until the year had expired, the Exposition had long been closed, and winter drawing to its end, before he sailed from Cherbourg, on January 19,1901, for home.

Descendant of Presidents of the United States, Henry Adams gives us the story of his education in his third-person autobiography, of history in *Mont Saint-Michel and Chartres,* and of America in history in his work on the Jefferson-Madison era. He evolved a theory of history based on cycles of growth and decay, and saw the medieval world as orderly, as in the vision of the virgin, the modern as fractured into the driving dynamo.

Conclusion

FROM *Studies in the History of the Renaissance (1873)*
BY ***Walter Pater*** *(1839-1894)*

Λέγει που Ἡράκλειτος ὅτι πάντα χωρεῖ καὶ οὐδὲν μένει.[1]

To regard all things and principles of things as inconstant modes or fashions has more and more become the tendency of modern thought. Let us begin with that which is without—our physical life. Fix upon it in one of its more exquisite intervals, the moment, for instance, of delicious recoil from the flood of water in summer heat. What is the whole physical life in that moment but a combination of natural elements to which science gives their names? But those elements, phosphorus and lime and delicate fibres, are present not in the human body alone: we detect them in places most remote from it. Our physical life is a perpetual motion of them—the passage of the blood, the wasting and repairing of the lenses of the eye, the modification of the tissues of the brain under every ray of light and sound—processes which science reduces to simpler and more elementary forces. Like the elements of which we are composed, the action of these forces extends beyond us: it rusts iron and ripens corn. Far out on every side of us those elements are broadcast,[2] driven in many currents; and birth and gesture and death and the springing of violets from the grave are but a few out of ten thousand resultant combinations. That clear, perpetual outline of face and limb is but an image of ours, under which we group

[1] Somewhere Heraclitus says that everything passes along and nothing stands still
[2] scattered widely

them—a design in a web, the actual threads of which pass out beyond it. This at least of flamelike[3] our life has, that it is but the concurrence, renewed from moment to moment, of forces parting sooner or later on their ways.

Or if we begin with the inward world of thought and feeling, the whirlpool is still more rapid, the flame more eager and devouring. There it is no longer the gradual darkening of the eye, the gradual fading of colour from the wall—movements of the shore-side, where the water flows down indeed, though in apparent rest—but the race of the midstream, a drift of momentary acts of sight and passion and thought. At first sight experience seems to bury us under a flood of external objects, pressing upon us with a sharp and importunate reality, calling us out of ourselves in a thousand forms of action. But when reflection begins to play upon those objects they are dissipated under its influence; the cohesive force seems suspended like some trick of magic; each object is loosed into a group of impressions—colour, odour, texture—in the mind of the observer. And if we continue to dwell in thought on this world, not of objects in the solidity with which language invests them, but of impressions, unstable, flickering, inconsistent, which burn and are extinguished with our consciousness of them, it contracts still further: the whole scope of observation is dwarfed into the narrow chamber of the individual mind. Experience, already reduced to a group of impressions, is ringed round for each one of us by that thick wall of personality through which no real voice has ever pierced on its way to us, or from us to that which we can only conjecture to be without. Every one of those impressions is the impression of the individual in his isolation, each mind keeping as a solitary prisoner its own dream of a world. Analysis goes a step farther still, and assures us that those impressions of the individual mind to which, for each one of us, experience dwindles down, are in perpetual flight; that each of them is limited by time, and that as time is infinitely divisible, each of them is infinitely divisible also; all that is actual in it being a single moment, gone while we try to apprehend it, of which it may ever be more truly said that it has ceased to be than that it is. To such a tremulous wisp constantly

[3] of what is like flame

reforming itself on the stream, to a single sharp impression, with a sense in it, a relic more or less fleeting, of such moments gone by, what is real in our life fines itself down. It is with this movement, with the passage and dissolution of impressions, images, sensations, that analysis leaves off—that continual vanishing away, that strange, perpetual weaving and unweaving of ourselves.

Philosophiren,[4] says Novalis,[5] *ist dephlegmatisiren vivificiren.* The service of philosophy, of speculative culture, towards the human spirit, is to rouse, to startle it to a life of constant and eager observation. Every moment some form grows perfect in hand or face; some tone on the hills or the sea is choicer than the rest; some mood of passion or insight or intellectual excitement is irrestibly real and attractive to us—for that moment only. Not the fruit of experience, but experience itself, is the end. A counted number of pulses only is given to us of a variegated, dramatic life. How may we see in them all that is to be seen in them by the finest senses? How shall we pass most swiftly from point to point, and be present always at the focus where the greatest number of vital forces unite in their purest energy?

To burn always with this hard, gemlike flame, to maintain this ecstasy, is success in life. In a sense it might even be said that our failure is to form habits: for, after all, habit is relative to a stereotyped world, and meantime it is only the roughness of the eye that makes any two persons, things, situations, seem alike. While all melts under our feet, we may well grasp at any exquisite passion, or any contribution to knowledge that seems by a lifted horizon to set the spirit free for a moment, or any stirring of the senses, strange dyes, strange colours, and curious odours, or work of the artist's hands, or the face of one's friend. Not to discriminate every moment some passionate attitude in those about us, and in the very brilliancy of their gifts some tragic dividing of forces on their ways, is, on this short day of frost and sun, to sleep before evening. With this sense of the splendour of our experience and its awful brevity, gathering all we are into one desperate effort to see and touch, we

[4] to philosophize is to arouse to make live

[5] pseudonym of Friedrich von Hardenberg, (1772-1801), German lyric poet of the older Romantic school

shall hardly have time to make theories about the things we see and touch. What we have to do is to be for ever curiously testing new opinions and courting new impressions, never acquiescing in a facile orthodoxy of Comte,[6] or of Hegel,[7] or of our own. Philosophical theories or ideas, as points of view, instruments of criticism, may help us to gather up what might otherwise pass unregarded by us. "Philosophy is the microscope of thought." The theory or idea or system which requires of us the sacrifice of any part of this experience, in consideration of some interest into which we cannot enter, or some abstract theory we have not identified with ourselves, or of what is only conventional, has no real claim upon us.

One of the most beautiful passages of Rousseau[8] is that in the sixth book of the *Confessions,* where he describes the awakening in him of the literary sense. An undefinable taint of death had always clung about him, and now in early manhood he believed himself smitten by a mortal disease. He asked himself how he might make as much as possible of the interval that remained; and he was not biased by anything in his previous life when he decided that it must be by intellectual excitement, which he found just then in the clear, fresh writings of Voltaire. Well! we are all *condamnés,* as Victor Hugo says: we are all under sentence of death but with a sort of indefinite reprieve—*les hommes sont tous condamnés à mort avec des sursis indéfinis:* we have an interval, and then our place knows us no more. Some spend this interval in listlessness, some in high passions, the wisest, at least among "the children of this world," in art and song. For our one chance lies in expanding that interval, in getting as many pulsations as possible into the given time. Great passions may give us this quickened sense of life, ecstasy and sorrow of love, the various forms of enthusiastic activity, disinterested or otherwise, which come naturally to so many of us. Only be sure it is passion—that it does yield you this fruit of a quickened, multiplied consciousness. Of such wisdom, the poetic passion, the desire

[6]Isidore Auguste Marie François Xavier Comte, known as Auguste Comte (1798-1857), French philosopher, founder of positivism

[7]Georg Wilhelm Friedrich Hegel (1770-1831), German philosopher

[8]Jean-Jacques Rousseau (1712-1778), Swiss-French philosopher and writer of autobiographical *Confessions* and other literary works

of beauty, the love of art for its own sake, has most. For art comes to you proposing frankly to give nothing but the highest quality to your moments as they pass, and simply for those moments' sake.

❧ Walter Pater studied and taught at Oxford and in association with other Pre-Raphaelites devoted his life to art and the philosophy of art, especially that of Greece and of the Renaissance. *Marius the Epicurean,* a "philosophic romance" (1855), is one of his best-known works of intense prose.

On a certain blindness in human beings

FROM *Talks to Teachers on Psychology (1899)*

BY *William James (1842-1910)*

Our judgments concerning the worth of things, big or little, depend on the *feelings* the things arouse in us. Where we judge a thing to be precious in consequence of the *idea* we frame of it, this is only because the idea is itself associated already with a feeling. If we were radically feelingless, and if ideas were the only things our mind could entertain, we should lose all our likes and dislikes at a stroke, and be unable to point to any one situation or experience in life more valuable or significant than any other.

Now the blindness in human beings, of which this discourse will treat, is the blindness with which we all are afflicted in regard to the feelings of creatures and people different from ourselves.

We are practical beings, each of us with limited functions and duties to perform. Each is bound to feel intensely the importance of his own duties and the significance of the situations that call these forth. But this feeling is in each of us a vital secret, for sympathy with which we vainly look to others. The others are too much absorbed in their own vital secrets to take an interest in ours. Hence the stupidity and injustice of our opinions, so far as they deal with the significance of alien lives. Hence the falsity of our judgments, so far as they presume to decide in an absolute way on the value of other persons' conditions or ideals.

Take our dogs and ourselves, connected as we are by a tie more intimate than most ties in this world; and yet, outside of that tie of friendly fondness, how insensible, each of us, to all that makes life significant for the other! – we to the rapture of bones under hedges, or smells of trees and lamp-posts, they to the delights of literature and art. As you sit reading the most moving romance you ever fell upon, what sort of a judge is your fox-terrier of your behavior? With all his good will toward you, the nature of your conduct is absolutely excluded from his comprehension. To sit there like a senseless statue, when you might be taking him to walk and throwing sticks for him to catch! What queer disease is this that comes over you every day, of holding things and staring at them like that for hours together, paralyzed of motion and vacant of all conscious life? The African savages came nearer the truth; but they, too, missed it, when they gathered wonderingly round one of our American travellers who, in the interior, had just come into possession of a stray copy of the New York *Commercial Advertiser,* and was devouring it column by column. When he got through, they offered him a high price for the mysterious object; and, being asked for what they wanted it, they said: "For an eye medicine," – that being the only reason they could conceive of for the protected bath which he had given his eyes upon its surface.

The spectator's judgment is sure to miss the root of the matter, and to possess no truth. The subject judged knows a part of the world of reality which the judging spectator fails to see, knows more while the spectator knows less; and, wherever there is conflict of opinion and difference of vision, we are bound to believe that the truer side is the side that feels the more, and not the side that feels the less.

Let me take a personal example of the kind that befalls each one of us daily: –

Some years ago, while journeying in the mountains of North Carolina, I passed by a large number of "coves," as they call them there, or heads of small valleys between the hills, which had been newly cleared and planted. The impression on my mind was one of unmitigated squalor. The settler had in every case cut down the more manageable trees, and left their charred stumps standing. The larger trees he had girdled and killed, in order that their foliage should not cast a shade. He had then built a log cabin, plastering its chinks with clay, and had set up a tall zigzag rail fence around the scene of his havoc, to keep the pigs and cattle out. Finally, he had irregularly planted the intervals between the stumps and trees with Indian corn, which grew among the chips; and there he dwelt with his wife and babes—an axe, a gun, a few utensils, and some pigs and chickens feeding in the woods, being the sum total of his possessions.

The forest had been destroyed; and what had "improved" it out of existence was hideous, a sort of ulcer, without a single element of artificial grace to make up for the loss of Nature's beauty. Ugly, indeed, seemed the life of the squatter, scudding,[1] as the sailors say, under bare poles, beginning again away back where our first ancestors started, and by hardly a single item the better off for all the achievements of the intervening generations.

Talk about going back to nature! I said to myself, oppressed by the dreariness, as I drove by. Talk of a country life for one's old age and for one's children! Never thus, with nothing but the bare ground and one's bare hands to fight the battle! Never, without the best spoils of culture woven in! The beauties and commodities gained by the centuries are sacred. They are our heritage and birthright. No modern person ought to be willing to live a day in such a state of rudimentariness and denudation.

Then I said to the mountaineer who was driving me, "What sort of people are they who have to make these new clearings?" "All of us," he replied. "Why, we ain't happy here, unless we are getting one of these coves under cultivation." I instantly felt that I had been losing the whole inward significance of the situation. Because to me the clearings spoke of naught but denudation, I thought that to those whose sturdy arms and obedient axes had made them they could tell no other story. But, when *they* looked on the hideous stumps, what they thought of was personal victory. The chips, the girdled trees, and the vile split rails spoke of honest sweat, persistent toil, and final reward. The cabin was a warrant of safety for self and wife and babes. In short, the clearing, which to me was a mere ugly picture on the retina, was to them a symbol redolent with[2]

[1] driven or running before the wind

[2] fragrant, used here as opposite to reeking

moral memories and sang a very paean of duty, struggle, and success.

I had been as blind to the peculiar ideality of their conditions as they certainly would also have been to the ideality of mine, had they had a peep at my strange indoor academic ways of life at Cambridge.[3]

Wherever a process of life communicates an eagerness to him who lives it, there the life becomes genuinely significant. Sometimes the eagerness is more knit up with the motor activities, sometimes with the perceptions, sometimes with the imagination, sometimes with reflective thought. But, wherever it is found, there is the zest, the tingle, the excitement of reality; and there *is* "importance" in the only real and positive sense in which importance ever anywhere can be.

Robert Louis Stevenson[4] has illustrated this by a case, drawn from the sphere of the imagination, in an essay which I really think deserves to become immortal, both for the truth of its matter and the excellence of its form.

"Toward the end of September," Stevenson writes, "when school-time was drawing near, and the nights were already black, we would begin to sally from our respective villas, each equipped with a tin bull's-eye lantern.[5] The thing was so well known that it had worn a rut in the commerce of Great Britain; and the grocers, about the due time, began to garnish their windows with our particular brand of luminary. We wore them buckled to the waist upon a cricket[6] belt, and over them, such was the rigor of the game, a buttoned top-coat. They smelled noisomely of blistered tin. They never burned aright, though they would always burn our fingers. Their use was naught, the pleasure of them merely fanciful, and yet a boy with a bull's-eye under his top-coat asked for nothing more. The fishermen used lanterns about their boats, and it was from them, I suppose, that we had got the hint; but theirs were not bull's-eyes, nor did we ever play at being fishermen. The police carried them at their belts, and we had plainly copied them in that; yet we

[3] Cambridge, Massachusetts, or in short Harvard

[4] Scottish novelist, essayist (1850-1894)

[5] lantern with a lens for concentrating light

[6] very popular English outdoor sport, vaguely comparable to baseball

did not pretend to be policemen. Burglars, indeed, we may have had some haunting thought of; and we had certainly an eye to past ages when lanterns were more common, and to certain story-books in which we had found them to figure very largely. But take it for all in all, the pleasure of the thing was substantive;[7] and to be a boy with a bull's-eye under his top-coat was good enough for us.

"When two of these asses met, there would be an anxious 'Have you got your lantern?' and a gratified 'Yes!' That was the shibboleth,[8] and very needful, too; for, as it was the rule to keep our glory contained, none could recognize a lantern-bearer unless (like the polecat) by the smell. Four or five would sometimes climb into the belly of a ten-man lugger, with nothing but the thwarts above them, —for the cabin was usually locked,—or choose out some hollow of the links where the wind might whistle overhead. Then the coats would be unbuttoned, and the bull's-eyes discovered; and in the chequering[9] glimmer, under the huge, windy hall of the night, and cheered by a rich steam of toasting tinware, these fortunate young gentlemen would crouch together in the cold sand of the links,[10] or on the scaly bilges of the fishing-boat, and delight them with inappropriate talk. Woe is me that I cannot give some specimens! . . . But the talk was but a condiment, and these gatherings themselves only accidents in the career of the lantern-bearer. The essence of this bliss was to walk by yourself in the black night, the slide shut, the top-coat buttoned, not a ray escaping, whether to conduct your footsteps or to make your glory public,—a mere pillar of darkness in the dark; and all the while, deep down in the privacy of your fool's heart, to know you had a bull's-eye at your belt, and to exult and sing over the knowledge.

"It is said that a poet has died young in the breast of the most stolid. It may be contended rather that a (somewhat minor) bard in almost every case survives, and is the spice of life to his possessor. Justice is not done to the versatility and the unplumbed childishness of men's imagination. His life from without may seem but a

[7] existing independently

[8] password, the word itself being used by the Gileadites, in the Bible, to distinguish the escaping Ephraimites who could not pronounce the initial *sh*

[9] checkered, alternating light and dark

[10] Scottish word, flat or slightly rolling land, especially along a seashore

rude mound of mud: there will be some golden chamber at the heart of it, in which he dwells delighted; and for as dark as his pathway seems to the observer, he will have some kind of bull's-eye at his belt.

..."There is one fable that touches very near the quick of life,—the fable of the monk who passed into the woods, heard a bird break into song, hearkened for a trill or two, and found himself at his return a stranger at his convent gates; for he had been absent fifty years, and of all his comrades there survived but one to recognize him. It is not only in the woods that this enchanter carols, though perhaps he is native there. He sings in the most doleful places. The miser hears him and chuckles, and his days are moments. With no more apparatus than an evil-smelling lantern, I have evoked him on the naked links. All life that is not merely mechanical is spun out of two strands,—seeking for that bird and hearing him. And it is just this that makes life so hard to value, and the delight of each so incommunicable. And it is just a knowledge of this, and a remembrance of those fortunate hours in which the bird *has* sung to *us,* that fills with such wonder when we turn to the pages of the realist. There, to be sure, we find a picture of life in so far as it consists of mud and of old iron, cheap desires and cheap fears, that which we are ashamed to remember and that which we are careless whether we forget; but of the note of that time-devouring nightingale we hear no news.

..."Say that we came in such a realistic romance] on some such business as that of my lantern-bearers on the links, and described the boys as very cold, spat upon by flurries of rain, and drearily surrounded, all of which they were; and their talk as silly and indecent, which it certainly was. To the eye of the observer they *are* wet and cold and drearily surrounded; but ask themselves, and they are in the heaven of a recondite pleasure, the ground of which is an ill-smelling lantern.

"For, to repeat, the ground of a man's joy is often hard to hit. It may hinge at times upon a mere accessory, like the lantern; it may reside in the mysterious inwards of psychology... It has so little bond with externals... that it may even touch them not, and the man's true life, for which he consents to live, lie altogether in the field of fancy... In such a case the poetry runs underground.

The observer (poor soul, with his documents!) is all abroad. For to look at the man is but to court deception. We shall see the trunk from which he draws his nourishment; but he himself is above and abroad in the green dome of foliage, hummed through by winds and nested in by nightingales. And the true realism were that of the poets, to climb up after him like a squirrel, and catch some glimpse of the heaven for which he lives. And the true realism, always and everywhere, is that of the poets: to find out where joy resides, and give it a voice far beyond singing.

"For to miss the joy is to miss all. In the joy of the actors lies the sense of any action. That is the explanation, that the excuse. To one who has not the secret of the lanterns the scene upon the links is meaningless. And hence the haunting and truly spectral unreality of realistic books ... In each we miss the personal poetry, the enchanted atmosphere, that rainbow work of fancy that clothes what is naked and seems to ennoble what is base; in each, life falls dead like dough, instead of soaring away like a balloon into the colors of the sunset; each is true, each inconceivable; for no man lives in the external truth, among salts and acids, but in the warm, phantasmagoric chamber of his brain, with the painted windows and the storied walls."

These paragraphs are the best thing I know in all Stevenson. "To miss the joy is to miss all." Indeed, it is. Yet we are but finite, and each one of us has some single specialized vocation of his own. And it seems as if energy in the service of its particular duties might be got only by hardening the heart toward everything unlike them. Our deadness toward all but one particular kind of joy would thus be the price we inevitably have to pay for being practical creatures. Only in some pitiful dreamer, some philosopher, poet, or romancer, or when the common practical man becomes a lover, does the hard externality give way, and a gleam of insight into the ejective world, as Clifford[11] called it, the vast world of inner life beyond us, so different from that of outer seeming, illuminate our mind. Then the whole scheme of our customary values gets confounded, then our self is riven and its narrow interests fly to pieces, then a new centre and a new perspective must be found.

[11] William Kingdon Clifford (1845-1879), English mathematician and philosophical writer

The change is well described by my colleague, Josiah Royce:[12] —

"What, then, is our neighbor? Thou hast regarded his thought, his feeling, as somehow different from thine. Thou hast said, 'A pain in him is not like a pain in me, but something far easier to bear.' He seems to thee a little less living than thou; his life is dim, it is cold, it is a pale fire beside thy own burning desires ... So, dimly and by instinct hast thou lived with thy neighbor, and hast known him not, being blind. Thou hast made of him] a thing, no Self at all. Have done with this illusion, and simply try to learn the truth. Pain is pain, joy is joy, everwhere, even as in thee. In all the songs of the forest birds; in all the cries of the wounded and dying, struggling in the captor's power; in the boundless sea where the myriads of water-creatures strive and die; amid all the countless hordes of savage men; in all sickness and sorrow; in all exultation and hope, everywhere, from the lowest to the noblest, the same conscious, burning, wilful life is found, endlessly manifold as the forms of the living creature, unquenchable as the fires of the sun, real as these impulses that even now throb in thine own little selfish heart. Lift up thy eyes, behold that life, and then turn away, and forget it as thou canst; but, if thou hast *known* that, thou hast begun to know thy duty."

This higher vision of an inner significance in what, until then, we had realized only in the dead external way, often comes over a person suddenly; and, when it does so, it makes an epoch in his history. As Emerson says, there is a depth in those moments that constrains us to ascribe more reality to them than to all other experiences. The passion of love will shake one like an explosion, or some act will awaken a remorseful compunction that hangs like a cloud over all one's later day.

This mystic sense of hidden meaning starts upon us often from non-human natural things. I take this passage from "Obermann,"[13] a French novel that had some vogue in its day: "Paris, March 7.—It was dark and rather cold. I was gloomy, and walked because I had nothing to do. I passed by some flowers placed breast-high upon a wall. A jonquil in bloom was there. It is the strongest expression of

[12] American philosopher (1855-1916)

[13] a psychological romance by Etienne Pivert de Senancourt, published in 1894

desire: it was the first perfume of the year. I felt all the happiness destined for man. This unutterable harmony of souls, the phantom of the ideal world, arose in me complete. I never felt anything so great or so instantaneous. I know not what shape, what analogy, what secret of relation it was that made me see in this flower a limitless beauty . . . I shall never enclose in a conception this power, this immensity that nothing will express; this form that nothing will contain; this ideal of a better world which one feels, but which it would seem that nature has not made."

Wordsworth and Shelley are similarly full of this sense of a limitless significance in natural things. In Wordsworth it was a somewhat austere and moral significance,—a "lonely cheer."

> To every natural form, rock, fruit, or flower,
> Even the loose stones that co the highway,
> I gave a moral life: I saw them feel
> Or linked them to some feeling: the great mass
> Lay bedded in some quickening soul, and all
> That I beheld respired with inward meaning.

"Authentic tidings of invisible things!" Just what this hidden presence in nature was, which Wordsworth so rapturously felt, and in the light of which he lived, tramping the hills for days together, the poet never could explain logically or in articulate conceptions. Yet to the reader who may himself have had gleaming moments of a similar sort the verses in which Wordsworth simply proclaims the fact of them come with a heart-satisfying authority:—

> Magnificent
> The morning rose, in memorable pomp,
> Glorious as ere I had beheld. In front
> The sea lay laughing at a distance; near
> The solid mountains shone, bright as the clouds
> Grain-tinctured, drenched in empyrean light;
> And in the meadows and the lower grounds
> Was all the sweetness of a common dawn,—
> Dews, vapors, and the melody of birds,
> And laborers going forth to till the fields.

Ah! need I say, dear Friend,[14] that to the brim
My heart was full; I made no vows, but vows
Were then made for me; bond unknown to me
Was given, that I should be, else sinning greatly,
A dedicated Spirit. On I walked,
In thankful blessedness, which yet survives.

As Wordsworth walked, filled with this strange inner joy, responsive thus to the secret life of nature round about him, his rural neighbors, tightly and narrowly intent upon their own affairs, their crops and lambs and fences, must have thought him a very insignificant and foolish personage. It surely never occurred to any one of them to wonder what was going on inside of *him* or what it might be worth. And yet that inner life of his carried the burden of a significance that has fed the souls of others, and fills them to this day with inner joy.

Richard Jefferies[15] has written a remarkable autobiographic document entitled, "The Story of My Heart." It tells, in many pages, of the rapture with which in youth the sense of the life of nature filled him. On a certain hill-top he says: —

"I was utterly alone with the sun and the earth. Lying down on the grass, I spoke in my soul to the earth, the sun, the air, and the distant sea, far beyond sight . . . With all the intensity of feeling which exalted me, all the intense communion I held with the earth, the sun and sky, the stars hidden by the light, with the ocean, — in no manner can the thrilling depth of these feelings be written, — with these I prayed as if they were the keys of an instrument . . . The great sun, burning with light, the strong earth, — dear earth, — the warm sky, the pure air, the thought of ocean, the inexpressible beauty of all filled me with a rapture, an ectasy, an inflatus.[16] With this inflatus, too, I prayed . . . The prayer, this soul-emotion, was in itself, not for an object: it was a passion. I hid my face in the grass. I

[14] Samuel Taylor Coleridge (1772-1834), English poet and critic, friend of Wordsworth

[15] John Richard Jefferies (1848-1887), English writer, noted for his descriptions of nature [16] upraising and elation of spirits

was wholly prostrated, I lost myself in the wrestle, I was rapt and carried away ... Had any shepherd accidentally seen me lying on the turf, he would only have thought I was resting a few minutes. I made no outward show. Who could have imagined the whirlwind of passion that was going on in me as I reclined there!"

Surely, a worthless hour of life, when measured by the usual standards of commercial value. Yet in what other *kind* of value can the preciousness of any hour, made precious by any standard, consist, if it consist not in feelings of excited significance like these, engendered in some one, by what the hour contains?

Yet so blind and dead does the clamor of our own practical interests make us to all other things, that it seems almost as if it were necessary to become worthless as a practical being, if one is to hope to attain to any breadth of insight into the impersonal world of worths as such, to have any perception of life's meaning on a large objective scale. Only your mystic, your dreamer, or your insolvent tramp or loafer, can afford so sympathetic an occupation, an occupation which will change the usual standards of human value in the twinkling of an eye, giving to foolishness a place ahead of power, and laying low in a minute the distinctions which it takes a hard-working conventional man a lifetime to build up. You may be a prophet, at this rate; but you cannot be a worldly success.

Walt Whitman, for instance, is accounted by many of us a contemporary prophet. He abolishes the usual human distinctions, brings all conventionalisms into solution, and loves and celebrates hardly any human attributes save those elementary ones common to all members of the race. For this he becomes a sort of ideal tramp, a rider on omnibus-tops and ferry-boats, and, considered either practically or academically, a worthless, unproductive being. His verses are but ejaculations—things mostly without subject or verb, a succession of interjections on an immense scale. He felt the human crowd as rapturously as Wordsworth felt the mountains, felt it as an overpoweringly significant presence, simply to absorb one's mind in which should be business sufficient and worthy to fill the days of a serious man. As he crosses Brooklyn Ferry, this is what he feels:—

Flood-tide below me! I watch you, face to face;
Clouds of the west! sun there half an hour high! I see you also face to face.
Crowds of men and women attired in the usual costumes! how curious you are to me!
On the ferry-boats, the hundreds and hundreds that cross, returning home, are more curious to me than you suppose;
And you that shall cross from shore to shore hence, are more to me and more in my meditations, than you might suppose.
Others will enter the gates of the ferry, and cross from shore to shore;
Others will watch the run of the flood-tide;
Others will see the shipping of Manhattan north and west, and the heights of Brooklyn to the south and east;
Others will see the islands large and small;
Fifty years hence, others will see them as they cross, the sun half an hour high.
A hundred years hence, or ever so many hundred years hence, others will see them,
Will enjoy the sunset, the pouring in of the flood-tide, the falling back to the sea of the ebb-tide.
It avails not, neither time or place—distance avails not.
Just as you feel when you look on the river and sky, so I felt;
Just as any of you is one of a living crowd, I was one of a crowd;
Just as you are refresh'd by the gladness of the river and the bright flow, I was refresh'd;
Just as you stand and lean on the rail, yet hurry with the swift current, I stood, yet was hurried;
Just as you look on the numberless masts of ships, and the thick-stemmed pipes of steamboats, I looked.
I too many and many a time cross'd the river, the sun half an hour high;
I watched the Twelfth-month sea-gulls—I saw them high in the air, with motionless wings, oscillating their bodies,

I saw how the glistening yellow lit up parts of their bodies,
 and left the rest in strong shadow,
I saw the slow-wheeling circles, and the gradual edging to-
 ward the south.
Saw the white sails of schooners and sloops, saw the ships at
 anchor,
The sailors at work in the rigging, or out astride the spars;
The scallop-edged waves in the twilight, the ladled cups, the
 frolicsome crests and glistening;
The stretch afar growing dimmer and dimmer, the gray walls
 of the granite store-houses by the docks;
On the neighboring shores, the fires from the foundry chim-
 neys burning high ... into the night,
Casting their flicker of black ... into the clefts of streets.
These, and all else, were to me the same as they are to you.

And so on, through the rest of a divinely beautiful poem. And, if you wish to see what this hoary loafer considered the most worthy way of profiting by life's heaven-sent opportunities, read the delicious volume of his letters to a young car-conductor who had become his friend: –

"New York, Oct. 9, 1868.

"Dear *Pete,* – It is splendid here this forenoon – bright and cool. I was out early taking a short walk by the river only two squares from where I live ... Shall I tell you about [my life] just to fill up? I generally spend the forenoon in my room writing, etc., then take a bath, fix up and go out about twelve and loafe somewhere or call on someone down town or on business, or perhaps if it is very pleasant and I feel like it ride a trip with some driver friend on Broadway from 23rd Street to Bowling Green, three miles each way. (Every day I find I have plenty to do, every hour is occupied with something.) You know it is a never ending amusement and study and recreation for me to ride a couple of hours on a pleasant afternoon on a Broadway stage in this way. You see everything as you pass, a sort of living, endless panorama – shops and splendid buildings and great windows: on the broad sidewalks crowds of women richly dressed continually passing, altogether different, superior in style and looks from any to be seen anywhere else—in fact a perfect stream of people—men too dressed in high style, and plenty of foreigners—and then in the streets the thick crowd of carriages, stages, carts, hotel and private coaches, and in fact all sorts of vehicles and many first class teams, mile after mile, and the splendor of such a great street and so many tall, ornamental, noble buildings many of them of white marble, and the gayety and motion on every side; you will not wonder how much attraction all this is on a fine day, to a great loafer like me, who enjoys so much seeing the busy world move by him, and exhibiting itself for his amusement, while he takes it easy and just looks on and observes."

Truly a futile way of passing the time, some of you may say, and not altogether creditable to a grown-up man. And yet, from the deepest point of view, who knows the more of truth, and who knows the less,—Whitman on his omnibus-top full of the inner joy with which the spectacle inspires him, or you, full of the disdain which the futility of his occupation excites?

When your ordinary Brooklynite or New Yorker, leading a life replete with too much luxury, or tired and careworn about his personal affairs, crosses the ferry or goes up Broadway, *his* fancy does not thus "soar away into the colors of the sunset" as did Whitman's, nor does he inwardly realize at all the indisputable fact that this world never did anywhere or at any time contain more of essential divinity, or of eternal meaning, than is embodied in the fields of vision over which his eyes so carelessly pass. There is life; and there, a step away, is death. There is the only kind of beauty there ever was. There is the old human struggle and its fruits together. There is the text and the sermon, the real and the ideal in one. But to the jaded and unquickened eye it is all dead and common, pure vulgarism, flatness, and disgust. "Hech! it is a sad sight!" says Carlyle, walking at night with some one who appears to him to note the splendor of the stars. And that very repetition of the scene to new generations of men *in secula seculorum,*[17] that eternal recurrence of the common order, which so fills a Whitman with mystic satisfaction, is to a Schopenhauer,[18] with the emotional anaesthesia, the feeling of "awful inner emptiness" form out of which he views it

[17] unto eternity [18] Arthur Schopenhauer (1788-1860), German philosopher

all, the chief ingredient of the tedium it instils. What is life on the largest scale, he asks, but the same recurrent inanities, the same dog barking, the same fly buzzing, forevermore? Yet of the kind of fibre of which such inanities consist is the material woven of all the excitements, joys, and meanings that ever were, or ever shall be, in this world.

To be rapt with satisfied attention, like Whitman, to the mere spectacle of the world's presence, is one way, and the most fundamental way, of confessing one's sense of its unfathomable significance and importance. But how can one attain to the feeling of the vital significance of an experience, if one have it not to begin with? There is no receipt which one can follow. Being a secret and a mystery, it often comes in mysteriously unexpected ways. It blossoms sometimes from out of the very grave wherein we imagined that our happiness was buried. Benvenuto Cellini,[19] after a life all in the outer sunshine, made of adventures and artistic excitements, suddenly finds himself cast into a dungeon in the Castle of San Angelo. The place is horrible. Rats and wet and mould possess it. His leg is broken and his teeth fall out, apparently with scurvy. But his thoughts turn to God as they have never turned before. He gets a Bible, which he reads during the one hour in the twenty-four in which a wandering ray of daylight penetrates his cavern. He has religious visions. He sings psalms to himself, and composes hymns. And thinking, on the last day of July, of the festivities customary on the morrow in Rome, he says to himself: "All these past years I celebrated this holiday with the vanities of the world: from this year henceforth I will do it with the divinity of God. And then I said to myself, 'Oh, how much more happy I am for this present life of mine than for all those things remembered!' "

But the great understander of these mysterious ebbs and flows is Tolstoi.[20] They throb all through his novels. In his "War and Peace," the hero, Peter, is supposed to be the richest man in the Russian empire. During the French invasion he is taken prisoner, and dragged through much of the retreat. Cold, vermin, hunger, and

[19] Italian sculptor and worker in gold and silver (1500-1571), perhaps most celebrated for his worldly *Autobiography*

[20] Count Leo Tolstoi (1828-1910), Russian novelist and social reformer

every form of misery assail him, the result being a revelation to him of the real scale of life's values. "Here only, and for the first time, he appreciated, because he was deprived of it, the happiness of eating when he was hungry, of drinking when he was thirsty, of sleeping when he was sleepy, and of talking when he felt the desire to exchange some words... Later in life he always recurred with joy to this month of captivity, and never failed to speak with enthusiasm of the powerful and ineffaceable sensations, and especially of the moral calm which he had experienced at this epoch. When at daybreak, on the morrow of his imprisonment, he saw [I abridge here Tolstoi's description] the mountains with their wooded slopes disappearing in the grayish mist; when he felt the cool breeze caress him; when he saw the light drive away the vapors, and the sun rise majestically behind the clouds and cupolas, and the crosses, the dew, the distance, the river, sparkle in the splendid, cheerful rays,—his heart overflowed with emotion. This emotion kept continually with him, and increased a hundred-fold as the difficulties of his situation grew graver... He learnt that man is meant for happiness, and that this happiness is in him, in the satisfaction of the daily needs of existence, and that unhappiness is the fatal result, not of our need, but of our abundance... When calm reigned in the camp, and the embers paled, and little by little went out, the full moon had reached the zenith. The woods and the fields roundabout lay clearly visible; and, beyond the inundation of light which filled them, the view plunged into the limitless horizon. Then Peter cast his eyes upon the firmament, filled at that hour with myriads of stars. 'All that is mine,' he thought. 'All that is in me, is me! And that is what they have taken prisoner! That is what they have shut up in a cabin.' So he smiled, and turned in to sleep among his comrades."

The occasion and the experience, then, are nothing. It all depends on the capacity of the soul to be grasped, to have its life-currents absorbed by what is given. "Crossing a bare common," says Emerson, "in snow puddles, at twilight, under a clouded sky, without having in my thoughts any occurrence of special good fortune, I have enjoyed a perfect exhilaration. I am glad to the brink of fear."

Life is always worth living, if one have such responsive sensibilities. But we of the highly educated classes (so called) have most of us got far, far away from Nature. We are trained to seek the choice, the rare, the exquisite exclusively, and to overlook the common. We are stuffed with abstract conceptions, and glib with verbalities and verbosities; and in the culture of these higher functions the peculiar sources of joy connected with our simpler functions often dry up, and we grow stoneblind and insensible to life's more elementary and general goods and joys.

The remedy under such conditions is to descend to a more profound and primitive level. To be imprisoned or shipwrecked or forced into the army would permanently show the good of life to many an overeducated pessimist. Living in the open air and on the ground, the lopsided beam of the balance slowly rises to the level line; and the over-sensibilities and insensibilities even themselves out. The good of all the artificial schemes and fevers fades and pales; and that of seeing, smelling, tasting, sleeping, and daring and doing with one's body, grows and grows. The savages and children of nature, to whom we deem ourselves so much superior, certainly are alive where we are often dead, along these lines; and could they write as glibly as we do, they would read us impressive lectures on our impatience for improvement and on our blindness to the fundamental static goods of life. "Ah! my brother," said a chieftain to his white guest, "thou wilt never know the happiness of both thinking of nothing and doing nothing. This, next to sleep, is the most enchanting of all things. Thus we were before our birth, and thus we shall be after death. Thy people . . . when they have finished reaping one field, they begin to plough another; and, if the day were not enough, I have seen them plough by moonlight. What is their life to ours,—the life that is as naught to them? Blind that they are, they lose it all! But we live in the present."

The intense interest that life can assume when brought down to the non-thinking level, the level of pure sensorial perception, has been beautifully described by a man who *can* write,—Mr. W. H. Hudson,[21] in his volume, "Idle Days in Patagonia."

"I spent the greater part of one winter," says this admirable author, "at a point on the Rio Negro, seventy or eighty miles from the sea.

[21] William Henry Hudson (1841-1922), English naturalist and writer, born in Argentina

..."It was my custom to go out every morning on horseback with my gun, and, followed by one dog, to ride away from the valley; and no sooner would I climb the terrace, and plunge into the gray, universal thicket, than I would find myself as completely alone as if five hundred instead of only five miles separated me from the valley and river. So wild and solitary and remote seemed that gray waste, stretching away into infinitude, a waste untrodden by man, and where the wild animals are so few that they have made no discoverable path in the wilderness of thorns... Not once nor twice nor thrice, but day after day I returned to this solitude, going to it in the morning as if to attend a festival, and leaving it only when hunger and thirst and the westering sun compelled me. And yet I had no object in going,—no motive which could be put into words; for, although I carried a gun, there was nothing to shoot,—the shooting was all left behind in the valley... Sometimes I would pass a whole day without seeing one mammal, and perhaps not more than a dozen birds of any size. The weather at that time was cheerless, generally with a gray film of cloud spread over the sky, and a bleak wind, often cold enough to make my bridle-hand quite numb... At a slow pace, which would have seemed intolerable under other circumstances, I would ride about for hours together at a stretch. On arriving at a hill, I would slowly ride to its summit, and stand there to survey the prospect. On every side it stretched away in great undulations, wild and irregular. How gray it all was! Hardly less so near at hand than on the haze-wrapped horizon where the hills were dim and the outline obscured by distance. Descending from my outlook, I would take up my aimless wanderings again, and visit other elevations to gaze on the same landscape from another point; and so on for hours. And at noon I would dismount, and sit or lie on my folded poncho for an hour or longer. One day in these rambles I discovered a small grove composed of twenty or thirty trees, growing at a convenient distance apart, that had evidently been resorted to by a herd of deer or other wild animals. This grove was on a hill differing in shape from other hills in its neighborhood; and, after a time, I made a point of finding and using it as a resting-place every day at noon. I did not ask myself why I made choice of that one spot, sometimes going out of my way to sit there, instead of sitting down under any one of the millions of trees and bushes on any other hillside. I thought nothing about it, but acted unconsciously. Only afterward it seemed to me that, after having rested there once, each time I wished to rest again, the wish came associated with the image of that particular clump of trees, with polished stems and clean bed of sand beneath; and in a short time I formed a habit of returning, animal like, to repose at that same spot.

"It was, perhaps, a mistake to say that I would sit down and rest, since I was never tired; and yet, without being tired, that noon-day pause, during which I sat for an hour without moving, was strangely grateful. All day there would be no sound, not even the rustling of a leaf. One day, while *listening* to the silence, it occurred to my mind to wonder what the effect would be if I were to shout aloud. This seemed at the time a horrible suggestion, which almost made me shudder. But during those solitary days it was a rare thing for any thought to cross my mind. In the state of mind I was in, thought had become impossible. My state was one of *suspense* and *watchfulness;* yet I had no expectation of meeting an adventure, and felt as free from apprehension as I feel now while sitting in a room in London. The state seemed familiar rather than strange, and accompanied by a strong feeling of elation; and I did not know that something had come between men and ny intellect until I returned to my former self,—to thinking, and the old insipid existence [again].

"I had undoubtedly *gone back;* and that state of intense watchfulness or alertness, rather, with suspension of the higher intellectual faculties, represented the mental state of the pure savage. He thinks little, reasons little, having a surer guide in his mere sensory perceptions]. He is in perfect harmony with nature, and is nearly on a level, mentally, with the wild animals he preys on, and which in their turn sometimes prey on him."

For the spectator, such hours as Mr. Hudson writes of form a mere tale of emptiness, in which nothing happens, nothing is gained, and there is nothing to describe. They are meaningless and vacant tracts[22] of time. To him who feels their inner secret, they tingle with an importance that unutterably vouches for itself. I am sorry for the boy or girl, or man or woman, who has never been

[22] a period of time, poetic usage

touched by the spell of this mysterious sensorial[23] life, with its irrationality, if so you like to call it, but its vigilance and its supreme felicity. The holidays of life are its most vitally significant portions, because they are, or at least should be, covered with just this kind of magically irresponsible spell.

And now what is the result of all these considerations and quotations? It is negative in one sense, but positive in another. It absolutely forbids us to be forward in pronouncing on the meaninglessness of forms of existence other than our own; and it commands us to tolerate, respect, and indulge those whom we see harmlessly interested and happy in their own ways, however unintelligible these may be to us. Hands off: neither the whole of truth nor the whole of good is revealed to any single observer, although each observer gains a partial superiority of insight from the peculiar position in which he stands. Even prisons and sick-rooms have their special revelations. It is enough to ask of each of us that he should be faithful to his own opportunities and make the most of his own blessings, without presuming to regulate the rest of the vast field.

[23] sensory, pertaining to the senses

☙ At the end of the nineteenth century, America's leading psychologist and philosopher, William James, elder brother of the novelist Henry James, published his *Principles of Psychology,* relating intuition and logical demonstration, spirit and pragmatic experience.

On Democracy

FROM Preface to *The Apple Cart (1929)*
BY *George Bernard Shaw (1856-1950)*

I am going to talk to you about Democracy objectively: that is, as it exists and as we must all reckon with it equally, no matter what our points of view may be. Suppose I were to talk to you not about Democracy, but about the sea, which is in some respects rather like Democracy! We all have our own views of the sea. Some of us hate it and are never well when we are at it or on it. Others love it, and are never so happy as when they are in it or on it or looking at it. Some of us regard it as Britain's natural realm and surest bulwark: others want a Channel Tunnel. But certain facts about the sea are quite independent of our feelings towards it. If I take it for granted that the sea exists, none of you will contradict me. If I say that the sea is sometimes furiously violent and always uncertain, and that those who are most familiar with it trust it least, you will not immediately shriek out that I do not believe in the sea; that I am an enemy of the sea: that I want to abolish the sea; that I am going to make bathing illegal; that I am out to ruin our carrying trade and lay waste all our seaside resorts and scrap the British Navy. If I tell you that you cannot breathe in the sea, you will not take that as a personal insult and ask me indignantly if I consider you inferior to a fish. Well, you must please be equally sensible when I tell you some hard facts about Democracy. When I tell you that it is sometimes furiously violent and always dangerous and treacherous, and that those who are familiar with it as practical statesmen trust it least, you must not at once denounce me as a paid agent of Benito

Mussolini, or declare that I have become a Tory Die-hard in my old age, and accuse me of wanting to take away your votes and make an end of parliament, and the franchise, and free speech, and public meeting, and trial by jury. Still less must you rise in your places and give me three rousing cheers as a champion of medieval monarchy and feudalism. I am quite innocent of any such extravagances. All I mean is that whether we are Democrats or Tories, Catholics or Protestants, Communists or Fascists, we are all face to face with a certain force in the world called Democracy; and we must understand the nature of that force whether we want to fight it or to forward it. Our business is not to deny the perils of Democracy, but to provide against them as far as we can, and then consider whether the risks we cannot provide against are worth taking.

Democracy, as you know it, is seldom more than a long word beginning with a capital letter, which we accept reverently or disparage contemptuously without asking any questions. Now we should never accept anything reverently until we have asked it a great many very searching questions, the first two being What are you? and Where do you live? When I put these questions to Democracy the answer I get is "My name is Demos;[1] and I live in the British Empire, the United States of America, and wherever the love of liberty burns in the heart of man. You, my friend Shaw, are a unit of Democracy: your name is also Demos: you are a citizen of a great democratic community: you are a potential constituent of the Parliament of Man, the Federation of the World." At this I usually burst into loud cheers, which do credit to my enthusiastic nature. Tonight, however, I shall do nothing of the sort: I shall say "Don't talk nonsense. My name is not Demos: it is Bernard Shaw. My address is not the British Empire, nor the United States of America, nor wherever the love of liberty burns in the heart of man: it is at such and such a number in such and such a street in London; and it will be time enough to discuss my seat in the Parliament of Man when that celebrated institution comes into existence. I don't believe your name is Demos: nobody's name is Demos; and all I can make of your address is that you have no address, and are just a tramp—if indeed you exist at all."

[1]Greek word meaning the people, or a member of the people

You will notice that I am too polite to call Demos a windbag or a hot air merchant; but I am going to ask you to begin our study of Democracy by considering it first as a big balloon, filled with gas or hot air, and sent up so that you shall be kept looking up at the sky whilst other people are picking your pockets. When the balloon comes down to earth every five years or so you are invited to get into the basket if you can throw out one of the people who are sitting tightly in it; but as you can afford neither the time nor the money, and there are forty millions of you and hardly room for six hundred in the basket, the balloon goes up again with much the same lot in it and leaves you where you were before. I think you will admit that the balloon as an image of Democracy corresponds to the parliamentary facts.

Now let us examine a more poetic conception of Democracy. Abraham Lincoln is represented as standing amid the carnage of the battlefield of Gettysburg, and declaring that all that slaughter of Americans by Americans occurred in order that Democracy, defined as government *of* the people *for* the people *by* the people, should not perish from the earth. Let us pick this famous peroration to pieces and see what really is inside it. (By the way, Lincoln did not really declaim it on the field of Gettysburg; and the American Civil War was not fought in defence of any such principle, but, on the contrary, to enable one half of the United States to force the other half to be governed as they did not wish to be governed. But never mind that. I mentioned it only to remind you that it seems impossible for statesmen to make speeches about Democracy, or journalists to report them, without obscuring it in a cloud of humbug).

Now for the three articles of the definition. Number One: Government *of* the people: that, evidently, is necessary: a human community can no more exist without a government than a human being can exist without a co-ordinated control of its breathing and blood circulation. Number Two: Government *for* the people, is most important. Dean Inge put it perfectly for us when he called Democracy a form of society which means equal consideration for all. He added that it is a Christian principle, and that, as a Christian, he believes in it. So do I. That is why I insist on equality of income. Equal consideration for a person with a hundred a year and one with a hundred thousand is impossible. But Number Three: Government *by* the people, is quite a different matter. All the monarchs, all the tyrants, all the dictators, all the Die-hard Tories are agreed that we must be governed. Democrats like the Dean[2] and myself are agreed that we must be governed with equal consideration for everybody. But we repudiate Number Three on the ground that the people cannot govern. The thing is a physical impossibility. Every citizen cannot be a ruler any more then every boy can be an engine driver or a pirate king. A nation of prime ministers or dictators is as absurd as an army of field marshals. Government by the people is not and never can be a reality: it is only a cry by which demagogues humbug us into voting for them. If you doubt this—if you ask me "Why should not the people make their own laws?" I need only ask you "Why should not the people write their own plays?" They cannot. It is much easier to write a good play than to make a good law. And there are not a hundred men in the world who can write a play good enough to stand daily wear and tear as long as a law must.

Now comes the question, If we cannot govern ourselves, what can we do to save ourselves from being at the mercy of those who *can* govern, and who may quite possibly be thoroughpaced grafters and scoundrels? The primitive answer is that as we are always in a huge majority we can, if rulers oppress us intolerably, burn their houses and tear them to pieces. This is not satisfactory. Decent people never do it until they have quite lost their heads; and when they have lost their heads they are as likely as not to burn the wrong house and tear the wrong man to pieces. When we have what is called a popular movement very few people who take part in it know what it is all about. I once saw a real popular movement in London. People were running excitedly through the streets. Everyone who saw them doing it immediately joined in the rush. They ran simply because everyone else was doing it. It was most impressive to see thousands of people sweeping along at full speed like that. There could be no doubt that it was literally a popular movement. I ascertained afterwards that it was started by a runaway cow.

[2]William Ralph Inge (1860-1954), English theologian and author, Dean of St. Paul's, London, 1911-1934

That cow had an important share in my education as a political philosopher; and I can assure you that if you will study crowds, and lost and terrified animals, and things like that, instead of reading books and newspaper articles, you will learn a great deal about politics from them. Most general elections, for instance, are nothing but stampedes. Our last but one was a conspicuous example of this. The cow was a Russian one.

I think we may take it that neither mob violence nor popular movements can be depended on as checks upon the abuse of power by governments. One might suppose that at least they would act as a last resort when an autocrat goes mad and commits outrageous excesses of tyranny and cruelty. But it is a curious fact that they never do. Take two famous cases: those of Nero and Tsar Paul the First of Russia. If Nero had been an ordinary professional fiddler he would probably have been no worse a man than any member of the wireless orchestra. If Paul had been a lieutenant in a line regiment we should never have heard of him. But when these two poor fellows were invested with absolute powers over their fellow-creatures they went mad, and did such appalling things that they had to be killed like mad dogs. Only, it was not the people that rose up and killed them. They were dispatched quite privately by a very select circle of their own bodyguards. For a genuinely democratic execution of unpopular statesmen we must turn to the brothers De Witt,[3] who were torn to pieces by a Dutch mob in the seventeenth century. They were neither tyrants nor autocrats. On the contrary, one of them had been imprisoned and tortured for his resistance to the despotism of William of Orange;[4] and the other had come to meet him as he came out of prison. The mob was on the side of the autocrat. We may take it that the shortest way for a tyrant to get rid of a troublesome champion of liberty is to raise a hue and cry against him as an unpatriotic person, and leave the mob to do the rest after supplying them with a well tipped ring-leader. Nowadays this is called direct action by the revolutionary proletariat. Those who put their faith in it soon find that proletariats are never revolu-

[3]Cornelius De Witt (1623-1672) and Jan De Witt (1625-1672)

[4]William III, Prince of Orange (1650-1702), King of England 1689-1702, ruled jointly with his wife Mary II until 1694

tionary, and that their direct action, when it is controlled at all, is usually controlled by police agents.

Democracy, then, cannot be government by the people: it can only be government by consent of the governed. Unfortunately, when democratic statesmen propose to govern us by our own consent, they find that we don't want to be governed at all, and that we regard rates and taxes and rents and death duties as intolerable burdens. What we want to know is how little government we can get along with without being murdered in our beds. That question cannot be answered until we have explained what we mean by getting along. Savages manage to get along. Unruly Arabs and Tartars get along. The only rule in the matter is that the civilized way of getting along is the way of corporate action, not individual action; and corporate action involves more government than individual action.

Thus government, which used to be a comparatively simple affair, today has to manage an enormous development of Socialism and Communism. Our industrial and social life is set in a huge communistic framework of public roadways, streets, bridges, water supplies, power supplies, lighting, tramways, schools, dockyards, and public aids and conveniences, employing a prodigious army of police, inspectors, teachers, and officials of all grades in hundreds of departments. We have found by bitter experience that it is impossible to trust factories, workshops, and mines to private management. Only by stern laws enforced by constant inspection have we stopped the monstrous waste of human life and welfare it cost when it was left uncontrolled by the Government. During the war our attempt to leave the munitioning of the army to private enterprise led us to the verge of defeat and caused an appalling slaughter of our soldiers. When the Government took the work out of private hands and had it done in national factories it was at once successful. The private firms were still allowed to do what little they could; but they had to be taught to do it economically, and to keep their accounts properly, by Government officials. Our big capitalist enterprises now run to the Government for help as a lamb runs to its mother. They cannot even make an extension of the Tube railway in London without Government aid. Unassisted private capitalism is breaking down or getting left behind in all directions. If all our

Socialism and Communism and the drastic taxation of unearned incomes which finances it were to stop, our private enterprises would drop like shot stags, and we should all be dead in a month. When Mr. Baldwin tried to win the last election by declaring that Socialism had been a failure whenever and wherever it had been tried, Socialism went over him like a steam roller and handed his office to a Socialist Prime Minister. Nothing could save us in the war but a great extension of Socialism; and now it is clear enough that only still greater extensions of it can repair the ravages of the war and keep pace with the growing requirements of civilization.

What we have to ask ourselves, then, is not whether we will have Socialism and Communism or not, but whether Democracy can keep pace with the developments of both that are being forced on us by the growth of national and international corporate action.

Now corporate action is impossible without a governing body. It may be the central Government: it may be a municipal corporation, a county council, a district council, or a parish council. It may be the board of directors of a joint stock company, or of a trust made by combining several joint stock companies. Such boards, elected by the votes of the shareholders, are little States within the State, and very powerful ones, too, some of them. If they have not laws and kings, they have by-laws and chairmen. And you and I, the consumers of their services, are more at the mercy of the boards that organize them than we are at the mercy of parliament. Several active politicians who began as Liberals and are now Socialists have said to me that they were converted by seeing that the nation had to choose, not between governmental control of industry and control by separate private individuals kept in order by their competition for our custom, but between governmental control and control by gigantic trusts wielding great power without responsibility, and having no object but to make as much money out of us as possible. Our Government is at this moment having much more trouble with the private corporations on whom we are dependent for our coals and cotton goods than with France or the United States of America. We are in the hands of our corporate bodies, public or private, for the satisfaction of our everyday needs. Their powers are life and death powers. I need not labor this point: we all know it.

But what we do not all realize is that we are equally dependent on corporate action for the satisfaction of our religious needs. Dean Inge tells us that our general elections have become public auctions at which the contending parties bid against one another for our votes by each promising us a larger share than the other of the plunder of the minority. Now that is perfectly true. The contending parties do not as yet venture to put it exactly in those words; but that is what it comes to. And the Dean's profession obliges him to urge his congregation, which is much wider than that of St. Paul's (it extends across the Atlantic), always to vote for the party which pledges itself to go farthest in enabling those of us who have great possessions to sell them and give the price to the poor. But we cannot do this as private persons. It must be done by the Government or not at all. Take my own case. I am not a young man with great possessions; but I am an old man paying enough in income tax and surtax to provide doles for some hundreds of unemployed and old age pensioners. I have not the smallest objection to this: on the contrary, I advocated it strongly for years before I had any income worth taxing. But I could not do it if the Government did not arrange it for me. If the Government ceased taxing my superfluous money and redistributing it among people who have no incomes at all, I could do nothing by myself. What could I do? Can you suggest anything? I could send my war bonds to the Chancellor of the Exchequer and invite him to cancel the part of the National Debt that they represent; and he would undoubtedly thank me in the most courteous official terms for my patriotism. But the poor would not get any of it. The other payers of surtax and income tax and death duties would save the interest they now have to pay on it: that is all. I should only have made the rich richer and myself poorer. I could burn all my share certificates and inform the secretaries of the companies that they might write off that much of their capital indebtedness. The result would be a bigger dividend for the rest of the shareholders, with the poor out in the cold as before. I might sell my war bonds and share certificates for cash, and throw the money into the street to be scrambled for; but it would be snatched up, not by the poorest, but by the best fed and most able-bodied of the scramblers. Besides, if we all tried to sell our bonds and shares—and this is what you have to consider; for Christ's advice was not addressed to me alone but to all who have great possessions—the result would be that their value would fall to nothing, as the Stock Exchange would immediately become a market in which there were all sellers and no buyers. Accordingly, any spare money that the Government leaves me is invested where I can get the highest interest and the best security, as thereby I can make sure that it goes where it is most wanted and gives immediate employment. This is the best I can do without Government interference: indeed any other way of dealing with my spare money would be foolish and demoralizing; but the result is that I become richer and richer, and the poor become relatively poorer and poorer. So you see I cannot even be a Christian except through Government action; and neither can the Dean.

Now let us get down to our problem. We cannot govern ourselves; yet if we entrust the immense powers and revenues which are necessary in an effective modern Government to an absolute monarch or dictator, he goes more or less mad unless he is a quite extraordinary and therefore very seldom obtainable person. Besides, modern government is not a one-man job: it is too big for that. If we resort to a committee or parliament of superior persons, they will set up an oligarchy and abuse their power for their own benefit. Our dilemma is that men in the lump cannot govern themselves; and yet, as William Morris put it, no man is good enough to be another man's master. We need to be governed, and yet to control our governors. But the best governors will not accept any control except that of their own consciences; and, as we who are governed are also apt to abuse any power of control we have, our ignorance, our passions, our private and immediate interests are constantly in conflict with the knowledge, the wisdom, and the public spirit and regard for the future of our best qualified governors.

Still, if we cannot control our governors, can we not at least choose them and change them if they do not suit?

Let me invent a primitive example of democratic choice. It is always best to take imaginary examples: they offend nobody. Imagine then that we are the inhabitants of a village. We have to elect somebody for the office of postman. There are several candidates; but one stands out conspicuously, because he has frequently treated us at the public-house, has subscribed a shilling to our little flower show, has a kind word for the children when he passes, and is a victim of oppression by the squire because his late father was one of our most successful poachers. We elect him triumphantly; and he is duly installed, uniformed, provided with a red bicycle, and given a batch of letters to deliver. As his motive in seeking the post has been pure ambition, he has not thought much beforehand about his duties; and it now occurs to him for the first time that he cannot read. So he hires a boy to come round with him and read the addresses. The boy conceals himself in the lane whilst the postman delivers the letters at the house, takes the Christmas boxes, and gets the whole credit of the transaction. In course of time he dies with a high reputation for efficiency in the discharge of his duties; and we elect another equally illiterate successor on similar grounds. But by this time the boy has grown up and become an institution. He presents himself to the new postman as an established and indispensable feature of the postal system, and finally becomes recognized and paid by the village as such.

Here you have the perfect image of a popularly elected Cabinet Minister and the Civil Service department over which he presides. It may work very well; for our postman, though illiterate, may be a very capable fellow; and the boy who reads the addresses for him may be quite incapable of doing anything more. But this does not always happen. Whether it happens or not, the system is not a democratic reality: it is a democratic illusion. The boy, when he has ability enough to take advantage of the situation, is the master of the man. The person elected to do the work is not really doing it: he is a popular humbug who is merely doing what a permanent official tells him to do. That is how it comes about that we are now governed by a Civil Service which has such enormous power that its regulations are taking the place of the laws of England, though some of them are made for the convenience of the officials without the slightest regard to the convenience or even the rights of the public. And how are our Civil Servants selected? Mostly by an educational test which nobody but an expensively schooled youth can pass, thus making the most powerful and effective part of our government an irresponsible class government.

Now, what control have you or I over the Services? We have votes. I have used mine a few times to see what it is like. Well, it is like this. When the election approaches, two or three persons of whom I know nothing write to me soliciting my vote and enclosing a list of meetings, an election address, and a polling card. One of the addresses reads like an article in The Morning Post, and has a Union Jack on it. Another is like The Daily News or Manchester Guardian. Both might have been compiled from the editorial waste paper baskets of a hundred years ago. A third address, more up-to-date and much better phrased, convinces me that the sender has had it written for him at the headquarters of the Labor Party. A fourth, the most hopelessly out of date of them all, contains scraps of the early English translations of the Communist Manifesto of 1848. I have no guarantee that any of these documents were written by the candidates. They convey nothing whatever to me as to their character or political capacity. The half-tone photographic portraits which adorn the front pages do not even tell me their ages, having been taken twenty years ago. If I go to one of the meetings I find a schoolroom packed with people who find an election meeting cheaper and funnier than a theatre. On the platform sit one or two poor men who have worked hard to keep party politics alive in the constituency. They ought to be the candidates; but they have no more chance of such eminence than they have of possessing a Rolls-Royce car. They move votes of confidence in the candidate, though as the candidate is a stranger to them and to everybody else present nobody can possibly feel any such confidence. They lead the applause for him; they prompt him when questions are asked; and when he is completely floored they jump up and cry "Let me answer that, Mr. Chairman!" and then pretend that he has answered it. The old shibboleths are droned over; and nothing has any sense or reality in it except the vituperation of the opposition party, which is received with shouts of relief by the audience. Yet it is nothing but an exhibition of bad manners. If I vote for one of these candidates, and he or she is elected, I am supposed to be enjoying a democratic control of the government—to be exercising government *of* myself, *for* myself, *by* myself. Do you wonder that the Dean cannot believe such nonsense? If I believed it I should not be fit to vote at all. If this is Democracy, who can blame Signor Mussolini for describing it as a putrefying corpse?

The candidates may ask me what more they can do for me but

present themselves and answer any questions I may put to them. I quite admit that they can do nothing; but that does not mend matters. What I should like is a real test of their capacity. Shortly before the war a doctor in San Francisco discovered that if a drop of a candidate's blood can be obtained on a piece of blotting paper it is possible to discover within half an hour what is wrong with him physically. What I am waiting for is the discovery of a process by which on delivery of a drop of his blood or a lock of his hair we can ascertain what is right with him mentally. We could then have a graded series of panels of capable persons for all employments, public or private, and not allow any person, however popular, to undertake the employment of governing us unless he or she were on the appropriate panel. At the lower end of the scale there would be a panel of persons qualified to take part in a parish meeting; at the higher end a panel of persons qualified to act as Secretaries of State for Foreign Affairs or Finance Ministers. At present not more than two per thousand of the population would be available for the highest panel. I should then be in no danger of electing a postman and finding that he could neither read nor write. My choice of candidates would be perhaps more restricted than at present; but I do not desire liberty to choose windbags and nincompoops to represent me in parliament; and my power to choose between one qualified candidate and another would give me as much control as is either possible or desirable. The voting and counting would be done by machinery: I should connect my telephone with the proper office; touch a button; and the machinery would do the rest.

Pending such a completion of the American doctor's discovery, how are we to go on? Well, as best we can, with the sort of government that our present system produces. Several reforms are possible without any new discovery. Our present parliament is obsolete: it can no more do the work of a modern State than Julius Caesar's galley could do the work of an Atlantic liner. We need in these islands two or three additional federal legislatures, working on our municipal committee system instead of our parliamentary party system. We need a central authority to co-ordinate the federal work. Our obsolete little internal frontiers must be obliterated, and our units of local government enlarged to dimensions compatible with the recent prodigious advances in facility of communication and co-operation. Commonwealth affairs and supernational activities through the League of Nations or otherwise will have to be provided for, and Cabinet function to be transformed. All the pseudo-democratic obstructive functions of our political machinery must be ruthlessly scrapped, and the general problem of government approached from a positive viewpoint at which mere anarchic national sovereignty as distinguished from self-government will have no meaning.

I must conclude by warning you that when everything has been done that can be done, civilization will still be dependent on the consciences of the governors and the governed. Our natural dispositions may be good; but we have been badly brought up, and are full of anti-social personal ambitions and prejudices and snobberies. Had we not better teach our children to be better citizens than ourselves? We are not doing that at present. The Russians *are.* That is my last word. Think over it.

From Dublin, George Bernard Shaw came to work in London, for the socialist Fabian society in politics, and for various magazines in drama and music criticism. His *Quintessence of Ibsenism* was published in 1891, most of his own plays in the first decades of the twentieth century, including *Man and Superman* (1903), *Pygmalion* (1912), *St. Joan (1924)*. For many of these dramas he wrote introductory prefaces which argued points of theory, reversed plots and judgments, upset the audience's supposed reactions, and generally stressed the importance of thought in the theater.

Soliloquies on masks

FROM *Soliloquies in England, and Later Soliloquies (1922)*
BY *George Santayana (1863-1952)*

The Tragic Mask

Masks are arrested expressions and admirable echoes of feeling, at once faithful, discreet, and superlative. Living things in contact with the air must acquire a cuticle, and it is not urged against cuticles that they are not hearts; yet some philosophers seem to be angry with images for not being things, and with words for not being feelings. Words and images are like shells, no less integral parts of nature than are the substances they cover, but better addressed to the eye and more open to observation. I would not say that substance exists for the sake of appearance, or faces for the sake of masks, or the passions for the sake of poetry and virtue. Nothing arises in nature for the sake of anything else; all these phases and products are involved equally in the round of existence, and it would be sheer wilfulness to praise the germinal phase on the ground that it is vital, and to denounce the explicit phase on the ground that it is dead and sterile. We might as justly despise the seed for being merely instrumental, and glorify the full-blown flower, or the conventions of art, as the highest achievement and fruition of life. Substance is fluid, and, since it cannot exist without some form, is always ready to exchange one form for another; but sometimes it falls into a settled rhythm or recognizable vortex, which we call a nature, and which sustains an interesting form for a season. These sustained forms are enshrined in memory and worshipped in moral philosophy, which often assigns to them a power to create and to reassert themselves which their precarious status is very far from justifying. But they are all in all to the mind: art and happiness lie in pouring and repouring the molten metal of existence through some such tenable mould.

Masks are accordingly glorious things; we are instinctively as proud of designing and wearing them as we are of inventing and using words. The blackest tragedy is festive; the most pessimistic philosophy is an enthusiastic triumph of thought. The life which such expressions seem to arrest or to caricature would be incomplete without them; indeed, it would be blind and abortive. It is no interruption to experience to master experience, as tragedy aspires to do; nor is it an interruption to sink into its episodes and render them consummate, which is the trick of comedy. On the contrary, without such playful pauses and reflective interludes our round of motions and sensations would be deprived of that intellectual dignity which relieves it and renders it morally endurable—the dignity of knowing what we are doing, even if it be foolish in itself, and with what probable issue. Tragedy, the knowledge of death, raises us to that height. In fancy and for a moment it brings our mortal wills into harmony with our destiny, with the wages of existence, and with the silence beyond. These discoveries of reason have fixed the expression of the tragic mask, half horror and half sublimity. Such is the countenance of man when turned towards death and eternity and looking beyond all his endeavours at the Gorgon face of the truth. This is not to say that it is less human, or less legitimate, to look in other directions and to make other faces. But whether the visage we assume be a joyful or a sad one, in adopting and emphasizing it we define our sovereign temper. Henceforth, so long as we continue under the spell of this self-knowledge, we do not merely give but act; we compose and play our chosen character, we wear the buskin of deliberation, we defend and idealize our passions, we encourage ourselves eloquently to be what we are, devoted or scornful or careless or austere; we soliloquize (before an imaginary audience) and we wrap ourselves gracefully in the mantle of our inalienable part. So draped, we solicit applause and expect to die amid a universal hush. We profess to live up to the fine sentiments we have uttered, as we try to believe in the religion we profess. The greater our difficulties the greater our zeal. Under our published principles and plighted language we must assiduously hide all the inequalities of our moods and conduct, and this without hypocrisy, since our deliberate character is more truly ourself than is the flux of our involuntary dreams. The portrait we paint in this way and exhibit as our true person may well be in the grand manner, with column and curtain and distant landscape and finger pointing to the terrestrial globe or to the Yorick-skull of philosophy; but if this style is native to us and our art is vital, the more it transmutes its model the deeper and truer art it will be. The severe bust of an archaic sculpture, scarcely humanizing the block, will express a spirit more justly than the man's dull morning looks or casual grimaces. Every one who is sure of his mind, or proud of his office, or anxious about his duty assumes a tragic mask. He deputes it to be himself and transfers to it almost all his vanity. While still alive and subject, like all existing things, to the undermining flux of his own substance, he has crystallized his soul into an idea, and more in pride than in sorrow he has offered up his life on the altar of the Muses. Self-knowledge, like any art or science, renders its subject-matter in a new medium, the medium of ideas, in which it loses its old dimensions and its old pace. Our animal habits are transmuted by conscience into loyalties and duties, and we become "persons" or masks.[1] Art, truth, and death turn everything to marble.

That life should be able to reach such expression in the realm of eternal form is a sublime and wonderful privilege, but it is tragic, and for that reason distasteful to the animal in man. A mask is not responsive; you must not speak to it as to a living person, you must not kiss it. If you do, you will find the cold thing repulsive and ghastly. It is only a husk, empty, eyeless, brittle, and glazed. The more comic its expression the more horrible it will prove, being

that of a corpse. The animal in man responds to things according to their substance, edible, helpful, or plastic; his only joy is to push his

[1] the word "person" comes from the Latin *persona,* meaning mask as well as "person" or "character" and so Santayana, making person and mask interchangeable, is invoking the fullest meaning for each

way victoriously through the material world, till a death stops him which he never thought of and, in a sense, never experiences. He is not in the least interested in picturing what he is or what he will have been; he is intent only on what is happening to him now or may happen to him next. But when the passions see themselves in the mirror of reflection, what they behold is a tragic mask. This is the escutcheon[2] of human nature, in which its experience is emblazoned. In so far as men are men at all, or men of honour, they militate[3] under this standard and are true to their colours. Whatever refuses to be idealized in this way, they are obliged to disown and commit to instant oblivion. It will never do for a mind merely to live through its passions or its perceptions; it must discern recognizable objects, in which to centre its experience and its desires; it must choose names and signs for them, and these names and symbols, if they are to perform their function in memory and intercourse, must be tightly conventional. What could be more unseemly than a fault in grammar, or in many a case more laughable and disconcerting? Yet any solecism, if it were once stereotyped and made definitely significant, would become an idiom: it would become a good verbal mask. What is not covered in this way by some abiding symbol can never be recovered; the dark flood of existence carries it down bodily. Only in some word or conventional image can the secret of one moment be flashed to another moment; and even when there is no one ready to receive the message, or able to decipher it, at least the poet in his soliloquy has uttered his mind and raised his monument in his own eyes; and in expressing his life he has found it.

The Comic Mask

The clown is the primitive comedian. Sometimes in the exuberance of animal life a spirit of riot and frolic comes over a man; he leaps, he dances, he tumbles head over heels, he grins, shouts, or leers, possibly he pretends to go to pieces suddenly, and blubbers like a child. A moment later he may look up wreathed in smiles, and

[2] shield or surface on which a distinctive (heraldic) device is displayed, hence, badge or special sign [3] fight

hugely pleased about nothing. All this he does hysterically, without any reason, by a sort of mad inspiration and irresistible impulse. He may easily, however, turn his absolute histrionic impulse, his pure fooling, into mimicry of anything or anybody that at the moment happens to impress his senses; he will crow like a cock, simper like a young lady, or reel like a drunkard. Such mimicry is virtual mockery, because the actor is able to revert from those assumed attitudes to his natural self; whilst his models, as he thinks, have no natural self save that imitable attitude, and can never disown it; so that the clown feels himself immensely superior, in his role of universal satirist, to all actual men, and belabours and rails at them unmercifully. He sees everything in caricature, because he sees the surface only, with the lucid innocence of a child; and all these grotesque personages stimulate him, not to moral sympathy, nor to any consideration of their fate, but rather to boisterous sallies, as the rush of a crowd, or the hue and cry of a hunt, or the contortions of a jumping-jack might stimulate him. He is not at all amused intellectually; he is not rendered wiser or tenderer by knowing the predicaments into which people inevitably fall; he is merely excited, flushed, and challenged by an absurd spectacle. Of course this rush and suasion[4] of mere existence must never fail[5] on the stage, nor in any art; it is to the drama what the hypnotizing stone block is to the statue, or shouts and rhythmic breathing to the bard; but such primary magical influences may be qualified by reflection, and then rational and semi-tragic unities will supervene. When this happens the histrionic impulse creates the idyl or the tragic chorus; henceforth the muse of reflection follows in the train of Dionysus,[6] and the revel or the rude[7] farce passes into humane comedy.

Paganism was full of scruples and superstitions in matters of behaviour or of *cultus,* since the *cultus* too was regarded as a business or a magic craft; but in expression, in reflection, paganism was frank and even shameless; it felt itself inspired, and revered this inspiration. It saw nothing impious in inventing or recasting a myth about no matter how sacred a subject. Its inspiration, however, soon fell into classic moulds, because the primary impulses of na-

[4] persuasion [5] be absent
[6] in Greek mythology, god of wine and revelry [7] primitive, unrefined

ture, though intermittent, are monotonous and clearly defined, as are the gestures of love and of anger. A man who is unaffectedly himself turns out to be uncommonly like other people. Simple sincerity will continually rediscover the old right ways of thinking and speaking, and will be perfectly conventional without suspecting it. This classic iteration comes of nature, it is not the consequence of any revision or censorship imposed by reason. Reason, not being responsible for any of the facts or passions that enter into human life, has no interest in maintaining them as they are; any novelty, even the most revolutionary, would merely afford reason a fresh occasion for demanding a fresh harmony. But the Old Adam is conservative; he repeats himself mechanically in every child who cries and loves sweets and is imitative and jealous. Reason, with its tragic discoveries and restraints, is a far more precarious and personal possession than the trite animal experience and the ancestral grimaces on which it supervenes; and automatically even the philosopher continues to cut his old comic capers, as if no such thing as reason existed. The wiseacres too are comic, and their mask is one of the most harmlessly amusing in the human museum; for reason, taken psychologically, is an old inherited passion like any other, the passion for consistency and order; and it is just as prone as the other passions to overstep the modesty of nature and to regard its own aims as alone important. But this is ridiculous; because importance springs from the stress of nature, from the cry of life, not from reason and its pale prescriptions. Reason cannot stand alone; brute habit and blind play are at the bottom of art and morals, and unless irrational impulses and fancies are kept alive, the life of reason collapses for sheer emptiness. What tragedy could there be, or what sublime harmonies rising out of tragedy, if there were no spontaneous passions to create the issue, no wild voices to be reduced to harmony? Moralists have habitually aimed at suppression, wisely perhaps at first, when they were preaching to men of spirit; but why continue to harp on propriety and unselfishness and labour, when we are little but labour-machines already, and have hardly any self or any passions left to indulge? Perhaps the time has come to suspend those exhortations, and to encourage us to be sometimes a little lively, and see if we can invent something worth saying or doing. We should then be living in the spirit of comedy, and the world would grow young. Every occasion would don its comic mask, and make its bold grimace at the world for a moment. We should be constantly original without effort and without shame, somewhat as we are in dreams, and consistent only in sincerity; and we should gloriously emphasize all the poses we fell into, without seeking to prolong them.

Objections to the comic mask—to the irresponsible, complete, extreme expression of each moment—cut at the roots of all expression. Pursue this path, and at once you do away with gesture: we must not point, we must not pout, we must not cry, we must not laugh aloud; we must not only avoid attracting attention, but our attention must not be obviously attracted; it is silly to gaze, says the nursery-governess, and rude to stare. Presently words, too, will be reduced to a telegraphic code. A man in his own country will talk like the laconic tourist abroad; his whole vocabulary will be *Où?*[8] *Combien?*[9] *All right! Dear me!* Conversation in the quiet home will dispense even with these phrases; nothing will be required but a few pragmatic grunts and signals for action. Where the spirit of comedy has departed, company becomes constraint, reserve eats up the spirit, and people fall into a penurious melancholy in their scruple to be always exact, sane, and reasonable, never to mourn, never to glow, never to betray a passion or a weakness, nor venture to utter a thought they might not wish to harbour for ever.

Yet irony pursues these enemies of comedy, and for fear of wearing a mask for a moment they are hypocrites all their lives. Their very reserve becomes a pose, a convention imposed externally, and their mincing speech turns to cant. Sometimes this evasion of impulsive sentiment fosters a poignant sentimentality beneath. The comedy goes on silently behind the scenes, until perhaps it gets the upper hand and becomes positive madness; or else it breaks out in some shy, indirect fashion, as among Americans with their perpetual joking. Where there is no habitual art and no moral liberty, the instinct for direct expression is atrophied for want of exercise; and then slang and a humorous perversity of phrase or manner act as safety-valves to sanity; and you manage to express yourself in spite of the censor by saying something grotes-

[8] where [9] how much

quely different from what you mean. That is a long way round to sincerity, and an ugly one. What, on the contrary, could be more splendidly sincere than the impulse to play in real life, to rise on the rising wave of every feeling and let it burst, if it will, into the foam of exaggeration? Life is not a means, the mind is not a slave nor a photograph: it has a right to enact a pose, to assume[10] a *panache,*[11] and to create what prodigious allegories it will for the mere sport and glory of it. Nor is this art of innocent make-believe forbidden in the Decalogue, although Bible-reading Anglo-Saxondom might seem to think so. On the contrary, the Bible and the Decalogue[12] are themselves instances of it. To embroider upon experience is not to bear false witness against one's neighbour, but to bear true witness to oneself. Fancy is playful and may be misleading to those who try to take it for literal fact; but literalness is impossible in any utterance of spirit, and if it were possible it would be deadly. Why should we quarrel with human nature, with metaphor, with myth, with impersonation? The foolishness of the simple is delightful; only the foolishness of the wise is exasperating.

[10] put on [12] the Ten Commandments
[11] ornamental plume or tuft or feathers, on a helmet or cap

☙ Like James, the American-Spaniard George Santayana taught philosophy at Harvard and wrote speculations on the nature of experience, reason, and religion, and of the relation of the material and ideal. Santayana's style suggests a philosophical relish for substance as James' does for action and process.

Characteristics of scientific method

FROM *The Scientific Outlook,* Chapter II *(1931)*

BY ***Bertrand Russell*** *(born 1872)*

Scientific method has been often described, and it is not possible, at this date, to say anything very new about it. Nevertheless, it is necessary to describe it if we are to be in a position later to consider whether any other method of acquiring general knowledge exists.

In arriving at a scientific law there are three main stages: the first consists in observing the significant facts; the second in arriving at a hypothesis, which, if it is true, would account for these facts; the third in deducing from this hypothesis consequences which can be tested by observation. If the consequences are verified, the hypothesis is provisionally accepted as true, although it will usually require modification later on as the result of the discovery of further facts.

In the existing state of science, no facts and no hypotheses are isolated; they exist within the general body of scientific knowledge. The significance of a fact is relative to such knowledge. To say that a fact is significant in science, is to say that it helps to establish or refute some general law; for science, though it starts from observation of the particular, is not concerned essentially with the particular, but with the general. A fact, in science, is not a mere fact, but an instance. In this the scientist differs from the artist, who, if he deigns to notice facts at all, is likely to notice them in all their particularity. Science, in its ultimate ideal, consists of a set of propositions arranged in a hierarchy, the lowest level of the hierarchy being concerned with particular facts, and the highest with some general law, governing everything in the universe. The various levels in the hierarchy have a twofold logical connexion, travelling one up, one down; the upward connexion proceeds by induction, the downward by deduction. That is to say, in a perfected science, we should proceed as follows: the particular facts, A, B, C, D, etc., suggest as probable a certain general law, of which, if it is true, they are all instances. Another set of facts suggests another general law, and so on. All these general laws suggest, by induction, a law of a higher order of generality of which, if it is true, they are instances. There will be many such stages in passing from the particular facts observed to the most general law as yet ascertained. From this general law we proceed in turn deductively, until we arrive at the particular facts from which our previous induction had started. In textbooks the deductive order will be adopted, but in the laboratory the inductive order.

The only science which has, as yet, come anywhere near this perfection is physics. The consideration of physics may help us to give concreteness to the above abstract account of scientific method. Galileo, as we saw, discovered the law of falling bodies in the neighbourhood of the earth's surface. He discovered that, apart from the resistance of the air, they fall with a constant acceleration, which is the same for all. This was a generalization from a comparatively small number of facts, namely, the cases of actual falling bodies which Galileo had timed; but his generalization was confirmed by all subsequent experiments of a like nature. Galileo's result was a law of the lowest order of generality, as little removed from the crude facts as a general law could be. Meanwhile, Kepler[1] had observed the motions of the planets, and formulated his three laws as to their orbits. These, again, were laws of the lowest order of generality. Newton collected together Kepler's laws and Galileo's law of falling bodies, and the laws of the tides, and what was known as to the motions of comets, in one law, namely, the law of gravitation, which embraced them all. This law, moreover, as usually hap-

[1]Johann Kepler (1571-1630), German astronomer, chief founder of modern astronomy

pens with a successful generalization, showed not merely why the previous laws were right, but also why they were not quite right. Bodies near the earth's surface do not fall with an acceleration which is quite constant: as they approach the earth, the acceleration is slightly increased. Planets do not move exactly in ellipses: when they approach near to other planets, they are pulled a little out of their orbits. Thus Newton's law of gravitation superseded the older generalizations, but could scarcely have been arrived at except from them. For over two hundred years no new generalization was found to swallow up Newton's law of gravitation, as it had swallowed up Kepler's laws. When, at last, Einstein arrived at such a generalization it placed the law of gravitation in the most unexpected company. To everybody's surprise, it was found to be a law of geometry rather than of physics in the old sense. The proposition with which it has most affinity is the theorem of Pythagoras,[2] to the effect that the squares on the two shorter sides of a right-angled triangle are together equal to the square on the longest side. Every schoolboy learns the proof of this proposition, but only those who read Einstein learn the disproof. To the Greeks—and to the moderns until a hundred years ago geometry was an *a priori*[3] study like formal logic, not an empirical science based upon observation. Lobachevsky,[4] in the year 1829, demonstrated the falsehood of this opinion, and showed that the truth of Euclidean geometry could only be established by observation, not by reasoning. Although this view gave rise to important new branches of pure mathematics, it did not bear fruit in physics until the year 1915, when Einstein embodied it in his general theory of relativity. It now appears that the theorem of Pythagoras is not quite true, and that the exact truth which it adumbrates contains within itself the law of gravitation as an ingredient or consequence. Again, it is not quite Newton's law of gravitation, but a law whose observable consequences are slightly different. Where Einstein differs from Newton in an observable manner it is found that Einstein is right as against Newton. Einstein's law of gravitation is more general than Newton's, since it

[2] Greek philosopher and mathematician (c. 528-500 B.C.)

[3] previous to actual experience

[4] Nikolaus Ivanovitch Lobachevsky (1793-1856), Russian mathematician, founder of non-Euclidean geometry

applies not only to matter, but also to light and to every form of energy. Einstein's general theory of gravitation demanded as a preliminary not only Newton's theory, but also the theory of electromagnetism, the science of spectroscopy, observation of light pressure, and the power of minute astronomical observation, which we owe to large telescopes and the perfecting of the technique of photography. Without all these preliminaries, Einstein's theory could not have been both discovered and demonstrated. But when the theory is set forth in mathematical form we start with the generalized law of gravitation, and arrive at the end of our argument at those verifiable consequences upon which, in the inductive order, the law was based. In the deductive order, the difficulties of discovery are obscured, and it becomes hard to be aware of the immense extent of preliminary knowledge required for the induction which led to our major premise. The same sort of development has happened with a rapidity which is truly astonishing in regard to quantum theory. The first discovery that there were facts necessitating such a theory was made in 1900, yet already the subject can be treated in an utterly abstract way which scarcely reminds the reader that a universe exists.

Throughout the history of physics, from the time of Galileo onward, the importance of the *significant* fact has been very evident. The facts that are significant at any one stage in the development of a theory are quite different from those that are significant at another stage. When Galileo was establishing the law of falling bodies, the fact that in a vacuum a feather and a lump of lead fall equally fast, was more important than the fact that, in air, a feather falls more slowly, since the first step in understanding falling bodies consisted in realizing that, so far as the earth's attraction alone is concerned, all falling bodies have the same acceleration. The effect of the resistance of the air must be treated as something superadded to the earth's attraction. The essential thing is always to look for such facts as illustrate one law in isolation, or at any rate, only in combination with laws whose effects are well known. This is why experiment plays such an important part in scientific discovery. In an experiment the circumstances are artificially simplified, so that some one law in isolation may become observable. In most concrete situations, what actually happens requires for its explanation a number of laws of nature, but in order to discover these one by one it is usually necessary to invent circumstances such that only one of them is relevant. Moreover, the most instructive phenomena may be very difficult to observe. Consider, for example, how much our knowledge of matter has been enhanced by the discovery of X-rays and of radio-activity; yet both of these would have remained unknown but for the most elaborate experimental technique. The discovery of radio-activity was an accident due to the perfecting of photography. Becquerel[5] had some very sensitive photographic plates, which he was meaning to employ; but as the weather was bad, he put them away in a dark cupboard in which there happened to be some uranium. When they were taken out again they were found to have photographed the uranium, in spite of the complete darkness. It was this accident which led to the discovery that uranium is radio-active. This accidental photograph affords another illustration of the significant fact.

Outside physics, the part played by deduction is much less, while the part played by observation, and by laws immediately based upon observation, is much greater. Physics, owing to the simplicity of its subject matter, has reached a higher stage of development than any other science. I do not think it can be doubted that the ideal is the same for all sciences; but it can be doubted whether human capacity will ever be able to make physiology, for example, as perfect a deductive edifice as theoretical physics is now. Even in pure physics the difficulties of calculation swiftly become insuperable. In the Newtonian gravitation theory it was impossible to calculate how three bodies would move under their mutual attractions, except approximately when one of them was much larger than the other two. In the theory of Einstein, which is much more complicated than Newton's, it is impossible to work out with theoretical exactness even how two bodies will move under their mutual attraction, though it is possible to obtain a sufficiently good approximation for all practical purposes. Fortunately for physics there are methods of averaging, by which the behaviour of large bodies can be calculated with a quite sufficient approximation to the truth,

[5] Alexandre Edmond Becquerel (1820-1891), French physicist noted for researches on electric light and photography

although a wholly exact theory is utterly beyond human powers.

Although this may seem a paradox, all exact science is dominated by the idea of approximation. When a man tells you that he knows the exact truth about anything, you are safe in inferring that he is an inexact man. Every careful measurement in science is always given with the probable error, which is a technical term, conveying a precise meaning. It means: that amount of error which is just as likely to be greater than the actual error as to be less. It is characteristic of those matters in which something is known with exceptional accuracy that, in them, every observer admits that he is likely to be wrong, and knows about how much wrong he is likely to be. In matters where the truth is not ascertainable, no one admits that there is the slightest possibility of even the minutest error in his opinions. Whoever heard of a theologian prefacing his creed, or a politician concluding his speeches, with a statement as to the probable error in his opinions? It is an odd fact that subjective certainty is inversely proportional to objective certainty. The less reason a man has to suppose himself in the right, the more vehemently he asserts that there is no doubt whatever that he is exactly right. It is a practice of theologians to laugh at science because it changes. "Look at us," they say. "What we asserted at the Council of Nicea[6] we still assert; whereas what the scientists asserted only two or three years ago is already forgotten and antiquated." Men who speak in this way have not grasped the great idea of successive approximations. No man who has the scientific temper asserts that what is now believed in science is *exactly* right; he asserts that it is a stage on the road towards the exact truth. When a change occurs in science, as, for example, from Newton's law of gravitation to Einstein's, what had been done is not overthrown, but is replaced by something slightly more accurate. Suppose you measured yourself with a rough apparatus, and came to the conclusion that you were 6 ft. tall: you would not suppose, if you were wise, that your height was exactly 6 ft., but rather that your height was (say) between 5 ft. 11 in. and 6 ft. 1 in.; and if a very careful measurement showed that your height was (within a tenth of an inch) 5 ft. 11 9/10 in. you

[6] the first of two general councils which met at Nicea in Asia Minor, in 325, and which is almost universally recognized among Christians as authoritative

would not consider that that had overthrown the previous result. The previous result was that your height was *about* six ft., and this remains true. The case with the changes in science is precisely analogous.

The part played by measurement and quantity in science is very great, but is, I think, sometimes overestimated. Mathematical technique is powerful, and men of science are naturally anxious to be able to apply it whenever possible; but a law may be quite scientific without being quantitative. Pavlov's[7] laws concerning conditioned reflexes may serve as an illustration. It would probably be impossible to give quantitative precision to these laws; the number of repetitions required to establish conditioned reflexes depends upon many conditions, and varies not only with different animals, but with the same animal at different times. In the pursuit of quantitative precision we should be driven first to the physiology of the cortex and the physical nature of nerve-currents, and we should find ourselves unable to stop short of the physics of electrons and protons. There, it is true, quantitative precision may be possible, but to pass back by calculation from pure physics to the phenomena of animal behaviour is beyond human power, at any rate at present, and probably for many ages to come. We must, therefore, in dealing with such a matter as animal behaviour, be content in the meantime with qualitative laws which are none the less scientific for not being quantitative.

One advantage of quantitative precision, where it is possible, is that it gives much greater strength to inductive arguments. Suppose, for example, that you invent a hypothesis, according to which a certain observable quantity should have a magnitude which you work out to five significant figures; and suppose you then find by observation that the quantity in question has this magnitude. You will feel that such a coincidence between theory and observation can hardly be an accident, and that your theory must contain at least some important element of truth. Experience shows, however, that it is easy to attach too much importance to such coincidences. Bohr's[8] theory of the atom was originally commended by a re-

[7] Ivan Petrovich Pavlov (1849-1936) Russian physiologist
[8] Neils Henrik David Bohr (1885-1960), Danish physicist

markable power of calculating theoretically certain quantities which had until then been known only by observation. Nevertheless, Bohr's theory, though a necessary stage in progress, has already been virtually abandoned. The truth is, that men cannot frame sufficiently abstract hypotheses; imagination is always intruding upon logic, and causing men to make pictures of occurrences which are essentially incapable of being visualized. In Bohr's theory of the atom, for example, there was a highly abstract constituent, which was in all likelihood true, but this abstract element was embedded in imaginative details which had no inductive justification. The world that we can picture is the world that we see; but the world of physics is an abstract world that cannot be seen. For this reason, even a hypothesis which accounts with a minute exactitude for all known relevant facts must not be regarded as certainly true, since it is probably only some highly abstract aspect of the hypothesis that is logically necessary in the deductions which we make from it to observable phenomena.

All scientific laws rest upon induction, which, considered as a logical process, is open to doubt, and not capable of giving certainty. Speaking crudely, an inductive argument is of the following kind. If a certain hypothesis is true, then such and such facts will be observable; now these facts are observable; therefore the hypothesis is probably true. An argument of this sort will have varying degrees of validity according to circumstances. If we could prove that no other hypothesis was compatible with the observed facts we could arrive at certainty, but this is hardly ever possible. In general, there will be no method of thinking of all the possible hypotheses, or, if there is, it will be found that more than one of them is compatible with the facts. When this is the case, the scientist adopts the simplest as a working hypothesis, and only reverts to more complicated hypotheses if new facts show that the simplest hypothesis is inadequate. If you had never seen a cat without a tail, the simplest hypothesis to account for this fact would be: "all cats have tails"; but the first time that you saw a Manx cat,[9] you would be compelled to adopt a more complicated hypothesis. The man who argues that because all cats he has seen have tails,

[9] tailless variety of the domestic cat, indigenous to the Isle of Man

therefore all cats have tails, is employing what is called "induction by simple enumeration." This is a very dangerous form of argument. In its better forms, induction is based upon the fact that our hypothesis leads to consequences which are found to be true, but which, if they had not been observed, would seem extremely improbable. If you meet a man who has a pair of dice that always throw double sixes, it is possible that he is lucky; but there is another hypothesis which would make the observed facts less astonishing. You will therefore be well advised to adopt this other hypothesis. In all good inductions, the facts accounted for by the hypothesis are such as would be antecedently improbable, and the more improbable they would be, the greater becomes the probability of the hypothesis which accounts for them. This, as we remarked a moment ago, is one of the advantages of measurement. If something which might have any size, is found to have just the size that your hypothesis had led you to expect, you feel that your hypothesis must at least have something in it. As common sense this seems evident, but as logic it has certain difficulties. This, however, we will not consider until the next chapter.

There is one remaining characteristic of scientific method about which something must be said, namely, analysis. It is generally assumed by men of science, at any rate as a working hypothesis, that any concrete occurrence is the resultant of a number of causes, each of which, acting separately, might produce some different result from that which actually occurs; and that the resultant can be calculated when the effects of the separate causes are known. The simplest examples of this occur in mechanics. The moon is attracted both by the earth and by the sun. If the earth acted alone, the moon would describe one orbit; if the sun acted alone, it would describe another; but its actual orbit is calculable when we know the effects which the earth and the sun separately would produce. When we know how bodies fall in a vacuum, and also the law of the resistance of the air, we can calculate how bodies will fall in air. The principle that causal laws can, in this way, be separated, and then recombined, is in some degree essential to the procedure of science, for it is impossible to take account of everything at once, or to arrive at causal laws unless we can isolate them one at a time. It must be said, however, that there is no reason *a priori* to suppose that the effect of two causes, acting simultaneously, will be calculable from the effects which they have severally; and in the most modern physics, this principle is found to have less truth than was formerly supposed. It remains a practical and approximate principle in suitable circumstances, but it cannot be laid down as a general property of the universe. Undoubtedly, where it fails, science becomes very difficult; but, so far as can be seen at present, it retains sufficient truth to be employed as a hypothesis, except in the most advanced and delicate calculations.

⸎ The Third Earl Russell, Viscount Amberley, prefers to be known as Bertrand Russell. He holds unorthodox opinions on numerous subjects, political, social, and domestic. He is known as a philosopher and sociologist. *Principia Mathematica,* which he wrote in collaboration with A. N. Whitehead, is a classic in mathematical logic.

The rulers and the ruled

FROM *Political Freedom (1948)*

BY *Alexander Meiklejohn (1872-1964)*

The most general thesis of the argument is that, under the Constitution, there are two different freedoms of speech, and, hence, two different guarantees of freedom rather than only one.

More broadly, it may be asserted that our civil liberties, in general, are not all of one kind. They are of two kinds which, though radically different in constitutional status, are easily confused. And that confusion has been, and is, disastrous in its effect upon our understanding of the relations between an individual citizen and the government of the United States. The argument of these lectures is an attempt to clear away that confusion.

As an instance of the first kind of civil liberty I would offer that of religious or irreligious belief. In this country of ours, so far as the Constitution is effective, men are free to believe and to advocate or to disbelieve and to argue against, any creed. And the government is unqualifiedly forbidden to restrict that freedom. As an instance of the second kind, we may take the liberty of an individual to own, and to use the income from, his labor or his property. It is agreed among us that every man has a right, a liberty, to such ownership and use. And yet it is also agreed that the government may take whatever part of a man's income it deems necessary for the promoting of the general welfare. The liberty of owning and using property is, then, as contrasted with that of religious belief, a limited one. It may be invaded by the government. And the Constitution authorizes such invasion. It requires only that the procedure shall be properly and impartially carried out and that it shall be justified by public need.

Our Constitution, then, recognizes and protects two different sets of freedoms. One of these is open to restriction by the government. The other is not open to such restriction. It would be of great value to our argument and, in fact, to all attempts at political thinking in the United States, if there were available two sharply defined terms by which to identify these two fundamentally different kinds of civil liberty. But, alas, no such accurate use of words has been established among us. Men speak of the freedom of belief and the freedom of property as if, in the Constitution, the word "freedom," as used in these two cases, had the same meaning. Because of that confusion we are in constant danger of giving to a man's possessions the same dignity, the same status, as we give to the man himself. From that confusion our national life has suffered disastrous effects in all its phases. But for this disease of our minds there is, so far as I know, no specific semantic cure. All that we can do at present is to remember that such terms as liberty, freedom, civil rights, etc., are ambiguous. We must, then, in each specific case, try to keep clear what meaning we are using.

1

We Americans think of ourselves as politically free. We believe in self-government. If men are to be governed, we say, then that governing must be done, not by others, but by themselves. So far, therefore, as our own affairs are concerned, we refuse to submit to alien control. That refusal, if need be, we will carry to the point of rebellion, of revolution. And if other men, within the jurisdiction of our laws, are denied their right to political freedom, we will, in the same spirit, rise to their defense. Governments, we insist, derive their just powers from the consent of the governed. If that consent be lacking, governments have no just powers.

Now, this political program of ours, though passionately advocated by us, is not—as we all recognize—fully worked out in practice. Over one hundred and seventy years have gone by since the Declaration of Independence was written. But, to an unforgivable degree, citizens of the United States are still subjected to decisions in the making of which they have had no effective share. So far as that is true, we are not self-governed; we are not politically free. We are governed by others. And, perhaps worse, we are, without their consent, the governors of others.

But a more important point—which we Americans do not so readily recognize—is that of the intellectual difficulties which are inherent in the making and administering of this political program of ours. We do not see how baffling, even to the point of desperation, is the task of using our minds, to which we are summoned by our plan of government. That plan is not intellectually simple. Its victories are chiefly won, not by the carnage of battle, but by the sweat and agony of the mind. By contrast with it, the idea of alien government which we reject—whatever its other merits or defects—is easy to understand. It is suited to simple-minded people who are unwilling or unable to question their own convictions, who would defend their principles by suppressing that hostile criticism which is necessary for their clarification.

The intellectual difficulty of which I am speaking is sharply indicated by Professor Edward Hallett Carr, in his recent book, *The Soviet Impact on the Western World.* Mr. Carr tells us that our American political program, as we formulate it, is not merely unclear. It is essentially self-contradictory and hence, nonsensical. "Confusion of thought," he says, "is often caused by the habit common among politicans and writers of the English-speaking world, of defining democracy in formal and conventional terms as 'self-government' or 'government by consent.' " What these terms define, he continues, "is not democracy, but anarchy. Government of some kind is necessary in the common interest precisely because men will not govern themselves. 'Government by consent' is a contradiction in terms; for the purpose of government is to compel people to do what they would not do of their own volition. In short, government is a process by which some people exercise compulsion on others."*

Those words of Mr. Carr seem to me radically false. And, whatever else these lectures may do or fail to do, I hope that they may,

*Edward Hallett Carr, *The Soviet Impact on the Western World* (New York, Macmillan, 1947), p. 10.

in some measure, serve as a refutation of his contention. And yet the challenge of so able and well-balanced a mind cannot be ignored. If we believe in our principles we must make clear to others and to ourselves that self-government is not anarchy. We must show in what sense a free man, a free society, does practice self-direction. What, then, is the difference between a political system in which men do govern themselves and a political system in which men, without their consent, are governed by others? Unless we can make clear that distinction, discussion of freedom of speech or of any other freedom is meaningless and futile.

Alien government, we have said, is simple in idea. It is easy to understand. When one man or some self-chosen group holds control, without consent, over others, the relation between them is one of force and counterforce, of compulsion on the one hand and submission or resistance on the other. That relation is external and mechanical. It can be expressed in numbers—numbers of guns or planes or dollars or machines or policemen. The only basic fact is that one group "has the power" and the other group has not. In such a despotism, a ruler, by some excess of strength or guile or both, without the consent of his subjects, forces them into obedience. And in order to understand what he does, what they do, we need only measure the strength or weakness of the control and the strength or weakness of the resistance to it.

But government by consent—self-government—is not thus simple. It is, in fact, so complicated, so confusing, that, not only to the scholarly judgment of Mr. Carr, but also to the simple-mindedness which we call "shrewd, practical, calculating, common sense," it tends to seem silly, unrealistic, romantic, or—to use a favorite term of reproach—"idealistic." And the crux of the difficulty lies in the fact that, in such a society, the governors and the governed are not two distinct groups of persons. There is only one group—the self-governing people. Rulers and ruled are the same individuals. We, the People, are our own masters, our own subjects. But that inner relationship of men to themselves is utterly different in kind from the external relationship of one man to another. It cannot be expressed in terms of forces and compulsions. If we attempt to think about the political procedures of self-government by means of the ideas which are useful in describing the external control of a hammer over a nail or of a master over his slaves, the meaning slips through the fingers of our minds. For thinking which is done merely in terms of forces, political freedom does not exist.

At this point, a protest must be entered against the over-simplified advice which tells us that we should introduce into the realms of economics, politics, and morals the "methods" of the "sciences." Insofar as the advice suggests to us that we keep our beliefs within the limits of the evidence which warrants them, insofar as it tells us that our thinking about human relationships must be as exact and tentative, as orderly and inclusive, as is the work done by students of physical or biological fact, no one may challenge either its validity or its importance. To believe what one has no reason for believing is a crime of the first order. But, on the other hand, it must be urged that the chief source of our blundering ineptness in dealing with moral and political problems is that we do not know how to think about them except by quantitative methods which are borrowed from non-moral, non-political, non-social sciences. In this sense we need to be, not more scientific, but less scientific, not more quantitative but other than quantitative. We must create and use methods of inquiry, methods of belief which are suitable to the study of men as self-governing persons but not suitable to the study of forces or of machines. In the understanding of a free society, scientific thinking has an essential part to play. But it is a secondary part. We shall not understand the Constitution of the United States if we think of men only as pushed around by forces. We must see them also as governing themselves.

But the statement just made must be guarded against two easy misinterpretations. First, when we say that self-government is hard to interpret, we are not saying that it is mysterious or magical or irrational. Quite the contrary is true. No idea which we have is more sane, more matter-of-fact, more immediately sensible, than that of self-government. Whether it be in the field of individual or of social activity, men are not recognizable as men unless, in any given situation, they are using their minds to give direction to their behavior. But the point which we are making is that the externalized measuring of the play of forces which serves the purposes of business or of science is wholly unsuited to our dealing with problems of moral or political freedom. And we Americans seem characteristically blind to the distinction. We are at the top of the world in engineering. We are experts in the knowledge and manipulation of measurable forces, whether physical or psychological. We invent and run machines of ever new and amazing power and intricacy. And we are tempted by that achievement to see if we can manipulate men with the same skill and ingenuity. But the manipulation of men is the destruction of self-government. Our skill, therefore, threatens our wisdom. In this respect the United States with its "know-how" is, today, the most dangerous nation in the world.

And, second, what we have said must not be allowed to obscure the fact that a free government, established by common consent, may and often must use force in compelling citizens to obey the laws. Every government, as such, must have external power. It must, in fact, be more powerful than any one of its citizens, than any group of them. Political freedom does not mean freedom from control. It means self-control. If, for example, a nation becomes involved in war, the government must decide who shall be drafted to leave his family and home, to risk his life, his health, his sanity, upon the battlefield. The government must also levy and collect and expend taxes. In general, it must determine how far and in what ways the customs and privileges of peace are to be swept aside. In all these cases it may be taken for granted that, in a self-governing society, minorities will disagree with the decisions which are made. May a minority man, then, by appeal to the principle of "consent," refuse to submit to military control? May he evade payment of taxes which he thinks unwise or unjust? May he say, "I did not approve of this measure; therefore, as a self-governing man, I claim the right to disobey it"?

Certainly not! At the bottom of every plan of self-government is a basic agreement, in which all the citizens have joined, that all matters of public policy shall be decided by corporate action, that such decisions shall be equally binding on all citizens, whether they agree with them or not, and that, if need be, they shall, by due legal procedure, be enforced upon anyone who refuses to conform to them. The man who rejects that agreement is not objecting to tyranny or despotism. He is objecting to political freedom. He is not a democrat. He is the anarchist of whom Mr. Carr speaks. Self-government is nonsense unless the "self" which governs is able and determined to make its will effective.

2

What, then, is this compact or agreement which underlies any plan for political freedom? It cannot be understood unless we distinguish sharply and persistently between the "submission" of a slave and the "consent" of a free citizen. In both cases it is agreed that obedience shall be required. Even when despotism is so extreme as to be practically indistinguishable from enslavement, a sort of pseudo consent is given by the subjects. When the ruling force is overwhelming, men are driven not only to submit, but also to agree to do so. For the time, at least, they decide to make the best of a bad situation rather than to struggle against hopeless odds. And, coordinate with this "submission" by the people, there are "concessions" by the ruler. For the avoiding of trouble, to establish his power, to manipulate one hostile force against another, he must take account of the desires and interests of his subjects, must manage to keep them from becoming too rebellious. The granting of such "concessions" and the accepting of them are, perhaps, the clearest evidence that a government is not democratic but is essentially despotic and alien.

But the "consent" of free citizens is radically different in kind from this "submission" of slaves. Free men talk about their government, not in terms of its "favors" but in terms of their "rights." They do not bargain. They reason. Every one of them is, of course, subject to the laws which are made. But if the Declaration of Independence means what it says, if we mean what it says, then no man is called upon to obey a law unless he himself, equally with his fellows, has shared in making it. Under an agreement to which, in the closing words of the Declaration of Independence, "we mutually pledge to each other our Lives, our Fortunes, and our sacred Honor," the consent which we give is not forced upon us. It expresses a voluntary compact among political equals. We, the People, acting together, either directly or through our representatives, make and administer law. We, the People, acting in groups or separately, are subject to the law. If we could make that double agreement effective, we would have accomplished the American Revolution. If we could understand that agreement we would understand the Revolution, which is still in the making. But the agreement can have meaning for us only as we clarify the tenuous and elusive distinction between a political "submission" which we abhor and a political "consent" in which we glory. Upon the effectiveness of that distinction rests the entire enormous and intricate structure of those free political institutions which we have pledged ourselves to build. If we can think that distinction clearly, we can be self-governing. If we lose our grip upon it, if, rightly or wrongly, we fall back into the prerevolutionary attitudes which regard our chosen representatives as alien and hostile to ourselves, nothing can save us from the slavery which, in 1776, we set out to destroy.

3

I have been saying that, under the plan of political freedom, we maintain by common consent a government which, being stronger than any one of us, than any group of us, can take control over all of us. But the word "control" strikes terror into the hearts of many "free" men, especially if they are mechanically minded about their freedom. Out of that fear there arises the passionate demand that the government which controls us must itself be controlled. By whom, and in what ways?

In abstract principle, that question is easy to answer. A government of free men can properly be controlled only by itself. Who else could be trusted by us to hold our political institutions in check? Shall any single individual or any special group be allowed to take domination over the agencies of control? There is only one situation in which free men can answer "yes" to that question. If the government, as an institution, has broken down, if the basic agreement has collapsed, then both the right and the duty of rebellion are thrust upon the individual citizens. In that chaotic and desperate situation they must, for the sake of a new order, revolt and destroy, as the American colonies in 1776 revolted and destroyed. But, short of such violent lawlessness in the interest of a new law, there can be no doubt that a free government must be its own master. If We, the People are to be controlled, then We, the People, must do the controlling. As a corporate body, we must exercise control over our separate members. That principle is a flat denial of the suggestion that we, acting as an unorganized and irresponsible mob, may drive into submission ourselves acting as an organized government. What it means is that the body politic, organized as a nation, must recognize its own limitations of wisdom and of temper and of circumstance, and must, therefore, make adequate provision for self-criticism and self-restraint. The government itself must limit the government, must determine what it may and may not do. It must make sure that its attempts to make men free do not result in making them slaves.

Our own American constitutional procedure gives striking illustration of the double principle that no free government can submit to control other than its own and that, therefore, it must limit and control itself. For example, our agencies of government do their work under a scheme of mutual checks and balances. The Bill of Rights, also, sharply and explicitly defines boundaries beyond which acts of governing may not go. "Congress shall make no law..." it says. And again, "No person shall be held to answer for a capital or otherwise infamous crime unless..." And again, "Excessive bail shall not be required, nor excessive fines imposed, nor cruel and unusual punishments inflicted." All these and many other limits are set to the powers of government. But in every case—let it be noted—these limits are set by government. These enactments were duly proposed, discussed, adopted, interpreted, and enforced by regular political procedure. And, as the years have gone by, We, the People, who, by explicit compact, are the government, have maintained and interpreted and extended them. In some cases, we have reinterpreted them or have even abolished them. They are expressions of our own corporate self-control. They tell us that, by compact, explicit or implicit, we are self-governed.

Here, then, is the thesis upon which the argument of these lectures is to rest. At the bottom of our American plan of government there is, as Thomas Jefferson has firmly told us, a "compact." To Jefferson it is clear that as fellow citizens we have made and are continually remaking an agreement with one another, and that, whatever the cost, we are in honor bound to keep that agreement. The nature of the compact to which we "consent" is suggested by the familiar story of the meeting of the Pilgrims in the cabin of the Mayflower. "We whose names are underwritten, . . ." they said, ". . . Do by these Presents solemnly and mutually, in the presence of God, and one another, Covenant and Combine ourselves together into a Civil Body Politick, for our better ordering and preservation, and furtherance of the ends aforesaid; and by virtue hereof do enact, constitute, and frame such just and equal Laws, Ordinances, Acts, Constitutions, and Offices, from time to time, as shall be thought most meet and convenient for the general good of the Colony; unto which we promise all due submission and obedience . . . ." This is the same pledge of comradeship, of responsible cooperation in a joint undertaking, which was given in the concluding words of the Declaration of Independence already quoted—"We mutually pledge to each other our Lives, our Fortunes, and our sacred Honor." And, some years later, as the national revolution moved on from its first step to its second, from the negative task of destroying alien government to the positive work of creating self-government, the Preamble of the Constitution announced the common purposes in the pursuit of which we had become united. "We, the People of the United States," it says, "in order to form a more perfect Union, establish justice, insure domestic tranquillity, provide for the common defense, promote the general welfare, and secure the blessings of liberty to ourselves and our posterity, do ordain and establish this Constitution of the United States of America."

In those words it is agreed, and with every passing moment it is reagreed, that the people of the United States shall be self-governed. To that fundamental enactment all other provisions of the Constitution, all statutes, all administrative decrees, are subsidiary and dependent. All other purposes, whether individual or social, can find their legitimate scope and meaning only as they conform to the one basic purpose that the citizens of this nation shall make and shall obey their own laws, shall be at once their own subjects and their own masters.

Our preliminary remarks about the Constitution of the United States may, then, be briefly summarized. That Constitution is based upon a twofold political agreement. It is ordained that all authority to exercise control, to determine common action, belongs to "We, the People." We, and we alone, are the rulers. But it is ordained also that We, the People, are, all alike, subject to control. Every one of us may be told what he is allowed to do, what he is not allowed to do, what he is required to do. But this agreed-upon requirement of obedience does not transform a ruler into a slave. Citizens do not become puppets of the state when, having created it by common consent, they pledge allegiance to it and keep their pledge. Control by a self-governing nation is utterly different in kind from control by an irresponsible despotism. And to confuse these two is to lose all understanding of what political freedom is. Under actual conditions, there is no freedom for men except by the authority of government. Free men are not non-governed. They are governed—by themselves.

And now, after this long introduction, we are, I hope, ready for the task of interpreting the First Amendment to the Constitution, of trying to clear away the confusions by which its meaning has been obscured and even lost.

4

"Congress shall make no law . . . abridging the freedom of speech . . ." says the First Amendment to the Constitution. As we turn now to the interpreting of those words, three preliminary remarks should be made.

First, let it be noted that, by those words, Congress is not debarred from all action upon freedom of speech. Legislation which abridges that freedom is forbidden, but not legislation to enlarge and enrich it. The freedom of mind which befits the members of a self-governing society is not a given and fixed part of human nature. It can be increased and established by learning, by teaching, by the unhindered flow of accurate information, by giving men health and vigor and security, by bringing them together in activities of communication and mutual understanding. And the federal legislature is not forbidden to engage in that positive enterprise of cultivating the general intelligence upon which the success of self-government so obviously depends. On the contrary, in that positive field the Congress of the United States has a heavy and basic responsibility to promote the freedom of speech.

And second, no one who reads with care the text of the First Amendment can fail to be startled by its absoluteness. The phrase,

"Congress shall make no law . . . abridging the freedom of speech," is unqualified. It admits of no exceptions. To say that no laws of a given type shall be made means that no laws of that type shall, under any circumstances, be made. That prohibition holds good in war as in peace, in danger as in security. The men who adopted the Bill of Rights were not ignorant of the necessities of war or of national danger. It would, in fact, be nearer to the truth to say that it was exactly those necessities which they had in mind as they planned to defend freedom of discussion against them. Out of their own bitter experience they knew how terror and hatred, how war and strife, can drive men into acts of unreasoning suppression. They planned, therefore, both for the peace which they desired and for the wars which they feared. And in both cases they established an absolute, unqualified prohibition of the abridgment of the freedom of speech. That same requirement, for the same reasons, under the same Constitution, holds good today.

Against what has just been said it will be answered that twentieth-century America does not accept "absolutes" so readily as did the eighteenth century. But to this we must reply that the issue here involved cannot be dealt with by such twentieth-century a priori reasoning. It requires careful examination of the structure and functioning of our political system as a whole to see what part the principle of the freedom of speech plays, here and now, in that system. And when that examination is made, it seems to me clear that for our day and generation, the words of the First Amendment mean literally what they say. And what they say is that under no circumstances shall the freedom of speech be abridged. Whether or not that opinion can be justified is the primary issue with which this argument tries to deal.

But, third, this dictum which we rightly take to express the most vital wisdom which men have won in their striving for political freedom is yet—it must be admitted—strangely paradoxical. No one can doubt that, in any well-governed society, the legislature has both the right and the duty to prohibit certain forms of speech. Libellous assertions may be, and must be, forbidden and punished. So too must slander. Words which incite men to crime are themselves criminal and must be dealt with as such. Sedition and treason may be expressed by speech or writing.* And, in those cases, decisive repressive action by the government is imperative for the sake of the general welfare. All these necessities that speech be limited are recognized and provided for under the Constitution. They were not unknown to the writers of the First Amendment. That amendment, then, we may take it for granted, *does not forbid the abridging of speech.* But, at the same time, *does forbid the abridging of the freedom of speech.* It is to the solving of that paradox, that apparent self-contradiction, that we are summoned if, as free men, we wish to know what the right of freedom of speech is.

5

As we proceed now to reflect upon the relations of a thinking and speaking individual to the government which guards his freedom, we may do well to turn back for a few moments to the analysis of those relations given by Plato. The Athenian philosopher of the fourth century B.C. was himself caught in our paradox. He saw the connection between self-government and intelligence with a clarity and wisdom and wit which have never been excelled. In his two short dialogues, the *Apology*[1] and the *Crito*,[2] he grapples with the problem which we are facing.

In both dialogues, Plato is considering the right which a government has to demand obedience from its citizens. And in both dialogues, Socrates,[3] a thinker and teacher who had aroused Plato from dogmatic slumber, is the citizen whose relations are discussed. The question is whether or not Socrates is in duty bound to obey the government. In the *Apology* the answer is "No." In the *Crito* the

*I shall be grateful if the reader will eliminate from the sentence, "Sedition and treason may be expressed by speech or writing," the words "Sedition and." "Treason" is a genuine word, with an honest and carefully defined procedural meaning. But "sedition," as applied to belief or communication, is, for the most part, a tricky and misleading word. It is used chiefly to suggest that a "treasonable" crime has been committed in an area in which, under the Constitution, no such crime can exist. (Note added 1960.)

[1] Dialogue of Plato recounting Socrates' trial and defense of free inquiry and criticism

[2] Dialogue of Plato in which Socrates' defends obedience to civil law

[3] (469?-399 B.C.), Greek philosopher and teacher of Plato

answer is "Yes." Plato is obviously using one of the favorite devices of the teacher. He is seeming to contradict himself. He is thereby demanding of his pupils that they save themselves and him from contradiction by making clear a basic and elusive distinction.

In the *Apology,* Socrates is on trial for his life. The charge against him is that in his teaching he has "corrupted the youth" and has "denied the Gods." On the evidence presented by a kind of un-Athenian Subversive Activities Committee he is found guilty. His judges do not wish to put him to death, but they warn him that, unless he will agree to stop his teaching or to change its tenor, they must order his execution. And to this demand for obedience to a decree abridging his freedom of speech, Socrates replies with a flat and unequivocal declaration of disobedient independence. My teaching, he says, is not, in that sense, under the abridging control of the government. Athens is a free city. No official, no judge, he declares, may tell me what I shall, or shall not, teach or think. He recognizes that the government has the power and the legal right to put him to death. But so far as the content of his teaching is concerned, he claims unqualified independence. "Congress shall make no law abridging the freedom of speech," he seems to be saying. Present-day Americans who wish to understand the meaning, the human intention, expressed by the First Amendment, would do well to read and to ponder again Plato's *Apology,* written in Athens twenty-four centuries ago. It may well be argued that if the *Apology* had not been written—by Plato or by someone else—the First Amendment would not have been written. The relation here is one of trunk and branch.

But the argument of the *Crito* seems, at least, to contradict that of the *Apology.* Here Socrates, having been condemned to death, is in prison awaiting the carrying out of the sentence. His friend Crito urges him to escape, to evade the punishment. This he refuses to do. He has no right, he says, to disobey the decision of the government that he must drink the hemlock. That government has legal authority over the life and death of its citizens. Even though it is mistaken, and, therefore, unjust, they must, in this field, conform to its decisions. For Socrates, obedience to the laws which would abridge his life is here quite as imperative as was disobedience to laws which would abridge his belief and the expression of it. In passages of amazing beauty and insight, Socrates explains that duty to Crito. He represents himself as conversing with The Laws of Athens about the compact into which they and he have entered. The Laws, he says, remind him that for seventy years, he has "consented" to them, has accepted from them all the rights and privileges of an Athenian citizen. Will he now, they ask, because his own life is threatened, withdraw his consent, annul the compact? To do that would be a shameful thing, unworthy of a citizen of Athens.

Plato is too great a teacher to formulate for us, or for his more immediate pupils, the distinction which he is here drawing. He demands of us that we make it for ourselves. But that there is a distinction and that the understanding of it is essential for the practice of freedom, he asserts passionately and without equivocation. If the government attempts to limit the freedom of a man's opinions, he tells us, that man, and his fellows with him, has both the right and the duty of disobedience. But if, on the other hand, by regular legal procedure, his life or his property is required of him, he must submit; he must let them go willingly. In one phase of man's activities, the government may exercise control over him. In another phase, it may not. What, then, are those two phases? Only as we see clearly the distinction between them, Plato is saying, do we know what government by consent of the governed means.

6

The difficulties of the paradox of freedom as applied to speech may perhaps be lessened if we now examine the procedure of the traditional American town meeting. That institution is commonly, and rightly, regarded as a model by which free political procedures may be measured. It is self-government in its simplest, most obvious form.

In the town meeting the people of a community assemble to discuss and to act upon matters of public interest—roads, schools, poorhouses, health, external defense, and the like. Every man is free to come. They meet as political equals. Each has a right and a duty to think his own thoughts, to express them, and to listen to the arguments of others. The basic principle is that the freedom of speech shall be unabridged. And yet the meeting cannot even be opened unless, by common consent, speech is abridged. A chairman or moderator is, or has been, chosen. He "calls the meeting to order." And the hush which follows that call is a clear indication that restrictions upon speech have been set up. The moderator assumes, or arranges, that in the conduct of the business, certain rules of order will be observed. Except as he is overruled by the meeting as a whole, he will enforce those rules. His business on its negative side is to abridge speech. For example, it is usually agreed that no one shall speak unless "recognized by the chair." Also, debaters must confine their remarks to "the question before the house." If one man "has the floor," no one else may interrupt him except as provided by the rules. The meeting has assembled, not primarily to talk, but primarily by means of talking to get business done. And the talking must be regulated and abridged as the doing of the business under actual conditions may require. If a speaker wanders from the point at issue, if he is abusive or in other ways threatens to defeat the purpose of the meeting, he may be and should be declared "out of order." He must then stop speaking, at least in that way. And if he persists in breaking the rules, he may be "denied the floor" or, in the last resort, "thrown out" of the meeting. The town meeting, as it seeks for freedom of public discussion of public problems, would be wholly ineffectual unless speech were thus abridged. It is not a Hyde Park.[4] It is a parliament or congress. It is a group of free and equal men, cooperating in a common enterprise, and using for that enterprise responsible and regulated discussion. It is not a dialectical free-for-all. It is self-government.

These speech-abridging activities of the town meeting indicate what the First Amendment to the Constitution does not forbid. When self-governing men demand freedom of speech they are not saying that every individual has an unalienable right to speak whenever, wherever, however he chooses. They do not declare that any man may talk as he pleases, when he pleases, about what he pleases, about whom he pleases, to whom he pleases. The common sense of any reasonable society would deny the existence of that unqualified right. No one, for example, may, without consent of nurse or doctor, rise up in a sickroom to argue for his principles or his candidate. In the sickroom, that question is not "before the house."

[4]Public park in London noted for its open-air meetings and soap-box protests

The discussion is, therefore, "out of order." To you who now listen to my words, it is allowable to differ with me, but it is not allowable for you to state that difference in words until I have finished my reading. Anyone who would thus irresponsibly interrupt the activities of a lecture, a hospital, a concert hall, a church, a machine shop, a classroom, a football field, or a home, does not thereby exhibit his freedom. Rather, he shows himself to be a boor, a public nuisance, who must be abated, by force if necessary.

What, then, does the First Amendment forbid? Here again the town meeting suggests an answer. That meeting is called to discuss and, on the basis of such discussion, to decide matters of public policy. For example, shall there be a school? Where shall it be located? Who shall teach? What shall be taught? The community has agreed that such questions as these shall be freely discussed and that, when the discussion is ended, decision upon them will be made by vote of the citizens. Now, in that method of political self-government, the point of ultimate interest is not the words of the speakers, but the minds of the hearers. The final aim of the meeting is the voting of wise decisions. The voters, therefore, must be made as wise as possible. The welfare of the community requires that those who decide issues shall understand them. They must know what they are voting about. And this, in turn, requires that so far as time allows, all facts and interests relevant to the problem shall be fully and fairly presented to the meeting. Both facts and interests must be given in such a way that all the alternative lines of action can be wisely measured in relation to one another. As the self-governing community seeks, by the method of voting, to gain wisdom in action, it can find it only in the minds of its individual citizens. If they fail, it fails. That is why freedom of discussion for those minds may not be abridged.

The First Amendment, then, is not the guardian of unregulated talkativeness. It does not require that, on every occasion, every citizen shall take part in public debate. Nor can it even give assurance that everyone shall have opportunity to do so. If, for example, at a town meeting, twenty like-minded citizens have become a "party," and if one of them has read to the meeting an argument which they have all approved, it would be ludicrously out of order for each of the others to insist on reading it again. No competent moderator would tolerate that wasting of the time available for free discussion. What is essential is not that everyone shall speak, but that everything worth saying shall be said. To this end, for example, it may be arranged that each of the known conflicting points of view shall have, and shall be limited to, an assigned share of the time available. But however it be arranged, the vital point, as stated negatively, is that no suggestion of policy shall be denied a hearing because it is on one side of the issue rather than another. And this means that though citizens may, on other grounds, be barred from speaking, they may not be barred because their views are thought to be false or dangerous. No plan of action shall be outlawed because someone in control thinks it unwise, unfair, un-American. No speaker may be declared "out of order" because we disagree with what he intends to say. And the reason for this equality of status in the field of ideas lies deep in the very foundations of the self-governing process. When men govern themselves, it is they—and no one else—who must pass judgment upon unwisdom and unfairness and danger. And that means that unwise ideas must have a hearing as well as wise ones, unfair as well as fair, dangerous as well as safe, un-American as well as American. Just so far as, at any point, the citizens who are to decide an issue are denied acquaintance with information or opinion or doubt or disbelief or criticism which is relevant to that issue, just so far the result must be ill-considered, ill-balanced planning for the general good. *It is that mutilation of the thinking process of the community against which the First Amendment to the Constitution is directed.* The principle of the freedom of speech springs from the necessities of the program of self-government. It is not a Law of Nature or of Reason in the abstract. It is a deduction from the basic American agreement that public issues shall be decided by universal suffrage.

If, then, on any occasion in the United States it is allowable to say that the Constitution is a good document it is equally allowable, in that situation, to say that the Constitution is a bad document. If a public building may be used in which to say, in time of war, that the war is justified, then the same building may be used in which to say that it is not justified. If it be publicly argued that conscription for armed service is moral and necessary, it may likewise be publicly argued that it is immoral and unnecessary. If it may be said that

American political institutions are superior to those of England or Russia or Germany, it may, with equal freedom, be said that those of England or Russia or Germany are superior to ours. These conflicting views may be expressed, must be expressed, not because they are valid, but because they are relevant. If they are responsibly entertained by anyone, we, the voters, need to hear them. When a question of policy is "before the house," free men choose to meet it not with their eyes shut, but with their eyes open. To be afraid of ideas, any idea, is to be unfit for self-government. Any such suppression of ideas about the common good, the First Amendment condemns with its absolute disapproval. The freedom of ideas shall not be abridged.

A distinguished educator, Meiklejohn has written on the liberal college, freedom of speech, and the Bill of Rights in modern America, in such works as *The Experimental College, Freedom and the College,* and *Education between Two Worlds.* He was awarded the Freedom Medal in 1962.

What I believe

FROM *Two Cheers for Democracy (1951)*
BY *E. M. Forster (born 1879)*

I do not believe in Belief. But this is an age of faith, and there are so many militant creeds that, in self-defence, one has to formulate a creed of one's own. Tolerance, good temper and sympathy are no longer enough in a world which is rent by religious and racial persecution, in a world where ignorance rules, and science, who ought to have ruled, plays the subservient pimp. Tolerance, good temper and sympathy – they are what matter really, and if the human race is not to collapse they must come to the front before long. But for the moment they are not enough, their action is no stronger than a flower, battered beneath a military jack-boot. They want stiffening, even if the process coarsens them. Faith, to my mind, is a stiffening process, a sort of mental starch, which ought to be applied as sparingly as possible. I dislike the stuff. I do not believe in it, for its own sake, at all. Herein I probably differ from most people, who believe in Belief, and are only sorry they cannot swallow even more than they do. My law-givers are Erasmus[1] and Montaigne,[2] not Moses and St. Paul. My temple stands not upon Mount Moriah[3] but in that Elysian Field[4] where even the immortal are admitted. My motto is: "Lord, I disbelieve – help thou my unbelief."

[1]Desiderius Erasmus (c. 1466-1536), Renaissance scholar and humanist who urged tolerance and reason in an age of religious persecution

[2]Michel Eyquem de Montaigne (1533-1592), celebrated French essayist

[3]The hill on which Abraham was commanded to sacrifice Isaac

[4]The afterworld for the gods, the blessed and the immortals in Greek mythology

I have, however, to live in an Age of Faith—the sort of epoch I used to hear praised when I was a boy. It is extremely unpleasant really. It is bloody in every sense of the word. And I have to keep my end up in it. Where do I start?

With personal relationships. Here is something comparatively solid in a world full of violence and cruelty. Not absolutely solid, for Psychology has split and shattered the idea of a "Person," and has shown that there is something incalculable in each of us, which may at any moment rise to the surface and destroy our normal balance. We don't know what we are like. We can't know what other people are like. How, then, can we put any trust in personal relationships, or cling to them in the gathering political storm? In theory we cannot. But in practice we can and do. Though A is not unchangeably A or B unchangeably B, there can still be love and loyalty between the two. For the purpose of living one has to assume that the personality is solid, and the "self" is an entity, and to ignore all contrary evidence. And since to ignore evidence is one of the characteristics of faith, I certainly can proclaim that I believe in personal relationships.

Starting from them, I get a little order into the contemporary chaos. One must be fond of people and trust them if one is not to make a mess of life, and it is therefore essential that they should not let one down. They often do. The moral of which is that I must, myself, be as reliable as possible, and this I try to be. But reliability is not a matter of contract—that is the main difference between the world of personal relationships and the world of business relationships. It is a matter for the heart, which signs no documents. In other words, reliability is impossible unless there is a natural warmth. Most men possess this warmth, though they often have bad luck and get chilled. Most of them, even when they are politicians, *want* to keep faith. And one can, at all events, show one's own little light here, one's own poor little trembling flame, with the knowledge that it is not the only light that is shining in the darkness, and not the only one which the darkness does not comprehend. Personal relations are despised today. They are regarded as bourgeois luxuries, as products of a time of fair weather which is now past, and we are urged to get rid of them, and to dedicate ourselves to some movement or cause instead. I hate the idea of causes, and if I had to choose between betraying my country and betraying my friend, I hope I should have the guts to betray my country. Such a choice may scandalize the modern reader, and he may stretch out his patriotic hand to the telephone at once and ring up the police. It would not have shocked Dante,[5] though. Dante places Brutus[6] and Cassius[7] in the lowest circle of Hell because they had chosen to betray their friend Julius Caesar rather than their country Rome. Probably one will not be asked to make such an agonising choice. Still, there lies at the back of every creed something terrible and hard for which the worshipper may one day be required to suffer, and there is even a terror and a hardness in this creed of personal relationships, urbane and mild though it sounds. Love and loyalty to an individual can run counter to the claims of the State. When they do—down with the State, say I, which means that the State would down me.

This brings me along to Democracy, "even Love, the Beloved Republic, which feeds upon Freedom and lives." Democracy is not a Beloved Republic really, and never will be. But it is less hateful than other contemporary forms of government, and to that extent it deserves our support. It does start from the assumption that the individual is important, and that all types are needed to make a civilisation. It does not divide its citizens into the bossers and the bossed—as an efficiency-regime tends to do. The people I admire most are those who are sensitive and want to create something or discover something, and do not see life in terms of power, and such people get more of a chance under a democracy than elsewhere. They found religions, great or small, or they produce literature and art, or they do disinterested scientific research, or they may be what is called "ordinary people," who are creative in their private lives, bring up their children decently, for instance, or help their neighbours. All these people need to express themselves; they cannot do so unless society allows them to do so, and the society which allows them most liberty is a democracy.

Democracy has another merit. It allows criticism, and if there is

[5] Dante Alighieri (1265-1321), Italian poet, author of *The Divine Comedy*

[6] Marcus Julius Brutus (85-42 B.C.), leader of conspiracy against and an assassin of Julius Caesar

[7] Gaius Cassius Longinus (d. 42 B.C.), instigator of conspiracy against Caesar

not public criticism there are bound to be hushed-up scandals. That is why I believe in the Press, despite all its lies and vulgarity, and why I believe in Parliament. Parliament is often sneered at because it is a Talking Shop. I believe in it *because* it is a talking shop. I believe in the Private Member who makes himself a nuisance. He gets snubbed and is told that he is cranky or ill-informed, but he does expose abuses which would otherwise never have been mentioned, and very often an abuse gets put right just by being mentioned. Occasionally, too, a well-meaning public official starts losing his head in the cause of efficiency, and thinks himself God Almighty. Such officials are particularly frequent in the Home Office. Well, there will be questions about them in Parliament sooner or later, and then they will have to mind their steps. Whether Parliament is either a representative body or an efficient one is questionable, but I value it because it criticises and talks, and because its chatter gets widely reported.

So Two Cheers for Democracy: one because it admits variety and two because it permits criticism. Two cheers are quite enough: there is no occasion to give three. Only Love the Beloved Republic deserves that.

What about Force, though? While we are trying to be sensitive and advanced and affectionate and tolerant, an unpleasant question pops up: does not all society rest upon force? If a government cannot count upon the police and the army, how can it hope to rule? And if an individual gets knocked on the head or sent to a labour camp, of what significance are his opinions?

This dilemma does not worry me as much as it does some. I realise that all society rests upon force. But all the great creative actions, all the decent human relations, occur during the intervals when force has not managed to come to the front. These intervals are what matter. I want them to be as frequent and as lengthy as possible, and I call them "civilisation." Some people idealise force and pull it into the foreground and worship it, instead of keeping it in the background as long as possible. I think they make a mistake, and I think that their opposites, the mystics, err even more when they declare that force does not exist. I believe that it exists, and that one of our jobs is to prevent it from getting out of its box. It gets out sooner or later, and then it destroys us and all the lovely things which we have made. But it is not out all the time, for the fortunate reason that the strong are so stupid. Consider their conduct for a moment in the Niebelung's Ring.[8] The giants there have the guns, or in other words the gold; but they do nothing with it, they do not realise that they are all-powerful, with the result that the catastrophe is delayed and the castle of Walhalla,[9] insecure but glorious, fronts the storms. Fafnir,[10] coiled round his hoard, grumbles and grunts; we can hear him under Europe today; the leaves of the wood already tremble, and the Bird[11] calls its warnings uselessly. Fafnir will destroy us, but by a blessed dispensation he is stupid and slow, and creation goes on just outside the poisonous blast of his breath. The Nietzschean[12] would hurry the monster up, the mystic would say he did not exist, but Wotan,[13] wiser than either, hastens to create warriors before doom declares itself. The Valkyries[14] are symbols not only of courage but of intelligence; they represent the human spirit snatching its opportunity while the going is good, and one of them even finds time to love. Brünnhilde's[15] last song hymns the recurrence of love, and since it is the privilege of art to exaggerate, she goes even further, and proclaims the love which is eternally triumphant and feeds upon freedom, and lives.

So that is what I feel about force and violence. It is, alas! the ultimate reality on this earth, but it does not always get to the front. Some people call its absences "decadence"; I call them "civilisation" and find in such interludes the chief justification for the human experiment. I look the other way until fate strikes me. Whether this

[8] *Der Ring des Nibelungen,* Richard Wagner's cycle of four musical dramas based on the Germanic epic *Nibelungenlied;* in the epic, also a curse-laden ring that was made of gold stolen from the Rhinedaughters

[9] Home of the gods in early Germanic mythology

[10] Son of the magician Hreidmar, the giant Fafnir (or Fafner) turned himself into a dragon to guard the stolen gold from which the Niebelung's ring was made and was slain by Siegfried, son of Wotan

[11] Generally, symbol of prophecy; in Wagner's work, the birds warn Siegfried of treachery

[12] Follower of Friedrich Wilhelm Nietzsche (1844-1900), German philosopher

[13] Chief of the gods, father of Siegfried, symbol of greed for wealth and power

[14] Daughters of Wotan and Erda, godess of wisdom, who carry the bodies of slain heroes to Walhalla, where they revive and help defend Walhalla

[15] Leader of the Valkyries, whom Siegfried makes his wife.

is due to courage or to cowardice in my own case I cannot be sure. But I know that if men had not looked the other way in the past, nothing of any value would survive. The people I respect most behave as if they were immortal and as if society was eternal. Both assumptions are false: both of them must be accepted as true if we are to go on eating and working and loving, and are to keep open a few breathing holes for the human spirit. No millennium seems likely to descend upon humanity; no better and stronger League of Nations will be instituted; no form of Christianity and no alternative to Christianity will bring peace to the world or integrity to the individual; no "change of heart" will occur. And yet we need not despair, indeed, we cannot despair; the evidence of history shows us that men have always insisted on behaving creatively under the shadow of the sword; that they have done their artistic and scientific and domestic stuff for the sake of doing it, and that we had better follow their example under the shadow of the aeroplanes. Others, with more vision or courage than myself, see the salvation of humanity ahead, and will dismiss my conception of civilisation as paltry, a sort of tip-and-run game. Certainly it is presumptuous to say that we *cannot* improve, and that Man, who has only been in power for a few thousand years, will never learn to make use of his power. All I mean is that, if people continue to kill one another as they do, the world cannot get better than it is, and that since there are more people than formerly, and their means for destroying one another superior, the world may well get worse. What is good in people – and consequently in the world – is their insistence on creation, their belief in friendship and loyalty for their own sakes; and though Violence remains and is, indeed, the major partner in this muddled establishment, I believe that creativeness remains too, and will always assume direction when violence sleeps. So, though I am not an optimist, I cannot agree with Sophocles[16] that it were better never to have been born. And although, like Horace,[17] I see no evidence that each batch of births is superior to the last, I leave the field open for the more complacent view. This is such a difficult moment to live in, one cannot help getting gloomy and also a bit rattled, and perhaps short-sighted.

[16] (c. 496-406 B.C.), famous Greek tragedian

[17] Quintus Horatius Flaccus (65-8 B.C.), Roman poet

In search of a refuge, we may perhaps turn to hero-worship. But here we shall get no help, in my opinion. Hero-worship is a dangerous vice, and one of the minor merits of a democracy is that it does not encourage it, or produce that unmanageable type of citizen known as the Great Man. It produces instead different kinds of small men—a much finer achievement. But people who cannot get interested in the variety of life, and cannot make up their own minds, get discontented over this, and they long for a hero to bow down before and to follow blindly. It is significant that a hero is an integral part of the authoritarian stock-in-trade today. An efficiency-regime cannot be run without a few heroes stuck about it to carry off the dullness—much as plums have to be put into a bad pudding to make it palatable. One hero at the top and a smaller one each side of him is a favourite arrangement, and the timid and the bored are comforted by the trinity, and, bowing down, feel exalted and strengthened.

No, I distrust Great Men. They produce a desert of uniformity around them and often a pool of blood too, and I always feel a little man's pleasure when they come a cropper. Every now and then one reads in the newspapers some such statement as: "The coup d'etat appears to have failed, and Admiral Toma's whereabouts is at present unknown." Admiral Toma had probably every qualification for being a Great Man—an iron will, personal magnetism, dash, flair, sexlessness—but fate was against him, so he retires to unknown whereabouts instead of parading history with his peers. He fails with a completeness which no artist and no lover can experience, because with them the process of creation is itself an achievement, whereas with him the only possible achievement is success.

I believe in aristocracy, though—if that is the right word, and if a democrat may use it. Not an aristocracy of power, based upon rank and influence, but an aristocracy of the sensitive, the considerate and the plucky. Its members are to be found in all nations and classes, and all through the ages, and there is a secret understanding between them when they meet. They represent the true human tradition, the one permanent victory of our queer race over cruelty and chaos. Thousands of them perish in obscurity, a few are great names. They are sensitive for others as well as for themselves, they are considerate without being fussy, their pluck is not swankiness but the power to endure, and they can take a joke. I give no examples—it is risky to do that—but the reader may as well consider whether this is the type of person he would like to meet and to be, and whether (going farther with me) he would prefer that this type should *not* be an ascetic one. I am against asceticism myself. I am with the old Scotsman who wanted less chastity and more delicacy. I do not feel that my aristocrats are a real aristocracy if they thwart their bodies, since bodies are the instruments through which we register and enjoy the world. Still, I do not insist. This is not a major point. It is clearly possible to be sensitive, considerate and plucky and yet be an ascetic too, if anyone possesses the first three qualities, I will let him in! On they go—an invincible army, yet not a victorious one. The aristocrats, the elect, the chosen, the Best People—all the words that describe them are false, and all attempts to organise them fail. Again and again Authority, seeing their value, has tried to net them and to utilise them as the Egyptian Priesthood or the Christian Church or the Chinese Civil Service or the Group movement, or some other worthy stunt. But they slip through the net and are gone; when the door is shut, they are no longer in the room; their temple, as one of them remarked, is the Holiness of the Heart's Affection, and their kingdom, though they never possess it, is the wide-open world.

With this type of person knocking about, and constantly crossing one's path if one has eyes to see or hands to feel, the experiment of earthly life cannot be dismissed as a failure. But it may well be hailed as a tragedy, the tragedy being that no device has been found by which these private decencies can be transmitted to public affairs. As soon as people have power they go crooked and sometimes dotty as well, because the possession of power lifts them into a region where normal honesty never pays. For instance, the man who is selling newspapers outside the Houses of Parliament can safely leave his papers to go for a drink and his cap beside them: anyone who takes a paper is sure to drop a copper into the cap. But the men who are inside the Houses of Parliament—they cannot trust one another like that, still less can the Government they compose trust other governments. No caps upon the pavement here, but suspicion, treachery and armaments. The more highly public life is organised the lower does its morality sink; the nations of today behave to each other worse than they ever did in the past, they cheat, rob, bully and bluff, make war without notice, and kill as many women and children as possible; whereas primitive tribes were at all events restrained by taboos. It is a humiliating outlook—though the greater the darkness, the brighter shine the little lights, reassuring one another, signaling: "Well, at all events, I'm still here. I don't like it very much, but how are you?" Unquenchable lights of my aristocracy! Signals of the invincible army! "Come along—anyway, let's have a good time while we can." I think they signal that too.

The Saviour of the future—if ever he comes—will not preach a new Gospel. He will merely utilise my aristocracy, he will make effective the good will and the good temper which are already existing. In other words, he will introduce a new technique. In economics, we are told that if there was a new technique of distribution, there need be no poverty, and people would not starve in one place while crops were being ploughed under in another. A similar change is needed in the sphere of morals and politics. The desire for it is by no means new; it was expressed, for example, in theological terms by Jacopone da Todi[18] over six hundred years ago. "Ordina questo amore, O tu che m'ami," he said; "O thou who lovest me—set this love in order." His prayer was not granted, and I do not myself believe that it ever will be, but here, and not through a change of heart, is our probable route. Not by becoming better, but by ordering and distributing his native goodness, will Man shut up Force into its box, and so gain time to explore the universe and to set his mark upon it worthily. At present he only explores it at odd moments, when Force is looking the other way, and his divine creativeness appears as a trivial by-product, to be scrapped as soon as the drums beat and the bombers hum.

Such a change, claim the orthodox, can only be made by Christianity, and will be made by it in God's good time: man always has failed and always will fail to organise his own goodness, and it is presumptuous of him to try. This claim—solemn as it is—leaves me cold. I cannot believe that Christianity will ever cope with the present world-wide mess, and I think that such influence as it re-

[18](c. 1230-1306) Italian religious poet

tains in modern society is due to the money behind it, rather than to its spiritual appeal. It was a spiritual force once, but the indwelling spirit will have to be restated if it is to calm the waters again, and probably restated in a non-Christian form. Naturally a lot of people, and people who are not only good but able and intelligent, will disagree here; they will vehemently deny that Christianity has failed, or they will argue that its failure proceeds from the wickedness of men, and really proves its ultimate success. They have Faith, with a large F. My faith has a very small one, and I only intrude it because these are strenuous and serious days, and one likes to say what one thinks while speech is comparatively free: it may not be free much longer.

The above are the reflections of an individualist and a liberal who has found liberalism crumbling beneath him and at first felt ashamed. Then, looking around, he decided there was no special reason for shame, since other people, whatever they felt, were equally insecure. And as for individualism – there seems no way of getting off this, even if one wanted to. The dictator-hero can grind down his citizens till they are all alike, but he cannot melt them into a single man. That is beyond his power. He can order them to merge, he can incite them to mass-antics, but they are obliged to be born separately, and to die separately, and, owing to these unavoidable termini, will always be running off the totalitarian rails. The memory of birth and the expectation of death always lurk within the human being, making him separate from his fellows and consequently capable of intercourse with them. Naked I came into the world, naked I shall go out of it! And a very good thing too, for it reminds me that I am naked under my shirt, whatever its colour.

☙ After completing his studies at Cambridge, Edward Morgan Forster wrote short stories in London, travelled to Italy (the setting of his novels *Where Angels Fear to Tread* and *A Room with a View*), and worked as a civil servant in Alexandria during World War I. After a return to India in 1921 his best-known novel (*A Passage to India*) was written.

How should one read a book?

FROM *The Second Common Reader (1932)*

BY *Virginia Woolf (1885-1941)*

In the first place, I want to emphasise the note of interrogation at the end of my title. Even if I could answer the question for myself, the answer would apply only to me and not to you. The only advice, indeed, that one person can give another about reading is to take no advice, to follow your own instincts, to use your own reason, to come to your own conclusions. If this is agreed between us, then I feel at liberty to put forward a few ideas and suggestions because you will not allow them to fetter that independence which is the most important quality that a reader can possess. After all, what laws can be laid down about books? The battle of Waterloo was certainly fought on a certain day; but is *Hamlet* a better play than *Lear?* Nobody can say. Each must decide that question for himself. To admit authorities however heavily furred and gowned, into our libraries and let them tell us how to read, what to read, what value to place upon what we read, is to destroy the spirit of freedom which is the breath of those sanctuaries. Everywhere else we may be bound by laws and conventions – there we have none.

But to enjoy freedom, if the platitude is pardonable, we have of course to control ourselves. We must not squander our powers, helplessly and ignorantly, squirting half the house in order to water a single rose-bush; we must train them, exactly and powerfully, here on the very spot. This, it may be, is one of the first difficulties that faces us in a library. What is "the very spot"? There may well seem to be nothing but a conglomeration and huddle of confusion. Poems and novels, histories and memoirs, dictionaries and blue-books; books written in all languages by men and women of all tempers, races, and ages jostle each other on the shelf. And outside the donkey brays, the women gossip at the pump, the colts gallop across the fields. Where are we to begin? How are we to bring order into this multitudinous chaos and so get the deepest and widest pleasure from what we read?

It is simple enough to say that since books have classes—fiction, biography, poetry—we should separate them and take from each what it is right that each should give us. Yet few people ask from books what books can give us. Most commonly we come to books with blurred and divided minds, asking of fiction that it shall be true, of poetry that it shall be false, of biography that it shall be flattering, of history that it shall enforce our own prejudices. If we could banish all such preconceptions when we read, that would be an admirable beginning. Do not dictate to your author; try to become him. Be his fellow-worker and accomplice. If you hang back, and reserve and criticise at first, you are preventing yourself from getting the fullest possible value from what you read. But if you open your mind as widely as possible, then signs and hints of almost imperceptible fineness, from the twist and turn of the first sentences, will bring you into the presence of a human being unlike any other. Steep yourself in this, acquaint yourself with this, and soon you will find that your author is giving you, or attempting to give you, something far more definite. The thirty-two chapters of a novel—if we consider how to read a novel first—are an attempt to make something as formed and controlled as a building: but the words are more impalpable than bricks; reading is a longer and more complicated process than seeing. Perhaps the quickest way to understand the elements of what a novelist is doing is not to read, but to write; to make your own experiment with the dangers and difficulties of words. Recall, then, some event that has left a distinct impression on you—how at the corner of the street, perhaps, you passed two people talking. A tree shook; an electric light danced; the tone of the talk was comic, but also tragic; a whole vision, an entire conception, seemed contained in that moment.

But when you attempt to reconstruct it in words, you will find that it breaks into a thousand conflicting impressions. Some must be subdued; others emphasized; in the process you will lose, probably, all grasp upon the emotion itself. Then turn from your blurred and littered pages to the opening pages of some great novelist—Defoe, Jane Austen, Hardy. Now you will be better able to appreciate their mastery. It is not merely that we are in the presence of a different person—Defoe, Jane Austen, or Thomas Hardy—but that we are living in a different world. Here, in *Robinson Crusoe,* we are trudging a plain high road; one thing happens after another; the fact and the order of the fact is enough. But if the open air and adventure mean everything to Defoe they mean nothing to Jane Austen. Hers is the drawing-room, and people talking, and by the many mirrors of their talk revealing their characters. And if, when we have accustomed ourselves to the drawing-room and its reflections, we turn to Hardy, we are once more spun round. The moors are round us and the stars are above our heads. The other side of the mind is now exposed—the dark side that comes uppermost in solitude, not the light side that shows in company. Our relations are not towards people, but toward Nature and destiny. Yet different as these worlds are, each is consistent with itself. The maker of each is careful to observe the laws of his own perspective, and however great a strain they may put upon us they will never confuse us, as lesser writers so frequently do, by introducing two different kinds of reality into the same book. Thus to go from one great novelist to another—from Jane Austen to Hardy, from Peacock to Trollope, from Scott to Meridith—is to be wrenched and uprooted; to be thrown this way and then that. To read a novel is a difficult and complex art. You must be capable not only of great fineness of perception, but of great boldness of imagination if you are going to make use of all that the novelist—the great artist—gives you.

But a glance at the heterogeneous company on the shelf will show you that writers are very seldom "great artists"; far more often a book makes no claim to be a work of art at all. These biographies and autobiographies, for example, lives of great men, of men long dead and forgotten, that stand cheek by jowl with the novels and poems, are we to refuse to read them because they are not "art"? Or shall we read them, but read them in a different way, with a different aim? Shall we read them in the first place to satisfy that curiosity which possesses us sometimes when in the evening we linger in front of a house where the lights are lit and the blinds are not yet drawn, and each floor of the house shows us a different section of human life in being? Then we are consumed with curiosity about the lives of these people—the servants gossiping, the gentlemen dining, the girl dressing for a party, the old woman at the window with her knitting. Who are they, what are they, what are their names, their occupations, their thoughts, and adventures?

Biographies and memoirs answer such questions, light up innumerable such houses; they show us people going about their daily affairs, toiling, failing, succeeding, eating, hating, loving, until they die. And sometimes as we watch, the house fades and the iron railings vanish and we are out at sea; we are hunting, sailing, fighting; we are among savages and soldiers; we are taking part in great campaigns. Or if we like to stay here in England, in London, still the scene changes; the street narrows; the house becomes small, cramped, diamond-paned, and malodorous. We see a poet, Donne, driven from such a house because the walls were so thin that when the children cried their voices cut through them. We can follow him, through the paths that lie in the pages of books, to Twickenham;[1] to Lady Bedford's Park, a famous meeting-ground for nobles and poets; and then turn our steps to Wilton,[2] the great house under the downs, and hear Sidney[3] read the *Arcadia* to his sister; and ramble among the very marshes and see the very herons that figure in that famous romance; and then again travel north with that other Lady Pembroke,[4] Anne Clifford,[5] to her wild moors, or plunge into the city and control our merriment at the sight of Gabriel Harvey[6] in his black velvet suit arguing about poetry with Spenser. Nothing is more fascinating than to grope and stumble in the alternate darkness and splendour of Elizabethan London. But

[1] city on the Thames, near London

[2] town in England

[3] Sir Philip Sidney (1554-1586), English poet, soldier, and statesman

[4] Sidney's sister was Mary, Countess of Pembroke, whose country house was at Wilton

[5] Anne Clifford Herbert, Countess of Pembroke (1590-1676); her diary was published in 1923

[6] English author (c. 1545-1630)

there is no staying there. The Temples[7] and the Swifts,[8] the Harleys[9] and the St. Johns[10] beckon us on; hour upon hour can be spent disentangling their quarrels and deciphering their character; and when we tire of them we can stroll on, past a lady in black wearing diamonds, to Samuel Johnson and Goldsmith[11] and Garrick,[12] or cross the channel, if we like, and meet Voltaire[13] and Diderot,[14] Madame du Deffand;[15] and so back to England and Twickenham—how certain places repeat themselves and certain names!—where Lady Bedford had her Park once and Pope lived later, to Walpole's home at Strawberry Hill. But Walpole[16] introduces us to such a swarm of new acquaintances, there are so many houses to visit and bells to ring that we may well hesitate for a moment, on the Miss Berrys'[17] doorstep, for example, when behold up comes Thackeray; he is the friend of the woman whom Walpole loved; so that merely by going from friend to friend, from garden to garden, from house to house, we have passed from one end of English literature to another and wake to find ourselves here again in the present, if we can so differentiate this moment from all that have gone before. This, then, is one of the ways in which we can read these lives and letters; we can make them light up the many windows of the past; we can watch the famous dead in their familiar habits and fancy sometimes that we are very close and can surprise their secrets, and sometimes we may pull out a play or a poem that they have written and see whether it reads differently in the presence of the author. But this again rouses other questions. How far, we must ask ourselves, is a book influenced by its writer's life—how far is it safe to

[7] Sir William Temple (1628-1699), English author and statesman

[8] Jonathan Swift, *cf.* "A Modest Proposal" above

[9] Robert Harley, first Earl of Oxford (1661-1724), English statesman, left a valuable collection of manuscripts and pamphlets

[10] Henry St. John, first Viscount Bolingbroke (1678-1751), English statesman and writer [11] Oliver Goldsmith (1728-1784), English poet, novelist, and dramatist

[12] David Garrick (1717-1779), English actor [13] François Marie Arouet (1694-1778) French satirist philosopher dramatist, and historian [14] Denis Diderot (1713-1784) French philosopher and encyclopedist

[15] Marie de Vichy-Chamrond Marquise du Deffand (1697-1780) witty and cynical Frenchwoman, leader in Parisian literary and philosophical circles

[16] Horace Walpole, fourth Earl of Oxford (1717-1797), English author

[17] Mary Berry (1763-1852), English authoress and Agnes Berry (1764-1852), were both friends of Horace Walpole

let the man interpret the writer? How far shall we resist or give way to the sympathies and antipathies that the man himself rouses in us —so sensitive are words, so receptive of the character of the author? These are questions that press upon us when we read lives and letters, and we must answer them for ourselves, for nothing can be more fatal than to be guided by the preferences of others in a matter so personal.

But also we can read such books with another aim, not to throw light on literature, not to become familiar with famous people, but to refresh and exercise our own creative powers. Is there not an open window on the right hand of the bookcase? How delightful to stop reading and look out! How stimulating the scene is, in its unconsciousness, its irrelevance, its perpetual movement—the colts galloping round the field, the woman filling her pail at the well, the donkey throwing back his head and emitting his long, acrid moan. The greater part of any library is nothing but the record of such fleeting moments in the lives of men, women, and donkeys. Every literature, as it grows old, has its rubbish-heap, its record of vanished moments and forgotten lives told in faltering and feeble accents that have perished. But if you give yourself up to the delight of rubbish-reading you will be surprised, indeed you will be overcome, by the relics of human life that have been cast out to moulder. It may be one letter—but what a vision it gives! It may be a few sentences—but what vistas they suggest! Sometimes a whole story will come together with such beautiful humour and pathos and completeness that it seems as if a great novelist had been at work, yet it is only an old actor, Tate Wilkinson,[18] remembering the strange story of Captain Jones; it is only a young subaltern[19] serving under Arthur Wellesley[20] and falling in love with a pretty girl at Lisbon; it is only Maria Allen[21] letting fall her sewing in the empty

[18] English actor (1739-1803), fond of telling stories of real people, author of *Memoirs of His Own Life;* see V. Woolf's *Death of the Moth*

[19] See *Memoirs and Literary Remains* of Lieutenant-General Sir Edward Henry Bunbury, bart. (1868)

[20] Duke of Wellington, English general and statesman (1769-1852)

[21] See William S. Allen, *Memoirs of Mrs. Allen of Woodbread Hall, Staffordshire,* 1871; mentioned by V. Woolf in two essays in *Granite and Rainbow.* (With thanks to Professors James Hafley, Donald Weeks, J. J. Wilson, for these and following identifications.)

drawing-room and sighing how she wishes she had taken Dr. Burney's good advice and had never eloped with her Rishy. None of this has any value; it is negligible in the extreme; yet how absorbing it is now and again to go through the rubbish-heaps and find rings and scissors and broken noses buried in the huge past and try to piece them together while the colt gallops round the field, the woman fills her pail at the well, and the donkey brays.

But we tire of rubbish-reading in the long run. We tire of searching for what is needed to complete the half-truth which is all that the Wilkinsons, the Bunburys and the Maria Allens are able to offer us. They had not the artist's power of mastering and eliminating; they could not tell the whole truth even about their own lives; they have disfigured the story that might have been so shapely. Facts are all that they can offer us, and facts are a very inferior form of fiction. Thus the desire grows upon us to have done with half-statements and approximations; to cease from searching out the minute shades of human character, to enjoy the greater abstractness, the purer truth of fiction. Thus we create the mood, intense and generalised, unaware of detail, but stressed by some regular, recurrent beat, whose natural expression is poetry; and that is the time to read poetry when we are almost able to write it.

> Western wind, when wilt thou blow?
> The small rain down can rain.
> Christ, if my love were in my arms,
> And I in my bed again![22]

The impact of poetry is so hard and direct that for the moment there is no other sensation except that of the poem itself. What profound depths we visit then—how sudden and complete is our immersion! There is nothing here to catch hold of; nothing to stay us in our flight. The illusion of fiction is gradual; its effects are prepared; but who when they read these four lines stops to ask who wrote them, or conjures up the thought of Donne's house or Sidney's secretary; or enmeshes them in the intricacy of the past and the succession of generations? The poet is always our contemporary. Our being for the moment is centred and constricted, as in any violent shock of personal emotion. Afterwards, it is true, the

[22] Anonymous Renaissance lyric

sensation begins to spread in wider rings through our minds; remoter senses are reached; these begin to sound and to comment and we are aware of echoes and reflections. The intensity of poetry covers an immense range of emotion. We have only to compare the force and directness of

> I shall fall like a tree, and find my grave,
> Only remembering that I grieve,[23]

with the wavering modulation of

> Minutes are numbered by the fall of sands,
> As by an hour glass; the span of time
> Doth waste us to our graves, and we look on it;
> An age of pleasure, revelled out, comes home
> At last, and ends in sorrow; but the life,
> Weary of riot, numbers every sand,
> Wailing in sighs, until the last drop down,
> So to conclude calamity in rest,[23]

or place the meditative calm of

> whether we be young or old,
> Our destiny, our being's heart and home,
> Is with infinitude, and only there;
> With hope it is, hope that can never die,
> Effort, and expectation, and desire,
> And something evermore about to be,[24]

beside the complete and inexhaustible loveliness of

> The moving Moon went up the sky,
> And nowhere did abide:
> Softly she was going up,
> And a star or two beside—[25]

[23] From John Ford's *Lovers' Melancholy*
[24] From Wordsworth's *Prelude,* Book VI
[25] From Coleridge's *Ancient Mariner*

or the splendid fantasy of

> And the woodland haunter
> Shall not cease to saunter
>   When, far down some glade,
> Of the great world's burning
> One soft flame upturning
> Seems, to his discerning,
>   Crocus in the shade,[26]

to bethink us of the varied art of the poet; his power to make us at once actors and spectators; his power to run his hand into character as if it were a glove, and be Falstaff or Lear; his power to condense, to widen, to state, once and for ever.

"We have only to compare"—with those words the cat is out of the bag, and the true complexity of reading is admitted. The first process, to receive impressions with the utmost understanding, is only half the process of reading; it must be completed, if we are to get the whole pleasure from a book, by another. We must pass judgment upon these multitudinous impressions; we must make of these fleeting shapes one that is hard and lasting. But not directly. Wait for the dust of reading to settle; for the conflict and the questioning to die down; walk, talk, pull the dead petals from a rose, or fall asleep. Then suddenly without our willing it, for it is thus that Nature undertakes these transitions, the book will return, but differently. It will float to the top of the mind as a whole. And the book as a whole is different from the book received currently in separate phrases. Details now fit themselves into their places. We see the shape from start to finish; it is a barn, a pig-sty, or a cathedral. Now then we can compare book with book as we compare building with building. But this act of comparison means that our attitude has changed; we are no longer the friends of the writer, but his judges; and just as we cannot be too sympathetic as friends, so as judges we cannot be too severe. Are they not criminals, books that have wasted our time and sympathy; are they not the most insidious enemies of society, corrupters, defilers, the writers of false books, faked books, books that fill the air with decay and disease? Let us

[26] From Ebenezer Jones' *When the World Is Burning*

then be severe in our judgments; let us compare each book with the greatest of its kind. There they hang in the mind the shapes of the books we have read solidified by the judgments we have passed on them—*Robinson Crusoe, Emma, The Return of the Native.* Compare the novels with these—even the latest and least of novels has a right to be judged with the best. And so with poetry—when the intoxication of rhythm has died down and the splendour of words has faded, a visionary shape will return to us and this must be compared with *Lear,* with *Phedre,* with *The Prelude;* or if not with these, with whatever is the best or seems to us to be the best in its own kind. And we may be sure that the newness of new poetry and fiction is its most superficial quality and that we have only to alter slightly, not to recast, the standards by which we have judged the old.

It would be foolish, then, to pretend that the second part of reading, to judge, to compare, is as simple as the first—to open the mind wide to the fast flocking of innumerable impressions. To continue reading without the book before you, to hold one shadow-shape against another, to have read widely enough and with enough understanding to make such comparisons alive and illuminating—that is difficult; it is still more difficult to press further and to say, "Not only is the book of this sort, but it is of this value; here it fails; here it succeeds; this is bad; that is good." To carry out this part of a reader's duty needs such imagination, insight, and learning that it is hard to conceive any one mind sufficiently endowed; impossible for the most self-confident to find more than the seeds of such powers in himself. Would it not be wiser, then, to remit this part of reading and to allow the critics, the gowned and furred authorities of the library, to decide the question of the book's absolute value for us? Yet how impossible! We may stress the value of sympathy; we may try to sink our own identity as we read. But we know that we cannot sympathise wholly or immerse ourselves wholly; there is always a demon in us who whispers, "I hate, I love," and we cannot silence him. Indeed, it is precisely because we hate and we love that our relation with the poets and novelists is so intimate that we find the presence of another person intolerable. And even if the results are abhorrent and our judgments are wrong, still our taste, the nerve of sensation that sends shocks through us, is our chief illuminant; we learn through feeling; we cannot suppress our own idiosyncrasy without improvising it. But as time goes on perhaps we can train our taste; perhaps we can make it submit to some control. When it has fed greedily and lavishly upon books of all sort—poetry, fiction, history, biography—and has stopped reading and looked for long spaces upon the variety, the incongruity of the living word, we shall find that it is changing a little; it is not so greedy, it is more reflective. It will begin to bring us not merely judgments on particular books, but it will tell us that there is a quality common to certain books. Listen, it will say, what shall we call *this?* And it will read us perhaps *Lear* and then perhaps the *Agamemnon* in order to bring out that common quality. Thus, with our taste to guide us, we shall venture beyond the particular book in search of qualities that group books together; we shall give them names and thus frame a rule that brings order into our perceptions. We shall gain a further and a rarer pleasure from that discrimination. But as a rule only lives when it is perpetually broken by contact with the books themselves—nothing is easier and more stultifying than to make rules which exist out of touch with facts, in a vacuum—now at last, in order to steady ourselves in this difficult attempt, it may be well to turn to the very rare writers who are able to enlighten us upon literature as an art. Coleridge and Dryden and Johnson, in their considered criticism, the poets and novelists themselves in their unconsidered sayings, are often surprisingly relevant; they light up and solidify the vague ideas that have been tumbling in the misty depths of our minds. But they are only able to help us if we come to them laden with questions and suggestions won honestly in the course of our own reading. They can do nothing for us if we herd ourselves under their authority and lie down like sheep in the shade of a hedge. We can only understand their ruling when it comes in conflict with our own and vanquishes it.

If this is so, if to read a book as it should be read calls for the rarest qualities of imagination, insight, and judgment, you may perhaps conclude that literature is a very complex art and that it is unlikely that we shall be able, even after a lifetime of reading, to make any valuable contribution to its criticism. We must remain readers; we shall not put on the further glory that belongs to those rare beings who are also critics. But still we have our responsibilities as readers and even our importance. The standards we raise and the judgment we pass steal into the air and become part of the atmosphere which writers breathe as they work. An influence is created which tells upon them even if it never finds its way into print. And that influence, if it were well instructed, vigorous and individual and sincere, might be of great value now when criticism is necessarily in abeyance; when books pass in review like the procession of animals in a shooting gallery, and the critic has only one second in which to load and aim and shoot and may well be pardoned if he mistakes rabbits for tigers, eagles for barndoor fowls, or misses altogether and wastes his shot upon some peaceful cow grazing in a further field. If behind the erratic gunfire of the press the author felt that there was another kind of criticism, the opinion of people reading for the love of reading, slowly and unprofessionally, and judging with great sympathy and yet with great severity, might this not improve the quality of his work? And if by our means books were to become stronger, richer, and more varied, that would be an end worth reaching.

Yet who reads to bring about an end, however desirable? Are there not some pursuits that we practise because they are good in themselves, and some pleasures that are final? And is not this among them? I have sometimes dreamt, at least, that when the Day of Judgment dawns and the great conquerors and lawyers and statesmen come to receive their rewards—their crowns, their laurels, their names carved indelibly upon imperishable marble—the Almighty will turn to Peter and will say, not without a certain envy when He sees us coming with our books under our arms, "Look, these need no reward. We have nothing to give them here. They have loved reading."

Virginia Woolf is best known as a novelist, experimenting in form, time, and sensibility as she does in *Mrs. Dalloway* and *To the Lighthouse.* In the literary allegory of *Orlando* and the prose of *A Room of One's Own* and *The Common Reader,* she develops some of her themes of reality more directly.

The spirit of place

FROM *Studies in Classic American Literature (1924)*

BY *D. H. Lawrence (1885-1930)*

We like to think of the old-fashioned American classics as children's books. Just childishness, on our part.

The old American art-speech contains an alien quality, which belongs to the American continent and to nowhere else. But, of course, so long as we insist on reading the books as children's tales, we miss all that.

One wonders what the proper high-brow Romans of the third and fourth or later centuries read into the strange utterances of Lucretius or Apuleius[1] or Tertullian,[2] Augustine[3] or Athanasius.[4] The uncanny voice of Iberian Spain, the weirdness of old Carthage, the passion of Libya and North Africa; you may bet the proper old Romans never heard these at all. They read old Latin inference over the top of it, as we read old European inference over the top of Poe or Hawthorne.

It is hard to hear a new voice, as hard as it is to listen to an

[1] Lucius Apuleius (born c. 125 A.D.), Latin Platonic philosopher and rhetorician, author of *The Golden Ass,* a romance

[2] Quintus Septimus Florens Tertullianus (c. 150 - c. 230 A.D.), ecclesiastical writer, one of the fathers of the Latin Church

[3] Saint Augustine (354-430), most renowned father of the Latin Church

[4] one of the fathers of the Christian church (c. 296-373 A.D.), called "The Father of Orthodoxy"

unknown language. We just don't listen. There is a new voice in the old American classics. The world has declined to hear it, and has blabbed about children's stories.

Why?—Out of fear. The world fears a new experience more than it fears anything. Because a new experience displaces so many old experiences. And it is like trying to use muscles that have perhaps never been used, or that have been going stiff for ages. It hurts horribly.

The world doesn't fear a new idea. It can pigeon-hole any idea. But it can't pigeon-hole a real new experience. It can only dodge. The world is a great dodger, and the Americans the greatest. Because they dodge their own very selves. There is a new feeling in the old American books, far more than there is in the modern American books, which are pretty empty of any feeling, and proud of it. There is a "different" feeling in the old American classics. It is the shifting over from the old psyche to something new, a displacement. And displacements hurt. This hurts. So we try to tie it up, like a cut finger. Put a rag around it.

It is a cut, too. Cutting away the old emotions and consciousness. Don't ask what is left.

Art-speech is the only truth. An artist is usually a damned liar, but his art, if it be art, will tell you the truth of his day. And that is all that matters. Away with eternal truth. Truth lives from day to day, and the marvellous Plato of yesterday is chiefly bosh to-day.

The old American artists were hopeless liars. But they were artists, in spite of themselves. Which is more than you can say of most living practitioners.

And you can please yourself, when you read *The Scarlet Letter,* whether you accept what that sugary, blue-eyed little darling of a Hawthorne has to say for himself, false as all darlings are, or whether you read the impeccable truth of his art-speech.

The curious thing about art-speech is that it prevaricates so terribly, I mean it tells such lies. I suppose because we always all the time tell ourselves lies. And out of a pattern of lies art weaves the truth. Like Dostoevsky posing as a sort of Jesus, but most truthfully revealing himself all the while as a little horror.

Truly art is a sort of subterfuge. But thank God for it, we can see through the subterfuge if we choose. Art has two great functions.

First, it provides an emotional experience. And then, if we have the courage of our own feelings, it becomes a mine of practical truth. We have had the feelings *ad nauseam.* But we've never dared dig the actual truth out of them, the truth that concerns us, whether it concerns our grandchildren or not.

The artist usually sets out—or used to—to point a moral and adorn a tale. The tale, however, points the other way, as a rule. Two blankly opposing morals, the artist's and the tale's. Never trust the artist. Trust the tale. The proper function of a critic is to save the tale from the artist who created it.

Now we know our business in these studies; saving the American tale from the American artist.

Let us look at this American artist first. How did he ever get to America, to start with? Why isn't he a European still, like his father before him?

Now listen to me, don't listen to him. He'll tell you the lie you expect. Which is partly your fault for expecting it.

He didn't come in search of freedom of worship. England had more freedom of worship in the year 1700 than America had. Won by Englishmen who wanted freedom, and so stopped at home and fought for it. And got it. Freedom of worship? Read the history of New England during the first century of its existence.

Freedom anyhow? The land of the free! This the land of the free! Why, if I say anything that displeases them, the free mob will lynch me, and that's my freedom. Free? Why I have never been in any country where the individual has such an abject fear of his fellow countrymen. Because, as I say, they are free to lynch him the moment he shows he is not one of them.

No, no, if you're so fond of the truth about Queen Victoria, try a little about yourself.

Those Pilgrim Fathers and their successors never came here for freedom of worship. What did they set up when they got here? Freedom, would you call it?

They didn't come for freedom. Or if they did, they sadly went back on themselves.

All right then, what did they come for? For lots of reasons. Perhaps least of all in search of freedom of any sort: positive freedom, that is.

They came largely to get *away*—that most simple of motives. To get away. Away from what? In the long run, away from themselves. Away from everything. That's why most people have come to America, and still do come. To get away from everything they are and have been.

"Henceforth be masterless."

Which is all very well, but it isn't freedom. Rather the reverse. A hopeless sort of constraint. It is never freedom till you find something you really *positively want to be.* And people in America have always been shouting about the things they are *not.* Unless of course they are millionaires, made or in the making.

And after all there is a positive side to the movement. All that vast flood of human life that has flowed over the Atlantic in ships from Europe to America has not flowed over simply on a tide of revulsion from Europe and from the confinements of the European ways of life. This revulsion was, and still is, I believe, the prime motive in emigration. But there was some cause, even for the revulsion.

It seems as if at times man had a frenzy for getting away from any control of any sort. In Europe the old Christianity was the real master. The Church and the true aristocracy bore the responsibility for the working out of the Christian ideals: a little irregularly, maybe, but responsible nevertheless.

Mastery, kingship, fatherhood had their power destroyed at the time of the Renaissance.

And it was precisely at this moment that the great drift over the Atlantic started. What were men drifting away from? The old authority of Europe? Were they breaking the bonds of authority, and escaping to a new more absolute unrestrainedness? Maybe. But there was more to it.

Liberty is all very well, but men cannot live without masters. There is always a master. And men either live in glad obedience to the master they believe in, or they live in a frictional opposition to the master they wish to undermine. In America this frictional opposition has been the vital factor. It has given the Yankee his kick. Only the continual influx of more servile Europeans has provided America with an obedient labouring class. The true obedience never outlasting the first generation.

But there sits the old master over in Europe. Like a parent. Somewhere deep in every American heart lies a rebellion against the old parenthood of Europe. Yet no American feels he has completely escaped its mastery. Hence the slow, smouldering patience of American opposition. The slow, smouldering, corrosive obedience to the old master Europe, the unwilling subject, the unremitting opposition.

Whatever else you are, be masterless.

> "Ca Ca Caliban
> Get a new master, be a new man."

Escaped slaves, we might say, people the republics of Liberia or Haiti. Liberia enough! Are we to look at America in the same way? A vast republic of escaped slaves. When you consider the hordes from eastern Europe, you might well say it: a vast republic of escaped slaves. But one dare not say this of the Pilgrim Fathers, and the great old body of idealist Americans, the modern Americans tortured with thought. A vast republic of escaped slaves. Look out, America! And a minority of earnest, self-tortured people.

The masterless.

> "Ca Ca Caliban
> Get a new master, be a new man."

What did the Pilgrim Fathers come for, then, when they came so gruesomely over the black sea? Oh, it was in a black spirit. A black revulsion from Europe, from the old authority of Europe, from kings and bishops and popes. And more. When you look into it, more. They were black, masterful men, they wanted something else. No kings, no bishops maybe. Even no God Almighty. But also, no more of this new "humanity" which followed the Renaissance. None of this new liberty which was to be so pretty in Europe. Something grimmer, by no means free-and-easy.

America has never been easy, and is not easy to-day. Americans have always been at a certain tension. Their liberty is a thing of sheer will, sheer tension: a liberty of THOU SHALT NOT. And it has been so from the first. The land of THOU SHALT NOT. Only the first commandment is: THOU SHALT NOT PRESUME TO BE A MASTER. Hence democracy.

"We are the masterless." That is what the American Eagle shrieks. It's a Hen-Eagle.

The Spaniards refused the post-Renaissance liberty of Europe. And the Spaniards filled most of America. The Yankees, too, refused, refused the post-Renaissance humanism of Europe. First and foremost, they hated masters. But under that, they hated the flowing ease of humour in Europe. At the bottom of the American soul was always a dark suspense, at the bottom of the Spanish-American soul the same. And this dark suspense hated and hates the old European spontaneity, watches it collapse with satisfaction.

Every continent has its own great spirit of place. Every people is polarized in some particular locality, which is home, the homeland. Different places on the face of the earth have different vital effluence, different vibration, different chemical exhalation, different polarity with different stars: call it what you like. But the spirit of place is a great reality. The Nile valley produced not only the corn, but the terrific religions of Egypt. China produces the Chinese, and will go on doing so. The Chinese in San Francisco will in time cease to be Chinese, for America is a great melting pot.

There was a tremendous polarity in Italy, in the city of Rome. And this seems to have died. For even places die. The Island of Great Britain had a wonderful terrestrial magnetism or polarity of its own, which made the British people. For the moment, this polarity seems to be breaking. Can England die? And what if England dies?

Men are less free than they imagine; ah, far less free. The freest are perhaps least free.

Men are free when they are in a living homeland, not when they are straying and breaking away. Men are free when they are obeying some deep, inward voice of religious belief. Obeying from within. Men are free when they belong to a living, organic, *believing* community, active in fulfilling some unfulfilled, perhaps unrealized purpose. Not when they are escaping to some wild west. The most unfree souls go west, and shout of freedom. Men are freest when they are most unconscious of freedom. The shout is a rattling of chains, always was.

Men are not free when they are doing just what they like. The moment you can do just what you like, there is nothing you care about doing. Men are only free when they are doing what the deepest self likes.

And there is getting down to the deepest self! It takes some diving.

Because the deepest self is way down and the conscious self is an obstinate monkey. But of one thing we may be sure. If one wants to be free, one has to give up the illusion of doing what one likes, and seek what IT wishes done.

But before you can do what IT likes, you must first break the spell of the old mastery, the old IT.

Perhaps at the Renaissance, when kingship and fatherhood fell, Europe drifted into a very dangerous half-truth: of liberty and equality. Perhaps the men who went to America felt this, and so repudiated the old world altogether. Went one better than Europe. Liberty in America has meant so far the breaking away from *all* dominion. The true liberty will only begin when Americans discover IT, and proceed possibly to fulfill IT. IT being the deepest *whole* self of man, the self in its wholeness, not idealistic halfness.

That's why the Pilgrim Fathers came to America, then; and that's why we come. Driven by IT. We cannot see that invisible winds carry us, as they carry swarms of locusts, that invisible magnetism brings us as it brings the migrating birds to their unforeknown goal. But it is so. We are not the marvellous choosers and deciders we think we are. IT chooses for us, and decides for us. Unless of course we are just escaped slaves, vulgarly cocksure of our ready-made destiny. But if we are living people, in touch with the source, IT drives us and decides us. We are free only so long as we obey. When we run counter, and think we will do as we like, we just flee around like Orestes pursued by the Eumenides.

And still, when the great day begins, when Americans have at last discovered America and their own wholeness, still there will be the vast number of escaped slaves to reckon with, those who have no cocksure, ready-made destinies.

Which will win in America, the escaped slaves, or the new whole men?

The real American day hasn't begun yet. Or at least, not yet sunrise. So far it has been the false dawn. That is, in the progressive American consciousness there has been the one dominant desire, to do away with the old thing. Do away with masters, exalt the will of the people. The will of the people being nothing but a figment, the exalting doesn't count for much. So, in the name of the will of the people, get rid of masters. When you have got rid of masters, you are left with this mere phrase of the will of the people. Then you pause and bethink yourself, and try to recover your own wholeness.

So much for the conscious American motive, and for democracy over here. Democracy in America is just the tool with which the old mastery of Europe, the European spirit, is undermined. Europe destroyed, potentially, American democracy will evaporate. America will begin.

American consciousness has so far been a false dawn. The negative ideal of democracy. But underneath, and contrary to this open ideal, the first hints and revelations of IT. IT, the American whole soul.

You have got to pull the democratic and idealistic clothes off American utterance, and see what you can of the dusky body of IT underneath.

"Henceforth be masterless."

Henceforth be mastered.

David Herbert Lawrence is best known for his novels and stories from *Sons and Lovers* (1913) on, but he was also a poet and essayist, writing with a fine sense of place, atmosphere, and meaning such studies as *Twilight in Italy* and *Mornings in Mexico,* and *Fantasia of the Unconscious.*

Tradition and the individual talent

FROM *The Sacred Wood*
BY *T. S. Eliot (1888-1965)*

I

In English writing we seldom speak of tradition, though we occasionally apply its name in deploring its absence. We cannot refer to "the tradition" or to "a tradition"; at most, we employ the adjective in saying that the poetry of So-and-so is "traditional" or even "too traditional." Seldom, perhaps, does the word appear except in a phrase of censure. If otherwise, it is vaguely approbative, with the implication, as to the work approved, of some pleasing archaeological reconstruction. You can hardly make the word agreeable to English ears without this comfortable reference to the reassuring science of archaeology.

Certainly the word is not likely to appear in our appreciations of living or dead writers. Every nation, every race, has not only its own creative, but its own critical turn of mind; and is even more oblivious of the shortcomings and limitations of its critical habits than of those of its creative genius. We know, or think we know, from the enormous mass of critical writing that has appeared in the French language the critical method or habit of the French; we only conclude (we are such unconscious people) that the French are "more critical" than we, and sometimes even plume ourselves a little with the fact, as if the French were the less spontaneous. Perhaps they are; but we might remind ourselves that criticism is as inevitable as breathing, and that we should be none the worse for articulating what passes in our minds when we read a book and feel an emotion about it, for criticizing our own minds in their work of criticism. One of the facts that might come to light in this process is our tendency to insist, when we praise a poet, upon those aspects of his work in which he least resembles anyone else. In these aspects or parts of his work we pretend to find what is individual, what is the peculiar essence of the man. We dwell with satisfaction upon the poet's difference from his predecessors, especially his immediate predecessors; we endeavour to find something that can be isolated in order to be enjoyed. Whereas if we approach a poet without this prejudice we shall often find that not only the best, but the most individual parts of his work may be those in which the dead poets, his ancestors, assert their immortality most vigorously. And I do not mean the impressionable period of adolescence, but the period of full maturity.

Yet if the only form of tradition, of handing down, consisted in following the ways of the immediate generation before us in a blind or timid adherence to its successes, "tradition" should positively be discouraged. We have seen many such simple currents soon lost in the sand; and novelty is better than repetition. Tradition is a matter of much wider significance. It cannot be inherited, and if you want it you must obtain it by great labour. It involves, in the first place, the historical sense, which we may call nearly indispensable to anyone who would continue to be a poet beyond his twenty-fifth year; and the historical sense involves a perception, not only of the pastness of the past, but of its presence; the historical sense compels a man to write not merely with his own generation in his bones, but with a feeling that the whole of the literature of Europe from Homer and within it the whole of the literature of his own country has a simultaneous existence and composes a simultaneous order. This historical sense, which is a sense of the timeless as well as of the temporal and of the timeless and of the temporal together, is what makes a writer traditional. And it is at the same time what makes a writer most acutely conscious of his place in time, of his contemporaneity.

No poet, no artist of any art, has his complete meaning alone. His significance, his appreciation is the appreciation of his relation to the dead poets and artists. You cannot value him alone; you must set him, for contrast and comparison, among the dead. I mean this as a principle of aesthetic, not merely historical, criticism. The necessity that he shall conform, that he shall cohere, is not one-sided; what happens when a new work of art is created is something that happens simultaneously to all the works of art which preceded it. The existing monuments form an ideal order among themselves, which is modified by the introduction of the new (the really new) work of art among them. The existing order is complete before the new work arrives; for order to persist after the supervention of novelty, the *whole* existing order must be, if ever so slightly, altered; and so the relations, proportions, values of each work of art toward the whole are readjusted; and this is conformity between the old and the new. Whoever has approved this idea of order, of the form of European, of English literature, will not find it preposterous that the past should be altered by the present as much as the present is directed by the past. And the poet who is aware of this will be aware of great difficulties and responsibilities.

In a peculiar sense he will be aware also that he must inevitably be judged by the standards of the past. I say judged, not amputated, by them; not judged to be as good as, or worse or better than, the dead; and certainly not judged by the canons of dead critics. It is a judgment, a comparison, in which two things are measured by each other. To conform merely would be for the new work not really to conform at all; it would not be new, and would therefore not be a work of art. And we do not quite say that the new is more valuable because it fits in; but its fitting in is a test of its value—a test, it is true, which can only be slowly and cautiously applied, for we are none of us infallible judges of conformity. We say: it appears to conform, and is perhaps individual, or it appears individual, and may conform; but we are hardly likely to find that it is one and not the other.

To proceed to a more intelligible exposition of the relation of the poet to the past: he can neither take the past as a lump, an indiscriminate bolus, nor can he form himself wholly on one or two private admirations, nor can he form himself wholly upon one preferred period. The first course is inadmissible, the second is an important experience of youth, and the third is a pleasant and highly desirable supplement. The poet must be very conscious of the main current, which does not at all flow invariably through the most distinguished reputations. He must be quite aware of the obvious fact that art never improves, but that the material of art is never quite the same. He must be aware that the mind of Europe—the mind of his own country—a mind which he learns in time to be much more important than his own private mind—is a mind which changes, and that this change is a development which abandons nothing *en route,* which does not superannuate either Shakespeare, or Homer, or the rock drawing of the Magdalenian[1] draughtsmen. That this development, refinement perhaps, complication certainly, is not, from the point of view of the artist, any improvement. Perhaps not even an improvement from the point of view of the psychologist or not to the extent which we imagine; perhaps only in the end based upon a complication in economics and machinery. But the difference between the present and the past is that the conscious present is an awareness of the past in a way and to an extent which the past's awareness of itself cannot show.

Some one said: "The dead writers are remote from us because we *know* so much more than they did." Precisely, and they are that which we know.

I am alive to a usual objection to what is clearly part of my programme for the *métier*[2] of poetry. The objection is that the doctrine requires a ridiculous amount of erudition (pedantry), a claim which can be rejected by appeal to the lives of poets in any pantheon. It will even be affirmed that much learning deadens or perverts poetic sensibility. While, however, we persist in believing that a poet ought to know as much as will not encroach upon his necessary receptivity and necessary laziness, it is not desirable to confine knowledge to whatever can be put into a useful shape for examinations, drawing-rooms, or the still more pretentious modes of publicity. Some can absorb knowledge, the more tardy must sweat for it. Shakespeare acquired more essential history from Plu-

[1] of a late period of the Old Stone age: named after La Madeleine in west-central France, where pertinent cave art and tools of polished stone or bone were found

[2] occupation or profession

tarch than most men could from the whole British Museum. What is to be insisted upon is that the poet must develop or procure the consciousness of the past and that he should continue to develop this consciousness throughout his career.

What happens is a continual surrender of himself as he is at the moment to something which is more valuable. The progress of an artist is a continual self-sacrifice, a continual extinction of personality.

There remains to define this process of depersonalization and its relation to the sense of tradition. It is in this depersonalization that art may be said to approach the condition of science. I shall, therefore, invite you to consider, as a suggestive analogy, the action which takes place when a bit of finely filiated platinum is introduced into a chamber containing oxygen and sulphur dioxide.

II

Honest criticism and sensitive appreciation is directed not upon the poet but upon the poetry. If we attend to the confused cries of the newspaper critics and the susurrus of popular repetition that follows, we shall hear the names of poets in great numbers; if we seek not Blue-book knowledge but the enjoyment of poetry, and ask for a poem, we shall seldom find it. In the last article I tried to point out the importance of the relation of the poem to other poems by other authors, and suggested the conception of poetry as a living whole of all the poetry that has ever been written. The other aspect of this Impersonal theory of poetry is the relation of the poem to its author. And I hinted, by an analogy, that the mind of the mature poet differs from that of the immature one not precisely in any valuation of "personality," not being necessarily more interesting, or having "more to say," but rather by being a more finely perfected medium in which special, or very varied, feelings are at liberty to enter into new combinations.

The analogy was that of the catalyst. When the two gases previously mentioned are mixed in the presence of a filament of platinum, they form sulphurous acid. This combination takes place only if the platinum is present; nevertheless the newly formed acid contains no trace of platinum, and the platinum itself is apparently unaffected; has remained inert, neutral, and unchanged. The mind of the poet is the shred of platinum. It may partly or exclusively operate upon the experience of the man himself; but, the more perfect the artist, the more completely separate in him will be the man who suffers and the mind which creates; the more perfectly will the mind digest and transmute the passions which are its material.

The experience, you will notice, the elements which enter the presence of the transforming catalyst, are of two kinds: emotions and feelings. The effect of a work of art upon the person who enjoys it is an experience different in kind from any experience not of art. It may be formed out of one emotion, or may be a combination of several; and various feelings, inhering for the writer in particular words or phrases or images, may be added to compose the final result. Or great poetry may be made without the direct use of any emotion whatever: composed out of feelings solely. Canto XV of the *Inferno* (Brunetto Latini) is a working up of the emotion evident in the situation; but the effect, though single as that of any work of art, is obtained by considerable complexity of detail. The last quatrain gives an image, a feeling attaching to an image, which "came," which did not develop simply out of what precedes, but which was probably in suspension in the poet's mind until the proper combination arrived for it to add itself to. The poet's mind is in fact a receptacle for seizing and storing up numberless feelings, phrases, images, which remain there until all the particles which can unite to form a new compound are present together.

If you compare several representative passages of the greatest poetry you see how great is the variety of types of combination, and also how completely any semi-ethical criterion of "sublimity" misses the mark. For it is not the "greatness," the intensity, of the emotions, the components, but the intensity of the artistic process, the pressure, so to speak, under which the fusion takes place, that counts. The episode of Paolo and Francesca[3] employs a definite emotion, but the intensity of the poetry is something quite different from whatever intensity in the supposed experience it may give the impression of. It is no more intense, furthermore, than Canto

[3]Francesca da Rimini and Paolo Malatesta, whose love makes up an episode in the "Inferno" of Dante's *Divina Commedia*

XXVI, the voyage of Ulysses, which has not the direct dependence upon an emotion. Great variety is possible in the process of transmutation of emotion: the murder of Agamemnon, or the agony of Othello, gives an artistic effect apparently closer to a possible original than the scenes from Dante. In the *Agamemnon,* the artistic emotion approximates to the emotion of an actual spectator; in *Othello* to the emotion of the protagonist himself. But the difference between art and the event is always absolute; the combination which is the murder of Agamemnon is probably as complex as that which is the voyage of Ulysses. In either case there has been a fusion of elements. The ode of Keats contains a number of feelings which have nothing particular to do with the nightingale, but which the nightingale, partly, perhaps, because of its attractive name, and partly because of its reputation, served to bring together.

The point of view which I am struggling to attack is perhaps related to the metaphysical theory of the substantial unity of the soul: for my meaning is, that the poet has, not a "personality" to express, but a particular medium, which is only a medium and not a personality, in which impressions and experiences combine in peculiar and unexpected ways. Impressions and experiences which are important for the man may take no place in the poetry, and those which become important in the poetry may play quite a negligible part in the man, the personality.

I will quote a passage which is unfamiliar enough to be regarded with fresh attention in the light—or darkness—of these observations:

> And now methinks I could e'en chide myself
> For doting on her beauty, though her death
> Shall be revenged after no common action.
> Does the silkworm expend her yellow labours
> For thee? For thee does she undo herself?
> Are lordships sold to maintain ladyships
> For the poor benefit of a bewildering minute?
> Why does yon fellow falsify highways,
> And put his life between the judge's lips,
> To refine such a thing—keeps horse and men
> To beat their valours for her? . . .

In this passage (as is evident if it is taken in its context) there is a combination of positive and negative emotions: an intensely strong attraction toward beauty and an equally intense fascination by the ugliness which is contrasted with it and which destroys it. This balance of contrasted emotion is in the dramatic situation to which the speech is pertinent, but that situation alone is inadequate to it. This is, so to speak, the structural emotion, provided by the drama. But the whole effect, the dominant tone, is due to the fact that a number of floating feelings, having an affinity to this emotion by no means superficially evident, have combined with it to give us a new art emotion.

It is not in his personal emotions, the emotions provoked by particular events in his life, that the poet is in any way remarkable or interesting. His particular emotions may be simple, or crude, or flat. The emotion in his poetry will be a very complex thing, but not with the complexity of the emotions of people who have very complex or unusual emotions in life. One error, in fact, of eccentricity in poetry is to seek for new human emotions to express; and in this search for novelty in the wrong place it discovers the perverse. The business of the poet is not to find new emotions, but to use the ordinary ones and, in working them up into poetry, to express feelings which are not in actual emotions at all. And emotions which he has never experienced will serve his turn as well as those familiar to him. Consequently, we must believe that "emotion recollected in tranquillity"[4] is an inexact formula. For it is neither emotion, nor recollection, nor, without distortion of meaning, tranquillity. It is a concentration, and a new thing resulting from the concentration, of a very great number of experiences which to the practical and active person would not seem to be experiences at all; it is a concentration which does not happen consciously or of deliberation. These experiences are not "recollected," and they finally unite in an atmosphere which is "tranquil" only in that it is a passive attending upon the event. Of course this is not quite the whole story. There is a great deal, in the writing of poetry, which must be conscious and deliberate. In fact, the bad poet is usually unconscious where he ought to be conscious, and conscious where he ought to be unconscious. Both errors tend to make him "personal."

[4]Wordsworth's phrase for poetry

Poetry is not a turning loose of emotion, but an escape from emotion; it is not the expression of personality, but an escape from personality. But, of course, only those who have personality and emotions know what it means to want to escape from these things.

III

ὁ δὲ νοῦς, ἴσως, θειότερόν τι καὶ ἀπαθές ἐστιν[5]

This essay proposes to halt at the frontier of metaphysics or mysticism, and confine itself to such practical conclusions as can be applied by the responsible person interested in poetry. To divert interest from the poet to the poetry is a laudable aim: for it would conduce to a juster estimation of actual poetry, good and bad. There are many people who appreciate the expression of sincere emotion in verse, and there is a smaller number of people who can appreciate technical excellence. But very few know when there is expression of *significant* emotion, emotion which has its life in the poem and not in the history of the poet. The emotion of art is impersonal. And the poet cannot reach this impersonality without surrendering himself wholly to the work to be done. And he is not likely to know what is to be done unless he lives in what is not merely the present, but the present moment of the past, unless he is conscious, not of what is dead, but of what is already living.

[5] But the mind, perhaps, is more divine and indifferent

§ T. S. Eliot was born in Missouri, educated in philosophy at Harvard and in Europe, became editor of *the Criterion* in London, and starting in 1917 published poems *(Waste Land, Four Quartets)*, plays *(Family Reunion, The Cocktail Party)*, and essays *(The Sacred Wood, Notes Toward a Definition of Culture)*.

Shooting an elephant

FROM *Shooting an Elephant, and Other Essays (1945)*
BY *George Orwell (1903-1950)*

In Moulmein, in Lower Burma, I was hated by large numbers of people – the only time in my life that I have been important enough for this to happen to me. I was sub-divisional police officer of the town, and in an aimless, petty kind of way anti-European feeling was very bitter. No one had the guts to raise a riot, but if a European woman went through the bazaars alone somebody would probably spit betel juice over her dress. As a police officer I was an obvious target and was baited whenever it seemed safe to do so. When a nimble Burman tripped me up on the football field and the referee (another Burman) looked the other way, the crowd yelled with hideous laughter. This happened more than once. In the end the sneering yellow faces of young men that met me everywhere, the insults hooted after me when I was at a safe distance, got badly on my nerves. The young Buddhist priests were the worst of all. There were several thousands of them in the town and none of them seemed to have anything to do except stand on street corners and jeer at Europeans.

All this was perplexing and upsetting. For at that time I had already made up my mind that imperialism was an evil thing and the sooner I chucked up my job and got out of it the better. Theoretically – and secretly, of course – I was all for the Burmese and all against their oppressors, the British. As for the job I was doing, I hated it more bitterly than I can perhaps make clear. In a job like that you see the dirty work of Empire at close quarters. The wretched prisoners huddling in the stinking cages of the lock-ups, the grey, cowed faces of the long-term convicts, the scarred buttocks of the men who had been flogged with bamboos—all these oppressed me with an intolerable sense of guilt. But I could get nothing into perspective. I was young and ill-educated and I had had to think out my problems in the utter silence that is imposed on every Englishman in the East. I did not even know that the British Empire is dying, still less did I know that it is a great deal better than the younger empires that are going to supplant it. All I knew was that I was stuck between my hatred of the empire I served and my rage against the evil-spirited little beasts who tried to make my job impossible. With one part of my mind I thought of the British Raj[1] as an unbreakable tyranny, as something clamped down, *in saecula saeculorum,* upon the will of prostrate peoples; with another part I thought that the greatest joy in the world would be to drive a bayonet into a Buddhist priest's guts. Feelings like these are the normal by-products of imperialism; ask any Anglo-Indian offical, if you can catch him off duty.

One day something happened which in a roundabout way was enlightening. It was a tiny incident in itself, but it gave me a better glimpse than I had had before of the real nature of imperialism—the real motives for which despotic governments act. Early one morning the sub-inspector at a police station the other end of the town rang me up on the 'phone and said that an elephant was ravaging the bazaar. Would I please come and do something about it? I did not know what I could do, but I wanted to see what was happening and I got on to a pony and started out. I took my rifle, an old .44 Winchester and much too small to kill an elephant, but I thought the noise might be useful *in terrorem.*[2] Various Burmans stopped me on the way and told me about the elephant's doings. It was not, of course, a wild elephant, but a tame one which had gone "must."[3] It had been chained up, as tame elephants always are when their attack of "must" is due, but on the previous night it had

[1] in India, rule [2] for causing fright

[3] state of frenzy in an animal, especially the male elephant

broken its chain and escaped. Its mahout,[4] the only person who could manage it when it was in that state, had set out in pursuit, but had taken the wrong direction and was now twelve hours' journey away, and in the morning the elephant had suddenly reappeared in the town. The Burmese population had no weapons and were quite helpless against it. It had already destroyed somebody's bamboo hut, killed a cow and raided some fruit-stalls and devoured the stock; also it had met the municipal rubbish van and, when the driver jumped out and took to his heels, had turned the van over and inflicted violences upon it.

The Burmese sub-inspector and some Indian constables were waiting for me in the quarter where the elephant had been seen. It was a very poor quarter, a labyrinth of squalid bamboo huts, thatched with palmleaf, winding all over a steep hillside. I remember that it was a cloudy, stuffy morning at the beginning of the rains. We began questioning the people as to where the elephant had gone and, as usual, failed to get any definite information. That is invariably the case in the East; a story always sounds clear enough at a distance, but the nearer you get to the scene of events the vaguer it becomes. Some of the people said that the elephant had gone in one direction, some said that he had gone in another, some professed not even to have heard of any elephant. I had almost made up my mind that the whole story was a pack of lies, when we heard yells a little distance away. There was a loud, scandalized cry of "Go away, child! Go away this instant!" and an old woman with a switch in her hand came round the corner of a hut, violently shooing away a crowd of naked children. Some more women followed, clicking their tongues and exclaiming; evidently there was something that the children ought not to have seen. I rounded the hut and saw a man's dead body sprawling in the mud. He was an Indian, a black Dravidian[5] coolie, almost naked, and he could not have been dead many minutes. The people said that the elephant had come suddenly upon him round the corner of the hut, caught him with its trunk, put its foot on his back and ground him into the earth. This was the rainy season and the ground was soft, and his face had scored a trench a foot deep and a couple of yards long. He was lying

[4]elephant driver or elephant keeper

[5]member of a group of intermixed races in southern India and southern Ceylon

on his belly with arms crucified and head sharply twisted to one side. His face was coated with mud, the eyes wide open, the teeth bared and grinning with an expression of unendurable agony. (Never tell me, by the way, that the dead look peaceful. Most of the corpses I have seen looked devilish.) The friction of the great beast's foot had stripped the skin from his back as neatly as one skins a rabbit. As soon as I saw the dead man I sent an orderly to a friend's house nearby to borrow an elephant rifle. I had already sent back the pony, not wanting it to go mad with fright and throw me if it smelt the elephant.

The orderly came back in a few minutes with a rifle and five cartridges, and meanwhile some Burmans had arrived and told us that the elephant was in the paddy fields below, only a few hundred yards away. As I started forward practically the whole population of the quarter flocked out of the houses and followed me. They had seen the rifle and were all shouting excitedly that I was going to shoot the elephant. They had not shown much interest in the elephant when he was merely ravaging their homes, but it was different now that he was going to be shot. It was a bit of fun to them, as it would be to an English crowd; besides they wanted the meat. It made me vaguely uneasy. I had no intention of shooting the elephant – I had merely sent for the rifle to defend myself if necessary – and it is always unnerving to have a crowd following you. I marched down the hill, looking and feeling a fool, with the rifle over my shoulder and an ever-growing army of people jostling at my heels. At the bottom, when you got away from the huts, there was a metalled road and beyond that a miry waste of paddy fields a thousand yards across, not yet ploughed but soggy from the first rains and dotted with coarse grass. The elephant was standing eight yards from the road, his left side towards us. He took not the slightest notice of the crowd's approach. He was tearing up bunches of grass, beating them against his knees to clean them and stuffing them into his mouth.

I had halted on the road. As soon as I saw the elephant I knew with perfect certainty that I ought not to shoot him. It is a serious matter to shoot a working elephant – it is comparable to destroying a huge and costly piece of machinery – and obviously one ought not to do it if it can possibly be avoided. And at that distance, peacefully eating, the elephant looked no more dangerous than a cow. I thought then and I think now that his attack of "must" was already passing off; in which case he would merely wander harmlessly about until the mahout came back and caught him. Moreover, I did not in the least want to shoot him. I decided that I would watch him for a little while to make sure that he did not turn savage again, and then go home.

But at that moment I glanced round at the crowd that had followed me. It was an immense crowd, two thousand at the least and growing every minute. It blocked the road for a long distance on either side. I looked at the sea of yellow faces above the garish clothes—faces all happy and excited over this bit of fun, all certain that the elephant was going to be shot. They were watching me as they would watch a conjurer about to perform a trick. They did not like me, but with the magical rifle in my hand I was momentarily worth watching. And suddenly I realized that I should have to shoot the elephant after all. The people expected it of me and I had got to do it; I could feel their two thousand wills pressing me forward, irresistibly. And it was at this moment, as I stood there with the rifle in my hands, that I first grasped the hollowness, the futility of the white man's dominion in the East. Here was I, the white man with his gun, standing in front of the unarmed native crowd—seemingly the leading actor of the piece; but in reality I was only an absurd puppet pushed to and fro by the will of those yellow faces behind. I perceived in this moment that when the white man turns tyrant it is his own freedom that he destroys. He becomes a sort of hollow, posing dummy, the conventionalized figure of a sahib. For it is the condition of his rule that he shall spend his life in trying to impress the "natives," and so in every crisis he has got to do what the "natives" expect of him. He wears a mask, and his face grows to fit it. I had got to shoot the elephant. I had committed myself to doing it when I sent for the rifle. A sahib has got to act like a sahib; he has got to appear resolute, to know his own mind and do definite things. To come all that way, rifle in hand, with two thousand people marching at my heels, and then to trail feebly away, having done nothing—no, that was impossible. The crowd would laugh at me. And my whole life, every white man's life in the East, was one long struggle not to be laughed at.

But I did not want to shoot the elephant. I watched him beating his bunch of grass against his knees, with that preoccupied grandmotherly air that elephants have. It seemed to me that it would be murder to shoot him. At that age I was not squeamish about killing animals, but I had never shot an elephant and never wanted to. (Somehow it always seems worse to kill a *large* animal.) Besides, there was the beast's owner to be considered. Alive, the elephant was worth at least a hundred pounds; dead, he would only be worth the value of his tusks, five pounds, possibly. But I had got to act quickly. I turned to some experienced-looking Burmans who had been there when we arrived, and asked them how the elephant had been behaving. They all said the same thing: he took no notice of you if you left him alone, but he might charge if you went too close to him.

It was perfectly clear to me what I ought to do. I ought to walk up to within, say, twenty-five yards of the elephant and test his behavior. If he charged, I could shoot; if he took no notice of me, it would be safe to leave him until the mahout came back. But also I knew that I was going to do no such thing. I was a poor shot with a rifle and the ground was soft mud into which one would sink at every step. If the elephant charged and I missed him, I should have about as much chance as a toad under a steam-roller. But even then I was not thinking particularly of my own skin, only of the watchful yellow faces behind. For at that moment, with the crowd watching me, I was not afraid in the ordinary sense, as I would have been if I had been alone. A white man mustn't be frightened in front of "natives"; and so, in general, he isn't frightened. The sole thought in my mind was that if anything went wrong those two thousand Burmans would see me pursued, caught, trampled on and reduced to a grinning corpse like that Indian up the hill. And if that happened it was quite probable that some of them would laugh. That would never do. There was only one alternative. I shoved the cartridges into the magazine and lay down on the road to get a better aim.

The crowd grew very still, and a deep, low, happy sigh, as of people who see the theatre curtain go up at last, breathed from innumerable throats. They were going to mave their bit of fun after all. The rifle was a beautiful German thing with cross-hair sights. I did not then know that in shooting an elephant one would shoot to cut an imaginary bar running from ear-hole to ear-hole. I ought, therefore, as the elephant was sideways on, to have aimed straight at his ear-hole; actually I aimed several inches in front of this, thinking the brain would be further forward.

When I pulled the trigger I did not hear the bang or feel the kick – one never does when a shot goes home – but I heard the devilish roar of glee that went up from the crowd. In that instant, in too short a time, one would have thought, even for the bullet to get there, a mysterious, terrible change had come over the elephant. He neither stirred nor fell, but every line of his body had altered. He looked suddenly stricken, shrunken, immensely old, as though the frightful impact of the bullet had paralysed him without knocking him down. At last, after what seemed a long time – it might have been five seconds, I dare say – he sagged flabbily to his knees. His mouth slobbered. An enormous senility seemed to have settled upon him. One could have imagined him thousands of years old. I fired again into the same spot. At the second shot he did not collapse but climbed with desperate slowness to his feet and stood weakly upright, with legs sagging and head drooping. I fired a third time. That was the shot that did for him. You could see the agony of it jolt his whole body and knock the last remnant of strength from his legs. But in falling he seemed for a moment to rise, for as his hind legs collapsed beneath him he seemed to tower upward like a huge rock toppling, his trunk reaching skywards like a tree. He trumpeted, for the first and only time. And then down he came, his belly towards me, with a crash that seemed to shake the ground even where I lay.

I got up. The Burmans were already racing past me across the mud. It was obvious that the elephant would never rise again, but he was not dead. He was breathing very rhythmically with long rattling gasps, his great mound of a side painfully rising and falling. His mouth was wide open – I could see far down into caverns of pale pink throat. I waited a long time for him to die, but his breathing did not weaken. Finally I fired my two remaining shots into the spot where I thought his heart must be. The thick blood welled out of him like red velvet, but still he did not die. His body did not even jerk when the shots hit him, the tortured breathing continued without a pause. He was dying, very slowly and in great agony, but in some world remote from me where not even a bullet could damage him further. I felt that I had got to put an end to that dreadful noise. It seemed dreadful to see the great beast lying there, powerless to move and yet powerless to die, and not even to be able to finish him. I sent back for my small rifle and poured shot after shot into his heart and down his throat. They seemed to make no impression. The tortured gasps continued as steadily as the ticking of a clock.

In the end I could not stand it any longer and went away. I heard later that it took him half an hour to die. Burmans were bringing dahs and baskets even before I left, and I was told they had stripped his body almost to the bones by the afternoon.

Afterwards, of course, there were endless discussions about the shooting of the elephant. The owner was furious, but he was only an Indian and could do nothing. Besides, legally I had done the right thing, for a mad elephant has to be killed, like a mad dog, if its owner fails to control it. Among the Europeans opinion was divided. The older men said I was right, the younger men said it was a damn shame to shoot an elephant for killing a coolie, because an elephant was worth more than any damn Coringhee coolie. And afterwards I was very glad that the coolie had been killed; it put me legally in the right and it gave me a sufficient pretext for shooting the elephant. I often wondered whether any of the others grasped that I had done it solely to avoid looking a fool.

George Orwell is the nom de plume of Eric Blair, an Englishman born in India, where his father was a member of the Bengal Civil Service. Rather than go to a university on leaving Eton, he went to Burma to serve for five years in the Imperial Police.

Orwell's interests, largely social and political, show through his best known works, *Burmese Days, Homage to Catalonia, Animal Farm,* and *Nineteen Eighty-four,* a vision of the doom of man under a mechanized totalitarian state.

Prospects in the arts and sciences

FROM *The Open Mind (1960)*

BY ***J. Robert Oppenheimer** (born 1904)*

The words "prospects in the arts and sciences" mean two quite different things to me. One is prophecy: What will the scientists discover and the painters paint, what new forms will alter music, what parts of experience will newly yield to objective description? The other meaning is that of a view: What do we see when we look at the world today and compare it with the past? I am not a prophet; and I cannot very well speak to the first subject, though in many ways I should like to. I shall try to speak to the second, because there are some features of this view which seem to me so remarkable, so new and so arresting, that it may be worth turning our eyes to them; it may even help us to create and shape the future better, though we cannot foretell it.

In the arts and in the sciences, it would be good to be a prophet. It would be a delight to know the future. I had thought for a while of my own field of physics and of those nearest to it in the natural sciences. It would not be too hard to outline the questions which natural scientists today are asking themselves and trying to answer. What, we ask in physics, is matter, what is it made of, how does it behave when it is more and more violently atomized, when we try to pound out of the stuff around us the ingredients which only violence creates and makes manifest? What, the chemist asks, are those special features of nucleic acids and proteins which make life possible and give it its characteristic endurance and mutability? What subtle chemistry, what arrangements, what reactions and controls make the cells of living organisms differentiate so that they may perform functions as oddly diverse as transmitting information throughout our nervous systems or covering our heads with hair? What happens in the brain to make a record of the past, to hide it from consciousness, to make it accessible to recall? What are the physical features which make consciousness possible?

All history teaches us that these questions that we think the pressing ones will be transmuted before they are answered, that they will be replaced by others, and that the very process of discovery will shatter the concepts that we today use to describe our puzzlement.

It is true that there are some who profess to see in matters of culture, in matters precisely of the arts and sciences, a certain macrohistorical pattern, a grand system of laws which determines the course of civilization and gives a kind of inevitable quality to the unfolding of the future. They would, for instance, see the radical, formal experimentation which characterized the music of the last half-century as an inevitable consequence of the immense flowering and enrichment of natural science; they would see a necessary order in the fact that innovation in music precedes that in painting and that in turn in poetry, and point to this sequence in older cultures. They would attribute the formal experimentation of the arts to the dissolution, in an industrial and technical society, of authority—of secular, political authority, and of the catholic authority of the church. They are thus armed to predict the future. But this, I fear, is not my dish.

If a prospect is not a prophecy, it is a view. What does the world of the arts and sciences look like? There are two ways of looking at it: One is the view of the traveler, going by horse or foot, from village to village to town, staying in each to talk with those who live there and to gather something of the quality of its life. This is the intimate view, partial, somewhat accidental, limited by the limited life and strength and curiosity of the traveler, but intimate and human, in a human compass. The other is the vast view, showing the earth with its fields and towns and valleys as they appear to a camera carried in a high-altitude rocket. In one sense this prospect will be more complete; one will see all branches of knowledge, one will see all the arts, one will see them as part of the vastness and complication of the whole of human life on earth. But one will miss a great deal; the beauty and warmth of human life will largely be gone from that prospect.

It is in this vast high-altitude survey that one sees the general surprising quantitative features that distinguish our time. This is where the listings of science and endowments and laboratories and books published show up; this is where we learn that more people are engaged in scientific research today then ever before, that the Soviet world and the free world are running neck and neck in the training of scientists, that more books are published per capita in England than in the United States, that the social sciences are pursued actively in America, Scandinavia, and England, that there are more people who hear the great music of the past, and more music composed and more paintings painted. This is where we learn that the arts and sciences are flourishing. This great map, showing the world from afar and almost as to a stranger, would show more: It would show the immense diversity of culture and life, diversity in place and tradition for the first time clearly manifest on a world-wide scale, diversity in technique and language, separating science from science and art from art, and all of one from all of the other. This great map, world-wide, culture-wide, remote, has some odd features. There are innumerable villages. Between the villages there appear to be almost no paths discernible from this high altitude. Here and there passing near a village, sometimes through its heart, there will be a superhighway, along which windy traffic moves at enormous speed. The superhighways seem to have little connection with villages, starting anywhere, ending anywhere, and sometimes appearing almost by design to disrupt the quiet of the village. This view gives us no sense of order or of unity. To find these we must visit the villages, the quiet, busy places, the laboratories and studies and studios. We must see the paths that are barely discernible; we must understand the superhighways and their dangers.

In the natural sciences these are and have been and are likely to continue to be heroic days. Discovery follows discovery, each both raising and answering questions, each ending a long search, and each providing the new instruments for a new search. There are radical ways of thinking unfamiliar to common sense and connected with it by decades or centuries of increasingly specialized and unfamiliar experience. There are lessons of how limited, for all its variety, the common experience of man has been with regard to natural phenomena, and hints and analogies as to how limited may be his experience with man. Every new finding is a part of the instrument kit of the sciences for further investigation and for penetrating into new fields. Discoveries of knowledge fructify technology and the practical arts, and these in turn pay back refined techniques, new possibilities of observation and experiment.

In any science there is harmony between practitioners. A man may work as an individual, learning of what his colleagues do through reading or conversation; he may be working as a member of a group on problems whose technical equipment is too massive for individual effort. But whether he is a part of a team or solitary in his own study, he, as a professional, is a member of a community. His colleagues in his own branch of science will be grateful to him for the inventive or creative thoughts he has, will welcome his criticism. His world and work will be objectively communicable; and he will be quite sure that if there is error in it, that error will not long be undetected. In his own line of work he lives in a community where common understanding combines with common purpose and interest to bind men together both in freedom and in cooperation.

This experience will make him acutely aware of how limited, how inadequate, how precious is this condition of his life; for in his relations with a wider society, there will be neither the sense of community nor of objective understanding. He will sometimes find, in returning to practical undertakings, some sense of community with men who are not expert in his science, with other scientists whose work is remote from his, and with men of action and men of art. The frontiers of science are separated now by long years of study, by specialized vocabularies, arts, techniques, and knowledge from the common heritage even of a most civilized society; and anyone working at the frontier of such science is in that sense a very long way from home, a long way too from the practical arts that were its matrix and origin, as indeed they were of what we today call art.

The specialization of science is an inevitable accompaniment of progress; yet it is full of dangers, and it is cruelly wasteful, since so much that is beautiful and enlightening is cut off from most of the world. Thus it is proper to the role of the scientist that he not merely find new truth and communicate it to his fellows, but that he teach, that he try to bring the most honest and intelligible account of new knowledge to all who will try to learn. This is one reason—it is the decisive organic reason—why scientists belong in universities. It is one reason why the patronage of science by and through universities is its most proper form; for it is here, in teaching, in the association of scholars and in the friendships of teachers and taught, of men who by profession must themselves be both teachers and taught, that the narrowness of scientific life can best be moderated, and that the analogies, insights, and harmonies of scientific discovery can find their way into the wider life of man.

In the situation of the artist today there are both analogies to and differences from that of the scientist; but it is the differences which are the most striking and which raise the problems that touch most on the evil of our day. For the artist it is not enough that he communicate with others who are expert in his own art. Their fellowship, their understanding, and their appreciation may encourage him; but that is not the end of his work, nor its nature. The artist depends on a common sensibility and culture, on a common meaning of symbols, on a community of experience and common ways of describing and interpreting it. He need not write for everyone or paint or play for everyone. But his audience must be man; it must be man, and not a specialized set of experts among his fellows. Today that is very difficult. Often the artist has an aching sense of great loneliness, for the community to which he addresses himself is largely not there; the traditions and the culture, the symbols and the history, the myths and the common experience, which it is his function to illuminate, to harmonize, and to portray, have been dissolved in a changing world.

There is, it is true, an artificial audience maintained to moderate between the artist and the world for which he works: the audience of the professional critics, popularizers, and advertisers of art. But though, as does the popularizer and promoter of science, the critic fulfills a necessary present function and introduces some order and some communication between the artist and the world, he cannot add to the intimacy and the directness and the depth with which the artist addresses his fellow men.

To the artist's loneliness there is a complementary great and terrible barrenness in the lives of men. They are deprived of the illumination, the light and tenderness and insight of an intelligible interpretation, in contemporary terms, of the sorrows and wonders and gaieties and follies of man's life. This may be in part offset, and is, by the great growth of technical means for making the art of the past available. But these provide a record of past intimacies between art and life; even when they are applied to the writing and painting and composing of the day, they do not bridge the gulf between a society, too vast and too disordered, and the artist trying to give meaning and beauty to its parts.

In an important sense this world of ours is a new world, in which the unity of knowledge, the nature of human communities, the order of society, the order of ideas, the very notions of society and culture have changed and will not return to what they have been in the past. What is new is new not because it has never been there before, but because it has changed in quality. One thing that is new is the prevalence of newness, the changing scale and scope of change itself, so that the world alters as we walk in it, so that the years of man's life measure not some small growth or rearrangement or moderation of what he learned in childhood, but a great upheaval. What is new is that in one generation our knowledge of the natural world engulfs, upsets, and complements all knowledge of the natural world before. The techniques, among which and by which we live, multiply and ramify, so that the whole world is bound together by communication, blocked here and there by the immense synapses of political tyranny. The global quality of the world is new: our knowledge of and sympathy with remote and diverse people, our involvement with them in practical terms, and our commitment to them in terms of brotherhood. What is new in the world is the massive character of the dissolution and corruption of authority, in belief, in ritual, and in temporal order. Yet this is the world that we have come to live in. The very difficulties which it presents derive from growth in understanding, in skill, in power. To assail the changes that have unmoored us from the past is futile, and in a deep sense, I think, it is wicked. We need to recognize the change and learn what resources we have.

Again I will turn to the schools and, as their end and as their center, the universities. For the problem of the scientist is in this respect not different from that of the artist or of the historian. He needs to be a part of the community, and the community can only with loss and peril be without him. Thus it is with a sense of interest and hope that we see a growing recognition that the creative artist is a proper charge on the university, and the university a proper home for him; that a composer or a poet or a playwright or painter needs the toleration, understanding, the rather local and parochial patronage that a university can give; and that this will protect him from the tyranny of man's communication and professional promotion. For here there is an honest chance that what the artist has of insight and of beauty will take root in the community, and that some intimacy and some human bonds can mark his relations with his patrons. For a university rightly and inherently is a place where the individual man can form new syntheses, where the accidents of friendship and association can open a man's eyes to a part of science or art which he had not known before, where parts of human life, remote and perhaps superficially incompatible, can find in men their harmony and their synthesis.

These, then, in rough and far too general words, are some of the things we see as we walk through the villages of the arts and of the sciences and notice how thin are the paths that lead from one to another, and how little in terms of human understanding and pleasure the work of the villages comes to be shared outside.

The superhighways do not help. They are the mass media—from the loud-speakers in the deserts of Asia Minor and the cities of Communist China to the organized professional theater of Broadway. They are the purveyors of art and science and culture for the millions upon millions—the promoters who represent the arts and sciences to humanity and who represent humanity to the arts and sciences; they are the means by which we are reminded of the famine in remote places or of war or trouble or change; they are the means by which the great earth and its peoples have become one to one another, the means by which the news of discovery or honor and the stories and songs of today travel and resound throughout the world. But they are also the means by which the true human community, the man knowing man, the neighbor understanding neighbor, the schoolboy learning a poem, the woman dancing, the individual curiosity, the individual sense of beauty are being blown dry and issueless, the means by which the passivity of the disengaged spectator presents to the man of art and science the bleak face of unhumanity.

For the truth is that this is indeed, inevitably and increasingly, an open and, inevitably and increasingly, an eclectic world. We know too much for one man to know much, we live too variously to live as one. Our histories and traditions – the very means of interpreting life – are both bonds and barriers among us. Our knowledge separates as well as it unites; our orders disintegrate as well as bind; our art brings us together and sets us apart. The artist's loneliness, the scholar despairing because no one will any longer trouble to learn what he can teach, the narrowness of the scientist – these are unnatural insignia in this great time of change.

For what is asked of us is not easy. The openness of this world derives its character from the irreversibility of learning; what is once learned is part of human life. We cannot close our minds to discovery; we cannot stop our ears so that the voices of far-off and strange people can no longer reach them. The great cultures of the East cannot be walled off from ours by impassable seas and defects of understanding based on ignorance and unfamiliarity. Neither our integrity as men of learning nor our humanity allows that. In this open world, what is there, any man may try to learn.

This is no new problem. There has always been more to know than one man could know; there have always been modes of feeling that could not move the same heart; there have always been deeply held beliefs that could not be composed into a synthetic union. Yet never before today have the diversity, the complexity, the richness so clearly defied hierarchical order and simplification; never before have we had to understand the complementary, mutually not compatible ways of life and recognize choice between them as the only course of freedom. Never before today has the integrity of the intimate, the detailed, the true art, the integrity of craftsmanship and the preservation of the familiar, of the humorous and the beautiful stood in more massive contrast to the vastness of life, the greatness of the globe, the otherness of people, the otherness of ways, and the all-encompassing dark.

This is a world in which each of us, knowing his limitations, knowing the evils of superficiality and the terrors of fatigue, will have to cling to what is close to him, to what he knows, to what he can do, to his friends and his tradition and his love, lest he be dissolved in a universal confusion and know nothing and love nothing. It is at the same time a world in which none of us can find hieratic prescription or general sanction for any ignorance, any insensitivity, any indifference. When a friend tells us of a new discovery we may not understand, we may not be able to listen without jeopardizing the work that is ours and closer to us; but we cannot find in a book or canon—and we should not seek—grounds for hallowing our ignorance. If a man tells us that he sees differently than we, or that he finds beautiful what we find ugly, we may have to leave the room, from fatigue or trouble; but that is our weakness and our default. If we must live with a perpetual sense that the world and the men in it are greater than we and too much for us, let it be the measure of our virtue that we know this and seek no comfort. Above all, let us not proclaim that the limits of our powers correspond to some special wisdom in our choice of life, of learning, or of beauty.

This balance, this perpetual, precarious, impossible balance between the infinitely open and the intimate, this time—our twentieth century—has been long in coming; but it has come. It is, I think, for us and our children, our only way.

This is for all men. For the artist and for the scientist there is a special problem and a special hope, for in their extraordinarily different ways, in their lives that have increasingly divergent character, there is still a sensed bond, a sensed analogy. Both the man of science and the man of art live always at the edge of mystery, surrounded by it; both always, as the measure of their creation, have had to do with the harmonization of what is new with what is familiar, with the balance between novelty and synthesis, with the struggle to make partial order in total chaos. They can, in their work and in their lives, help themselves, help one another, and help all men. They can make the paths that connect the villages of arts and sciences with each other and with the world at large the multiple, varied, precious bonds of a true and world-wide community.

This cannot be an easy life. We shall have a rugged time of it to keep our minds open and to keep them deep, to keep our sense of beauty and our ability to make it, and our occasional ability to see it in places remote and strange and unfamiliar; we shall have a rugged time of it, all of us, in keeping these gardens in our villages, in keeping open the manifold, intricate, casual paths, to keep these flourishing in a great, open, windy world; but this, as I see it, is the condition of man; and in this condition we can help, because we can love, one another.

Julius Robert Oppenheimer has taught physics at the University of California at Berkeley, and the California Institute of Technology, and is head of the Institute for Advanced Studies at Princeton. Known for his leadership of the project to develop the atomic bomb at Los Alamos, New Mexico, he received the Atomic Energy Commission's Enrico Fermi Award in 1963.

Meditations on a hobby horse or the roots of artistic form

FROM *Meditations on a Hobby Horse and Other Essays on the Theory of Art (1963)*

BY *E. H. Gombrich (born 1909)*

The subject of this article is a very ordinary hobby horse. It is neither metaphorical nor purely imaginary, at least not more so than the broomstick on which Swift[1] wrote his meditations. It is usually content with its place in the corner of the nursery and it has no aesthetic ambitions. Indeed it abhors frills. It is satisfied with its broomstick body and its crudely carved head which just marks the upper end and serves as holder for the reins. How should we address it? Should we describe it as an "image of a horse"? The compliers of the *Pocket Oxford Dictionary* would hardly have agreed. They defined *image* as "imitation of object's external form" and the "external form" of a horse is surely not "imitated" here. So much the worse, we might say, for the "external form," that elusive remnant of the Greek Philosophical tradition which has dominated our aesthetic language for so long. Luckily there is another word in the *dictionary* which might prove more accommodating: *representation.* To *represent,* we read, can be used in the sense of "call up by description or portrayal or imagination, figure, place likeness of before mind or senses, serve or be meant as likeness of . . . stand for, be specimen of, fill place of, be substitute for." A portrayal of a horse?

[1]Jonathan Swift (1667-1745), see p. 124

Surely not. A substitute for a horse? Yes. That it is. Perhaps there is more in this formula than meets the eye.

I

Let us first ride our wooden steed into battle against a number of ghosts which still haunt the language of art criticism. One of them we even found entrenched in the *Oxford Dictionary.* The implication of its definition of an image is that the artist "imitates" the "external form" of the object in front of him, and the beholder, in his turn, recognizes the "subject" of the work of art by this "form." This is what might be called the traditional view of representation. Its corollary is that a work of art will either be a faithful copy, in fact a complete replica, of the object represented, or will involve some degree of "abstraction." The artist, we read, abstracts the "form" from the object he sees. The sculptor usually abstracts the three-dimensional form, and abstracts *from* colour; the painter abstracts contours and colours, and *from* the third dimension. In this context one hears it said that the draughtsman's line is a "tremendous feat of abstraction" because it does not "occur in nature." A modern sculptor of Brancusi's[2] persuasion may be praised or blamed for "carrying abstraction to its logical extreme." Finally the label of "abstract art" for the creation of "pure" forms carries with it a similar implication. Yet we need only look at our hobby horse to see that the very idea of abstraction as a complicated mental act lands us in curious absurdities. There is an old music hall joke describing a drunkard who politely lifts his hat to every lamp-post he passes. Should we say that the liquor has so increased his power of abstraction that he is now able to isolate the formal quality of uprightness from both lamp-post and the human figure? Our mind, of course, works by differentiation rather than by generalization, and the child will for long call all four-footers of a certain size "gee-gee" before it learns to distinguish breeds and "forms"!

II

Then there is that age-old problem of universals as applied to art. It has received its classical formulation in the Platonizing theories of

[2]Constantin Brancusi (born 1876), Rumanian abstract sculptor

the Academicians.[3] "A history-painter," says Reynolds,[4] "paints men in general; a portrait-painter a particular man, and therefore a defective model." This, of course, is the theory of abstraction applied to one specific problem. The implications are that the portrait, being an exact copy of a man's "external form" with all "blemishes" and "accidents," refers to the individual person exactly as does the proper name. The painter, however, who wants to "elevate his style" disregards the particular and "generalizes the forms." Such a picture will no longer represent a particular man but rather the class or concept "man." There is a deceptive simplicity in this argument, but it makes at least one unwarranted assumption: that every image of this kind necessarily refers to something outside itself—be it individual or class. But nothing of the kind need be implied when we point to an image and say "this is a man." Strictly speaking that statement may be interpreted to mean that the image itself is a member of the class "man." Nor is that interpretation as farfetched as it may sound. In fact our hobby horse would submit to no other interpretation. By the logic of Reynolds's reasoning it would have to represent the most generalized idea of horseness. But if the child calls a stick a horse it obviously means nothing of the kind. The stick is neither a sign signifying the concept horse nor is it a portrait of an individual horse. By its capacity to serve as a "substitute" the stick becomes a horse in its own right, it belongs in the class of "gee-gees" and may even merit a proper name of its own.

When Pygmalion[5] blocked out a figure from his marble he did not at first represent a "generalized" human form, and then gradually a particular woman. For as he chipped away and made it more lifelike the block was not turned into a portrait—not even in the unlikely case that he used a live model. So when his prayers were heard and the statue came to life she was Galatea and no one else—and that regardless of whether she had been fashioned in an archaic, idealistic, or naturalistic style. The question of reference, in fact, is

[3] a usually pejorative term for those who claim that art concerns the universal and the general, rather than the particular

[4] Sir Joshua Reynolds (1723-1792), English painter

[5] in Greek mythology, Pygmalion was a Cyprian king who carved an ivory statue of Galatea and fell in love with it. In answer to his prayer, Aphrodite brought the statue to life and he married Galatea

totally independent of the degree of differentiation. The witch who made a "generalized" wax dummy of an enemy may have meant it to refer to someone in particular. She would then pronounce the right spell to establish this link—much as we may write a caption under a generalized picture to do the same. But even those proverbial replicas of nature, Madame Tussaud's[6] effigies, need the same treatment. Those in the galleries which are labelled are "portraits of the great." The figure on the staircase made to hoax the visitor simply represents "an" attendant, one member of a class. It stands there as a "substitute" for the expected guard—but it is not more "generalized" in Reynolds's sense.

III

The idea that art is "creation" rather than "imitation" is sufficiently familiar. It has been proclaimed in various forms from the time of Leonardo,[7] who insisted that the painter is "Lord of all Things," to that of Klee,[8] who wanted to create as Nature does. But the more solemn overtones of metaphysical power disappear when we leave art for toys. The child "makes" a train either of a few blocks or with pencil on paper. Surrounded as we are by posters and newspapers carrying illustrations of commodities or events, we find it difficult to rid ourselves of the prejudice that all images should be "read" as referring to some imaginary or actual reality. Only the historian knows how hard it is to look at Pygmalion's work without comparing it with nature. But recently we have been made aware how thoroughly we misunderstand primitive or Egyptian art whenever we make the assumption that the artist "distorts" his motif or that he even want us to see in his work the record of any specific experience. In many cases these images "represent" in the sense of being substitutes. The clay horse or servant, buried in the tomb of the mighty, takes the place of the living. The idol takes the place of the god. The question whether it represents the "external form" of the particular divinity or, for that matter, of a class of demons is quite

[6]founder of waxworks museum of notable persons

[7]Leonardo da Vinci (1452-1519), Italian painter, sculptor, musician and engineer

[8]Paul Klee (1879-1940), Swiss modernist painter and etcher

inappropriate. The idol serves as the substitute of the God in worship and ritual—it is a man-made god in precisely the sense that the hobby horse is a man-made horse; to question it further means to court deception.

There is another misunderstanding to be guarded against. We often try instinctively to save our idea of "representation" by shifting it to another plane. Where we cannot refer the image to a motif in the outer world we take it to be a portrayal of a motif in the artist's inner world. Much critical (and uncritical) writing on both primitive and modern art betrays this assumption. But to apply the naturalistic idea of portrayal to dreams and visions—let alone to unconscious images—begs a whole number of questions. The hobby horse does not portray our idea of a horse. The fearsome monster or funny face we may doodle on our blotting pad is not projected out of our mind as paint is "ex-pressed" out of a paint tube. Of course any image will be in some way symptomatic of its maker, but to think of it as of a photograph of a pre-existing reality is to misunderstand the whole process of image-making.

IV

Can our substitute take us further? Perhaps, if we consider how it could become a substitute. The "first" hobby horse (to use eighteenth-century language) was probably no image at all. Just a stick which qualified as a horse because one could ride on it. The *tertium comparationis,* the common factor, was function rather than form. Or, more precisely, that formal aspect which fulfilled the minimum requirement for the performance of the function—for any "ridable" object could serve as a horse. If that is true we may be enabled to cross a boundary which is usually regarded as closed and sealed. For in this sense "substitutes" reach deep into biological functions that are common to man and animal. The cat runs after the ball as if it were a mouse. The baby sucks its thumb as if it were the breast. In a sense the ball "represents" a mouse to the cat, the thumb a breast to the baby. But here too "representation" does not depend on formal similarities, beyond the minimum requirements of function. The ball has nothing in common with the mouse except that it is chasable. The thumb nothing with the breast except that it is suckable.

As "substitutes" they fulfill certain demands of the organism. They are keys which happen to fit into biological or psychological locks, or counterfeit coins which make the machine work when dropped into the slot.

In the language of the nursery the psychological function of "representation" is still recognized. The child will reject a perfectly naturalistic doll in favour of some monstrously "abstract" dummy which is "cuddly." It may even dispose of the element of "form" altogether and take to a blanket or an eiderdown as its favourite "comforter"—a substitute on which to bestow its love. Later in life, as the psychoanalysts tell us, it may bestow this same love on a worthy or unworthy living substitute. A teacher may "take the place" of the mother, a dictator or even an enemy may come to "represent" the father. Once more the common denominator between the symbol and the thing symbolized is not the "external form" but the function; the mother symbol would be lovable, the father-imago fearable, or whatever the case may be.

Now this psychological concept of symbolization seems to lead so very far away from the more precise meaning which the word "representation" has acquired in the figurative arts. Can there be any gain in throwing all these meanings together? Possibly: for anything seems worth trying, to get the function of symbolizing out of its isolation.

The "origin of art" has ceased to be a popular topic. But the origin of the hobby horse may be a permitted subject for speculation. Let us assume that the owner of the stick on which he proudly rode through the land decided in a playful or magic mood—and who could always distinguish between the two?—to fix "real" reins and that finally he was even tempted to "give" it two eyes near the top end. Some grass could have passed for a mane. Thus our inventor "had a horse." He had made one. Now there are two things about this fictitious event which have some bearing on the idea of the figurative arts. One is that, contrary to what is sometimes said, communication need not come into this process at all. He may not have wanted to show his horse to anyone. It just served as a focus for his fantasies as he galloped along—though more likely than not it fulfilled this same function for a tribe to which it "represented" some horse-demon of fertility and power. We may sum up the moral of this "Just So Story" by saying that substitution may precede portrayal, and creation communication. It remains to be seen how such a general theory can be tested. If it can, it may really throw light on some concrete questions. Even the origin of language, that notorious problem of speculative history, might be investigated from this angle. For what if the "pow-wow" theory, which sees the root of language in imitation, and the "pooh-pooh" theory, which sees it in emotive interjection, were to be joined by yet another? We might term it the "niam-niam" theory postulating the primitive hunter lying awake through hungry winter nights and making the sound of eating, not for communication but as a substitute for eating—being joined, perhaps, by a ritualistic chorus trying to conjure up the phantasm of food.

V

There is one sphere in which the investigation of the "representational" function of forms has made considerable progress of late, that of animal psychology. Pliny,[9] and innumerable writers after him, have regarded it as the greatest triumph of naturalistic art for a painter to have deceived sparrows or horses. The implication of these anecdotes is that a human beholder easily recognizes a bunch of grapes in a painting because for him recognition is an intellectual art. But for the birds to fly at the painting is a sign of a complete "objective" illusion. It is a plausible idea, but a wrong one. The merest outline of a cow seems sufficient for a tsetse trap, for somehow it sets the apparatus of attraction in motion and "deceives" the fly. To the fly, we might say, the crude trap has the "significant" form—biologically significant, that is. It appears that visual stimuli of this kind play an important part in the animal world. By varying the shapes of "dummies" to which animals were seen to respond, the "minimum image" that still sufficed to release a specific reaction has been ascertained. Thus little birds will open their beak when they see the feeding parent approaching the nest, but they will also do so when they are shown two darkish roundels of different size, the silhouette of the head and body of the bird "represented" in its

[9] Gaius Plinius Secundus (23-79 A.D.), Roman naturalist

most "generalized" form. Certain young fishes can even be deceived by two simple dots arranged horizontally, which they take to be the eyes of the mother fish, in whose mouth they are accustomed to shelter against danger. The fame of Zeuxis[10] will have to rest on other achievements than his deception of birds.

An "image" in this biological sense is not an imitation of an object's external form but an imitation of certain privileged or relevant aspects. It is here that a wide field of investigation would seem to open. For man is not exempt from this type of reaction. The artist who goes out to represent the visible world is not simply faced with a neutral medley of forms he seeks to "imitate." Ours is a structured universe whose main lines of force are still bent and fashioned by our biological and psychological needs, however much they may be overlaid by cultural influences. We know that there are certain privileged motifs in our world to which we respond almost too easily. The human face may be outstanding among them. Whether by instinct or by very early training, we are certainly ever disposed to single out the expressive features of a face from the chaos of sensations that surrounds it, and to respond to its slightest variations with fear or joy. Our whole perceptual apparatus is somehow hypersensitized in this direction of physiognomic vision and the merest hint suffices for us to create an expressive physiognomy that "looks" at us with suprising intensity. In a heightened state of emotion, in the dark, or in a feverish spell, the looseness of this trigger may assume pathological forms. We may see faces in the pattern of a wallpaper, and three apples arranged on a plate may stare at us like two eyes and a clownish nose. What wonder that it is so easy to "make" a face with two dots and a stroke even though their geometrical constellation may be greatly at variance with the "external form" of a real head? The well-known graphic joke of the "reversible face" might well be taken as a model for experiments which could still be made in this direction. It shows to what extent the group of shapes that can be read as a physiognomy has priority over all other readings. It turns the side which is the right way up into a convincing face and disintegrates the one that is upside down into a mere jumble of forms which is

[10] Greek painter, flourished at close of fifth century B.C.

accepted as a strange headgear. In good pictures of this kind it needs a real effort to see both faces at the same time, and perhaps we never quite succeed. Our automatic response is stronger than our intellectual awareness.

Seen in the light of the biological examples discussed above there is nothing surprising in this observation. We may venture the guess that this type of automatic recognition is dependent on the two factors of resemblance and biological relevance, and that the two may stand in some kind of inverse ratio. The greater the biological relevance an object has for us the more will we be attuned to its recognition—and the more tolerant will therefore be our standards of formal correspondence. In an erotically charged atmosphere the merest hint of formal similarity with sexual functions creates the desired response and the same is true of the dream symbols investigated by Freud.[11] The hungry man will be similarly attuned to the discovery of food—he will scan the world for the slightest promise of nourishment. The starving may even project food into all sorts of dissimilar objects—as Chaplin[12] does in *Gold Rush*[13] when his huge companion suddenly appears to him as a chicken. Can it have been some such experience which stimulated our "niam-niam" chanting hunters to see their longed-for prey in the patches and irregular shapes on the dark cave walls? Could they perhaps gradually have sought this experience in the deep mysterious recesses of the rocks, much as Leonardo sought out crumbling walls to aid his visual fantasies? Could they, finally, have been prompted to fill in such "readable" outlines with coloured earth—to have at least something "spearable" at hand which might "represent" the eatable in some magic fashion? There is no way of testing such a theory, but if it is true that cave artists often "exploited" the natural formations of the rocks, this, together with the "eidetic"[14] character of their works, would at least not contradict our fantasy. The great naturalism of cave paintings may after all be a very late flower. It may correspond to our late, derivative, and naturalistic hobby horse.

[11] Sigmund Freud (1856-1939), founder of psychoanalysis

[12] Charles Spencer Chaplin (born 1889), American movie comedian

[13] movie starring Chaplin

[14] imagistic

VI

It needed two conditions, then, to turn a stick into our hobby horse: first, that its form made it just possible to ride on it; secondly —and perhaps decisively—that riding mattered. Fortunately it still needs no great effort of the imagination to understand how the horse could become such a focus of desires and aspirations, for our language still carries the metaphors moulded by a feudal past when to be chival-rous was to be horsy. The same stick that had to represent a horse in such a setting would have become the substitute of something else in another. It might have become a sword, sceptre, or—in the context of ancestor worship—a fetish representing a dead chieftain. Seen from the point of view of "abstraction," such a convergence of meanings onto one shape offers considerable difficulties, but from that of psychological "projection" of meanings it becomes more easily intelligible. After all a whole diagnostic technique has been built up on the assumption that the meanings read into identical forms by different people tell us more about the readers than about the forms. In the sphere of art it has been shown that the same triangular shape which is the favourite pattern of many adjoining American Indian tribes is given different meanings reflecting the main preoccupations of the peoples concerned. To the student of styles this discovery that one basic form can be made to represent a variety of objects may still become significant. For while the idea of realistic pictures being deliberately "stylized" seems hard to swallow, the opposite idea of a limited vocabulary of simple shapes being used for the building up of different representations would fit much better into what we know of primitive art.

VII

Once we get used to the idea of "representation" as a two-way affair rooted in psychological dispositions we may be able to refine a concept which has proved quite indispensable to the historian of art and which is nevertheless rather unsatisfactory: that of the "conceptual image." By this we mean the mode of representation which is more or less common to children's drawings and to various forms of primitive and primitivist art. The remoteness of this type of imagery from any visual experience has often been described. The explanation of this fact which is most usually advanced is that the child (and the primitive) do not draw what they "see" but what they "know." According to this idea the typical children's drawing of a manikin is really a graphic enumeration of those human features the child remembered. It represents the content of the childish "concept" of man. But to speak of "knowledge" or "intellectual realism" (as the French do) brings us dangerously near to the fallacy of "abstraction." So back to our hobby horse. Is it quite correct to say that it consists of features which make up the "concept" of a horse or that it reflects the memory image of horses seen? No—because this formulation omits one factor: the stick. If we keep in mind that representation is originally the creation of substitutes out of given material we may reach safer ground. The greater the wish to ride, the fewer may be the features that will do for a horse. But at a certain stage it must have eyes—for how else could it see? At the most primitive level, then, the conceptual image might be identified with what we have called the minimum image—that minimum, that is, which will make it fit into a psychological lock. The form of the key depends on the material out of which it is fashioned, and on the lock. It would be a dangerous mistake, however, to equate the "conceptual image" as we find it used in the historical styles with this psychologically grounded minimum image. On the contrary. One has the impression that the presence of these schemata is always felt but that they are as much avoided as exploited. We must reckon with the possibility of a "style" being a set of conventions born out of complex tensions. The man-made image must be complete. The servant for the grave must have two hands and two feet. But he must not become a double under the artist's hands. Image-making is beset with dangers. One false stroke and the rigid mask of the face may assume an evil leer. Strict adherence to conventions alone can guard against such danger. And thus primitive art seems often to keep on that narrow ledge that lies between the lifeless and the uncanny. If the hobby horse became too lifelike it might gallop away on its own.

VIII

The contrast between primitive art and "naturalistic" or "illusionist" art can easily be overdrawn. All art is "image-making" and all image-making is rooted in the creation of substitutes. Even the artist of an "illusionist" persuasion must make the man-made, the "conceptual" image of convention his starting point. Strange as it may seem he cannot simply "imitate an object's external form" without having first learned how to construct such a form. If it were otherwise there would be no need for the innumerable books on "how to draw the human figure" or "how to draw ships." Wölfflin[15] once remarked that all pictures owe more to other pictures than they do to nature. It is a point which is familiar to the student of pictorial traditions but which is still insufficiently understood in its psychological implications. Perhaps the reason is that, contrary to the hopeful belief of many artists, the "innocent eye" which should see the world afresh would not see it at all. It would smart under the painful impact of a chaotic medley of forms and colours. In this sense the conventional vocabulary of basic forms is still indispensable to the artist as a starting point, as a focus of organization.

How, then, should we interpret the great divide which runs through the history of art and sets off the few islands of illusionist styles, of Greece, of China, and of the Renaissance, from the vast ocean of "conceptual" art?

One difference, undoubtedly, lies in a change of function. In a way the change is implicit in the emergence of the idea of the image as a "representation" in our modern sense of the word. As soon as it is generally understood that an image need not exist in its own right, that it may refer to something outside itself and therefore be the record of a visual experience rather than the creation of a substitute, the basic rules of primitive art can be transgressed with impunity. No longer is there any need for that completeness of essentials which belongs to the conceptual style, no longer is there the fear of the casual which dominates the archaic conception of art. The picture of a man on a Greek vase no longer needs a hand or a foot in full view. We know it is meant as a shadow, a mere record of what the artist saw or might see, and we are quite ready to join in the game and to supplement with our imagination what the real motif undoubtedly possessed. Once this idea of the picture suggest-

[15] Heinrich Wölfflin (1864-1945), German art historian

ing something beyond what is really there is accepted in all its implications—and this certainly did not happen overnight—we are indeed forced to let our imagination play around it. We endow it with "space" around its forms which is only another way of saying that we understand the reality which it evokes as three-dimensional, that the man could move and that even the aspect momentarily hidden "was there." When medieval art broke away from that narrative conceptual symbolism into which the formulas of classical art had been frozen, Giotto[16] made particular use of the figure seen from behind which stimulates our "spatial" imagination by forcing us to imagine the other side.

Thus the idea of the picture as a representation of a reality outside itself leads to an interesting paradox. On the one hand it compels us to refer every figure and every object shown to that imaginary reality which is "meant." This mental operation can only be completed if the picture allows us to infer not only the "external form" of every object represented but also its relative size and position. It leads us to that "rationalization of space" we call scientific perspective by which the picture plane becomes a window through which we look into the imaginary world the artist creates there for us. In theory, at least, painting is then conceived in terms of geometrical projection.

The paradox of the situation is that, once the whole picture is regarded as the representation of a slice of reality, a new context is created in which the conceptual image plays a different part. For the first consequence of the "window" idea is that we cannot conceive of any spot on the panel which is not "significant," which does not represent something. The empty patch thus easily comes to signify light, air, and atmosphere, and the vague form is interpreted as enveloped by air. It is this confidence in the representational context which is given by the very convention of the frame, which makes the development of impressionist methods possible. The artists who tried to rid themselves of their conceptual knowledge, who conscientiously became beholders of their own work and never ceased matching their created images against their impressions by stepping back and comparing the two—these artists could

[16] Giotto di Bondone (1276-1337), Italian painter, architect, and sculptor

only achieve their aim by shifting something of the load of creation on to the beholder. For what else does it mean if we are enjoined to step back in turn and watch the coloured patches of an impressionist landscape "spring to life"? It means that the painter relies on our readiness to take hints, to read contexts, and to call up our conceptual image under his guidance. The blob in the painting by Manet[17] which stands for a horse is no more an imitation of its external form than is our hobby horse. But he has so cleverly contrived it that it evokes the image in us—provided, of course, we collaborate.

Here there may be another field for independent investigation. for those "privileged" objects which play their part in the earliest layers of image-making recur—as was to be expected—in that of image-reading. The more vital the feature that is indicated by the context and yet omitted, the more intense seems to be the process that is started off. On its lowest level this method of "suggestive veiling" is familiar to erotic art. Not, of course, to its Pygmalion phase, but to its illusionist applications. What is here a crude exploitation of an obvious biological stimulus may have its parallel, for instance, in the representation of the human face. Leonardo achieved his greatest triumphs of lifelike expression by blurring precisely the features in which the expression resides, thus compelling us to complete the act of creation. Rembrandt[18] could dare to leave the eyes of his most moving portraits in the shade because we are thus stimulated to supplement them. The "evocative" image, like its "conceptual" counterpart, should be studied against a wider psychological background.

IX

My hobby horse is not art. At best it can claim the attention of iconology, that emerging branch of study which is to art criticism what linguistics is to the criticism of literature. But has not modern art experimented with the primitive image, with the "creation" of forms, and the exploitation of deep-rooted psychological forces? It has. But whatever the nostalgic wish of their makers, the meaning

[17] Edouard Manet (1833-1883), French painter, founder of Impressionism

[18] (1607-1669), Dutch painter and etcher

of these forms can never be the same as that of their primitive models. For that strange precinct we call "art" is like a hall of mirrors or a whispering gallery. Each form conjures up a thousand memories and after-images. No sooner is an image presented as art than, by this very act, a new frame of reference is created which it cannot escape. It becomes part of an institution as surely as does the toy in the nursery. If—as might be conceivable—a Picasso[19] would turn from pottery to hobby horses and send the products of this whim to an exhibition, we might read them as demonstrations, as satirical symbols, as a declaration of faith in humble things or as self-irony—but one thing would be denied even to the greatest of contemporary artists: he could not make the hobby horse mean to us what it meant to its first creator. That way is barred by the angel with a flaming sword.

[19] Pablo Picasso (born 1881), Spanish cubist painter and sculptor

☙ Ernst Hans Gombrich studied in Vienna and England and is presently Director of the Warburg Institute and Professor of the Classical Tradition at the University of London. An art historian and aesthetician, he has written *Story of Art, Art and Illusion,* and many essays on the theory of art.

The discovery of what it means to be an American

FROM *Nobody Knows My Name (1961)*
BY ***James Baldwin** (born 1924)*

"It is a complex fate to be an American," Henry James[1] observed, and the principal discovery an American writer makes in Europe is just how complex this fate is. America's history, her aspirations, her peculiar triumphs, her even more peculiar defeats, and her position in the world—yesterday and today—are all so profoundly and stubbornly unique that the very word "America" remains a new, almost completely undefined and extremely controversial proper noun. No one in the world seems to know exactly what it describes, not even we motley millions who call ourselves Americans.

I left America because I doubted my ability to survive the fury of the color problem here. (Sometimes I still do.) I wanted to prevent myself from becoming *merely* a Negro; or, even, merely a Negro writer. I wanted to find out in what way the *specialness* of my experience could be made to connect me with other people instead of dividing me from them. (I was as isolated from Negroes as I was from whites, which is what happens when a Negro begins, at bottom, to believe what white people say about him.)

In my necessity to find the terms on which my experience could

[1](1843-1916), American novelist and critic

be related to that of others, Negroes and whites, writers and non-writers, I proved, to my astonishment, to be as American as any Texas G.I. And I found my experience was shared by every American writer I knew in Paris. Like me, they had been divorced from their orgins, and it turned out to make little difference that the origins of white Americans were European and mine were African —they were no more at home in Europe than I was.

The fact that I was the son of a slave and they were the sons of free men meant less, by the time we confronted each other on European soil, than the fact that we were both searching for our separate identities. When we had found these, we seemed to be saying, why, then, we would no longer need to cling to the shame and bitterness which had divided us so long.

It became terribly clear in Europe, as it never had been here, that we knew more about each other than any European ever could. And it also became clear that, no matter where our fathers had been born, or what they had endured, the fact of Europe had formed us both, was part of our identity and part of our inheritance.

I had been in Paris a couple of years before any of this became clear to me. When it did, I, like many a writer before me upon the discovery that his props have all been knocked out from under him, suffered a species of breakdown and was carried off to the mountains of Switzerland. There, in that absolutely alabaster landscape, armed with two Bessie Smith[2] records and a typewriter, I began to try to re-create the life that I had first known as a child and from which I had spent so many years in flight.

It was Bessie Smith, through her tone and her cadence, who helped me to dig back to the way I myself must have spoken when I was a pickaninny,[3] and to remember the things I had heard and seen and felt. I had buried them very deep. I had never listened to Bessie Smith in America (in the same way that, for years, I would not touch watermelon), but in Europe she helped to reconcile me to being a "nigger."

I do not think that I could have made this reconciliation here. Once I was able to accept my role—as distinguished, I must say, from my "place"—in the extraordinary drama which is America, I was released from the illusion that I hated America.

[2](c. 1900-1937), American jazz and blues singer [3]Negro child

The story of what can happen to an American Negro writer in Europe simply illustrates, in some relief, what can happen to any American writer there. It is not meant, of course, to imply that it happens to them all, for Europe can be very crippling, too; and, anyway, a writer, when he has made his first breakthrough, has simply won a crucial skirmish in a dangerous, unending and unpredictable battle. Still, the breakthrough is important, and the point is that an American writer, in order to achieve it, very often has to leave this country.

The American writer, in Europe, is released, first of all, from the necessity of apologizing for himself. It is not until he *is* released from the habit of flexing his muscles and proving that he is just a "regular guy" that he realizes how crippling this habit has been. It is not necessary for him, there, to pretend to be something he is not, for the artist does not encounter in Europe the same suspicion he encounters here. Whatever the Europeans may actually think of artists, they have killed enough of them off by now to know that they are as real—and as persistent—as rain, snow taxes or businessmen.

Of course, the reason for Europe's comparative clarity concerning the different functions of men in society is that European society has always been divided into classes in a way that American society never has been. A European writer considers himself to be part of an old and honorable tradition—of intellectual activity, of letters—and his choice of a vocation does not cause him any uneasy wonder as to whether or not it will cost him all his friends. But this tradition does not exist in America.

On the contrary, we have a very deep-seated distrust of real intellectual effort (probably because we suspect that it will destroy, as I hope it does, that myth of America to which we cling so desperately). An American writer fights his way to one of the lowest rungs on the American social ladder by means of pure bull-headedness and an indescribable series of odd jobs. He probably *has* been a "regular fellow" for much of his adult life, and it is not easy for him to step out of that lukewarm bath.

We must, however, consider a rather serious paradox: though American society is more mobile than Europe's, it is easier to cut across social and occupational lines there than it is here. This has something to do, I think, with the problem of status in American life. Where everyone has status, it is also perfectly possible, after all, that no one has. It seems inevitable, in any case, that a man may become uneasy as to just what his status is.

But Europeans have lived with the idea of status for a long time. A man can be as proud of being a good waiter as of being a good actor, and in neither case feel threatened. And this means that the actor and the waiter can have a freer and more genuinely friendly relationship in Europe than they are likely to have here. The waiter does not feel, with obscure resentment, that the actor has "made it," and the actor is not tormented by the fear that he may find himself, tomorrow, once again a waiter.

This lack of what may roughly be called social paranoia causes the American writer in Europe to feel—almost certainly for the first time in his life—that he can reach out to everyone, that he is accessible to everyone and open to everything. This is an extraordinary feeling. He feels, so to speak, his own weight, his own value.

It is as though he suddenly came out of a dark tunnel and found himself beneath the open sky. And, in fact, in Paris, I began to see the sky for what seemed to be the first time. It was borne in on me—and it did not make me feel melancholy—that this sky had been there before I was born and would be there when I was dead. And it was up to me, therefore, to make of my brief opportunity the most that could be made.

I was born in New York, but have lived only in pockets of it. In Paris, I lived in all parts of the city—on the Right Bank and the Left, among the bourgeoisie and among *les miserables,*[4] and knew all kinds of people, from pimps and prostitutes in Pigalle to Egyptian bankers in Neuilly. This may sound extremely unprincipled or even obscurely immoral: I found it healthy. I love to talk to people, all kinds of people, and almost everyone, as I hope we still know, loves a man who loves to listen.

This perpetual dealing with people very different from myself caused a shattering in me of preconceptions I scarcely knew I held. The writer is meeting in Europe people who are not American, whose sense of reality is entirely different from his own. They may

[4]poor wretches, probably referring to Parisian underworld types in the novel of the same name by the French author Victor Hugo (1802-1885)

love or hate or admire or fear or envy this country—they see it, in any case, from another point of view, and this forces the writer to reconsider many things he had always taken for granted. This reassessment, which can be very painful, is also very valuable.

This freedom, like all freedom, has its dangers and its responsibilities. One day it begins to be borne in on the writer, and with great force, that he is living in Europe as an American. If he were living there as a European, he would be living on a different and far less attractive continent.

This crucial day may be the day on which an Algerian taxi-driver tells him how it feels to be an Algerian in Paris. It may be the day on which he passes a cafe terrace and catches a glimpse of the tense, intelligent and troubled face of Albert Camus.[5] Or it may be the day on which someone asks him to explain Little Rock and he begins to feel that it would be simpler—and, corny as the words may sound, more honorable—to *go* to Little Rock than sit in Europe, on an American passport, trying to explain it.

This is a personal day, a terrible day, the day to which his entire sojourn has been tending. It is the day he realizes that there are no untroubled countries in this fearfully troubled world; that if he has been preparing himself for anything in Europe, he has been preparing himself—for America. In short, the freedom that the American writer finds in Europe brings him, full circle, back to himself, with the responsibility for his development where it always was: in his own hands.

Even the most incorrigible maverick has to be born somewhere. He may leave the group that produced him—he may be forced to—but nothing will efface his origins, the marks of which he carries with him everywhere. I think it is important to know this and even find it a matter for rejoicing, as the strongest people do, regardless of their station. On this acceptance, literally, the life of a writer depends.

The charge has often been made against American writers that they do not describe society, and have no interest in it. They only describe individuals in opposition to it, or isolated from it. Of course, what the American writer is describing is his own situation.

[5](1913-1960), French novelist, dramatist and philosopher

But what is *Anna Karenina*[6] describing if not the tragic fate of the isolated individual, at odds with her time and place?

The real difference is that Tolstoy[7] was describing an old and dense society in which everything seemed—to the people in it, though not to Tolstoy—to be fixed forever. And the book is a masterpiece because Tolstoy was able to fathom, and make us see, the hidden laws which really governed this society and made Anna's doom inevitable.

American writers do not have a fixed society to describe. The only society they know is one in which nothing is fixed and in which the individual must fight for his identity. This is a rich confusion, indeed, and it creates for the American writer unprecedented opportunities.

That the tensions of American life, as well as the possibilities, are tremendous is certainly not even a question. But these are dealt with in contemporary literature mainly compulsively; that is, the book is more likely to be a symptom of our tension than an examination of it. The time has come, God knows, for us to examine ourselves, but we can only do this if we are willing to free ourselves of the myth of America and try to find out what is really happening here.

Every society is really governed by hidden laws, by unspoken but profound assumptions on the part of the people, and ours is no exception. It is up to the American writer to find out what these laws and assumptions are. In a society much given to smashing taboos without thereby managing to be liberated from them, it will be no easy matter.

It is no wonder, in the meantime, that the American writer keeps running off to Europe. He needs sustenance for his journey and the best models he can find. Europe has what we do not have yet, a sense of the mysterious and inexorable limits of life, a sense, in a word, of tragedy. And we have what they sorely need: a new sense of life's possibilities.

In this endeavor to wed the vision of the Old World with that of the New, it is the writer, not the statesman, who is our strongest

[6] novel by Tolstoy

[7] Count Leo Tolstoy (1828-1910), Russian novelist and social reformer

arm. Though we do not wholly believe it yet, the interior life is a real life, and the intangible dreams of people have a tangible effect on the world.

☙ James Arthur Baldwin has established himself as a leading literary spokesman for American Negroes in his essays *(Notes of a Native Son, The Fire Next Time)* and in his novels *(Giovanni's Room, Another Country). Nobody Knows My Name* records the last months of his ten-year exile on the continent and his return to America.

Alternative tables of contents

A collection of essays is more than a collection of ideas, more than an historical sequence of concerns; it is also a collection of ways of apprehension, each individual in its combination of traits, yet each sharing with others certain emphases of manner and belief. So we can make alternative groupings, tables of contents alternative to the chronological: a thematic grouping, or a stylistic grouping, for example. For theme:

POLITICAL

ARTISTIC

Conclusion, Walter Pater
On Biography, Samuel Johnson
The Action of an Heroic Poem, John Dryden
How to Tell a Story, Mark Twain
How a Gallant Should Behave Himself in a Play-House, Thomas Dekker
On Literature and Science, Matthew Arnold
Prospects in the Arts and Sciences, J. Robert Oppenheimer
On Tragedy, David Hume
Soliloquies on Masks, George Santayana
How Should One Read a Book? Virginia Woolf
Tradition and the Individual Talent, T. S. Eliot
Meditations on a Hobby Horse, E. H. Gombrich

PHILOSOPHICAL

Ecclesiastes
Three Meditations, John Donne
A Sceptic in Religion, John Earle
Conclusion, Sir Thomas Browne
Melancthon and Calvin, Walter Savage Landor
Levana and Our Ladies of Sorrow, Thomas De Quincey
Labour, Thomas Carlyle
On Self-Reliance, Ralph Waldo Emerson
Conclusion, Henry David Thoreau
Of Friendship, Sir Francis Bacon
Characteristics of Scientific Method, Bertrand Russell
Worms and the Soil, Charles Darwin
A Conference, Izaak Walton
On a Certain Blindness in Human Beings, William James
Of Pleasure, Sir Thomas More
Of Learning and Experience, Roger Ascham

And for examples of style:

PREDICATIVE

On Familiar Style, William Hazlitt
On Pleasure, Sir Thomas More

For the writer and reader of essays

A SUMMARY OF SUGGESTIONS ON COMPOSING, EVALUATING, AND RECOMPOSING

In the essay: What is the controlling theme or idea? That is, what is the predication of the subject in the theme-sentence? And how do the separate sentences, and the groups of sentences in paragraphs, support and develop the idea? (Logic and Grammar)

Relations of ideas: Logic
- Their character: definition; comparison and contrast.
  - Positive evidence, necessary for definition and support: identification, example, allusion, analogy, authority.
  - Negative evidence, sufficient for definition and argument: anticipating and negating possible expectations.
- Their sequence: order and form.
  - Temporal or spatial, narrative or descriptive: then-then-then; and-and-and, first-second-third; negative, but-but-but; coordinate.
  - Alternative or choice: -either-or; negative, -neither-nor; coordinate.

Explanatory or causal: -if-then; because-therefore; negative, though-however-yet; subordinate.

Relations within statements of ideas: Grammar

Substance: Concrete and abstract, specific and general, literal and figurative, neutral and evaluative, denotative and connotative.

Predication: bases of organization; time, voice, person.

Qualification: adjectival and adverbial, phrasal and clausal.

Connection: guides to organization; coordinate, subordinate.

Substitution: one form to function as another; noun to function as adjective, clause as noun, phrase as adverb, and so on.

Signs of relation; spelling and punctuation.

Morphemes and syntactic units: roots; affixes, derivational and inflectional; agreement, reference, word-order.

Punctuation: intonation patterns of stress and pitch as partially indicated; punctuation marks and spaces as boundaries.

From the essay: What is the controlling tone toward reader, the purport and effect? (Rhetoric)

Location of main point in essay's own terms, and focus by controlling point of view.

Meeting other possible expectations, such as the reader's.

Relation of understanding of essay in its own terms to reader's reception of it in his terms.

Use of knowledge of work's context—history, occasion, effects—for establishing relevant expectations.

On the essay: How are judgments made by the critic and self-critic? (Evaluation)

Criteria or standards of value:

By criterion of coherence, internal consistency, relations of main characteristics, evaluate:

Main theme, and steps of development.

Use of evidence, both positive and negative, for adequacy and relevance.

Specific uses of language, use of a specific word, sentence structure, reference, or order.

By criterion of correspondence, external relation to facts, evaluate adequacy of evidence.

By criterion of communication, effectiveness, evaluate relation of work to reader, the satisfying of the expectations it establishes.

Recomposition: toward closer meeting of standards:

Reconsideration and restatement of main theme in the light of completed composition.

Addition to and clarification of evidence; elimination of unnecessary and irrelevant detail.

Pointing up and sharpening of the details of presentation.

- Heightening of emphasis at important points: the central statement, the transitions between it and supporting statements.
- Use of structural devices of similarity and difference: parallel structure in series and like elements, contrast in opposed elements.
- Strengthening of details to clarify the whole design.